1,000,000 Books
are available to read at

www.ForgottenBooks.com

Read online
Download PDF
Purchase in print

ISBN 978-0-282-38234-6
PIBN 10847888

This book is a reproduction of an important historical work. Forgotten Books uses state-of-the-art technology to digitally reconstruct the work, preserving the original format whilst repairing imperfections present in the aged copy. In rare cases, an imperfection in the original, such as a blemish or missing page, may be replicated in our edition. We do, however, repair the vast majority of imperfections successfully; any imperfections that remain are intentionally left to preserve the state of such historical works.

Forgotten Books is a registered trademark of FB &c Ltd.
Copyright © 2018 FB &c Ltd.
FB &c Ltd, Dalton House, 60 Windsor Avenue, London, SW19 2RR.
Company number 08720141. Registered in England and Wales.

For support please visit www.forgottenbooks.com

1 MONTH OF FREE READING

at
www.ForgottenBooks.com

By purchasing this book you are eligible for one month membership to ForgottenBooks.com, giving you unlimited access to our entire collection of over 1,000,000 titles via our web site and mobile apps.

To claim your free month visit: www.forgottenbooks.com/free847888

* Offer is valid for 45 days from date of purchase. Terms and conditions apply.

English
Français
Deutsche
Italiano
Español
Português

www.forgottenbooks.com

Mythology Photography **Fiction** Fishing Christianity **Art** Cooking Essays **Buddhism** Freemasonry Medicine **Biology** Music **Ancient Egypt** Evolution Carpentry Physics Dance Geology **Mathematics** Fitness Shakespeare **Folklore** Yoga Marketing **Confidence** Immortality Biographies Poetry **Psychology** Witchcraft Electronics Chemistry History **Law** Accounting **Philosophy** Anthropology Alchemy Drama Quantum Mechanics Atheism Sexual Health **Ancient History Entrepreneurship** Languages Sport Paleontology Needlework Islam **Metaphysics** Investment Archaeology Parenting Statistics Criminology **Motivational**

THE CATEGORICAL IMPERATIVE

A Study in Kant's Moral Philosophy

By
H. J. PATON

THE UNIVERSITY OF CHICAGO PRESS
CHICAGO · ILLINOIS

TO MY WIFE

PUBLISHED IN ENGLAND BY
HUTCHINSON & COMPANY, LTD.

THE UNIVERSITY OF CHICAGO PRESS, CHICAGO 37
Cambridge University Press, London, N.W. 1, England
W. J. Gage & Co., Limited, Toronto 2B, Canada

Copyright 1948 by The University of Chicago
All rights reserved. Published 1948

CONTENTS

	Page
REFERENCES AND ABBREVIATIONS	13
PREFACE	15

Book I

THE APPROACH TO THE CATEGORICAL IMPERATIVE

Chapter
I THE CRITICAL METHOD
1. The need for understanding Kant's method. 19
2. Moral judgements are *a priori*. 20
3. The marks of *a priori* judgement. 21
4. Composite knowledge. 22
5. The task of philosophy. 23
6. The need for pure ethics. 24
7. The method of analysis. 25
8. Analytic and synthetic arguments. 26
9. The Critical method. 27
10. The method of synthesis. 29
11. The importance of Kant. 29
    Appendix: The Divisions of Kant's Moral Philosophy. 31

II THE GOOD WILL
1. A good will is good without limitation. 34
2. Other possible views. 35
3. Are all goods good without limitation? 36
4. Are many goods good without limitation? 38
5. Is a good will good without limitation? 39
6. The highest good. 41
7. A good will and its objects. 43
8. The function of reason. 44
9. Goodness is fundamental. 45

[5]

Chapter
III DUTY
1. A good will and duty.
2. The method of isolation.
3. Misunderstandings.
4. Is duty the motive of a good will?
5. Is goodness the motive of a good will?
6. Are generous emotions the motive of a good will?
7. Conclusion.
   Appendix: Inclinations, Happiness, and Moral Worth.

IV THE MAXIM OF MORALITY
1. Moral value does not depend on results.
2. Practical principles—subjective and objective.
3. Two kinds of maxim—formal and material.
4. The maxim of duty.

V REVERENCE
1. Reverence for the law.
2. The description of reverence.
3. The function of reverence.
   Appendix: Reverence as a Motive.

VI THE LAW
1. Law as such.
2. Law as command.
3. The moral motive.
4. Formal maxim and moral law.
5. The categorical imperative.

VII MISUNDERSTANDINGS
1. Criticisms.
2. Kant's formalism.
3. Kant's legalism.
4. The ignoring of consequences.
5. The soundness of Kant's doctrine.

CONTENTS

Book II

THE BACKGROUND OF THE CATEGORICAL IMPERATIVE

Chapter   Page
VIII PRACTICAL REASON AND ITS SUBJECTIVE PRINCIPLES
1. The practical function of reason.   78
2. Two senses of 'reason'.   79
3. The approach to practical reason.   79
4. Theoretical reason and action.   81
5. Practical reason.   81
6. Impulsive action.   82
7. Means and end.   83
8. The pursuit of happiness.   85
9. The denial of practical reason.   87
10. Morality.   88

IX PRACTICAL REASON AND ITS OBJECTIVE PRINCIPLES
1. Subjective and objective principles.   89
2. The principle of skill.   90
3. The principle of self-love.   91
4. The principle of morality.   93
5. Conditioned and unconditioned principles.   95
Appendix: Kant's View of Reason.
    1. Different senses of 'reason'.   96
    2. The category of cause and effect.   97
    3. The schema of regular succession.   98
    4. The Idea of freedom.   99
    5. Different kinds of concept.   100
    6. Intuitive understanding.   100

X THE GOOD
1. The good in general.   103
2. 'Good for' and 'good at'.   104
3. My good.   105
4. The moral good.   107
5. The teleological view of good.   108
6. The realistic view of good.   110

Chapter		Page
XI	IMPERATIVES	
	1. Imperatives in general.	113
	2. Definition of an imperative.	114
	3. Three kinds of imperative.	114
	4. Rules, counsels, and laws.	115
	5. Obligation and goodness.	116
	6. The duty to act morally.	117
XII	HOW ARE IMPERATIVES POSSIBLE?	
	1. The meaning of the question.	120
	2. Analytic propositions.	120
	3. Synthetic propositions.	122
	4. Synthetic *a priori* propositions.	122
	5. Difficulties.	123
	6. Imperatives of skill are analytic propositions.	123
	7. Synthetic propositions are presupposed.	125
	8. Imperatives of prudence are analytic propositions.	126
	9. Categorical imperatives are synthetic *a priori* propositions.	127

BOOK III

THE FORMULATION OF THE CATEGORICAL IMPERATIVE

XIII	THE FIVE FORMULAE	
	1. The five formulae.	129
	2. The relations between the five formulae.	130
	3. The purpose and structure of the argument.	130
	4. The application of the formulae.	131
XIV	THE FORMULA OF UNIVERSAL LAW	
	1. Formula I.	133
	2. The one categorical imperative.	134
	3. Universal law.	135
	4. Maxims.	135
	5. Material maxims.	137
	6. The canon of moral judgement.	137
	7. Contradiction in the will.	139
	8. The coherence of rational wills.	139
	9. The rational will as arbiter.	140
	10. The permissible and the obligatory.	141
	Appendix: The Spontaneity of Mind.	
	1. Intellectual spontaneity.	142
	2. Aesthetic spontaneity.	144

CONTENTS

Chapter		Page
XV	THE FORMULA OF THE LAW OF NATURE	
	1. Formula Ia.	146
	2. Perfect and imperfect duties.	147
	3. The causal law of nature.	148
	4. Teleological law in nature.	149
	5. The perfection of nature.	150
	6. The appeal to teleological law.	150
	7. Kindness.	152
	8. Promises to repay loans.	152
	9. Suicide.	154
	10. Culture.	155
	11. Practical reason and purpose.	155
	12. The principles of moral action.	156
	Appendix: The Law of Nature as a Type of the Moral Law.	
	1. The form of law.	157
	2. The problem of 'exhibition'.	158
	3. Symbolic exhibition.	159
	4. The 'type' of moral law.	160
	5. The natural order.	161
	6. Practical exhibition.	162
XVI	THE FORMULA OF THE END IN ITSELF	
	1. Formula II.	165
	2. The nature of ends.	166
	3. Ends in themselves.	167
	4. Grounds and ends.	169
	5. The approach to Formula II.	170
	6. Kinds of duty.	171
	7. Kant's illustrations.	172
	8. The soundness of Kant's view.	173
	9. Special characteristics of Formula II.	175
	Appendix: Arguments in Support of Formula II.	
	1. Argument from the essence of the categorical imperative.	175
	2. Argument from the nature of rational agents.	176
	3. Argument from the character of a good will.	177
	4. Argument from the Formula of Universal Law.	177
	5. Summary.	178
XVII	THE FORMULA OF AUTONOMY	
	1. Formula III.	180
	2. The approach to Formula III.	181

Chapter
XVII   3. The exclusion of pathological interest.
        4. Legislating through maxims.
        5. The application of Formula III.

XVIII   THE FORMULA OF THE KINGDOM OF ENDS
        1. Formula IIIa.
        2. The approach to Formula IIIa.
        3. The kingdom of ends.
        4. Kingdom or realm.
        5. The supreme head.
        6. Dignity and price.
        7. The kingdom of nature.
        8. The realisation of the kingdom of ends.
        9. The application of Formula IIIa.
       10. Moral progress.
       11. Kant's historical background.
       12. Kant's personality.

Book IV

THE JUSTIFICATION OF THE CATEGORICAL IMPERATIVE

XIX   THE PROBLEM
        1. The question to be answered.
        2. An alternative question.
        3. The purpose of a transcendental deduction.
        4. A different view.
        5. Possible misunderstandings.
        6. Kant's method.

XX   FREEDOM AND AUTONOMY
        1. Kant as a pioneer.
        2. Freedom as the key to the moral problem.
        3. Will as causality.
        4. Freedom and natural necessity.
        5. The positive concept of freedom.
        6. Freedom and autonomy.
        7. Is only a good will free?
        8. Two kinds of heteronomy.
        9. Degrees of freedom.

Chapter		Page
XXI	FREEDOM AS A NECESSARY PRESUPPOSITION	
	1. Freedom and rational agents.	217
	2. The presupposition of freedom.	217
	3. Theoretical reason and its presupposition.	218
	4. Practical reason and its presupposition.	218
	5. The self-consciousness of reason.	220
	6. The position of the argument.	221
XXII	THE INTELLIGIBLE WORLD	
	1. Side issues.	223
	2. Moral interest.	223
	3. The alleged vicious circle.	224
	4. The way of escape.	225
	5. The two standpoints.	226
	6. The argument from the passivity of sense.	228
	7. Other arguments.	230
	8. Conclusion.	231
XXIII	MEMBERSHIP OF THE INTELLIGIBLE WORLD	
	1. Inner sense and mental states.	233
	2. The noumenal self.	234
	3. The mind affects itself.	235
	4. Knowledge of mental activity.	236
	5. The activity of reason.	238
	6. Membership of the intelligible world.	240
	7. The principles of reason.	240
XXIV	HOW IS A CATEGORICAL IMPERATIVE POSSIBLE?	
	1. The deduction.	242
	2. The additional argument.	242
	3. The conclusion.	243
	4. The failure of the deduction.	244
	5. Direct insight into the principle of autonomy.	245
	6. Is the principle of autonomy analytic?	246
	7. The imperative of autonomy.	247
	8. The objective principles of reason.	247
	9. Reason and the unconditioned.	249
	Appendix: Kant's Additional Argument.	250
XXV	SOME FURTHER QUESTIONS	
	1. Further questions to be considered.	253
	2. The real self.	253
	3. The conflict of reason and desire.	254
	4. Ethics and metaphysics.	255

Chapter			Page
XXV	5.	Moral interest.	256
	6.	Interest and obligation.	258
	7.	Practical insight.	258
	8.	Modern intellectualism.	259
	9.	Kant's teleology.	261
	10.	The self-consciousness of practical reason.	262
	11.	Thought and action.	263
	12.	Some practical objections.	265
XXVI	THE DEFENCE OF FREEDOM		
	1.	The antinomy of freedom and necessity.	266
	2.	The solution of the antinomy.	266
	3.	The two standpoints.	267
	4.	How is freedom possible?	268
	5.	Phenomena and noumena.	269
	6.	The thought of the intelligible world.	271
	7.	There is no explanation of freedom.	273
	8.	Timeless action.	273
	9.	Freedom to act badly.	275
	10.	Freedom and necessity.	276
	11.	The defence of freedom.	277
INDEX OF PROPER NAMES			279
GENERAL INDEX			280

REFERENCES AND ABBREVIATIONS

There is unfortunately no generally accepted method for referring to passages in Kant's works. The *first* number in my references is the page number in the complete edition published by the Berlin Academy. This number is for some of Kant's works given also in the margin of the complete edition published by Meiner in the *Philosophische Bibliothek*, which on the whole is the most convenient German edition for ordinary use. It is given, for example, in Vorländer's editions of the *Grundlegung* and the *Metaphysik der Sitten* in that series. It is also given in the margin of Meredith's translations of the *Critique of Judgement*.

Many English readers are likely to use Abbott's translations of Kant's ethical works, and the *second* page number in my references, *where it is not enclosed in brackets*, has been added for their benefit. Here, however, there is a difficulty; for the paging of the *Groundwork*—or, as he calls it, *Fundamental Principles of the Metaphysic of Morals*—is different in the small edition published separately and in the larger work which he calls '*Kant's Theory of Ethics*'. I have endeavoured to meet this difficulty by making use of the small page numbers which in both works he inserts in the body of the text; and for the sake of consistency I have adhered to this practice for the other works, or portions of works, which he translates in *Kant's Theory of Ethics*. These numbers are taken by Abbott from the complete edition of Kant's works by Rosenkrantz and Schubert, and so may be of use to those who consult that edition.

It would be enormously more convenient if all editions and commentaries on Kant could refer to the pages of the *original editions*. This is already the practice for the *Critique of Pure Reason*, where the first edition is commonly known as A and the second as B. This practice I have followed for the *Critique of Pure Reason* (*K.r.V.*), and where such page numbers are readily available for other works I have given them also; but in order to mark their character and to distinguish them from the references to Abbott *I have enclosed them in brackets*. These numbers are printed in the margin of some of the works published in the *Philosophische Bibliothek* and even in the Academy edition of the *Kritik der praktischen Vernunft* and the *Kritik der Urteilskraft* as printed in 1913 (though not earlier).

In the case of the *First Introduction* (*Erste Einleitung*) to the *Critique of Judgement* the page references are to Lehmann's edition in the *Philosophische Bibliothek*.

[13]

List of Chief Abbreviations

		Volume in the Academy Edition
Beobachtungen	= *Beobachtungen über das Gefühl des Schönen und Erhabenen.*	II
Das Ende	= *Das Ende aller Dinge.*	VIII
Gr.	= *Grundlegung zur Metaphysik der Sitten.*	IV
K.p.V.	= *Kritik der praktischen Vernunft.*	V
K.r.V.	= *Kritik der reinen Vernunft.*	III–IV
K.U.	= *Kritik der Urteilskraft.*	V
Logik	= *Immanuel Kants Logik.*	IX
M.A.d.N.	= *Metaphysische Anfangsgründe der Naturwissenschaft.*	IV
M.d.S.	= *Metaphysik der Sitten.*	VI
Prol.	= *Prolegomena zu jeder künftigen Metaphysik.*	IV
Religion	= *Die Religion innerhalb der Grenzen der blossen Vernunft.*	VI

Where necessary I refer to the edition of the Berlin Academy as *Ak.* and to that of the *Philosophische Bibliothek* as *Phil. Bib.* I refer also to my own book—*Kant's Metaphysic of Experience*—as *K.M.E.*

PREFACE

KANT contrived to say something new about morality. This remarkable achievement has compelled every subsequent writer on moral philosophy to examine his views even if only in order to refute his errors. The curious thing is that Kant himself makes no claim to propound a philosophical revolution in moral thinking as he did in speculative thinking. He knew, of course, that he was trying to do something which no one had succeeded in doing before—namely, to set forth the first principles of morality apart from all considerations of self-interest and even apart from their application to particular human problems. Yet he maintained that he was only putting forward a new formula for the principle by which good men had always judged moral excellence—even if they had been unable to make this principle clear to themselves or to separate it off sharply from other principles concerned with the happiness of the individual and the benefits arising from the moral life.

It is impossible to exaggerate the importance of grasping the supreme principle of morality; and because Kant's *Groundwork of the Metaphysic of Morals* (as I call his *Grundlegung zur Metaphysik der Sitten*) treats of this topic, and of this topic alone, it is an indispensable book for all who profess to think seriously about moral problems. Yet many readers find it difficult to understand, and the main purpose of my present book is to make understanding easier. This is all the more necessary because—as I believe—a whole series of misinterpretations has become traditional and stands in the way of an unprejudiced approach. It is indeed a strange thing that so many of those who either explicitly or implicitly regard Kant as a great, or at least an influential, thinker, ascribe to him views which can hardly be considered as anything but silly. Thus he is commonly supposed to maintain that no action can be moral if we have any natural inclination towards it or if we obtain the slightest pleasure from its performance; and again that a good man must take no account whatever of the consequences of his actions but must deduce all the manifold duties of life from the bare conception of moral law as such—without any regard for the characteristics of human nature or the circumstances of human life. These doctrines and others equally paradoxical, if they were held by Kant, would not indicate that he had any very profound insight into the nature of morality: they can hardly but suggest that his moral philosophy may be dismissed as negligible, if not diseased. It is my hope to show, by a careful examination of the text, that such interpretations are a distortion of his actual teaching, which is always reasonable, even if it may not always be correct.

From what I have said it will be clear that I regard the proper interpretation of Kant's doctrine as of vital importance, not merely to students of Kant, but to all students of moral philosophy, and indeed to all who seek to lead a good life intelligently and are not content to follow blindly what they consider to be the wisdom of their forefathers. For this reason I have endeavoured in the earlier sections of my book to deal with the more technical aspects of Kant's teaching in appendices, which can be ignored by those whose interests are limited. This device is no longer open to me in the final section—Book IV—which, since it is concerned with the metaphysical defence of moral principles, cannot be treated without reference to Kant's philosophy as a whole. But this section too can be ignored—though not, I think, without some loss—by those who are more anxious to understand what morality is than to consider how it is to be defended.

For students of Kant I have tried to show how his moral philosophy fits in with other parts of his Critical doctrine. Though I have taken the *Groundwork*, so to speak, as my text, I have sought to confirm my interpretation by references to his other works. As a reviewer of my previous book on Kant complained that his eyes were dazzled by having to look down so often to the footnotes, perhaps it is necessary to explain that these are intended, as a rule, for Kantian scholars who may wish to check my interpretation: they are not meant to be examined on a first reading, or indeed by anyone who is more interested in the doctrine that is expounded than in the evidence on which it is based. I may add that I have made no attempt to deal with the gradual evolution of Kant's thought on these subjects, since this has already been done most admirably by Professor P. A. Schilpp in *Kant's Pre-Critical Ethics*—a book which I should like to see widely used as a companion to my own.

Kant's moral philosophy is not nearly so difficult as his theoretical philosophy, and I hope I have presented no insuperable difficulties to any one who is able and willing to do some hard thinking. In writing *Kant's Metaphysic of Experience* I often felt as if I were fighting my way through a thicket, thankful at times if I could attach any clear meaning to what he was saying. Even in the *Groundwork* there are passages which became clear to me only after years of study, but—perhaps because I had already written the earlier book—I have not found the difficulties so great, and I have been able to use a greater freedom of expression, which I hope will make things easier for my readers. With the same end in view I hope also to publish later a fresh translation of the *Groundwork* with a few explanatory notes where the meaning is obscure.

I have chosen as my title '*The Categorical Imperative*' because this looms so large, both in Kant's thinking and in the commonly accepted views about him; but it will become clear in the course of my book that for Kant the supreme principle of morality is something higher even than the categorical imperative: it appears to us as a categorical imperative only because of our human frailty. It is necessary to grasp this if we are to understand his doctrine in its fulness and to get rid of the view that his moral philosophy is essentially harsh and Puritanic.

Perhaps I may be allowed also to confess that when, some twenty

PREFACE

years ago, I wrote about moral philosophy in '*The Good Will*', I had not freed myself from the traditional interpretation of Kant, and I supposed that I was dealing with factors in the moral life—particularly teleological factors—which he had neglected or overlooked. A fuller study has shown me my error—an error which, I think, is by no means confined to myself. One of the last things which I discovered in my study of him, though it now seems to have been staring me in the face all the time, is that in his *application* of moral principles Kant takes into account most fully the desires and purposes and potentialities of men, and indeed that it is on a teleological view of man and of the universe that his application of moral principles is based. At one time I intended to add a further section on '*The Application of the Categorical Imperative*' and to examine the *method* of application employed in his neglected *Metaphysic of Morals*; but I found that this would make my present book too long, and indeed it requires a separate book to itself. I hope that some student of Kant will one day undertake this very necessary task. I do not doubt that in so doing he will find in Kant's particular judgements considerable blemishes, due in part to personal limitations, but in greater part to the age in which he lived; but he will also find much of permanent value; and if he approaches his task sympathetically—instead of first attributing to Kant a mass of traditional absurdities and then complaining of inconsistency when he finds these everywhere contradicted—he will throw a flood of light, not only on Kant's method of applying his principles, but on the proper interpretation of these principles themselves.

In these days when the pillars of European society are shaken, and when even the British race, after displaying a magnificence in action almost without parallel, is assailed on every side by prophets of unreason for whom moral splendour is so much illusion, I hope that this new interpretation of Kant's doctrine may help men to reflect more deeply on objective principles of action, on the nature of obligation, and on the value of the moral life.

I have to thank my wife for typing the whole of this difficult manuscript in spite of the heavy burden laid on housewives by a six years' war and its oppressive aftermath. I must also thank Mr. W. F. R. Hardie, Mr. L. J. Beck, and Mr. C. B. H. Barford for their kindness in reading the proofs.

H. J. PATON.

Corpus Christi College, Oxford.
August, 1946.

BOOK I

THE APPROACH TO THE CATEGORICAL IMPERATIVE

CHAPTER I

THE CRITICAL METHOD

§1. *The need for understanding Kant's method.*[1]

ONE of the reasons why philosophy is difficult is that in philosophical thinking we ought to know exactly what it is that we are doing. This does not apply in the same sense to other thinkers: it does not apply to the mathematician, to the physicist, or (if we may regard as also a thinker him who is so much more) to the artist. No doubt each of these knows very well what he is doing: he understands his problem, and he alone can solve it. But among the questions that he asks and answers, there is one question not asked—the question 'What is mathematics?' or 'What is physics?' or 'What is art?' These are philosophical questions; and if the mathematician or the physicist or the artist asks these questions, he has taken the first step towards being something more than a mathematician or physicist or artist; he is, in short, becoming a philosopher.

If it is the part of a philosopher to ask these questions, it is still more the part of a philosopher to ask 'What is philosophy?' According to Kant, what was wrong with philosophy before his time was this—that philosophers blundered along trying to solve philosophical problems without ever asking themselves what it was that they were doing and whether what they were doing was something that could be done. He may have been unduly hard on his predecessors—most philosophers are—but in any case this was what he thought. For him a sound philosopher must know clearly and reflectively what he is doing, and only so was philosophy likely to succeed. This is one reason why Kant's philosophy is called the Critical Philosophy. It is also one reason why we must begin by trying to see what Kant was doing as a moral philosopher. In other words we must begin by trying to understand the Critical method, although we are bound to understand it imperfectly until we have followed it in its actual working.

[1] Since this is a difficult topic, beginners are advised on a first reading to go straight on to Chapter II.

§2. *Moral judgements are* a priori.

We all make moral judgements: that is, we judge some men to be good and some bad; some actions to be right and some wrong. However much or however little such judgements influence our own actions—and surely they do influence our actions to some extent—we commonly regard these judgements as capable of being either true or false. Such is certainly the view of the ordinary good man. In this he may no doubt be mistaken, though it seems odd that so many men of so many races and so many ages should have fallen into the same mistake. There have been, and there still are, philosophers who tell us that moral judgements, if true at all, are true only as asserting that at a particular time we happen to experience a particular kind of feeling; or even that they cannot be either true or false, since they assert nothing, but are mere expressions of emotion, comparable to a cry of horror or of grief. Kant admits provisionally, at least in the *Groundwork*, that all moral judgements may be illusory, but he assumes that they at any rate claim to assert something, and he proposes to make clear what is implied in their assertion. Having done this, he hopes to be in a position to justify and defend, not of course every individual moral judgement, but the principles in accordance with which such judgements can be truly made. Even those who are sceptical about all moral judgements should therefore be able to follow his argument.

There is a sharp difference between moral judgements and judgements of fact such as 'This carpet is red' or 'That table is square.' The latter judgements are based on sense: they can be verified by means of our senses, or by what may be called sensuous experience. Moral judgements cannot be so verified. If we hold, as some sharp-sighted thinkers hold, that only judgements which can be verified by sensuous experience are true, we must either say that moral judgements are neither true nor false, or else that they are true or false only if, in spite of appearances, they are judgements about pleasure and pain and consequently can be verified by our sensuous experience of pleasure and pain. These theories, which may be called positivistic theories, rest on the supposition that only judgements which can be verified by sense are true—a supposition which incidentally can itself never be verified by sense. of course not.

Kant meets the difficulty in another way. Agreeing with the positivists that moral judgements cannot be verified by sensuous experience, but supposing also with the ordinary man that moral judgements can be true or false, he asserts that moral judgements—if they are to be true—must be *a priori* judgements. By this he means that they are judgements which are not based on sensuous experience, and he holds that such judgements may be true although they are not verifiable by sensuous experience. Judgements based on sensuous experience (and consequently verifiable by sensuous experience) he calls *a posteriori* or empirical judgements.

To say that judgements are *a priori*—in the sense that they are not based on experience or are independent of experience—is thus a negative description. It does not mean that we make moral judgements before experience begins. It does not mean that an infant knows all about moral goodness before it begins to see colours and hear sounds. Such absurdities have been attributed to Kant even by distinguished thinkers, but I do not propose to discuss them. Kant holds expressly that no knowledge is prior to experience *in time* and that with experience all knowledge begins.[1]

If, however, *a priori* judgements are not based on experience, we may well ask on what they can be based. Are moral judgements possible, and if so, how? It is the main purpose of Kant's philosophy to answer these questions. At present we must ask 'What are the characteristics which lead us to suppose that there are *a priori* judgements at all?'

§3. *The marks of* a priori *judgement.*

Empirical judgements are always judgements of fact. Experience can tell us what is, and it cannot tell us anything more. Moral judgements tell us what ought to be, or what ought to be done, or what we ought to do. Such judgements are distinct from empirical judgements and cannot be inferred from empirical judgements: no one supposes that men always do what they ought to do; nor are we justified in arguing—as some philosophers have done—that because men are self-seeking, it is therefore a duty to be self-seeking. Words like 'ought' and 'duty' and 'right' and 'good' indicate that the speaker is making not an empirical, but an *a priori* judgement, if he is making a judgement at all.

Moral judgements are not, however, the only *a priori* judgements. Since experience tells us only what is, and not what must be, all judgements of *necessity* must be *a priori*: they cannot be based merely on sensuous experience. Hence if we can say that a triangle *must* have its interior angles equal to two right angles or that an event *must* have a cause, this must be an *a priori* judgement.

Judgements of necessity may also be called truly *universal* judgements. When we say that an event must have a cause, we can equally say that every event, or that all events, must have a cause. Experience cannot give us such truly universal judgements. We can indeed say loosely that all swans are white, and this is an empirical judgement. It means, however, merely that all swans hitherto seen have been white; and this is only a compendious way of saying 'This swan is white, and that swan is white,' and so on till the list is complete. If it means more than this, it is a generalisation, the result of an inductive inference from the swans we have seen to other swans. The judgement may then be described as general; but the sight of one black swan is enough to refute its claim to be universal. 'All swans are white' could be a strictly universal judgement only if we could grasp a *necessary* connexion between being a swan and being white, and this we can never do merely by looking at white swans or indeed in any other way.

Hence we may say that all judgements of necessity and all truly universal judgements are *a priori* and not empirical.

[1] *K.r.V.*, A1, B1. For a clear distinction between logical and temporal priority see *K.r.V.*, A452 n. = B480 n.

Kant himself, as we shall see later, regards duty as a kind of necessity, and so connects the two kinds of *a priori* judgement—the moral or practical, and the theoretical or scientific. But when we say that we ought to tell the truth, we suppose that it is possible not to tell the truth. Hence to say that men *ought* to tell the truth and to say that they *must* tell the truth are two quite different statements. Indeed 'ought' and 'must' seem to be opposed in such a way that when one is present, the other must be absent. Hence even although Kant's view gets some support from the fact that 'must' is sometimes used for 'ought' in ordinary speech, we must for the present assume that 'must' and 'ought' indicate different kinds of judgement. Both these words, however, are used to express judgements which are not based on sensuous experience, and so must be called *a priori*. The connexion, if there is one, between duty and necessity must be considered later.

§4. *Composite knowledge.*

Some of our knowledge is partly based on sensuous experience and is partly not so based. Such knowledge may be called composite knowledge: it contains in itself both empirical and *a priori* elements. For example, we judge that the striking of this match caused a flame. Such a judgement is obviously empirical: it is dependent on sensuous experience. Nevertheless it is also a judgement of necessity: it asserts a necessary connexion between the flame and the striking of the match, and such a necessary connexion is not anything that we see or touch. Ultimately the judgement rests on the presupposition that every event *must* have a cause.

Kant sometimes speaks as if experience were merely sensing, because sensing is an essential element in experience. Strictly speaking, however, his doctrine is that experience is composite: it contains both empirical and *a priori* elements. Thus experience, on his view, is not merely a gaping at colours and sounds: it is a knowing of real objects such as this red carpet and this square table. We have experience when we hold together before the mind different sensible qualities as qualities of one object. This could not happen unless these qualities were given to sense. But equally it could not happen unless these qualities, given to different senses at different times, were held together before the mind in accordance with certain principles which cannot be given to sense at all and so are *a priori*. Among these principles he includes the principle that what today are called sense-data are changing accidents of a permanent substance, and that every event (including every change in the qualities of a substance) must have a cause.

Some of our ethical knowledge is equally composite. Thus if I can say that I ought not to kill John Smith, who is my enemy, my judgement contains empirical elements. I could not make this statement unless I had experience both of myself and of John Smith, and unless I knew that John Smith was a man and that men are mortal beings whose lives can be brought to an end by artificial means. Nevertheless my statement asserts an obligation, and neither obligation in general nor this particular obligation can be known merely from experience of the way in which men actually behave.

§5. *The task of philosophy.*

According to Kant, the task of philosophy is to distinguish from one another the *a priori* and empirical elements in our knowledge, and to consider what is our justification for accepting the *a priori* elements. We have, for example, to consider by what right we assume that every event must have a cause. As regards ethics in particular, the task of the philosopher is to seek out, and if possible to justify, the supreme principle of morality. To put the question for a moment in its simplest form, we have to ask what is meant by duty or moral obligation, and what is our justification for supposing that we have duties at all.[1]

Such a question is very far removed from the question whether I ought or ought not to kill John Smith; but unless I can answer it, I am hardly in a position to give a satisfactory answer to the question about John Smith—or even to a more general question about the rightness or wrongness of killing.

The question as to the supreme principle of morality or the nature of duty as such belongs to the branch of ethics which we may call 'pure' or 'unmixed' or 'rational' ethics. The application of the supreme principle of morality to the problems of action presented by human nature may be called 'applied' ethics. Such application clearly demands knowledge of human nature, which Kant calls 'anthropology' and we should call 'psychology'. Strictly speaking, the *Groundwork of the Metaphysic of Morals* and the *Critique of Practical Reason* belong to pure ethics, though they may occasionally bring in problems of applied ethics by way of illustration. Kant's later work, the *Metaphysic of Morals*, belongs, in great part at least, to applied ethics.

One difficulty in Kant's moral philosophy, as indeed in his theoretical philosophy, is the problem of the line to be drawn between the pure and the applied. Pure ethics, as I have said, must strictly be concerned with the supreme principle of morality alone; but Kant has a dangerous tendency to extend it in such a way as to cover what may be called moral laws, such as 'Thou shalt not lie.'[2] We ought to distinguish (1) moral principles; (2) moral laws, like the ten commandments, which apply to men as men;[3] (3) moral rules, such as the statement that it may be the duty of a soldier or an executioner to kill; and (4) singular moral judgements, such as the judgement that I ought not to kill John Smith. Singular moral judgements cannot be a part of philosophy. Moral rules and moral laws alike must belong to applied ethics: they all have a reference to human nature, as can be easily seen by considering

---

[1] We shall see later that this is not an adequate way of putting our question.
[2] See, for example, the confused statements in *Gr.*, 389 = 5–6.
[3] Compare *M.d.S.*, *Tugendlehre*, §45, 468.

in what sense they could be binding upon non-human rational beings, such as angels, for example, are supposed to be. If angels are immortal, it is ridiculous to say that they ought not to kill one another. Only principles, supposed to be valid for all rational agents as such, can belong to pure ethics. An empirical element must enter in as soon as we begin to derive moral laws from our supreme principles.

§6. *The need for pure ethics.*

Kant is insistent on the need for pure ethics, and again and again he pours scorn on a merely 'popular' philosophy which mixes up the *a priori* and the empirical and gropes its way by means of examples. Such a procedure merits condemnation as being intellectually confused; but Kant maintains that it is also morally deleterious.

The reason for the latter contention is this. A morally good action must not only accord with duty, but it must be willed for the sake of duty.[1] If we fail to grasp the nature of duty in its purity, we may be tempted to act merely for the sake of pleasure or convenience. Actions so grounded may at times accord with our duty, but at times they will be contrary to our duty; and in any case they will never be morally good actions, since they will proceed from a non-moral motive.[2]

Such a view may appear hard on the ordinary good man, who is unaccustomed to philosophical abstractions. Kant, however, believes that human reason in morals, as opposed to speculation, can easily be set on the right path. This is indeed only to be expected, since if we all have a duty to do, it must be possible for us to know what our duty is.[3] On his view, every man ought to have, and indeed has, however obscurely, a pure philosophy of duty.[4] Kant claims to do no more than formulate clearly the moral principle already at work in our ordinary moral judgements.[5] The need for an explicit ethical philosophy arises because the ordinary man may be tempted to let the pure principles of duty be obscured by the attractions of pleasure: he may become sophistical about the strict laws of duty, and may seek to cast doubt upon their validity, or at least upon their strictness and purity.[6] This can be corrected only by pure ethics.

As to the use of examples, Kant is far from repudiating this in the moral education of the young, provided it is directed towards separating the moral motive from motives of pleasure and self-interest.[7] The danger of basing ethical teaching on examples is this: it may give the impression that the concept of duty is a generalisation from experience, a concept of how men actually behave; and this in turn may lead to a confusion of

---

[1] Kant himself speaks—rightly—of the moral law, and this we shall find to be wider than duty. I have spoken of duty, because we have not yet heard of the moral law (as distinct from particular moral laws).
[2] *Gr.*, 389–90 = 6–7. [3] *Gr.*, 391 = 8; 404 = 25.
[4] *M.d.S., Rechtslehre. Einl.* II, 216 = 16; *Tugendlehre, Vorrede*, 376 = 219.
[5] *K.p.V.*, 8 n. = 111 n. (= 14 n.) [6] *Gr.*, 405 = 26.
[7] *K.p.V.*, 154 ff. = 303 ff. (= 275 ff.); *Gr.*, 411 n. = 34 n.

moral with non-moral motives, or even to the view that duty is a mere phantom of the mind. Kant's attack on this use of examples is supported by three main reasons.[1] Firstly, we can have no certain examples of moral action, since the motives of human action are always obscure. Secondly, the moral law must be valid, not merely for men but for all rational agents as such, and no experience could entitle us to assert such a necessary law. Thirdly, examples must all be judged in the light of *a priori* principles, and consequently they cannot enable us to dispense with an examination of these *a priori* principles. Morality is not mere imitation, and examples serve only to encourage us; that is, they may show our ideal to be not impracticable, and they may make it more vivid to our imagination.

Of these arguments the first is at least plausible, if not altogether consistent with the alleged power of examples to show the practicableness of our ideals. The second must be reserved for consideration later. The third is, however, conclusive. Moral judgements are not judgements of fact and cannot be derived from judgements of fact. When we judge a man to be good or an action to be right, we are not making a statement of fact: we are appealing to an *a priori* standard. It is absolutely vital to morality to justify such a standard and to recognise that it cannot be justified by any judgement of fact. We may of course hold that we have no binding duty, that the whole concept of duty is a mere illusion, a relic of primitive tabus, a cover for self-interest, and so on. What is philosophically deplorable is that we should continue to talk and act as if we had duties, and yet should explain them away as due to convention or tradition or self-interest. Only pure ethics can clear away this confusion and justify a belief in duty, if it can be justified at all. Otherwise confusion of mind may easily lead to degeneration in conduct.

§7. *The method of analysis.*

If pure ethics is not based upon experience, on what can it be based? Indeed if we cannot begin our enquiry from experience, how can we even begin it at all?

Undoubtedly we must begin, as Kant does himself, 'from the common use of our practical reason';[2] and this means that we must begin with our ordinary moral experience, though Kant himself avoids this usage, presumably because for him experience is confined to experience of facts. It should also perhaps be said that moral judgements are not really ours unless to some extent they influence our actions. We act morally only in so far as we act according to moral judgements, and a justification of moral judgements will also be a justification of moral actions.

It may be objected that we are now lapsing back into some kind of empirical ethics. This, however, is a mistake. Our moral judgements have an *a priori* element in them, and it is with this *a priori* element that we are concerned. What we want to discover is the *a priori* principle upon which moral judgements are based. This principle Kant believes to be actually

[1] *Gr.*, 405 ff. = 2 ff.   [2] *Gr.*, 406 = 28.

used by the ordinary man as a standard for his judgements, although it is not conceived by him in its abstract or universal form.[1] What Kant seeks to do is to formulate this principle clearly before he considers its justification.

Thus far Kant's method may be described as a method of analysis, whereby the *a priori* element in ordinary moral judgements is made explicit and is examined in separation from the empirical element. Such an analysis must be sharply distinguished from other kinds of analysis. It is not to be confused with the analysis whereby we separate out common characteristics found in different individual things and use these common characteristics as the basis for empirical concepts. Still less is it to be confused with an analysis which professes to set forth the successive stages in the supposed development of moral judgements. It is on the contrary concerned only with the *a priori* element which must be present in moral judgements unless these are mere illusions.

The *a priori* element in moral judgements is expressed, as we saw above, by such words as 'good' and 'evil', 'right' and 'wrong'. We may apply these words wrongly in particular cases; but no moral judgement can be valid, unless the concepts corresponding to these words are valid. Hence in separating out the *a priori* element in moral judgements we are determining the condition, the *sine qua non*, of the validity of moral judgements.

We so commonly identify the condition of a thing with its cause and regard the cause of a thing as outside it (either in time or in space or in both) that it may seem absurd to speak as if the condition of the validity of a judgement could be an element in the judgement itself. It certainly raises logical problems, the discussion of which belongs to a study of Kant's logic, not of his ethics. Nevertheless, it is surely obvious *both* that the concept of 'good' is employed in the judgement that St. Francis was a good man *and* that the judgement cannot be valid unless the concept of 'good' is valid.[2]

§8. *Analytic and synthetic arguments.*

If by analysis we have separated out the *a priori* element which is the condition of the validity of a moral judgement, we may be able, at least theoretically, to pass by a similar analysis from this condition to a still prior condition. For example, if we have separated out the concept of moral goodness, we may be able to say that no action is morally good unless it is done for the sake of duty. Acting for the sake of duty is then the precondition of moral goodness and consequently of all judgements in which moral goodness is predicated of individual actions. We can then

[1] *Gr.*, 403 = 24.
[2] It should be noted that this implication of the analytic method characterises Kant's Critical Philosophy as a whole. Thus he deals in abstraction with categories which are *both* present in all experience *and* conditions of the validity of all experience. Failure to grasp this makes Kant unintelligible.

go on to ask whether there is a still further condition apart from which no action can be done for the sake of duty.

An argument of this kind is called by Kant both an 'analytic' and also a 'regressive' argument. It starts from something conditioned (such as a particular moral judgement), and it seeks to go back to its condition, and from this to still remoter conditions. It is opposed to a 'synthetic' or 'progressive' argument, which goes in the reverse direction; that is, which starts from a condition and goes forward to the conditioned.[1]

The word 'regressive' may appear more appropriate than the word 'analytic' for the kind of argument we have described. The word 'analytic' has, however, this merit: it suggests that the conditions (or series of conditions) made explicit are somehow contained in (or are somehow a part of) the moral judgements from which we start. How this can be so, and how each step in a regressive argument can be justified, are questions full of difficulty and requiring more examination than they receive from Kant. For example, it is not clear whether each step in the argument requires a separate intuition, nor how such intuition (if any) is to be characterised. Without such examination even the Critical philosopher has not attained his ideal of knowing exactly what it is that he is doing. Nevertheless we have at least the external plan of Kant's argument, and we must understand this plan if we are to follow each step as it is made.

All this, however, is only one aspect of Kant's method, and a similar method may be found in other philosophers besides Kant. Indeed it may be doubted whether any other method is possible in moral philosophy. Perhaps, however, it should also be said that in the case of Kant the method involves a gradual clarification of statements which to begin with are relatively vague and obscure. Kant does not believe, as some philosophers do, that we can begin with clear definitions and gradually build a structure on this foundation. He believes, on the contrary, that in philosophy adequate definitions can be given, not at the beginning, but only at the end, when our analysis is complete.[2]

§9. *The Critical method.*

It looks as if the method of analysis, even if we are justified at every step of the argument, can give us no more certainty than that of the original judgements from which we start; or at least as if it can give us only the certainty of bringing separate judgements under one principle, the certainty which belongs to a system rather than to isolated judgements. On the other hand, there is the possibility that in a regressive series of judgements we might be able to do more than see that the truth of each new judgement is the necessary condition of the truth of the previous judgement: we might also have the same kind of insight into the truth

---

[1] See *Prol., Vorw.* and §4 (263 and 274–5). This distinction must never be confused with either (1) the distinction between analytic and synthetic judgements or (2) the distinction between the analysis and synthesis which are present in all judgements. See *K.M.E.*, I, 130 and 219.

[2] *K.r.V.*, A731 = B759; *K.p.V.*, 9 n. = 113 n. (= 15 n.).

of each new judgement as we had into the truth of the judgement from which we started. This is, I think, Kant's view of what actually takes place. Finally we might arrive regressively at a judgement into whose truth we had some special kind of insight, a judgement whose truth was established with complete certainty. In such a case our whole argument would be greatly strengthened, and our previous judgements would be corroborated and justified. We should be able to reverse our direction and proceed progressively (or synthetically) to our original starting point without falling into a vicious circle.

The most obvious way, if not indeed the only way, in which our argument might be thus strengthened would have been found if in our regression we could arrive at a judgement whose truth is self-evident. This may, in a sense, be Kant's own view, but if so, he holds it with a difference. He believes that a philosopher should be very wary of alleged self-evident propositions.[1] They are too often the deliverances of common sense or tradition and are, in his language, the cushion of a lazy philosophy. He admits, it is true, that *a priori* principles (*Grundsätze*) are so called, not merely because they contain the grounds (*Gründe*) of other judgements, but also because they themselves are not grounded in any higher or more universal cognitions of *objects*. Nevertheless he holds that all such principles (apart from those that are tautologous) must be subject to criticism and require a proof or at least a justification (which he calls a 'deduction'). This applies, in his view, even to the principles of mathematics, which he believes to be grasped by direct intuition and to possess apodeictic certainty. Even so, we have still to ask how knowledge of this kind is possible, and we have still to explain and justify this possibility.[2]

How can we offer such an explanation and justification of *a priori* knowledge? It is at this point that we come to the distinguishing characteristic of Kant's philosophy. He holds that when we come to *a priori* principles which are not grounded in any higher knowledge of *objects*—we must forgive him for making the ground higher than what rests upon it—we still have to consider their *subjective* origin in the nature of reason itself and so to justify them and explain their possibility. This is why his greatest works are called the *Critique of Pure Reason* and the *Critique of Practical Reason*; and this is the main ground for calling his philosophy the *Critical* Philosophy.

It must not be thought that whenever he arrives at a first principle which appears to be self-evident, he merely asserts that our reason, or some other faculty, is capable of grasping such a self-evident principle. To say this might be true, but it would be unimportant and would carry us no further in the way of explanation or justification. If he is to be successful, we must be able so to understand the necessary working of reason that the possibility of grasping such a first principle is rendered intelligible.

Kant's procedure is so subtle and complicated, and it varies so much with different problems, that no general account of it can be given here.

---

[1] *K.r.V.*, A233 = B285–6.   [2] *K.r.V.*, A148–9 = B188–9.

Indeed the account I have so far given is unduly simplified—though not, I hope, as regards his moral philosophy. All we need say here is that his method has at least an initial plausibility. We certainly cannot go beyond or behind the activity of our own self-critical reason, and it may well be supposed that the working of reason is, in a very special sense, transparent to itself. On the other hand his view has many difficulties, and it apparently introduces us to a new kind of self-evidence, which, however, Kant seems to take for granted rather than to discuss.

When we follow an analytic argument of Kant, it is well to remember that amid its apparent twistings and windings it is always moving deliberately towards some possible explanation or justification in the nature of reason itself.

§10. *The method of synthesis.*

The method of analysis is the method of discovery, but if we arrive at a first principle, we must be able to reverse the process; and if our first principle is independently established, whether on grounds of self-evidence or otherwise, we have a new kind of argument which, as we have seen above, may be called 'progressive' or 'synthetic'. The synthetic method is the method of exposition rather than of discovery.

This in turn raises logical problems, and the very word 'synthetic' suggests that in our descent from a first principle we must bring in further elements not themselves contained in the first principle. It looks as if we re-create the whole which hitherto we have been breaking up into a series of logically dependent parts. This in turn might mean that we cannot make our descent unless we have previously made an ascent.[1] Here it need only be noted that the same subject may be treated by an analytic argument in one book and by a synthetic argument in another; or both methods may be combined in the same book. Thus in the first two chapters of the *Groundwork* Kant proceeds analytically from common knowledge to the supreme principle of morality—the categorical imperative. In the third chapter he proceeds synthetically from the examination of this principle *and its sources*—that is, its sources in practical reason itself—to the common knowledge in which it is employed. Such at least is his own account of the matter,[2] and it is substantially correct, although he does not in fact pay any attention to the lower stages of the descent.

§11. *The importance of Kant.*

To those who are influenced by modern theories of empiricism and positivism Kant's procedure must inevitably seem to belong to an obsolete rationalism. Historically it is a mistake to consider him as primarily an

---
[1] Compare Plato's account in the *Republic* of the way in which dialectic mounts to the Idea of the Good and then descends; and also Aristotle's account of the difference between arguing to an ἀρχή and arguing from an ἀρχή (*Eth. Nic.*, 1095 a 34).
[2] *Gr.*, 392 = 9.

exponent of rationalism: his great service was to break away from a one-sided rationalism and to do justice to the empirical element in human knowledge. On the other hand he was also endeavouring to answer the one-sided empiricism of Hume in spite of his very great admiration for that philosopher. His central doctrine, as we have seen, is that we must distinguish clearly the empirical and *a priori* elements in our knowledge in order to do justice to both; and he considers it as much an error to 'intellectualise' empirical appearances with the rationalists as to 'sensify' the concepts of the understanding with the empiricists.[1] It is only by a combination of the empirical and the *a priori* that we can have knowledge.

It is precisely in this that his importance is to be found for the present day. He believes that an unmitigated empiricism is bound to end in a complete scepticism and that the only way to avoid this is to consider the activity which belongs to reason in its own right. At a time like the present, when so-called knowledge is being reduced to the apprehension of tautologies and the reception of sense-data, it is hard to see how the world can be made intelligible—even as intelligible as it seems to the ordinary man. It is still harder to see how we can have any principles of conduct; and indeed the problem of moral action tends to be treated as a problem of explaining—or explaining away—moral beliefs in terms of a theory of knowledge which has been adopted on quite other, and purely theoretical, grounds. The result must inevitably be that our wills, instead of being guided by intelligible principles, are delivered up to mere caprice or self-indulgence or tradition or even fanaticism, the last three being merely particular forms of caprice. And the whole doctrine must lead, as it already did in the case of Hume, to scepticism as regards the very existence of such a thing as a human mind.

However much we may respect the thoroughness of empirical philosophers in working out their theory to its logical conclusions, it is not easy to believe that men will long be satisfied with their account of knowledge and above all with their account of moral action. Kant believes that they can be answered only by an examination of the activity of reason itself, and his attempts to do so are at least worthy of serious study. This is particularly true of moral philosophy; for apart from questions of purely theoretical interest it is a bleak look-out for the world if we are all to be convinced that reason has no part to play in action.

From another and non-empirical point of view Kant is criticised on the ground that his work has been superseded by Hegel and his followers. I have no wish to deny that Hegel and others have found weaknesses in Kant's doctrines (including many of which he was never guilty) or that they have made advances on him in certain respects. On the other hand Hegel in particular has added a good many mistakes of his own, and his school is far from finding general approbation at the present time. If we want to avoid these mistakes, it may be a good thing to go back to Kant, who started the whole modern movement, and try to see what his doctrine really was—for I agree with Professor Schilpp that many of the absurdities

---

[1] *K.r.V.*, A271 = B297.

usually attributed to him are the fault of his interpreters.[1] A good understanding of Kant may well be, as it has so often been before, the condition of a new advance, and one of which we are in great need at the present time.

APPENDIX
THE DIVISIONS OF KANT'S MORAL PHILOSOPHY

It does not matter much what names we give to the different parts of Kant's philosophy, and I have ignored his account of the relations between logic, physics, and ethics; but a brief note may be added on the difference between the *Groundwork*, the *Critique of Practical Reason*, and the *Metaphysic of Morals*.

The *Groundwork* may be regarded as setting forth the core or kernel of a critique of practical reason: it considers only some of the topics peculiar to a critique and ignores others, such as the relation of practical to theoretical reason, a topic not of immediate importance for moral philosophy. Kant believed that practical reason was less in need of a critique than pure reason, and he may have intended to go straight on to a metaphysic of morals. If so, the general failure to understand the *Groundwork* may have led to a change in his plan. In any case he published the *Critique of Practical Reason* three years later (in 1788), while the *Metaphysic of Morals* was not published till 1797, when he was already 73 years old.

Kant commonly regards his two great *Critiques* as either propaedeutics to, or parts of, the corresponding metaphysic. Neither of these views is satisfactory, since if we suppose metaphysics to be pure *a priori* knowledge, there is little or no such knowledge outside of the *Critiques* themselves. The metaphysic is supposed to fill up into a complete system the framework set forth in the critique; but such fillings up are made only by bringing in empirical elements. We can, if we like, regard a critique of practical reason as concerned only with the *origin* of the categorical imperative in practical reason, and a metaphysic of morals as concerned with the different *formulations* of the categorical imperative. Kant himself suggests this by his titles for the second and third chapters of the *Groundwork*—the second chapter being called a 'transition' to the metaphysic of morals, and the third chapter a 'transition' to the critique of pure practical reason. But such a division is somewhat arbitrary, and is not strictly adhered to in practice. It seems to me better to regard a critique of practical reason and a metaphysic of morals as the same thing.

Kant's own *Metaphysic of Morals* is something different from what he says it ought to be, namely pure ethics. He explicitly recognises that it contains empirical elements;[2] and he calls his Theory of Law and

---

[1] *Kant's Pre-Critical Ethics*, pp. xiii–xiv.   [2] *M.d.S., Rechtslehre, Vorrede*, 205.

Theory of Virtue—the two parts into which it is divided—not a metaphysic, but 'metaphysical rudiments' (*Metaphysische Anfangsgründe*). Exactly the same thing happens to the *Critique of Pure Reason*: it is not followed up by a *Metaphysic of Nature*, but merely by the *Metaphysical Rudiments of Natural Science*. In both cases the phrase 'metaphysical rudiments' indicates the presence of empirical elements. Kant may have thought that more of his *Metaphysic of Morals* was 'pure ethics than is in fact the case. It does contain some ethics which may be called pure, but in the main it is applied ethics.

So far, applied ethics is concerned with the moral laws and moral rules which arise when we apply the supreme moral principles to the special conditions of human nature. Kant himself, however, speaks of applied ethics in a second and different sense; or perhaps he uses the term in a confused way covering the two different senses.[1] In the second sense 'applied ethics' is used for a special kind of moral or practical psychology (or anthropology as he calls it) concerned with the conditions which favour or hinder the moral life. It would be extremely useful both for education and for the guidance of our own lives if we could have an authoritative psychology of this kind. In its absence many parents today do not know—to take a crude example—whether discipline or a complete absence of discipline is the more likely to encourage moral excellence in their children. There is, however, no reason why we should regard such a psychology as practical:[2] it is a theoretical examination of the causes of certain morally desirable effects. Still less is there a reason why we should regard it with Kant as a kind of applied or empirical ethics.[3]

The application of moral principles is not only dependent on a psychology specially limited to the conditions favouring or hindering the moral life: it is also dependent on general psychology as knowledge of human nature. Without psychology, and indeed without empirical knowledge both of human nature and of the world in which we are, the application of moral principles would be impossible; and the more of such empirical knowledge we have, the better shall we be able to make sound moral judgements. This does not, however, alter the fact that the knowledge of moral principles, if there is such knowledge, is something quite distinct from empirical psychology, and cannot be derived from empirical psychology. To paraphrase Kant—pure ethics cannot be grounded on psychology, but it can be applied to psychology.[4]

There is, however, a further question whether the philosophy of moral action should not be preceded by a philosophy, or a philosophical psychology, of action as such. Before we consider what Kant calls a pure will, ought we not to examine the nature of will as such? Kant himself, before he examines what he calls pure thinking—that is, the *a priori* element in our knowledge of objects—has before him in formal logic a philosophical account of thinking as such, and indeed his account of pure *a priori*

---

[1] *Gr.*, 410 n. = 33 n.; *K.r.V.*, A55 = B79; *M.d.S.*, *Rechtslehre*, Einl. II, 217 = 16–17. Applied ethics can be regarded as parallel to the applied logic of *K.r.V.*, A52 ff. = B77 ff.
[2] See *K.U.*, *Erste Einleitung*, I, 7.   [3] *Gr.*, 388 = 4.
[4] *M.d.S.*, *Rechtslehre.*, Einl. II, 217 = 16.

thinking rests to a considerable extent on the doctrines of formal logic. The parallel may not commend itself to critics,[1] and there may be differences in the two cases; but at least it serves to raise the question. A philosophy of action as such would be comparable to the *Philosophia Practica Universalis* of Wolff, which Kant condemns for mixing up empirical and *a priori* elements;[2] but the fact that Wolff botched his job does not show that the undertaking is superfluous. Kant indeed argues that for moral philosophy it is not necessary to consider such topics as the grounds for pleasure and displeasure; the difference between the pleasures of the senses and those of taste and moral satisfaction; the way in which desires and inclinations spring from pleasures and pains, and in turn, with the co-operation of reason, give rise to maxims for action.[3] Nevertheless he does not wholly ignore such topics in his own moral philosophy, and it can hardly be doubted that he takes for granted a good many doctrines of this kind which it would have been well if he had set forth specifically. He does make contributions to this subject in his *Anthropologie* and elsewhere; but there is much to be said for the view that if he had set forth in detail a sound philosophy of action, this would have been a great help towards understanding his moral philosophy and might have modified it in certain respects.

---

[1] The traditional criticisms of Kant on this point were based on complete misunderstanding. Compare Dr. Klaus Reich in *Die Vollständigkeit der kantischen Urteilstafel*—a work which supersedes all previous discussions on this topic.
[2] *Gr.*, 390 = 7. The *philosophia practica universalis* of *M.d.S.*, *Rechtslehre*, *Einl.* IV, has a somewhat different character.
[3] *Gr.*, 427 = 54–5.

CHAPTER II

THE GOOD WILL

§1. *A good will is good without limitation.*

KANT begins his argument dramatically. 'It is impossible,' he says, 'to conceive anything in the world, or even out of it, which can be taken as good without limitation, save only a *good will*.'[1]

This, it must be confessed, although it professes to be an ordinary moral judgement, is not the kind of utterance in which the ordinary good man habitually indulges: it is already more like the statement of a principle which the ordinary good man may be supposed to follow in his judgements and actions, even if he does not formulate it explicitly. Nevertheless the question raised is one for ordinary moral insight; and without further analysis the statement is too vague to be regarded as a satisfactory moral principle. We very much want to be told, for example, what is meant (1) by 'good without limitation' and (2) by 'a good will'.

The first phrase offers little difficulty. To put Kant's assertion in other terms—we may say that a good will alone can be good in itself, or can be an absolute or unconditioned good. Words like 'absolute' and 'unconditioned' may today be obscure to the simple and repulsive to the sophisticated, but in the present context they are not difficult to understand. All Kant means is that a good will alone must be good in whatever context it may be found. It is not good in one context and bad in another. It is not good as means to one end and bad as means to another. It is not good if somebody happens to want it and bad if he doesn't. Its goodness is not conditioned by its relation to a context or to an end or to a desire. In this sense it is an unconditioned and absolute good: it is good in itself and not merely in its relation to something else. Its goodness is not limited to goodness in this or in that relation: it is, in short, good without limitation or qualification or restriction.

But what is meant by 'a good will'? This indeed is one of the questions which it is the purpose of our enquiry to answer; but at present we are concerned with 'a good will' as it is recognised and judged by ordinary moral consciousness. Hence the conception is necessarily vague, and it is deliberately left so at first by Kant.[2] We might, perhaps not improperly, describe it as 'a moral will', but this might have misleading associations. For example, many people today might regard a moral will as one which is bound by what they call 'conventional morality', and so as intellectually blind and practically misguided. Such a will, however, is then

[1] *Gr.*, 393 = 11.   [2] *K.p.V.*, 62–3 = 183 (= 110).

regarded as conventionally good but genuinely bad. What we are concerned with is a will which we can regard as *genuinely* good. If we admit, provisionally, that there can be such a thing and that it can be recognised, or at least conceived, then it is not unplausible to say with Kant that it must be good in whatever circumstances it may be found, and that therefore it must be an absolute and unconditioned good.

§2. *Other possible views.*

Even on this semi-philosophical level there are further questions about the nature of a good will which demand at least a provisional answer. But before considering these, it may be well to examine, first of all, some possible alternatives to Kant's doctrine.

Some theories which would render Kant's assertion meaningless or trivial or false must be here passed over. We might say, for example, that since the word 'good' means nothing,[1] Kant's assertion about a good will can mean nothing. This view seems to me an ingenious paradox based on logical prejudices rather than on a disinterested examination of moral judgements. Again we might say that since 'to be good' *means* 'to be pleasant', Kant's assertion is certainly trivial and probably false. This is an ancient fallacy requiring no refutation here. I propose to assume that 'good' means something, and that it does not mean 'pleasant'.

On this assumption Kant's statement has two sides, a positive side and a negative side. He asserts positively that a good will is good without limitation, and negatively that nothing but a good will is so. As against his negative assertion, we may affirm that other things than a good will are good without limitation; we may even affirm that all things which are good (in at least one sense of the word 'good') are good without limitation. As against his positive assertion we may deny that a good will is good without limitation; we may even deny that anything is good without limitation.

Let us first consider the position of goods other than a good will.

§3. *Are all goods good without limitation?*

A possible alternative to Kant's view is that all goods (in one sense of the word 'good') are good without limitation or are absolute and unconditioned goods. This view has very strong support at the present time.

A brief discussion of this view is hampered both by the fact that in ordinary usage the word 'good' has many meanings, and also by the fact that different philosophers express themselves in different terms. A detailed examination would here be out of place, and it will be sufficient if we can show that Kant's view in opposition to it is at least not unreasonable.[2]

---

[1] The ablest exposition of this view will be found in Ayer, *Language, Truth and Logic*, Chap. VI of the first edition.

[2] In *The Philosophy of G. E. Moore* I have discussed this topic in an essay entitled *The Alleged Independence of Goodness*. Compare also my paper on *Kant's Idea of the Good* in the *Proceedings of the Aristotelian Society*, 1944–5, pp. i–xxv.

If we consider various kinds of thing in isolation—that is, in abstraction from their context—we may properly say of them that they are good. Among these kinds of thing may be included, for example, pleasure, knowledge, and art. Most people would be inclined to agree that all these kinds of thing, when thus considered in isolation, are good, or even good in themselves. They are at least what Sir David Ross might call *prima facie* goods.

The view we are considering maintains that whatever goodness these *prima facie* goods have in isolation, that very same goodness they must have in any context in which they may be found. In other words *all* such *prima facie* goods are absolute and unconditioned goods. In this respect therefore a good will is by no means, as Kant supposes, unique.

Such a view is not, I think, consistent in all cases with our ordinary judgements. Thus pleasure is manifestly a *prima facie* good; yet in some contexts it is thoroughly bad; for example, pleasure in the pain of others seems thoroughly bad. Indeed it is not unreasonable to hold that the actual goodness of these *prima facie* goods generally varies with their context. It is not merely that art and knowledge are no good to a starving man. In such a context as the burning of Rome, one would have to be a Nero, and not a reasonable man, to think that art was a good thing to pursue. In certain contexts art and knowledge are out of place.

It may be objected that even in such contexts it is not art or knowledge, but rather the pursuit of them, that is bad. Perhaps. But when we say this,[1] are we not merely judging art and knowledge in isolation over again? Whatever these things are in isolation, they are not actually good or bad except as in some sense pursued. The goodness supposed to belong to things considered in isolation is an abstraction; and the only real goodness is the actual concrete goodness of a thing in a concrete situation.

However this may be, there is a plausible explanation of the way in which the goodness of things *seems* to vary with their context, although, as we are told, in reality it does not so vary. The goodness which varies, it is held, is not the goodness of the thing itself, but a quite other goodness which belongs to it as a means, or else the goodness (other than its own) which it contributes to a whole of which it is a part. We must distinguish its intrinsic goodness from (1) its goodness as a means (that is, its utility) and from (2) what we may call its contributory goodness.

It is certainly true that we must be on our guard against confusing the goodness of a thing with its mere usefulness for something else. It is also true and important to say that the goodness of a whole is greater than the sum of the goodness of its parts taken in isolation from one another and from the whole. The part may contribute to the whole more goodness than it has when it is considered in isolation, that is, when it is not a part. So far so good. But the question is whether the part in thus contributing an extra goodness to the whole is not itself immediately better than it would be if it were not a part, that is, if it were in a different context.

It can hardly be doubted that the part in contributing this extra goodness to the whole *seems* to be more valuable than it would be in isolation. For some purposes it may perhaps be convenient to divide up its apparent goodness into a goodness which belongs to it intrinsically and a goodness which arises from its being a part of this whole—although such a division is a matter of theory and does not result from an immediate judgement of value. What is questionable is the assertion that the extra contributory goodness belongs not to the part but to the whole. The whole is made up of parts, and it has no goodness which is not manifested in its parts (that is, in its parts as parts and not as isolated existents). The goodness contributed by a part to the whole must also be manifested in the parts and above all, one would think, in the part which makes the contribution. This indeed seems the direct utterance of our judgement of value, as is very obvious, for example, of the beauty which is contributed to a poem by the use, in a particular context, of a word which may have no great beauty in itself—our aesthetic judgements throw a great light on this problem. Furthermore, if *ex hypothesi* the part can add an extra goodness to a whole and so to the other parts, it seems impossible to deny on principle that the whole, and so the other parts, can add an extra goodness to the part. That is, the goodness of the part may vary with its context; and this, however much we may divide up goodness in theory, seems, as I have said, to be the direct utterance of the judgement of value. In our actual concrete judgements, while we can distinguish the goodness of a thing from its utility (or from the goodness of its consequences), we cannot, I think, so distinguish the goodness which it has in itself from the goodness which it has as part of a whole.

Hence the general allegation that all goodness (in one sense) is independent of its context[1] is not sufficiently grounded to dispose of Kant's view that the goodness of a good will is unique in being independent of its context. When we say that a good will is good without limitation, we do not mean merely that in its actual goodness we can by abstraction distinguish a goodness which would equally belong to it in isolation. Kant, at least, holds that a good will, if it is good without limitation, must have its full worth in itself, and that this worth cannot be diminished or increased, and cannot be outweighed or dimmed, either by any consequences or by the varying contexts in which it may be found.[2] Such a statement would not be true, for example, of pleasure; for even if we think it proper to attribute to pleasure in a concrete situation a goodness which would equally belong to it in isolation, this *prima facie* goodness may be more than outweighed by the badness of its consequences or by the badness which arises from its presence in this particular situation. The question on which we have to make up our minds is whether or not Kant is right in finding this difference between a good will and all other things which we recognise to be at least *prima facie* good.

[1] I have assumed that this doctrine means more than an intention to *call* 'intrinsic goodness' only the goodness which, as present in isolation, is attributed to the thing in whatever context it may be found. If the matter were only one of terminology, Kant would be entitled to use his own.

[2] *Gr.*, 394 = 13. See §6 below.

§4. *Are many goods good without limitation?*

Even if we refuse to accept the general principle that all goods (in one sense of the word 'good') are good without limitation, it is nevertheless possible that some goods other than a good will may be good without limitation. Kant himself discusses this possibility. He examines, and rejects, the view that certain things which 'are without doubt in many respects good and desirable' are good without limitation in the same way as a good will.[1] We are now concerned, not with their goodness in abstraction or their abstract goodness: we are concerned with their goodness in concrete situations or their concrete goodness.

The principle upon which Kant selects these *prima facie* goods for consideration is not altogether clear.[2] He appears to be interested, at least primarily, in goods which are not themselves the product of a good will, although a good will might aim at their development or—in certain cases—at their attainment. Thus he mentions first *gifts of nature*. Under these he includes *mental talents*, such as intelligence, wit, and judgement (to which we might be allowed to add humour, imagination, and artistic capacity);[3] and *qualities of temperament*, such as courage, resolution, and perseverance. He then passes to *gifts of fortune*, among which he includes power, riches, honour, health, and happiness. Finally, he returns to what are apparently also *qualities of temperament*, special qualities which he considers peculiarly helpful to a good will and so liable to be regarded as themselves possessing unconditioned value. These are moderation in affections and passions, self-control, and cool deliberation.

His criticism of these claimants to absolute goodness is in all cases the same. However good these things may be in some respects, they are not, like a good will, good in all respects and in all relations. On the contrary, when they accompany a bad will, they are themselves bad. They are then bad, not merely as producing bad consequences, but as themselves the source of an additional badness in the whole of which they are parts.[4] The coolness of a villain makes him not only far more dangerous: it makes him also *immediately* more abominable in our eyes than he would have been without it.[5]

This contention appears to me to be sound; and presumably on Kant's view it would apply equally to other *prima facie* goods which he does not consider, such as skill in arts and sciences, taste, and bodily agility.[6] None of these things is an absolute or unconditioned good.

We may, however, put Kant's doctrine more positively. For him all

---

[1] *Gr.*, 393–4 = 11–12.
[2] Klaus Reich suggests that it is due to the influence of Cicero's *De Officiis* (*Mind*, N.S., Vol. XLVIII, No. 192).
[3] See *Gr.*, 435 = 66.
[4] The distinction is clearly made in this discussion, although when Kant discusses kinds of good abstractly, he uses only the distinction between 'good as means' and 'good in itself'—presumably on the ground that when anything makes worse the whole of which it is a part, it is then bad immediately (or in itself) in that context. *Gr.*, 414 = 38.
[5] *Gr.*, 394 = 12. The italics are mine.   [6] *Religion, Vorrede*, 4 n. (= IV n.).

these *prima facie* goods are conditioned goods, and the condition of their goodness is said to be a good will.[1] This would be absurd if it meant that in a bad man nothing—not even artistic or scientific activity—could be good. Kant's meaning is, I think, expressed more accurately when he says that a conditioned good is one which is good only on condition that its use is not contrary to the moral law.[2] This would dispose of the view that Nero's fiddling was a good. In the case of happiness perhaps Kant's view varies unconsciously. He always recognises that happiness is in many respects good,[3] and even holds that in man reason has an office which it cannot refuse, the office of seeking happiness in this world and where possible in the next.[4] In the view of reason happiness as a good knows no other limitation than that which springs from our own immoral conduct.[5] But he also says that reason does not approve happiness (however much inclination may desire it) unless it is united with moral behaviour.[6] For the sake of consistency as well as truth we must say that all happiness is good except in so far as it is happiness in iniquity.

In all this we must remember that Kant is not offering us a general theory of value, but only a theory of goodness. Art and science have their own standards of excellence, but these are standards of beauty and truth, not of goodness. Success in the pursuit of art or science is no doubt a conditioned good; but this, as we have seen, means for Kant that it is good only if it is not contrary to the moral law. No matter how well Nero fiddled, what he did was not good. Indeed it might be argued—though I do not attribute this to Kant—that the better he fiddled, the worse his action was. To paraphrase Kant—the scientific skill and artistic gifts of a villain may not only make him more dangerous: they may make him also *immediately* more abominable in our eyes than he would have been without them.

Once the question is put clearly, ordinary judgement would, I think, agree with Kant that even very great goods of the kind we have considered are not necessarily good in any and every context. That is, they are not good without limitation.

§5. *Is a good will good without limitation?*

We can now return to the alleged absolute goodness of a good will. This might perhaps be denied on the general ground that no good can be good without limitation. It might be held that the nature of everything must depend on its context, and that consequently the goodness of everything must depend on its context. From this it must follow that even

---

[1] *Gr.*, 396 = 15. Their goodness may also be conditioned by our desires and needs; but that is another question.

[2] *Religion, Vorrede*, 4 n. (= IV n.). It is stated less clearly when Kant says (*Gr.*, 397 = 16) that the concept of a good will always stands first in estimating the whole value of any action and constitutes the condition of all other value.

[3] *Gr.*, 393 = 11.   [4] *K.p.V.*, 61 = 181 (= 108).
[5] *K.r.V.*, A814 = B842.   [6] *K.r.V.*, A813 = B841.

the goodness of a good will must depend on its context, and that it is therefore absurd to speak of a good will as having the same unique and absolute goodness in any and every context.

Since views of this kind have little acceptance at the present time, we may perhaps be allowed to pass over this *a priori* objection and to consider the goodness of a good will in the light of our ordinary judgements.

We are concerned, as I have said, only with a genuinely good will. We need not concern ourselves with busy-bodies and killjoys, with scribes and pharisees, with fanatics and persecutors, so far as their activities are inspired by envy and pride and malevolence; for such men are manifestly not possessed of a genuinely good will. These types may indeed shade off gradually into other types described by Kant as 'moral enthusiasts', who allow a lively sympathy with goodness to degenerate into a passion or fever; or as the 'fantastically virtuous', who can admit nothing whatever to be morally indifferent.[1] But perhaps we may agree with Kant that even such types belong to the pathology of human nature. The presence of a good will in them means that their excessive emotions are manifested in an unbalanced pursuit of moral ideals: but these emotions would have found some outlet anyhow, perhaps—as in the case of German anti-Semites—with even worse results. Morality, like religion, may attract to itself unbalanced emotions, but a genuinely good will will seek to moderate and control, not to encourage, such emotions.

If we set aside men whose professed goodness springs from moral badness or whose genuine goodness is overlaid with emotional abnormality, is it not true that good men may do a great deal of harm which, as is commonly said, has to be undone by the wise? And may not even a genuinely good will be at times out of place?

It is certainly true that good men may do a great deal of harm; and this harm may spring, not from officiousness and vanity (which belong to moral badness), but from mere silliness or stupidity. In intellectual matters Kant shows a very good understanding of stupidity, which he describes as a lack of judgement;[2] but in moral matters he tends to underrate the need for judgement and discrimination in deciding upon the right course of action.[3] I think, however, he would hold that the harm done by a stupid good man was due to his stupidity and not to his goodness: he certainly seems to hold that a good will as such cannot issue in wrong actions.[4] In any case it would be paradoxical if we maintained that it is better to be a stupid bad man than a stupid good one; and even if the stupid good man may produce some bad results which would not be produced by the stupid bad man, Kant would still hold that his good

---

[1] *M.d.S., Tugendlehre, Einl.* XVII, 409 = 258; 433 n. Compare also *K.p.V.* 157 = 306-7 (= 280). Kant himself, however, denies elsewhere—though perhaps in a somewhat different sense—that actions can be morally indifferent; *Religion*, 22 = 23 (= 9). An interesting study of the moral and religious enthusiast is to be found in *Heaven's My Destination*, by Thornton Wilder.

[2] *K.r.V.*, A133 n. = B172-3 n.   [3] E.g. *Gr.*, 403 = 24.

[4] He implies this by arguing that motives other than duty, which is the motive of a good will, sometimes issue in right actions and sometimes in wrong. *Gr.*, 411 = 34.

will had a unique and incomparable value which could not be outweighed by the evils resulting from his natural defects.[1]

The antithesis between goodness and wisdom is useful enough to describe an empirical situation with which we are only too familiar, but considered philosophically it is artificial. A man with a genuinely good will cannot but seek to develop such intelligence as he has—especially that intelligence in practical matters which is commonly called wisdom.[2] And a genuinely wise man cannot but seek genuine moral goodness. This is not altered by the empirical fact that a well-meaning clergyman may talk nonsense about economics.

We must not regard a good will as a mixture of moral enthusiasm and practical folly and personal conceit. A good will of this kind would be out of place, not sometimes, but always. The only kind of situation in which a genuinely good will may reasonably seem out of place is the situation which calls for spontaneous emotion or mutual entertainment without the overriding thought that this is a binding duty. Kant may not have given enough place for such spontaneity—few moralists do; but he was far from supposing, either in theory or in practice, that a good will could not manifest itself in the virtues of social intercourse.[3] It is a mere prejudice to identify a good will with sour-faced morality; and if we abandon this prejudice, it may reasonably be said that of all things in the world a genuinely good will is the only one which is never out of place.

It remains, however, an open question whether a good will as described by Kant is a genuinely good will.

§6. *The highest good.*

If a good will is the only thing which is an unconditioned or absolute good in the sense that it must be good in every possible context, can we go on to assert with Kant that it must therefore be the highest good?

The phrase 'highest good' is ambiguous. It may mean merely the good which is itself unconditioned and is the condition of all other goods.[4] In this sense 'highest good' and 'absolute good' mean precisely the same thing. But Kant is also making a judgement of value; for such a good is to be *esteemed* as 'beyond comparison higher' than any other good.[5] Its usefulness or fruitlessness can neither add to, nor subtract from, this unique and incomparable worth.

There seem to be two questions here: 'Are we, first of all, entitled to say that only a highest, and indeed an incomparable, good can be good in every context?' And, secondly, 'Is such an inference confirmed by a direct and enlightened judgement?'

It is difficult to estimate an inference of the kind suggested in our

---

[1] *Gr.*, 394 = 12–13.
[2] Compare *M.d.S., Tugendlehre, Einl.* VIII, 391 ff. = 237 ff.; and §19, 444 ff.
[3] *M.d.S., Tugendlehre*, §48, 473 ff.
[4] *K.p.V.*, 110 = 246 (= 198); *Gr.*, 396 = 15.   [5] *Gr.*, 394 = 12.

first question. If we were speaking of something like air, for example, whose goodness consists in its utility for man and other animals, we could not say that air, which is good always, is better than exercise, which is good only sometimes. But manifestly the utility of anything does depend on its context—namely, the needs of living organisms—and it cannot offer a parallel to our inference about a good will. It is certainly hard to see how a thing could be good in itself and the condition of all other goods without being incomparably more valuable than these conditioned goods. Nevertheless we may be inclined to suspect a snag in this kind of argument if its conclusion is not confirmed by independent testimony—and perhaps even if it is.

This brings us back to the question: 'Are we entitled, in the light of ordinary judgements, to rate a good will so far above artistic activity or the pursuit of knowledge? Is Kant's assertion due merely to the personal prejudice of a moralist?'

It is always difficult to be sure how far any particular judgement of value may be affected by personal prejudices. But it is interesting to observe that Kant himself at one time shared the prejudices, natural to a scholar, which attach the greatest value to knowledge, if not to art; and he was converted from this view, not by some grim Puritan, but by Jean Jacques Rousseau. 'I am myself,' he says, 'by inclination a researcher. There was a time when . . . I despised the masses, who know nothing. Rousseau has put me right. This blind prejudice disappears; I learn to honour men.'[1]

The honour which Kant thus learned to pay to men is, I think, honour for their good will. The passage may be compared with another from the *Critique of Practical Reason*,[2] in which he says that even against his will his spirit bows before a man, however humble and ordinary, in whom he finds integrity of character in a measure which he is not conscious of finding in himself. This feeling of reverence, as distinct from admiration, is felt for the good man, and for no one else.

To the modern intellectual, who tends to value moral goodness mainly as a means necessary to establish satisfactory conditions for the pursuit of art and science, it may seem that Rousseau has put Kant wrong rather than right. Nevertheless if we are discussing the goodness of things, we must do so from the point of view of an agent and not merely of a detached observer. Art and science have their own standards of beauty and truth, but they are also goods which a good man, according to his circumstances, will seek and ought to seek. Nevertheless not only do we regard goodness with a feeling of reverence which we do not give to success in art or science;[3] but we know—in these days almost too well—that even these great goods must at times be sacrificed at the call of duty; and this

---

[1] *Fragmente*, Phil. Bib., VIII, p. 322. See also Schilpp, *Kant's Pre-Critical Ethics*, pp. 47–8.
[2] *K.p.V.*, 76–7 = 202 (= 136).
[3] Kant holds that where we feel reverence for a person of great talents, this is not because of his ability, but because he is to us an example of one who has performed the duty of developing his talents. See *Gr.*, 401 n. = 22 n.

ould not be so, unless we held, as so many have held in action, that the
oodness of acting well outweighs the goodness even of the things which
e regard as the most precious.

In any case, whatever may be thought of Kant's position, this is the
assumption upon which his argument is based.

§7. *A good will and its objects.*

It was suggested in §3 above that the goodness supposed to belong to
things considered in isolation was a mere abstraction, and it may now be
objected that we are falling into this very same abstraction ourselves. A
good will considered in isolation from its objects is, it may be said, itself a
mere abstraction. A good will must have an object; and surely the goodness of a good will must be estimated by the goodness of the objects which
it attains, or at the very least by the goodness of the objects which it seeks
to attain. We cannot even begin to discuss the goodness of a good will
before we have discussed the goodness of different kinds of object.

Kant regards this objection as a fundamental error, fatal to any sound
moral philosophy and indeed to morality itself.[1] We may hope to understand his view better as we advance; but it should already be clear that if
the objects of a good will are conditioned goods, and a good will itself is
an unconditioned good, the goodness of a good will cannot possibly be
derived from the goodness of the objects at which it aims.[2] This contention
is in no way affected by the assertion, which Kant fully accepts,[3] that a
good will (like any other) must aim at objects or ends.

If the goodness of a good will is not derived from the goodness of the
ends at which it aims, still less can it be derived from success in attaining
these ends. Furthermore, success in action depends on many factors outside our control, and a goodness which varies according to success or
failure could not be described as unconditioned. And finally, if through
some misfortune, such as a stroke of paralysis, a good volition (not a mere
wish) had no outer effects at all, it would still retain its unique and
incomparable goodness.[4] This last assertion is surely borne out by ordinary
enlightened judgement.

To maintain the absolute value of a good will is by no means to deny
that other things, and in particular the objects sought or achieved by a
good will, may have value. A good will is the highest good, but Kant
always rejects the absurd view that it is the only good or the whole
good.[5] In order to have the complete good our good volitions must be
successful in realising their aim. This is what Kant expresses, not too
satisfactorily, when he says that in the whole or perfect good (*bonum
consummatum*) happiness must be included.[6] The common view that Kant
underrated the value of happiness is a complete mistake: if anything, he
rated it too high.

[1] *K.p.V.*, 58 ff. = 177 ff. (= 101 ff.) and especially 62–3 = 183–4 (= 110–111).
[2] *Gr.*, 400 = 19–20; 437 = 68.   [3] *K.p.V.*, 34 = 146 (= 60).
[4] *Gr.*, 394 = 12–13.   [5] *Gr.*, 396 = 15.
[6] *K.p.V.*, 110 = 246 (= 198–9).

§8. *The function of reason.*

Kant is well aware that his insistence on the absolute value of a mere will may appear paradoxical. In spite of the support it has from ordinary judgement we may suspect that it has its roots in some unconscious tendency to the high-flown and the fantastic, which of all things he most abominates. He therefore attempts to corroborate his doctrine by a teleological argument concerning the purpose or function of reason in human life.[1]

In this argument he assumes (1) that an organic being is a whole adapted to a purpose or end, namely, life; (2) that in such a being every organ is also adapted to a purpose or end which is an element in the total purpose or end; and (3) that every such organ is well fitted, and completely adequate, to attain its purpose or end.[2] Man is such an organic being, and he has as one organ a reason which is practical in the sense that it directs his will. Now if we assume that the natural end of man is a happy life (or the maximum satisfaction of desire), reason is ill adapted to secure such happiness; and nature would have done better to leave the choice of both ends and means to instinct rather than to reason. If we have to possess reason at all, its function should have been merely to appreciate the excellence of our instinctive nature as a means for securing happiness. Our actual experience shows that on the whole the more we confine the use of reason to the pursuit of pleasure—even of intellectual pleasure—the less happy we seem to be.

On these grounds, so Kant argues, if reason, like other organs, is to be well adapted to its end, its end or purpose must be something other than the attainment of happiness. The true function of reason on its practical side must be to produce a will good not as a means to something else such as happiness, but good absolutely and in itself. Only on this hypothesis can we understand how reason can interfere with the attainment of happiness and yet not be an exception to the general principle that every organ is well adapted to its end.

The argument raises questions about the supposed purposiveness of nature which are too complicated to consider here either in relation to Kant's philosophy or on their own merits; and even those who accept a doctrine of teleology in some sense or other may nowadays be doubtful whether all organs are well adapted to their purpose. Indeed they may even regard reason itself as some kind of cosmic mistake. The argument, however, is subsidiary, and its chief interest for our purpose is this—that it gives us our first introduction to the part which Kant conceives reason to play in action. He holds that reason does play a necessary part in the pursuit of happiness, both in conceiving the nature of happiness as an end and in guiding our choice of means to this end. The happiness thus sought is, however, a conditioned good: its goodness is relative, as we have seen, to the goodness of our will, and it is also relative to our desires and needs. Reason must also seek a greater good which is unconditioned by our

---

[1] *Gr.*, 394 = 13–15. [2] See also *K.r.V.*, B425.

desires and needs, and only so can it be adequate to its purpose in spite of its inadequacy for the pursuit of happiness. Such an unconditioned good can be only a will good in itself, not a will good in so far as it aims at satisfying certain desires or at attaining the objects of these desires.

These doctrines are here adumbrated vaguely, as is to be expected at this stage of the argument. We need not at present expect to understand Kant's view of the second and more important function of reason; but it is desirable to note that there are these two distinct functions of reason, and that both aim at a good, the first function at a conditioned good (namely, happiness), and the second at an unconditioned good (namely, a good will).

§9. *Goodness is fundamental.*

We have now completed the examination of Kant's starting-point and found it in the absolute and unique goodness of a good will. This requires to be stressed, because as the argument advances we shall find ourselves talking a great deal more about duty than about goodness. Kant is so commonly regarded as the apostle of duty that if we are to get his doctrine in true perspective we must remember that for him goodness is fundamental; and there is no warrant for supposing that he even entertained the conception of a duty divorced from goodness.

On the other hand our conception of a good will is as yet vague and popular and in need of clarification. It is to the task of clarification that we must now address ourselves.

CHAPTER III

DUTY

§1. *A good will and duty.*

IN order to make clear the nature of a good will Kant proposes to examine the concept of duty.[1] A will which acts for the sake of duty is a good will; but it must not be supposed that a good will is necessarily one which acts for the sake of duty. On the contrary, a completely good and perfect will would never act for the sake of duty; for in the very idea of duty there is the thought of desires and inclinations to be overcome. A completely good or 'holy' will, as Kant calls it, would be all of a piece: it would manifest itself in good actions without having to restrain or thwart natural inclinations, and so it would not act from a concept of duty at all. We may suppose that God's will is holy, and it would be absurd to speak of Him as doing His duty. But in finite creatures, or at any rate in a finite creature such as man, there are certain 'subjective limitations': man's will is not wholly good but is influenced by sensuous desires and inclinations, which may be hindrances and obstacles to the good will present in him. Hence the good actions in which, but for these obstacles, his good will would necessarily be shown appear to him as duties; that is, as actions that ought to be done in spite of these obstacles. A good will *under human conditions* is one which acts for the sake of duty. Such is the contention which we have now to examine.

It must not be thought that a will is good only because it overcomes obstacles. On the contrary, if we could attain to the ideal of complete goodness, we should have so disciplined our desires that there would be no further obstacles to overcome. Obstacles may serve to make the goodness of a good will more conspicuous, and we may be unable to measure goodness except by reference to such obstacles; but a good will must be good in itself apart from the obstacles it overcomes. If it were not so, holiness itself would be eclipsed by our imperfect struggles towards goodness.[2]

Our concern, however, is not with a holy will, but with a good will *under human conditions* and therefore a will which acts for the sake of duty. Hence the phrase 'under human conditions'—which it would be tedious to repeat—must be read into many of our sentences; but this must not lead us to forget that much, if not most, of what we say is *not* to be taken as true of all good wills without exception.

[1] *Gr.*, 397 = 16.   [2] *M.d.S., Tugendlehre*, Einl. X, 397 = 244.

§2. *The method of isolation.*

If we are to justify our contention that a good will—under human conditions—is one which acts for the sake of duty, we must first *isolate* actions done for the sake of duty and judge whether they possess the supreme worth which we have ascribed to a good will. It is true that actions cannot have precisely the same kind of absolute goodness as a good will, because a good action must be adjusted to a particular situation. Kant himself seems to hint at this difference when he speaks of an action as 'good in itself', but of a will as 'absolutely and in all respects good'.[1] Nevertheless if a good action is to be judged by the good will which is manifested in it, we may avoid fine distinctions and suppose that such an action has something of the same unique goodness as a good will.

In the case of actions which accord with duty Kant recognises three main types: (1) those done from immediate inclination; (2) those done, not from immediate inclination, but from self-interest; and (3) those done, not from immediate inclination or self-interest, but for the sake of duty. He thinks that actions done from self-interest are not likely to be confused with actions done for the sake of duty; but that actions done from immediate inclination are. The reason for this is presumably that in acting for the sake of duty and in acting from immediate inclination we do not look beyond the action itself to some remoter end or result. Hence in order to be quite certain that we are judging the value of actions done for the sake of duty, he asks us to remove the immediate inclination and assess the value of action in its absence. Thus, for example, he asserts that when we have through grief lost the immediate inclination to live and desire nothing so much as death, there still remains the duty of preserving our own life; and that in doing so, not from inclination, but for the sake of duty, the action has for the first time its genuine and unique moral worth.

Kant's method of isolation seems to me eminently rational and his conclusion wholly just. Most men would agree that there is no particular moral value in preserving one's own life merely because one has a desire to live; and most men would agree that the action has its moral value only when it is done for the sake of duty. The action in the first case would accord with duty, but would not be done for the sake of duty. Similarly—to take a case of self-interest—if a man paid his debt only for fear of arrest, his action would accord with duty, but it would not be done for the sake of duty, nor would it have moral worth.

Such is, as it seems to me, the simple doctrine which Kant expounds.[2] His contention is that an action has moral worth only so far as it is done for the sake of duty. He may be mistaken, but at least there is nothing absurd in what he says. Nevertheless his argument has laid itself open to the most strange interpretations which are now commonly accepted as an essential part of Kant's moral theory. It is only fair to add that the complication,

---

[1] *K.p.V.*, 62 = 182 (= 109).   [2] *Gr.*, 397–9 = 16–19.

and perhaps the looseness, of his language have not unnaturally led to these interpretations.

§3. *Misunderstandings.*

How early these misunderstandings arose can be seen from the well-known verses of Schiller:[1]

> Gladly I serve my friends, but alas I do it with pleasure.
> Hence I am plagued with doubt that I am not a virtuous person.

To this the answer is given:

> Sure, your only resource is to try to despise them entirely,
> And then with aversion to do what your duty enjoins you.

This is poor poetry and worse criticism. The common interpretation of Kant along these lines may be put more precisely as follows:

1. An action has no moral worth if any inclination to do the action is present or if any pleasure results from the satisfaction of this inclination; and

2. An action has no moral worth if any satisfaction arises from the consciousness of doing one's duty.

These two points are quite distinct, although they are sometimes confused. Both are absurd in themselves and mistaken as interpretations of Kant. It would be possible to fill a volume with citations[2] to show how remote such views are from Kant's doctrine. Here we must be content to state briefly Kant's own teaching on these topics. Some of the evidence for our assertions will be found in an appendix to this chapter.

Kant holds that in order to have moral worth an action must not merely accord with duty, but must be done for the sake of duty. In holding this he holds also that so far as an action is done merely from inclination—or even from such a motive as a rational desire for happiness—it has no moral worth. In this there is nothing in the least paradoxical. Can anyone maintain that an action must be good, or that it must be a duty, merely because we have an inclination to do it?

In order to establish his doctrine Kant adopts a method of isolation. He considers actions done solely from inclination *without* any motive of duty and says they have no moral worth. Similarly he considers actions done solely for the sake of duty *without* any inclination and says they have

---

[1] *Über die Grundlage der Moral*, §6. The translation, which I take from Rashdall, *The Theory of Good and Evil*, Vol. I, p. 120, is by A. B. Bullock.

[2] Professor Schroeder has collected a certain number in *Some Common Misinterpretations of the Kantian Ethics; The Philosophical Review*, July, 1940.

moral worth.[1] To use such a method of isolation is by no means to assert that where an inclination is present *as well as* a will to do one's duty, there can be no moral worth in an action. Kant means only (1) that an action is good precisely in so far as it springs from a will to do one's duty; (2) that we cannot confidently affirm an action to be good except in so far as we believe that the will to do one's duty could *by itself* have been sufficient to produce the action without the support of any inclination; and (3) that such a belief is hazardous except in the absence of direct inclination to perform the action.

Furthermore, in determining one's duty Kant starts—as we shall see from his formulation of the imperative of duty—with an action suggested to us by our inclinations. He then asks whether we can *at the same time* will an action of this kind as compatible with the universal moral law. If we decide upon our actions by this criterion, we are acting for the sake of duty, and our action is good. Kant's doctrine is that the motive of duty must be present *at the same time* as inclination and must be the determining factor, if our action is to be good. It is therefore a distortion of his view to say that for him an action cannot be good if inclination is present at the same time as the motive of duty.

On the other hand he certainly holds that *in determining our duty* we must take no account of our inclinations or even of our happiness (which is the maximum satisfaction of our inclinations). By this, however, he means that we cannot affirm an action to be a duty merely because we happen to have an inclination to do it or because we think it would make us happy. If we assert an action to be a duty on these irrelevant grounds, we are self-deceivers. We all know that to follow duty may mean the sacrifice of inclination and even of happiness. Nevertheless we have, on Kant's view, a right, though not a direct duty, to pursue our own happiness in our own way, so long as this is not incompatible with the moral law.

Kant recognises that inclinations have a part to play in the moral life. The advantages of virtue and the disadvantages of vice have to be used in order to prepare untutored minds for the paths of virtue. Some inclinations, such as natural sympathy, will greatly help us to perform our duties of benevolent action, and they ought to be cultivated for this reason. Even the happiness and the advantages which follow from a good life are properly stressed to *counterbalance* the attractions of vice and so to give the motive of duty a better chance to exert its influence. What we have to avoid is the substitution of the motive of personal happiness or personal advantage for the motive of duty. To do this is to undermine morality, for an action is not good in virtue of being done for the sake of personal happiness: it is good only if it is done for the sake of duty.

Apart from the everyday happiness which we naturally seek and which may be attained in leading a good life, there is also—and here we come to our second point—a special satisfaction which springs from

---

[1] As Kant says in *K.p.V.*, 156 = 305-6 (= 279), the purity of the moral principle can be strikingly shown only by removing from the motives of action everything that men may want as belonging only to happiness.

consciousness of having acted well. We may not call it pleasure, since it does not arise from the satisfaction of a particular inclination; and we may not call it happiness, since it does not involve the maximum possible satisfaction of our inclinations taken together; but it is something analogous to these. We may call it contentment or self-approval, and we might even say—though Kant himself at times denies this—that it may be an important element in happiness. Kant is far too sensible to say that the good man will necessarily be happy. Because we are sensitive finite creatures, the good man will not be happy on the rack: and it is a paradox to say, with Croce, that if this is so, it must be because he is not a sufficiently good man. Kant recognises that even if we have the consolation and inner peace which comes from knowing that we have acted well, we may nevertheless in our human weakness continue to be distressed at the results of our good action or at the loss which we might have avoided by means of a bad action.[1]

If we do an action merely to gain this feeling of moral self-approval, we shall lose the feeling; for the feeling arises from the recognition that we have acted, not to obtain a feeling, but for the sake of duty. An action done merely for the sake of this feeling would be a self-centred action without moral worth.

It should be added that on Kant's view it is a mark of genuine goodness if we do our duty with a cheerful heart. He deplores a 'Carthusian' or monkish morality of self-mortification.

From all this it is clear that for him an action does not cease to have moral worth if it is accompanied by pleasure or even by a desire for pleasure; it ceases to have moral worth if it is done only for the sake of pleasure or only to satisfy an inclination.

These thoroughly sensible doctrines are completely distorted by Schiller's epigram and by other interpretations of the same kind. Such interpretations arise from misunderstanding two quite different doctrines of Kant, (1) that virtue is most easily and surely recognised where duty is opposed to inclinations, and (2) that inclination must not be taken into account when we are trying to determine what our duty is.

§4. *Is duty the motive of a good will?*

Having set aside these misunderstandings, we are now in a position to consider the truth or otherwise of Kant's doctrine. And first we must ask whether acting for the sake of duty has the same unique goodness which we have ascribed to a good will. Is what we have called a *genuinely* good will manifested in acting for the sake of duty?

Our answer will depend on what is meant by 'acting for the sake of duty'. If we take the man who acts for the sake of duty to be a man who is unceasingly worrying about what his duty is, so that there is never ease or spontaneity in his actions, then this is not what we regard as a genuinely good man or a genuinely good will. Still less do we regard as showing a

---

[1] *K.p.V.*, 87–8 = 216 (= 156–7).

genuinely good will the man who approaches every situation with a series of rigid and iron rules which he proceeds conscientiously to apply. Perhaps this is too harsh a judgement; for such men may be trying to do their best and so may be worthy of respect. Nevertheless they are at least acting stupidly, and they ought to know better. And certainly no one would say that their actions shine like jewels for their own sake.

Some of us may believe that what Kant admired was this wooden or mechanical or rigid kind of goodness. Certainly Kant was in some ways an austere, and even at times a rigid, moralist. Nevertheless he was essentially a humane man; and I believe that the types we are considering would be condemned by him as 'fantastically virtuous' or as 'moral enthusiasts'.[1] If we remember his rigid rule against lying, we should also remember that in applying ethical rules we must leave room for the free play of choice,[2] a certain 'latitude', where judgements of prudence and not of morality are decisive.[3] I do not say that he lays adequate stress on the spontaneity of moral action, but he always insists that morality is not a matter of wooden imitation[4] or of mechanical habit.[5] His is no slavish morality; and no one could insist more strongly on the freedom and independence of the moral will. The good man, on his view, must obey only laws of which he is himself the author.

How then are we to understand 'acting for the sake of duty' if we are to interpret Kant at his best? We may get some guidance if we consider the man who is prudent rather than good. The prudent man is not the man whose mind is so concentrated on his personal advantage that he loses all spontaneity in action, nor is he the man who makes a rigid plan of his future conduct and applies it mechanically in all circumstances. Such a man is only superficially prudent, but genuinely imprudent; for this is no way to have a happy or successful life. Genuine prudence is rather a controlling influence which is permanently in the background, ready to emerge at any moment in order to check acts of folly and to see that varied spontaneous impulses work together harmoniously instead of thwarting one another. So it is, surely, with the motive of duty in the good man. His life is controlled by the idea of duty; he is watchful against unruly impulses which conflict with duty, and against insensitiveness to the moral claims arising from his situation; duty is the determining factor in his conduct, for there is always present the will to do what is right and to avoid what is wrong; but granted this fundamental scrupulousness, there is a great place left for the free play of spontaneous impulses; and a good man, like every other, has the right, as Kant always holds, to seek his happiness in his own individual way, so long as this is not in conflict with duty.

If we interpret duty in some such way as this, it should be clear—except to those who regard duty as an illusion—that Kant is right in holding a good will to be manifested in acting for the sake of duty. Even where an action seems to spring from immediate inclination or from

---
[1] See Chapter II §5.   [2] *M.d.S., Tugendlehre*, Einl. VII, 390 = 235.
[3] *M.d.S., Tugendlehre*, §10, 433 n.   [4] *Gr.*, 409 = 31.
[5] *M.d.S., Tugendlehre*, Einl. XV, 407 = 256.

prudence, duty is still the factor determining the action; for the good man would not perform the action if he believed that it was not in accordance with duty.

§5. *Is goodness the motive of a good will?*

If we agree—as, I take it, most men would—that a good will is shown in acting for the sake of duty, there is still a possibility that it might also be shown in acting from other motives. In particular a good man might be good in acting, not for the sake of duty, but for the sake of goodness itself. Good actions may be done, it is said, *sub ratione boni*; and Kant is harsh in stressing the motive of duty and the obstacles to be overcome. He forgets the good man's delight in goodness and good actions. Indeed goodness for its own sake, and not duty, is the motive of the really good man.

Perhaps there is some truth in this, but it must be observed that here we do not have two different moral theories: what we have is two different views of the empirical facts. Kant knows very well that the perfectly good or holy will must act spontaneously, and yet necessarily, from a sheer love of goodness, and not for the sake of duty. This he regards as the ultimate moral ideal to which we should for ever strive, but to which—under human conditions—we can never attain. What he doubts is the actual presence of such a holy will in himself and in his fellow men.

It is, however, only right to say that Kant has a high idea of holiness. For him a holy will would be wholly good; it would always issue in good actions and would never be tempted to sin.[1] Such a will may belong to God, but not to man; and if the goodness of an action is derived from the goodness of the will which wills it, there are no human actions which can be regarded as holy and so divorced from the idea of duty. It is because of the height of his standards that he refuses man admittance into the company of the Saints. If we adopt lower standards, we shall no doubt be able to take in more recruits.

It may be said that it is only reasonable to adopt lower standards and to recognise that at least some actions even of imperfect men may be inspired by a love of goodness without any thought of duty and may in this sense be holy. I confess that at times I have had sympathy with this view; and it may be held even if we accept Kant's belief that we can see too little into the secrets of our own hearts to be sure that such a motive, and not the 'dear self', inspires even the best of human actions. But even if we accept this, we ought to recognise the sound practical common sense which here, as so often, lies behind Kant's doctrine. He is rightly afraid that if we slur over the motive of duty in the interests of love of goodness, we shall lay ourselves open to all sorts of moral enthusiasm or *Schwärmerei*, to a windy, high-falutin, fantastic attitude of mind which will regard moral action as the meritorious manifestation of a bubbling

---

[1] *Gr.*, 414 = 37; 439 = 70. *K.p.V.*, 32 = 144 (= 57–8).

heart. This may easily lead to vanity, self-complacency, and arrogance; and although at first it may attract the young, it tends to produce a violent reaction. Our moral teaching should be manly, and not melting or sentimental or flattering or grandiose. We are not volunteers but conscripts in the moral struggle, and our state of mind therein is at the best virtue and not holiness.[1]

Kant's view may be austere and even rigorous, but in the main it is sound. It was certainly a very necessary warning against some of the weaknesses of the German temperament, though such weaknesses are by no means confined to Germans. Nor should it be thought to involve any harsh separation between duty and goodness. For him virtue, even as steadfastness in the struggle to do one's duty, is something beyond price, casting into the shade, if we can see it in its true nature, everything that attracts our sensuous inclinations.[2]

In any case the differences of opinion here are concerned, not with principles, but with empirical facts and with the practical side of moral teaching. Kant fully recognises that with the attainment of perfect goodness there would be no place left for duty.[3]

§6. *Are generous emotions the motive of a good will?*

Some thinkers believe that actions may have moral worth when they spring neither from devotion to duty nor from love of goodness, but simply from generous natural emotions, such as sympathy and love. Here we come to a real difference of principle; for Kant denies this outright.

We have seen above that such generous impulses and emotions are, in Kant's view, a help to the moral life and ought to be cultivated for this reason. In one of his earlier works[4] he even calls sympathy and obligingness 'adopted virtues'; they are, so to speak, ennobled by their kinship with virtue and so receive its name. He recognises that these adopted virtues have great similarity to true virtue, since they involve the feeling of an immediate pleasure in kind and benevolent deeds. To say of Kant that he treats generous emotions as on the same footing with the crudest animal impulses is downright false: it can at best be excused as a result of ignorance. In spite, however, of his admiration for good-heartedness, actions which spring from such motives are to him worthy of love, praise, and encouragement, but they are not properly described as having that unique worth which we have called moral. They are in some ways like actions which spring from desire for honour, a desire which, although it is on a lower level, may also lead us to acts which accord with virtue[5] and may itself be said to have about it a 'glimmer' of virtue.[6] On a still lower level perhaps—though Kant does not say so

---

[1] See especially *K.p.V.*, 84 ff. = 211 ff. (= 150 ff.); 157 ff. = 306 ff. (= 280 ff.); *Gr.*, 411 n. = 34 n.
[2] *Gr.*, 435 = 64–5; 426 n. = 53 n.   [3] *K.p.V.*, 84 = 211 (= 150).
[4] *Beobachtungen*, 217–18. See also Schilpp, *Kant's Pre-Critical Ethics*, p. 53.
[5] *Gr.*, 398 = 17.   [6] *Beobachtungen*, 218.

—they are like acts which spring from the enviable quality of animal courage, which, though it greatly helps a man to be brave, is still distinct from the genuine virtue of courage.

It is not harsh or unreasonable to make a distinction between the man who is good and the man who is good-natured or good-hearted. Indeed the good-hearted are themselves often eager to disclaim any kind of moral merit. This may perhaps only show how good-hearted they are; but perhaps it also marks a real truth. Moreover, natural good-heartedness may lead in some circumstances to very wrong actions, either because it is by itself an inadequate motive or because it is a wrong motive. Good-hearted mothers have spoilt many children through lack of other requisite qualities; and the man whose amiability is shown in being 'easily led' is far from a model of moral worth. Even with the still higher motive of love, although it is admirable to act for love of another, the man who needs the influence of a good woman to keep him straight may not be a bad fellow, but he does not inspire us with respect.

It may, however, seem harsh to say of such people, whether their actions accord or fail to accord with duty, that they are self-centred or that they are really seeking their own happiness. It would be harsh, if by this we meant that their generous impulses have no more value than quarrelsomeness or greed; but there is no hint of such a view in Kant. Such people may at times act more generously, and even be more self-forgetful, than people who are conscientious. Nevertheless, although they are not selfish, they are in a sense self-centred. Their conduct depends less on the claims of the situation than on the accidental presence of certain impulses; and if a particular situation arouses in them a wrong kind of impulse there is nothing more in them to which we can appeal. They will do the right thing in certain situations because this happens to fit in with their inclinations; but equally they will not do the right thing in other situations, because this does not so fit in. In living by impulse, their will is centred upon the self and its emotions, even although many of these emotions may happen to be generous: they act generously only because certain emotions happen to be *theirs*. If we are to judge the goodness of an action, as Kant does, by the goodness of the will manifested in the action, it is not unreasonable to say that even a generous action may be without moral goodness, though it has a certain value of its own.

Kant makes no attempt to grade such types of action; or at any rate he makes no attempt to grade them systematically on any clearly formulated principle. We cannot complain of this, since the topic does not belong to ethics as he understands it; and he has given us so much that we have no justification for blaming him because of the books he did not write. It is easy, however, to see that he estimates the value of certain impulses and emotions by the extent to which they can contribute to our happiness and facilitate our obedience to duty. But he also attaches to actions which spring from such motives—at least when they accord with duty—a certain aesthetic value. It is, he says, very beautiful to do good to men out of love and sympathy;[1] and again that if love to mankind

---

[1] *K.p.V.*, 82 = 209 (= 146).

were lacking, a great moral adornment would be absent from the world.[1] In the latter case he is perhaps thinking more of practical benevolence than of natural sympathy; but it may be suspected that for him it is the emotional or sensuous side of such benevolence which makes it beautiful.

§7. *Conclusion.*

Kant's doctrine, when rightly understood, accords with our ordinary enlightened moral judgements. Under human conditions a good will is one which acts for the sake of duty, and only the actions in which such a will is manifested have moral worth. Hence we have taken our first step in the regress which seeks to establish the conditions under which our judgements of good actions can be true. Although our discussion has been more abstract than is customary in ordinary moral judgements, we are still on the level of what Kant calls 'common rational knowledge' of morality. We have now to move to a more philosophical level by passing from the common concept of duty to the highly abstract concept of 'the law'. This further movement will be considered in the following chapters.

If there are any who still feel dissatisfied with the argument on the ground that some good actions spring not from the motive of duty but from sheer love of goodness, this consideration need not disturb them. The 'law' to which we are moving is the same for the holy will as for the merely virtuous will; and it can be reached without difficulty by the same type of argument, whether we start from the virtuous will which seeks to do its duty or from the holy will which is above duty altogether.

APPENDIX

INCLINATIONS, HAPPINESS, AND MORAL WORTH

Kant's doctrine on these matters has been so wildly misunderstood that it is necessary to give some specific references in order to make his position clear.

Let us consider first our natural inclinations (or habitual desires) and our desire for happiness (or the maximum possible satisfaction of our inclinations). According to Kant—though he sometimes speaks as if a rational man would wish to be wholly free from inclinations[2]—it would

---

[1] *M.d.S., Tugendlehre,* §35, 458.
[2] *Gr.,* 428 = 56; *K.p.V.,* 118 = 256 (= 212).

not only be futile, it would also be harmful and blameworthy, to want to root them out.[1] Pure practical reason does not demand that we should *renounce* all claims to happiness, but only that the moment duty is in question we should not *take it into account*. Indeed my own happiness is included in the complete good which it is my duty to seek and in which virtue is combined with a proportionate happiness;[2] and it would be self-contradictory if every man always sacrificed his own happiness, his own true needs, to further those of others.[3] This does not mean that it is a direct duty to seek our own happiness, since, according to Kant, we seek this by nature;[4] still less does it mean that it is a duty to seek the happiness of others on the ground that this will promote our own.

That moral action is compatible with the presence of inclination is, however, best shown in the very formulation of the imperative of duty itself. According to Kant every action has a maxim—that is, a principle actually at work in it—and this maxim arises normally from the co-operation of reason and inclination.[5] The good man will act only on maxims which he can *at the same time* will to be universal laws. When Kant says that in a morally good action the motive of duty must *always* be present *at the same time* as maxims and so as inclinations, it is remarkable that he should be interpreted as saying that it must *never* be present at the same time as inclinations.[6] It is of course true that in some cases maxims have to be rejected because they are incompatible with duty. Nevertheless when they are not rejected they are present along with the motive of duty. There is no inconsistency in saying this and yet in holding that only in so far as the motive of duty is by itself sufficient to determine our action are we entitled to attribute to the action *moral* worth.

It may be added that on Kant's view various inclinations and also the desire for happiness, though they can never determine what our duty is, have nevertheless their part to play in the moral life. He recognises that in order to bring an untrained and unmanageable spirit into the path of virtue we must at first attract it by a view of its own advantage or alarm it by a fear of loss.[7] The life of virtue may be combined with so many charms and satisfactions that it may be worth following from the point of view of prudence, and it may even be advisable to join this prospect of a cheerful enjoyment of life with the moral motive which is already by itself sufficient to determine action—but this must be done *only as a counterpoise* to the attractions of vice, not in order to substitute

---

[1] *Religion*, 58 (= 69).
[2] *K.p.V.*, 129–30 = 271 (= 234); *M.d.S.*, *Tugendlehre*, §27, 451.
[3] *M.d.S.*, *Tugendlehre*, *Einl.* VIII 2, 393 = 240: see also *Rechtslehre*, *Einl.* II, 216 = 15, and *Tugendlehre*, §27, 451.
[4] *M.d.S.*, *Tugendlehre*, *Einl.* VB, 388 = 233–4; *Einl.* IV, 386 = 230.
[5] *K.p.V.*, 67 = 189 (= 118); 79 = 205 (= 141).
[6] Similarly when Kant says that sensa can be given to us only *under* the forms of space and time, he is often supposed to mean that they must be given *apart* from the forms of space and time and subsequently brought under them!
[7] *K.p.V.*, 152 = 300 (= 271).

this motive for the motive of duty.[1] Furthermore, a natural inclination to that which accords with duty (e.g. to benevolence) can greatly facilitate the effectiveness of the moral maxim, although by itself it can produce no such maxim.[2] Indeed he even goes so far as not only to say that since we have a duty to act benevolently, we have an indirect duty to cultivate natural sympathy as a means to this end; but also to add as a reason for this that such sympathy is one of the impulses given to us by nature in order to do what the thought of duty alone would not do.[3] In all his writings Kant attaches great value to good-hearted inclinations and regards it as their chief function to counterbalance bad inclinations and so to give the motive of duty a better chance to determine action.[4]

As to any suggestion that on Kant's view a good man must always be unhappy, this is pure nonsense. He always insists that the moral life brings with it its own peculiar satisfaction or contentment (*Zufriedenheit*).[5] It is true that he interprets it rather negatively as a special kind of satisfaction in doing without, and regards it as something analogous to, but distinct from, happiness, which is the maximum satisfaction of inclination.[6] It is a kind of consolation or inner peace which a man may have even in distress, if he has acted well.[7] In his later writings he goes farther and recognises that it may well be called happiness.[8]

He also speaks of moral feeling as a capacity for finding pleasure in obedience to the law;[9] and describes a moral pleasure going beyond mere contentment with oneself (which may be merely negative).[10] Furthermore, he insists that cheerfulness of heart in the doing of one's duty is the sign of the genuineness of a virtuous sentiment.[11] If he rejects alike the Epicurean view that to seek happiness is to be virtuous and the Stoic view that to be conscious of virtue is to be happy, this only shows his common sense.[12] This moral satisfaction, it must be remembered, is distinct from the everyday happiness which every man has a right, and even an indirect duty, to seek in his own way, so long as this is not incompatible with duty. Can it be wondered that Kant vigorously denies that his doctrine leads to any 'Carthusian' spirit of self-mortification?[13]

Kant is certainly in his way an austere moralist, but we shall never be able to understand him unless we free our mind from caricatures of his doctrine.

---

[1] *K.p.V.*, 88 = 217 (= 158). See also *M.d.S., Rechtslehre, Einl.* II, 216 = 16.
[2] *K.p.V.*, 118 = 256 (= 212–13).
[3] *M.d.S., Tugendlehre*, §35, 457. This last statement should be only a concession to human weakness, but see the even stronger statement in *Das Ende*, 388, where he asserts that the motive of love is necessary to make up for the imperfection of human nature—and that without the assistance of this motive we could not in fact count very much on the motive of duty. Perhaps Kant was mellowing with old age.
[4] Compare Schilpp, *Kant's Pre-Critical Ethics*, p. 53.
[5] *Gr.*, 396 = 15.
[6] *K.p.V.*, 117 = 256 (= 212).
[7] *K.p.V.*, 88 = 216 (= 157).
[8] *M.d.S., Tugendlehre, Vorrede*, 377.
[9] *M.d.S., Tugendlehre, Einl.* XII, 399 = 246.
[10] *M.d.S., Tugendlehre, Einl.* VII, 391 = 237.
[11] *Religion*, 24 n. = 25 n. (= 11–12 n.).
[12] *K.p.V.*, 111 = 248 (= 200).
[13] *Religion*, 23 n. = 24 n. (= 10 n.). The whole passage should be studied.

CHAPTER IV

THE MAXIM OF MORALITY

§1. *Moral value does not depend on results.*

WE have seen that the moral value of an action depends on its being done for the sake of duty, not on its being done to satisfy any inclination. We must now add that the moral value of such an action does not depend on results sought or attained.[1] The results we seek to produce by our action are not necessarily the same as the results we in fact produce; and it might even be the case, as in a sudden stroke of paralysis, that a morally good volition would produce no external results at all. Kant holds that a morally good action does not depend for its value either on the results it produces or even on the results it seeks to produce. In holding this he rejects all forms of utilitarianism.

Kant's conclusion follows directly from what has already been said; for if an action depended for its moral value on results sought or attained, it would have this value even if it were done only from an inclination to produce these results; and this is a possibility which we have rejected.

Kant suggests also another argument against deriving moral value from results produced.[2] Other causes might produce the same results as a good will: they might, for example, produce happiness for ourselves or others. If a good will derived its absolute value merely from producing these results, other causes producing these results would have the same absolute value. If so, a good will could not have the unique value which, we have argued, it must have. Indeed if a good will had its value only as producing results, it would have value, not in itself, but merely as means to an end.

Kant's conclusion has moreover been already established, as we saw in Chapter II §7, by what has been said about a good will. If a good will is an unconditioned good, and if its possible objects are conditioned goods, a good will cannot derive its absolute goodness from the merely relative goodness of the objects which it attains or seeks to attain. This conclusion still holds, although we have now added that, under human conditions, a good will is one which acts for the sake of duty; and it applies also, to actions done for the sake of duty, if the value of these is to be estimated by the goodness of the will which is manifested in them.

Kant is not so foolish as to deny that an action done for the sake of duty will produce results and will seek to produce results. It always seeks to produce results, and normally it succeeds in doing so. All Kant is

[1] *Gr.*, 399–400 = 19. [2] *Gr.*, 401 = 21.

saying is that its distinctively moral value does not depend on the results sought or the results attained.

§2. *Practical principles—subjective and objective.*

We must now try to make this doctrine more positive. If an action does not derive its value from results sought or attained, it must derive its value from its motive (the motive of duty), and this motive must be other than a mere desire to produce certain results. Kant expresses this by saying that an action derives its value from its *maxim* and—although he does not put this too clearly[1]—that the maxim is not a maxim of producing results. To see the relation between a maxim and a motive we must understand some of Kant's technical terms.

A maxim is a particular kind of *principle*: it may be defined as a subjective principle of action. In order to understand this we must first consider what is meant by 'a principle'.[2] It is difficult to state this precisely without going into too much detail, and the present account must be taken as provisional and over-simplified.[3]

A principle is in general a universal proposition which has under it other propositions of which it is the ground: for this reason it is also called a 'ground proposition' (*Grundsatz*). Strictly speaking, a principle should have no higher ground (except in so far as it is grounded in the nature of reason itself): it is then an absolute or supreme principle. Kant's Critical method, as we have seen,[4] is concerned with the discovery and justification of such supreme principles, and the object of our present enquiry is the discovery and justification of the supreme principle of morality. But the word 'principle' is also used, in a relative sense, for universal propositions which are not supreme principles, but yet have under them other propositions of which they are the ground. In this relative sense the major premise of a syllogism may be called a principle. In the strict sense the term 'principle' should be confined to such an ultimate principle as the law of non-contradiction.

We are here, however, concerned only with practical principles or principles of action. Kant believes that human action is distinguished from animal behaviour by the fact that men act in accordance with principles. 'Everything in nature,' he says, 'works in accordance with laws. Only a rational being has the power to act *in accordance with his idea of laws*,' that is, in accordance with principles.'[5] Practical principles are still universal propositions; they are, however, the ground, not only of other propositions or of judgements, but ultimately of actions. In them also we must distinguish between strict or absolute or supreme principles, and principles, in a looser sense, which are relative and subordinate.

---

[1] *Gr.*, 400 = 19–20.
[2] A principle is said to be a beginning (*Anfang*); *Logik*, §34, 110. It is a translation of the Greek word ἀρχή.
[3] Compare, for example, *K.r.V.*, A299–302 = B356–9.
[4] See Chapter I §9.   [5] *Gr.* 412 = 36.

In practical principles there is, however, another and more immediately important difference. There are, first of all, principles actually at work in our action, principles which are the real ground of our action. These principles Kant calls '*subjective principles*'. Subjective principles are valid only for the individual subject or agent as the principles on which he chooses to act. Against these we must set '*objective principles*'; that is, principles on which any rational agent would act. if reason had full control over his passions.[1] Objective principles are thus valid for every rational agent, and they may be called 'principles of reason'.

A subjective principle, in order to be such, must be acted upon: it is a subjective principle only if it is a principle on which we act. Needless to say, we do not always act on objective principles, and objective principles are still objective whether we act on them or not. We may, however, act on an objective principle, and when we do, this becomes a subjective principle as well as an objective one.

Kant's technical term for a subjective principle is a '*maxim*'.[2] Although a maxim differs from an objective principle in being, *qua* maxim, valid only for the individual agent (not for all rational agents), it also differs from a motive in being more general than a motive; and this is why it is called a principle. An animal might be said to have a motive so far as it is moved on a particular occasion by a particular impulse of hunger or a particular smell of food; but it could not be said to generalise its motive and so to have a maxim. Only a rational agent can have a maxim. Thus if I commit suicide because my life offers more pain than pleasure my maxim is 'If life offers more pain than pleasure, I will commit suicide.'[3] Here not merely an impulse or motive, but a general principle, is supposed to be at work in my action, a principle which I would apply to any similar situation. My maxim, as it were, generalises my action, including my motive.[4] My maxim is the principle which is in fact the determining ground of my action; but it does not profess, like an objective principle, to be valid for any one else, and it may be good, or it may be evil.[5]

All this raises questions about the extent to which such subjective principles or maxims are consciously formulated by a rational agent. Nevertheless Kant is trying to mark a real difference between human conduct and animal behaviour. In acting, a human being does not, unless in very exceptional circumstances, respond blindly to impulse. He knows

---

[1] *Gr.*, 400 n. = 21 n.

[2] Compare Webb, *Kant's Philosophy of Religion*, p. 95. 'The origin of this use of the word is to be explained as follows. Every properly human—that is, deliberately willed —act is done for some *reason*, subsumed, as it were in a syllogism, under some general major premise or *major propositio*. That to which in any individual case an act is ultimately referred is thus the ultimate major premise, *maxima propositio* or *maxim*.'

[3] *Gr.* 422 = 48.

[4] *Religion*, 23–4 = 25 (= 11–12). In this passage, as in others, Kant asserts a connexion between acting on maxims and freedom of the will. A free will cannot be determined to action by any sensuous motive except in so far as a man has taken up the motive into his maxim. In *Logik, Einl.* III, 24, Kant understands by a maxim the inner principle of a choice between different ends.

[5] A maxim is not to be confused, as it often is by beginners, with what we call 'a copy book maxim'. It is something purely personal to myself.

what he is doing; he recognises the quality of his action; and he could not do this without some concept, however vague, of the principle on which he acts.[1]

§3. *Two kinds of maxim—formal and material.*

Kant speaks at times as if all maxims were grounded on sensuous inclinations, and consequently as if a divine or holy will could have no maxims.[2] A divine or holy will would have no maxims which were not also objective principles; but to say this is not to deny that it acts in accordance with maxims, if we interpret 'maxims' to mean principles manifested in action. It is all-important to recognize that while maxims are commonly based on inclinations (as in the case of suicide given above), it may nevertheless be possible to act on maxims which are not so based.

We have seen that a morally good action cannot have as its determining motive any mere inclination to produce certain results. If this is so, and if the maxim of an action is, as it were, a generalisation of the action and its motive, it follows at once that the moral maxim is not based on any mere inclination to produce certain results: it holds irrespective of the ends which the action is intended to produce.[3] In saying this we are not altering or modifying our previous contention: we are only putting it in a more technical way.

In order to distinguish the maxims based on inclination from the maxims not so based we require to use certain technical terms.

Maxims based on sensuous inclinations Kant calls empirical or *a posteriori* maxims: they depend on our experience of desire. Maxims not based on sensuous inclinations he calls *a priori* maxims: that is, they do not depend on experience of desire.

Empirical maxims are also called *material* maxims: they refer to the desired ends which the action attempts to realise, and these ends are the matter of the maxim.[4] *A priori* maxims are also called *formal* maxims. At present formal maxims are characterised only negatively: they do not refer to desired ends which the action attempts to realise. What they are positively we shall have to consider later.

Since in all actions the will is determined by a principle and so has a maxim, it must be determined either by a material maxim or by a formal maxim. There is no other possibility open.

§4. *The maxim of duty.*

We can now say, in Kant's technical terminology, that a man who shows his good will in acting for the sake of duty is acting on a formal, and not on a material, maxim. In less technical terms, a good man does

---

[1] We might adapt a famous assertion of Kant's by saying that principles without content are empty, impulses without concepts are blind. See *K.r.V.*, A51 = B75.
[2] *K.p.V.*, 67 = 189 (= 118); 79 = 205 (= 141).
[3] *Gr.*, 400 = 20.   [4] Compare *Gr.*, 436 = 66.

not act merely on the principle of producing certain results which he happens to desire.

This doctrine is already established by our previous argument, yet it causes so much difficulty to many readers that we may summarise the argument at this stage.

An action done for the sake of duty does not derive its moral value either from the fact that it produces certain results or from the fact that it seeks to produce certain results. If it does not derive its value from the fact that its intention or motive is to produce certain results, it does not derive its value from a material maxim—that is, from a maxim or principle of producing such results. Consequently its value must be derived from a formal maxim, a maxim independent of the desired ends which the action seeks to produce. The maxim of an action done for the sake of duty must therefore be formal and not material.

All this may appear so negative as to be almost unintelligible, and we must give a more positive account of the moral maxim, if our position is to be made clear. Yet Kant's doctrine can be put quite simply, and when so put becomes almost obvious. The good man's maxim, in virtue of which his action has moral worth, is not 'This is the kind of thing I will do if I happen to have an inclination for it.' His maxim is 'I will do my duty, whatever my duty may be.' This is what we mean when we say that a man acts for the sake of duty. This is what we mean when we say that he is a conscientious and good man. The formal maxim of duty, and not the material maxim of inclination, is what determines his conduct and gives it its value.

When the young Victoria was brought down from her bedroom in the early morning to be told that she was now the Queen, she is reported to have exclaimed 'I will be good.' Although no philosopher, she was able to express in its simplest form what Kant believed to be the formal maxim of a good life.

The difficulty of Kant's doctrine, so far, arises partly from his abstract way of putting it, but mainly from a whole series of presuppositions which we have been accustomed to read into it. We must try to rid our minds of such presuppositions. We have still to consider the positive side of his doctrine, but his argument, so far as we have gone, is surely sound.

CHAPTER V

REVERENCE

§1. *Reverence for the law.*

LET us now try to describe moral actions more positively. *To act for the sake of duty is to act out of reverence for the law.*[1]

Here we get two new points. Firstly, moral action has an emotional aspect, and the emotional aspect of it may be called 'reverence'. Secondly, in moral action we are seeking to follow a law which we reverence, and therefore the moral maxim must be '*I will follow the law.*' This assertion about our moral maxim continues the direct path of our argument and is essential to it. The discussion of reverence is not strictly necessary for the argument; but it is necessary if our view of moral action is to be complete and if we are to meet the objection that emotion cannot be excluded from moral action. Let us consider first the nature of this emotion.

It is a mistake to regard Kant's attitude to morality as cold and heartless. We have already seen that in his view—contrary to the common belief—inclination or emotion may be present in a moral action, although the action will have its distinctively moral value only so far as it is done for the sake of duty. We have seen that a good man has a right to seek his own happiness and a duty to seek the happiness of others. We have seen also that a special contentment or peace of mind may arise from the consciousness that we have tried to do our duty.[2] We must now see that there is a specific emotion which Kant believes to be present in actions done for the sake of duty. It is obvious to any attentive reader that Kant himself feels most intensely this emotion of reverence for the law, and that both from his description and from the language he uses the feeling in question is something almost akin to religious emotion.

For this reason I have translated the German word '*Achtung*' by 'reverence' and not by the word 'respect', which is commonly used by English translators.[3] This may be considered a mistake, and I may be told that the German word does not suggest any very profound emotion: it is indeed commonly used by railway porters when they wish you to get out of the way, and in this connexion is equivalent to 'Look out' or the

---

[1] Compare *K.p.V.*, 81 = 208 (= 145). I substitute this for Kant's unsatisfactory third proposition in *Gr.*, 400 = 20: *Duty is the necessity of acting out of reverence for the law.*

[2] Chapter III, especially §3 and the Appendix.

[3] After deciding on this translation I was pleased to find that it is also used by Edward Caird in *The Critical Philosophy of Kant.*

[63]

French '*Attention*'. Nevertheless Kant himself translates it by the Latin word '*reverentia*', and he expressly distinguishes it from '*Respekt*', which has in it an additional element, namely, fear.[1] He compares his emotion towards the moral law with his emotion towards the starry heavens.[2] In the *Critique of Judgment* he connects *Achtung* with our feeling for the sublime.[3] These and many other passages suggest that *Achtung* is akin to reverence, or even awe, and is very remote from a strictly limited emotion like respect.

We are, I think, entitled to treat the word '*Achtung*' as a technical term in Kant which may have an emotional atmosphere other than that in ordinary German usage. The feeling in question has no doubt degrees.[4] When, as in ordinary moral action, we are not greatly moved, it may well be akin to respect; but when it is present in its full force, it seems much more closely akin to reverence.[5]

§2. *The description of reverence.*

For Kant the emotion of reverence is unique.[6] It is not directed to any object given to sense nor is it connected with the satisfaction of our natural inclinations. The emotion of reverence arises because I am conscious that my will is subordinated to a law without the intervention of any object of sense. In Kant's language, it is a feeling 'self-produced through a concept of reason'.

Its similarity to religious emotion is shown, I think, by the fact that in it I feel at once humbled and also uplifted or exalted.[7] On the one hand the moral law is a check to my inclinations and a blow to my self-conceit, so that in being humbled my feeling of reverence is akin to pain. On the other hand—as we shall see more clearly later—I am also uplifted by consciousness that the constraint imposed on my inclinations comes from my own free and rational will. On this side my feeling is akin to pleasure. Yet it is so little a feeling of pleasure that I would gladly avoid feeling reverence for a good man or even for the law itself—my vanity stands in the way. And it is so little a feeling of pain that, once I have laid aside my vanity, I cannot weary of beholding the splendour of the law: the soul is itself uplifted as it sees the holy law uplifted above itself and its frailty. Kant also speaks of reverence as analogous to fear and inclination; but as inclination is not strictly a feeling, he must mean by it something more like attraction or delight.

[1] *M.d.S.*, *Tugendlehre*, Einl. XII, 402 = 250 ; §13, 438.
[2] *K.p.V.*, 161 = 312 (= 288). The whole passage bears out my contention.
[3] *K.U.*, §27, 257 (= 96–7). There he defines *Achtung* as a feeling of the inadequacy of our power for the attainment of an Idea *which for us is law*.
[4] Compare *K.p.V.*, 73 = 197–8 (= 130).
[5] Kant himself recognises in *Gr.*, 442 = 74 that feelings, and apparently also moral feelings, vary infinitely in degree.
[6] *Gr.*, 401 n. = 21 n.
[7] See the long account given in *K.p.V.*, 71 ff. = 195 ff. (= 126 ff.). Kant's language at times may lack mathematical precision, but what he says does not lack psychological insight.

All this belongs, not to ethics, but to moral psychology. It may have little or no meaning to those who have not been fortunate enough to experience the emotion in question; but even the little I have said is surely enough to dispose of the common belief that Kant is an unemotional moralist. He never seeks to substitute unction for philosophical analysis; but that is a merit and not a defect.

§3. *The function of reverence.*

On the supposition that we have experienced this emotion Kant expects us to agree that we cannot feel reverence for any mere product of our action or for any mere inclination in ourselves or in others. I can feel reverence only for something which determines my will and does not serve my inclinations, but rather outweighs them or at least takes no account of them in determining my choice. This something we have hitherto known as duty. We are now told that it must be law in and for itself.[1]

We must, however, remember that we may also feel reverence for those people and actions in which the law is exemplified.[2] And we must not forget that a being whose will was holy would not feel reverence for the law, but something more akin to love.

For the moral philosopher the most important point in our discussion is this. On Kant's view we feel reverence because we recognise that the law is binding upon our wills. The great error of the moral sense school is to suppose that the law is binding because we feel reverence. No feeling can be the basis of a binding moral law, but the moral law may be the ground of a specific moral emotion. For Kant, to act out of respect for the law is the same thing as to act out of duty or for the sake of duty or for the sake of the law itself:[3] It is very different from any attempt to gratify an emotion; and for this reason Kant classifies believers in a moral sense as unconscious, even if well-meaning, hedonists.[4]

---

[1] *Gr.*, 400 = 20.
[2] In Kant's later writings he speaks of *Achtung* as owed to all men simply as men (in virtue of their *capacity* for morality), and from this important duties follow. The Latin translation of '*Achtung*' in this connexion is not '*reverentia*' but '*observantia*', that is, 'respect' or 'consideration'. See *M.d.S.*, *Tugendlehre*, §37, 462.
[3] *K.p.V.*, 81 = 207 (= 144).   [4] *Gr.*, 442-3 = 74.

APPENDIX

REVERENCE AS A MOTIVE

There are certain difficulties about the function of reverence in moral action, and we may even be tempted to ask whether it is possible to regard reverence as a motive of good action on Kant's theory. He has certainly described good action as action done out of reverence for the law; but he has also described good action as action done for the sake of duty.[1] He indeed appears to regard these expressions as equivalent.[2] Nevertheless reverence, on his view, seems to result from, or even to be, consciousness that our will is determined by the law.[3] How can it also be a motive inducing our will to determine itself by the law?

At first sight the difficulty might be got over by means of Kant's distinction between objective and subjective principles of action.[4] Kant might mean something like this. We first recognise the law as an objective principle—that is, as a principle which any rational agent would follow if reason fully controlled his inclinations, and so as a principle which we ought to follow in spite of our inclinations. This recognition arouses our feeling of reverence. Reverence in turn induces us to adopt the law as our subjective principle or maxim and so to act for the sake of duty or the sake of the law. Reverence would then be the connecting link between our recognition of the law as an objective principle and our adopting it as a subjective principle or maxim.

Kant may have had something of this kind in view: he describes reverence as a motive for making the law our maxim.[5] There appears, however, to be another doctrine when he insists that the moral law must determine the will *immediately* without the intervention of a feeling of any kind.[6] Here it might indeed be argued that he does not intend to exclude reverence as understood by him, but only any feeling (including reverence) considered as the ground of the law and not as its result. But he also says expressly that the moral law by itself alone must be not only the *objective* ground determining our action, but also at the same time a sufficient *subjective* ground determining our action. The law by itself, without the aid of any feeling, seems to be the motive necessary for good moral action.[7] This is a stumbling block to those who hold that the will can be moved to action only by means of feeling.

---

[1] The contrast is sharper in the German, since a good action is done both '*aus Achtung*' (out of reverence) and '*aus Pflicht*' (out of duty).

[2] *K.p.V.*, 81 = 207 (= 144).

[3] *Gr.*, 401 n. = 21 n. Compare also *K.U.*, §5, 210 (= 15).

[4] See Chapter IV §2.

[5] *K.p.V.*, 76 = 201 (= 135). He also speaks of the law as determining our will objectively and of reverence as determining it subjectively; *Gr.*, 400 = 20 and *K.p.V.*, 81 = 207 (= 144). In the latter passage, however, this seems to mean something rather different.

[6] *K.p.V.*, 71 = 195 (= 126–7).

[7] *K.p.V.*, 72 = 195–6 (= 127). See also *Gr.*, 419 = 45, 'The will is here determined without any other motive merely by the law.'

Perhaps Kant himself was not conscious that he appears to be speaking of two different kinds of motive. The word 'motive' is itself ambiguous. A motive is what moves us; and many people seem to assume that it must therefore be something that, as it were, pushes or shoves us from behind, as a feeling may be said to do. They forget that we may also be moved by something that pulls or attracts us, as perhaps the idea of the law might be said to do.

These are crude metaphors, and we may ask ourselves whether the whole language of motive is not crude and metaphorical. The difficulty seems to arise from the fact that we regard actions from two different points of view. These points of view, as we shall see towards the end of our inquiry, are treated by Kant in a highly metaphysical way.[1] We may attempt to treat them on a humbler common-sense level.

First of all we can take an external and scientific view of action. On this view, which Kant regards as legitimate and even necessary, we 'explain' action as follows. First of all we apprehend something, whether it be a binding moral law or a glass of wine. This gives rise to a feeling, which in turn gives rise to an impulse, which in turn (in co-operation with reason) gives rise to an action (in accordance with a maxim). The whole process is explained as a chain of causes and effects. The only difference would be that the moral law is not, like the glass of wine, apprehended by means of sense.

But even on a humbler and common-sense level we have also a very different point of view, the point of view of the agent acting, a point of view which sees the action from within, not from without. From this point of view we feel the previous account to be totally inadequate: it omits the fundamental fact of our free choice. From this point of view willing is something other than a causal event, and an action cannot be explained as the effect of a previous cause. It is rather the direct product of our free will, whether we drink for the sake of pleasure or obey the law for the sake of obeying the law.[2]

Hence it may be the case that from an external or psychological point of view our motive is the feeling of reverence, whereas from the internal or practical point of view our motive is simply the moral law, the law of our own free and rational will, without the intervention of any kind of feeling. We may perhaps say that from one point of view reverence is the *cause* of our action, but from another point of view the moral law is its *ground*.

It should be added that if, as Kant holds, the feeling of reverence is, in finite human beings, bound up inseparably with apprehension of the moral law,[3] then to act for the sake of the moral law is also to act out of reverence for the law. We have indeed no duty to feel reverence; for if we did not feel reverence, we should be blind to duty, and so should

---

[1] *Gr.*, 450 = 83–4.
[2] Kant recognises these two kinds of action as springing respectively from practical reason or pure practical reason, from will or pure will, and, in his later books, from *Villkür* (*liberum arbitrium*) or *Wille* (will in a technical sense).
[3] *K.p.V.*, 80 = 206 (= 142).

have no duty at all.[1] But the law compels our reverence, and reverence is the emotional side of our recognition that the law is binding. We cannot excuse ourselves from acting for the sake of the law on the ground that reverence is a feeling which has to be conjured up. As we are always free to obey the law because we recognise it to be the law, so we are always free to act out of reverence for the law. The distinctively ethical command is not merely to do what accords with duty, but to do it for the sake of duty.[2]

---

[1] Compare *M.d.S.*, *Tugendlehre*, *Einl.* XII, 402=250—a passage primarily concern with a special kind of reverence.
[2] *M.d.S.*, *Tugendlehre*, *Einl.* VII, 391 = 236.

CHAPTER VI

THE LAW

§1. *Law as such.*

We have now to leave the comfortable levels of ordinary moral judgement, where we have hitherto maintained an uneasy footing. We climb beyond this level to the giddy heights and rarer atmosphere of philosophy when we say that the motive of the good man is to obey law as such. What is this mysterious law as such? And how can we maintain that a good will has its unique and absolute value only if it is determined by the thought of law as such?[1]

Universality is the essential characteristic of law as such. A law, in the strict sense of 'law', must hold for all cases and admit of no exceptions. A law of nature, for example, must hold of all events in time without exception. If the principle that every event must have a cause is a law of nature, then there can be no exceptions to it; and if we were convinced that any exceptions were possible, we should at once deny this principle to be a law of nature. So it is also with what Kant calls 'the law of freedom'—that is, the law in accordance with which a rational agent would act if reason had full control over his inclinations. This law of freedom, or moral law, cannot have exceptions without ceasing to be law. There cannot be one moral law for me and another for you. The law must be the same for all.[2]

In Kant's technical language, universality is the *form* of law. Whatever a law may be about—that is, whatever may be its matter—it must have the form of universality; for unless it is universal, it is not a law at all. Laws of freedom and laws of nature, in spite of fundamental differences, share in the common form of universality.

In spite of its abstractness Kant's view still finds an echo in ordinary moral consciousness. If we try to consider duty in general, duty apart from the particular duty to do this and that, what can we say about it? We can say that duty appears to us as a law which must be the same for all and can admit of no arbitrary exceptions in our favour or in favour of anyone else. This is only another way of saying that if there is such a

---

[1] *Gr.*, 402 = 22.
[2] It is extraordinary how early the human mind seems able to grasp the universality of moral law. A small boy of five, not specially conspicuous either for goodness or for intelligence, was presented on a flag-day with several flags. One of these he was kind enough to give to me. Later he gave another to his sister, who rewarded him with a sixpence. Whereupon—surely on the assumption that his sister's action was a manifestation of universal law (even if this was not without advantage to himself)—he asserted, 'If G. gives me a sixpence, the Professor will have to give me a sixpence too.'

[69]

said about morality: morality must have the form of a universal law valid for rational agents as such.

In all this we are talking about the one fundamental moral law of duty. When it comes to particular moral laws or rules, we have to face another problem. In a looser sense of 'law' we may say that 'Thou shalt not kill' is a law, but that nevertheless in some circumstances it may be our duty to kill. This does not mean that the moral law itself admits of exceptions. If it is the duty of a rational agent to kill in certain circumstances, then it is the duty of every rational agent to kill in these circumstances. It is fundamentally immoral to regard killing as a special privilege of my own from which other men are excluded.

§2. *Law as command.*

It might be suggested that a second characteristic of law as such is that it is a command; and Kant says that mere law in itself *can* be an object of reverence and therewith a command.[1] This, however, is not a characteristic of law as such, nor need it be true of the moral law. A law of nature is not a command; and to a holy will the moral law would not appear as a command, although the holy will, because of its essential rationality, would necessarily follow the moral law. It is a very common mistake to say of Kant that for him the moral law is always a command or an imperative. On the contrary, we must make a sharp distinction between the moral law and the moral imperative. The moral law appears to us *under human conditions* as a command or imperative, because in us reason has not full control over the inclinations; but this characteristic does not belong to the moral law as such. For the will of a perfect being the moral law is a law of *holiness*; for the will of every finite rational being it is a law of *duty*.[2]

This is the other side of Kant's statement that human beings reverence the law rather than love it. To say this is not to deny that it is possible to love the law.

Only because of this distinction between moral law and moral command is Kant able to say of the moral law, as a law of action, that it must be the same for *all* rational agents—that is, for all beings capable of action—and for men only as rational agents.[3] This does not mean that we need ascribe to Kant, as Schopenhauer does, an unhealthy interest in the morals of the angels. It means, as we shall see later, that the moral law holds for us solely in virtue of our rationality, not because as human beings we happen to desire certain ends, such as happiness. We can say

---
[1] *Gr.*, 400 = 20.
[2] *K.p.V.*, 82 = 108 (= 146). Compare also the distinction between a supreme practical principle and a categorical imperative in *Gr.*, 428 = 56.
[3] *Gr.*, 408 = 30–1.

indeed that the moral law must appear to us as an imperative because of our character as finite and sensuous beings whose rational will has imperfect control over inclinations; but the moral law is not based on this character. Indeed the moral law is in no way based on the special nature of man. The special nature of man has to be taken into account, not in determining the essence of the moral law, but solely in determining its particular applications.[1]

§3. *The moral motive.*

If a good action is one which is done for the sake of law as such, this must mean that the moral motive, the motive of duty, must be *law-abidingness*, and this must serve as the principle of our will unless duty is a purely chimerical concept.[2] To state it thus may appear paradoxical, but it is not difficult to see what Kant means. The morally good man seeks to obey the moral law as such whatever it may enjoin. If he obeys it only so far as he happens to desire some of the actions it enjoins, he is not a morally good man. Equally, if he recognises that the moral law is binding upon all rational agents and yet seeks to make exceptions in his own favour, he is not a morally good man.

§4. *Formal maxim and moral law.*

How are we to establish the connexion between law as such and our previous argument? Kant has maintained[3] that the maxim of the good man must be formal—that is, it is not a maxim or principle of producing certain results. How do we pass from this negative statement to the positive statement that the maxim of the good man is to obey law as such?

At first sight the argument looks incredibly weak. The maxim of the good man is a formal principle that excludes all reference to the desired ends which are the matter of a maxim. But if so, Kant seems to argue, it can be only the *form* of a principle, and this is the same as the form of law or law as such. The only characteristic of a formal principle from which all matter is excluded is its universality. Hence the formal principle of moral action is to act in accordance with universal law. 'Since I have robbed the will of every inducement which could accrue to it from the following of any particular law, there remains nothing over except the conformity of actions to universal law as such, and this alone must serve the will as a principle.'[4] 'The idea of the law in itself, so far as it, and not the expected result, determines the will, can alone constitute that pre-eminent good which we call moral.'[5]

Kant has an unfortunate tendency to make his crucial transitions in arguments that are much too hurried and condensed. The weakness of the present argument is as follows. A principle is certainly universal; and a maxim or subjective principle, which is valid only for the individual

---

[1] *Gr.*, 412 = 35. [2] *Gr.*, 402 = 22. [3] See Chapter IV-§4.
[4] *Gr.*, 402 = 22. [5] *Gr.*, 401 = 21.

it is fallacious when we consider it against the whole background of Kant's thought. We cannot clear this up until we have examined, as we shall later, the part which he believes reason to play in human action; but we can give a provisional interpretation of his line of thought. He is considering material maxims as a product of practical reason working 'at the service of inclination'.[1] Practical reason, as it were, generalises our actions together with the inclination which is their motive; and although these maxims make no profession to be valid for anyone but the agent, nevertheless even they would be valid for every rational agent *if* he were seeking to satisfy this inclination.[2] When we exclude from our maxim all reference to the satisfaction of inclinations and the attainment of results, and when we nevertheless suppose that our action must have a maxim, a purely formal maxim, which is the product of a practical reason no longer at the service of inclination, what could such a maxim be? All it would retain, as is indeed inevitable if it is a product of pure reason without reference to particular inclinations, would be its validity for every rational agent as such, validity no longer qualified by an 'if'. It would be merely a maxim of being reasonable; it would be completely impartial as between my inclinations and yours; and it would be acted on by every rational agent except in so far as his reason was thwarted by individual desires. It would in short be a universal law. A formal maxim can be only the maxim of following universal law as such.

To this topic we shall in due course return. But at least we now know where we are, and we should observe that however abstract Kant's language and however obscure his argument, his conclusion at least is in line with ordinary moral judgement. The moral law, if valid at all, must be valid for every rational agent; and the good man is a man who seeks to obey such a universal moral law—that is, to act in accordance with an objective standard which is independent of his personal desires and ends. Whatever we may think of the argument, the conclusion stands firm.

§5. *The categorical imperative.*

Even if we accept Kant's conclusion, we may still hold that it is empty and useless. How can we pass from the empty concept of law-abidingness to the manifold duties and virtues of the moral life?

---

[1] *Gr.*, 413 n. = 37 n.; *K.p.V.*, 25 = 133 (= 45); *Religion*, 45 n. = 52 n. (= 50 n.).
[2] This holds only so far as the agent acts rationally in seeking to satisfy this inclination; but even when he does not, his action is rational within arbitrarily imposed limits; rational, for example, if he is seeking to satisfy some other inclination. Here too the maxim is conditionally valid for every rational agent. See Chapter IX §1.

This is certainly a difficult problem, but we need not make it more difficult than it is. Kant at once makes it clear that there is no question—as is sometimes supposed—of deducing particular duties merely from the empty form of universal law. On the contrary, we have to consider the *matter* which has to be fitted into this empty form. The matter consists of our ordinary material maxims based on inclination for definite objects; and what we have to do is to accept or reject these maxims by the principle of universality. Thus we can express the ultimate principle of duty more concretely than we have hitherto done. '*I ought never to act except in such a way that I can also will the maxim of my action to be a universal law.*'[1] Emphasis should be put on the word 'also', because it is so commonly ignored.

This is a formulation of what Kant later calls the categorical imperative, although here it is put in a negative form. We shall have to examine it in more detail later. At present we need note only that Kant speaks as if by the help of this principle alone we could easily solve all our moral problems. This is manifestly untrue; we require to bring in many further suppositions, as Kant does himself when he comes to work out the application of the moral law in the *Metaphysic of Morals*. Nevertheless the principle itself is entirely sound, whatever we may think about Kant's method of applying it. To judge our own actions by the same universal standard which we apply to the actions of others is an essential condition of morality.

---

[1] *Gr.*, 402 = 22.

CHAPTER VII

MISUNDERSTANDINGS

§1. *Criticisms.*

IT may be thought that Kant's doctrine is paradoxical, and that we have somehow been tricked by the subtlety and complexity of the argument. We began with a good will 'shining like a jewel for its own sake'. We end with a merely formal maxim, a mysterious reverence for empty law as such, a vague principle of law-abidingness, and an unworkable test of universality for the maxims of our actions. All this formalism and legalism may leave us cold. Furthermore, it may be said, we have been argued gradually into a manifestly ludicrous view, the view that in determining our duty no account whatever is to be taken of the results sought or attained by our action.

These criticisms can be answered only by a re-examination of our previous argument and indeed of Kant's argument as a whole, but we may attempt to make brief comments on some of the points raised.

§2. *Kant's formalism.*

On the theoretical side there is little justification for complaining of Kant's formalism. We ought not to expect an abstract philosophical analysis of moral goodness to arouse the same warm emotion as may be aroused by the spectacle of a good man or a good action; nor is it the business of a moral philosopher to 'emotionalise the district'—to quote the phrase used by a disappointed American visitor to one of Professor Cook Wilson's lectures. Kant's terminology may be technical, but it was familiar in his time, if not in ours. It is well adapted to the expression of his meaning; nor is it on acquaintance more rebarbative than that of many modern philosophers.

It is hard to see why we should blame a philosopher for being too formal in dealing with the form of anything, even the form of morality. We do not blame Mr. Bertrand Russell because his logic is too formal, though some people may wish that he would write another kind of logic as well. Why should we complain that Kant's ethics is too formal, especially as he *has* written another kind of ethics, his *Metaphysic of Morals*, not to mention his *Lectures*? In the *Groundwork* Kant, as he says, is dealing with the supreme principle of morality: he is dealing with the *a priori* part of ethics in abstraction and considering the form of moral action apart from the matter. When Kant sets before himself a programme of this kind he is in the habit of sticking to it. It is hard to see why he should be blamed for keeping to his subject and excluding irrelevancies. It is still harder to see why he should be charged with forgetting that moral action has a matter as well as a form, an empirical as well as an *a priori* element, and an object as well as a supreme principle. Kant does not forget. He expects his readers to remember.

§3. *Kant's legalism.*

It may be replied that this answer does not really meet the criticism, which is concerned more with the formalism or legalism of his moral attitude than with his method of exposition. No doubt, it may be said, good men of a certain type may take a pride in obeying the law for the sake of law, and in controlling inclinations from the standpoint of a detached and unmoved reason; but it is a great mistake to identify such a type with the moral life at its best.

It is true that a man's philosophy, and especially his moral philosophy, takes a certain colour from his own individual moral attitude. This applies to Kant as to any one else, and may help to explain certain idiosyncrasies of emphasis and perspective; but I do not think it vitiates his analysis, and it certainly does not excuse us from meeting his arguments. Kant himself was a gentle and humane man with a passion for freedom and a hatred of intolerance: there is no evidence whatever to suggest that he was either cold or domineering or ascetic. I have tried to expose, in the course of my discussion, some of the misconceptions on which this charge of legalism is based; but there is one special point which must be added in the present connexion.

The main ground for charging Kant with legalism is the belief that he bids us perform our moral actions for the sake of a vague abstraction called the law, and thereby forbids us to perform moral actions for their own sake. Since this view is completely opposed to Kant's doctrine, and yet may easily be read into his language, I will try to make his position clear.

According to Kant every action aims at a result or end or object. In non-moral behaviour we perform the action because we desire the object; we then have what Kant calls a 'pathological' interest in the object, and our interest in the action is *mediate*—that is, it depends on our interest in the object. In moral behaviour we perform the action because the action, aiming as it does at certain results, is an embodiment of the moral law; but it must not be supposed that the action is then willed only as a means to an empty abstraction called 'the law'. On the contrary, we take an *immediate* interest in the action itself 'when the universal validity of its maxim is a sufficient determining ground of the will'.[1] One of Kant's strongest convictions is that we take an *immediate* interest in moral actions. This is the reason why on his view actions done out of immediate inclinations, such as sympathy and benevolence, are more difficult to distinguish from moral actions than are actions done from self-interest, where there is no immediate inclination to the action. This immediate moral interest is

[1] *Gr.*, 460 n. = 95 n. See also 413 n. = 37 n.

indeed another name for 'reverence',[1] which we may feel for actions, and still more for persons, in whom the law is embodied.

I do not believe that there need be any real inconsistency in Kant about this: he is entitled to say both that we take an immediate interest in a moral action and that we do the action for the sake of the law. The category of means and end is inadequate to action, and grossly inadequate to moral action. The law is not for Kant an end to which the action is a means: it is the form or principle of the action itself. Although it is the condition of the action's goodness, it is nevertheless an element in the action itself.[2]

§4. *The ignoring of consequences.*

Nothing, I suppose, will ever get rid of the illusion that for Kant a good man must take no account of consequences—in some sense which means that a good man must be a perfect fool. This interpretation rests on the ambiguities of language.[3] There is a sense in which the good man will take no account of consequences in deciding what he ought to do. He will not *begin* with the consequences and say that because an action will have certain consequences which he desires, therefore he will regard the action as his duty. He knows that it may be his duty not to produce results which he may greatly desire. Kant is right in saying that the expected consequences cannot be the *determining ground* of an action if it is to have moral worth. Nevertheless the good man begins with the *maxim* of a proposed action and asks himself whether the maxim can be willed as a universal law; and the maxim is always of the form 'if I am in certain circumstances, I will perform an action likely to have certain consequences'. How could we propose to steal or to kill or to act at all, if we ignored the fact that an action has consequences? Nevertheless we must not judge the action to be right or wrong according as we like or dislike the consequences. The test is whether the maxim of such an action is compatible with the nature of a universal law which is to hold for others as well as for myself. A good man aims at consequences because of the law: he does not obey the law merely because of the consequences.

Such is the simple and obvious truth so often caricatured. If Kant had said merely that we must not allow our desires for particular consequences to determine our judgement of what our duty is, he would have avoided a great deal of misunderstanding.

---

[1] *Gr.*, 401 n. = 22 n.

[2] Compare Chapter I §7, at the end. What Kant says about the highest good—in *K.p.V.*, 109–10 = 244–5 (= 196–7)—applies to any action or object. I will summarise and simplify. If our volition is determined by the thought of an action or object independently of the law, then our action is not moral. The moral law is the only determining ground of the pure will. But *it goes without saying (Es versteht sich von selbst)* that if the moral law is *included* in the concept of such an action or object as its supreme condition, then the concept of such an action or object and of its realisation by our will is *at the same time* the determining ground of the pure will.

[3] It is, however, also encouraged by a tendency in Kant to exaggerate the generally sound principle that in many cases remoter consequences ought to be ignored.

§5. *The soundness of Kant's doctrine.*

One of the great merits of Kant's doctrine is the sharp distinction which he makes between the *a priori* and the empirical, between duty and inclination. Since he wrote, there is no longer any excuse for the muddled thinking which confuses *my* good with *the* good and consciously or unconsciously substitutes for the moral motive mere desire for our own personal happiness either in this world or the next. A veiled and unconscious hedonism is as corrupting as it is confused. The primary aim of a good man is not to satisfy his own inclinations, however generous, but to obey a law which is the same for all, and only so does he cease to be self-centred and become moral. There is no more fundamental difference than that between a life of prudence or self-love and one of moral goodness.

We cannot give a general description of moral action by reference to its objects, both because the objects of moral action vary indefinitely and because they may be produced by action which is not moral. Moral action must be described, not by its objects, but by its motive or principle or maxim; and this principle or maxim, for the same reasons as before, cannot *merely* be one of producing certain objects. The only possibility is that it should be a maxim of obeying a law which is the same for all: in Kant's language, it must be a formal maxim.

A man who is guided by the formal maxim of morality must not be conceived as acting in a vacuum. In the light of this maxim he selects and controls his ordinary maxims of self-love and inclination. In this way he resembles the prudent man, who selects and controls his maxims of inclination in the light of the maxim of self-love.[1] The behaviour of the prudent man is familiar to us all, though we do not describe it in Kant's language; and it too is the work of practical reason. The work of reason in moral action is not very much more difficult to conceive than the work of reason in prudential action.

I will add one more point in anticipation of what is to follow. One of the reasons why Kant ascribes absolute value to a good will is that in obeying law for its own sake a good man is raised above the stream of events which we call nature: he is no longer at the mercy of his own natural instincts and desires. A good man is free in so far as he obeys the formal law which is the product of his rational will instead of being pulled about by desire, and it is this freedom which arouses Kant's veneration.[2] Whatever be our judgement of this, we do well to note that Kant's view of the formal character of the moral law is necessary to his doctrine of freedom. So far his philosophy has at least the merit of being consistent.

---

[1] Compare Chapter III §4.   [2] *Gr.*, 426 = 53.

BOOK II

THE BACKGROUND OF
THE CATEGORICAL IMPERATIVE

CHAPTER VIII

PRACTICAL REASON
AND ITS SUBJECTIVE PRINCIPLES

§1. *The practical function of reason.*

IT has been taken for granted hitherto that reason plays a part in human action and especially in moral action.[1] Two distinct practical functions have been ascribed to reason: (1) the pursuit of happiness and (2) the pursuit of goodness.[2] We must now attempt to explain and justify this assumption; and our task is the more necessary if, on Critical principles, we have to trace the concept of duty, and indeed of goodness, to its origin in reason itself.[3]

The view that reason has a part to play in action is not an innovation of Kant's: on the contrary, it has been the predominant doctrine of philosophy at least since the time of Plato. The widespread rejection of the doctrine at the present time is partly due to a distrust of reason as such. With this we have no concern, though it may be observed that if the distrust of reason professes to be based on reason, it is self-contradictory; and if it is not so based, then it is admittedly irrational, and it would be waste of time to argue about it. Such a thorough-based irrationalism or scepticism must inevitably make all values rest on mere feeling and so make them arbitrary: it must deny all objective standards of value. We are, however, supposing for the sake of argument that moral judgements, whether they are illusions or not, can be analysed *as if* they were objective: we are endeavouring to discover their implications and the conditions which would have to be fulfilled if there were to be a possibility of their being true. One of the conditions is manifestly that such judgements must be a product of reason, which is the only source of truth; and we have to face the contention that while reason may be concerned with truth, it

---
[1] I have discussed this question more generally in *Can Reason be Practical?*
[2] Chapter II §8. [3] Chapter I §9; *Gr.*, 412 = 36.

[78]

cannot have any connexion with value, in particular with moral value, nor can it have any bearing on action. This view, in part at least, seems to rest upon misunderstandings of Kant's doctrine.

§ 2. *Two senses of 'reason'.*

One of these misunderstandings is the common assumption that reason is to be regarded only as a power of inferring or reasoning. If this were so, it seems obvious enough that we cannot infer or demonstrate any particular action to be good or to be a duty; and indeed we cannot infer or demonstrate that there is such a thing as goodness or duty at all. Where could we possibly get the premises for such an inference?

There is a sense in which practical reason, on Kant's view, is connected with reason as a power of inference, although the connexion is very different from the simple-minded connexion we have just suggested.[1] But at present we must deal with this question on a lower level. Reason, in traditional usage, is the higher faculty of cognition and as such is opposed to sense and imagination.[2] Aristotle defines man as a rational animal; and in this definition rationality or the possession of reason is what differentiates man from the higher animals, who share with him the possession of sense and perhaps even, in some degree, of imagination. The cognitive power which man possesses in addition to sense and imagination is wider than a power of making inferences, though this is included.

In the wide traditional sense reason covers (1) the power of entertaining concepts (or '*understanding*' in Kant's terminology); (2) the power of applying concepts to given objects (the power of '*judgement*'); and (3) the power of making mediate inferences (the power of reasoning or of '*reason*' in a narrower sense). To say that reason in the wide sense plays no part in human actions is palpably untrue. All we need to consider is what is the precise part which such reason does play in human action.

§ 3. *The approach to practical reason.*

action only by considering the nature of action itself. This is Kant's own view, but he is sometimes misunderstood on this point. He says, for example, that we must *derive* (*ableiten*) moral laws from the universal concept of a rational being as such.[1] This might be taken to mean that we start with the concept of a rational being, in the sense of a being who thinks or even of a being who makes inferences; and that by mere analysis of this concept we arrive at certain propositions asserting, for example, that a rational being ought to act for the sake of duty, or even that he ought to fulfil such particular duties as the payment of debts, the display of gratitude, and the like. Such a procedure is manifestly impossible, nor is there any trace of such an argument in Kant. He explicitly rejects the fundamental assumption on which this procedure is based; for he asserts that a practical proposition (or moral law) connects a volition immediately with the concept of the will of a rational being *as something which is not contained in that concept*.[2]

We understand theoretical reason because we are beings capable of thinking, and we understand practical reason because we are beings capable of acting. Why should there be more difficulty in the one case than in the other? The only difference is that in understanding theoretical reason we are thinking about thinking, whereas in understanding practical reason we are thinking about something which is not itself thinking, but acting. Nevertheless in both cases we have, so to speak, an inside view of what we are thinking about.

At times Kant identifies practical reason with the will. At other times he speaks of reason as determining the will.[3] The former terminology is more satisfactory: it suggests that our willing is as rational as our thinking and is not merely something blind and unconscious which—*per impossibile*—is causally affected by our conscious thinking. Nevertheless when we speak of reason as determining the will, we indicate that volition has a cognitive aspect, which can be considered in abstraction. Similarly thinking has a volitional aspect which can also be considered in abstraction.

There is admittedly some danger in speaking of powers and faculties at all. Strictly, it is the whole man who thinks and feels and wills. Nevertheless it is often convenient to speak of powers of thinking, feeling, and willing, when we wish to discuss different functions within man's total activity. In fact, it is almost impossible to avoid doing so, and there is no harm in this so long as we remember that what we are trying to understand is always an element in a whole rational life.

---

[1] *Gr.*, 412 = 35.
[2] *Gr.*, 420 n. = 46 n. See also *Gr.*, 426-7 = 54 and 440 = 71. To connect the concept of a rational being with the moral law or the categorical imperative is to show how a categorical imperative is possible; and to do this, as we shall see more clearly later, is to justify a synthetic *a priori* proposition, not an analytic proposition. See Chapter XII §9.
[3] *Gr.*, 412 = 36.

§4. *Theoretical reason and action.*

Even in its theoretical aspect reason makes a vast difference to our actions. It is only by theoretical reason that we can be aware of the situation in which we must act and to which our action must be adapted; and in this situation we must include not only physical nature and the nature of other rational agents, but also our own nature, and especially our desires and needs. To the outside observer it may seem that all events happen, all organisms function, all animals behave, and all men act in one and the same world; but from the point of view of the agent men act in the world as it is known to them. This remains true although the agent knows that he knows incompletely the world in which he must act. Hence it may be said that for the agent the world, or the situation, in which he acts varies according to the extent of his knowledge. Since men act differently in different situations, our theoretical knowledge must affect the character of our actions. If, for example, we do not know the cup to be poisoned, we may drink; but if we do know it to be poisoned, we will not drink, unless it is our intention to commit suicide.

The last point illustrates very clearly the special importance of knowledge about causes and effects. Without such knowledge all action would be impossible. But although theoretical knowledge is a precondition of action, and although action is always willed in the light of theoretical knowledge, knowledge does not thereby cease to be theoretical and become practical. Practical reason must be manifested in something other than the acquisition of such theoretical knowledge as may be useful or even necessary for action.

§5. *Practical reason.*

If our reason is practical, we must be able to will our individual actions as instances of a concept, just as our theoretical reason, in the wide sense, knows individual objects as instances of a concept. Kant holds that on the side of action reason manifests itself in this way. Only a rational being, he says,[1] has the power of acting in accordance with his conception of laws—that is, in accordance with principles. And he contrasts such a being with things in nature, which work in accordance with laws, but do not act in accordance with their conception of laws.

Everything in nature works in accordance with laws so far as its working is governed by the laws of cause and effect; but although a stone, for example, falls in accordance with the law of gravitation, it does not (so far as we know) fall in accordance with its conception of this law. The movements and functions of man's body, and even—according to Kant—of his mind, are equally governed by laws of nature, including the law of cause and effect. But in action something more than this is present. We have already seen[2] that every action has its *maxim* or subjective principle;

---

[1] *Gr.*, 412 = 36.   [2] Chapter IV §2.

F

and this is the first thing Kant has in mind when he says that a rational being acts in accordance with principles, or in accordance with its conception of laws, and so only has it a will.

To have a maxim of action is something different from being aware of the law in accordance with which events happen to us or even in us. The physicist who falls from an aeroplane may reflect that he is now falling in accordance with the law of gravitation, but the law of gravitation cannot be regarded as the maxim of his action of falling; nor indeed in such a case is his falling an action. If we were in any precise sense moved by irresistible impulses, something of the same kind would happen to us: as Kant himself suggests,[1] we might be able to understand, and even to admire, the working of our own nature; but in this there would be neither a maxim nor an action. Although some psychologists speak as if all action were merely the result of a play of forces which they alone are able to understand—presumably even when, if ever, they are acting themselves—their view carries little conviction if we regard action from the agent's point of view. Even the murderer who pleads irresistible impulse seems generally to maintain that at one stage of the proceedings everything went black, and that only when he came to himself again did he find that the lady had been strangled. But however this may be, if we merely understood the law in accordance with which our nature worked, there would be no maxim and no action.

Practical reason is shown, not in understanding a law of our behaviour, but in willing in accordance with a principle or maxim—or, as I should be inclined to put it, in willing an action as an instance of a concept or rule.

At least in finite rational beings, there is no volition and no action without a maxim; and it is only because we act in accordance with maxims that we can be said to have a will. Indeed Kant defines a will as a power to determine oneself to action in accordance with the conception of certain laws[2]—that is, in accordance with maxims. And the same definition applies to practical reason since practical reason is identified with will.

§6. *Impulsive action.*

It follows from all this that practical reason, with a maxim or subjective principle, is present in every kind of human action—even in action that we call impulsive—provided that it is consciously willed. This is what distinguishes human action from animal behaviour, or again from what is called 'reflex action', which we do not regard as our action at all. In impulsive action the generality of the maxim, as a rule which we might apply to similar situations, is far from being conspicuous and may easily be overlooked; but even in such a case we are aware of the quality of our action and will it as an action having this quality. This would, I imagine,

---
[1] *Gr.*, 395 = 14.
[2] *Gr.*, 477 = 55. Compare *Religion*, 21 n. = 22 n. (= 7 n.), where Kant says that apart from a maxim no determining ground of free choice can or ought to be adduced.

be regarded by a British jury as the test of our responsibility—or the condition apart from which the action could not be called ours, and indeed could not be called an action.

In this there may well be degrees; and it may be hard to decide whether, for example, the avoidance of a sudden blow is an action or a mere reflex. But if it is an action, and if we are responsible for it, we are aware of its character, and we will it as having this character; and if this is so, our action has its maxim or principle.

Kant unfortunately does not consider a philosophy of action to be necessary for ethics,[1] and consequently he does not discuss these questions in any detail. Nevertheless he gives us a good many hints as to his view. In a rational being an animal *inclination*, in so far as it is conceived through reason, becomes what he calls a 'pathological *interest*', and on this interest a material *maxim* is based.[2] As he considers the pathological interest to be directed to the object, or intended results, of the action, he may possibly regard every material maxim as setting forth the kind of action necessary to secure the object.[3] If so, every material maxim may be regarded as stating the means to an end, the means being the action and the object being the end. In his actual usage, however, maxims express primarily the will to act in a certain kind of way in a certain kind of situation.

All this is important mainly in order to guard against misunderstandings. It is too commonly assumed that Kant opposes impulsive actions to actions based on a principle or maxim; he is said to fall into a dualism of reason and inclination; and he is alleged to recognise no difference in action other than that between pure moral action on the one hand and mere animal behaviour on the other. It is true that Kant recognises, as we all must, an antagonism between animal inclinations and pure reason in human action; but he also recognises that animal inclination can never issue in human action unless through the activity of reason it is transformed into an *interest* which gives rise to a *maxim* or rational principle of action. Here, as so often, the absurdities attributed to Kant arise only in the imagination of his interpreters. Animal inclination or impulse is never for Kant a motive of human action except in so far as 'taken up' by practical reason into its maxims.[4]

§7. *Means and end.*

Practical reason must be shown in adjusting action to different and changing situations as these become known to us. This side of action Kant assumes rather than discusses—he is not professing to offer us a general

---
[1] See Chapter I, Appendix (towards the end).
[2] *K.p.V.*, 79 = 205 (= 141); 67 = 189 (= 118); *Gr.*, 413 n. = 37 n.; 460 n. = 95 n.
[3] The object may be the result which the action seeks to produce (that is, a change in the actual world) or it may be the satisfaction of inclination (that is, a change in the self).
[4] *Religion*, 23–4 = 24–5 (= 12).

philosophy of action beyond what is necessary for his ethical theory. He may conceivably regard this side of action as falling under the concept of means and end: if I adjust myself to rain by taking shelter, this might be regarded as applying the means necessary to my aim of keeping dry. Anyhow he is interested primarily in the function of reason as looking forward and using means towards desired ends. This is something which is present in human beings, but not in the higher animals. Many of our maxims must take the form: '*I will do X as a means to Y.*'

In this there must be all sorts of gradations and even a kind of continuity with animal life. An animal may take shelter from the rain; and in this case, as in many others, such as eating and drinking, animal behaviour resembles human action, though we have no reason to suppose that the animal recognises the quality of what it is doing or that it regards its actions as means to a desired end. In human action, taking shelter may be relatively casual, or it may be part of what I call a 'policy', as when a man deliberately and systematically avoids any risk of getting wet. The most notable use of means to ends is in the exercise of skill, and it is in this that Kant is particularly interested.

It should be noted that while I may act on many particular maxims concerning the best means to my various ends, these actions may be considered as having a more general maxim, the maxim '*I will use the most effective means to any end I may have.*' This may be regarded as the controlling maxim when I use any particular means to a particular end. By itself this more general or higher maxim is empty, and it may not be consciously formulated; but we may nevertheless be said to act in accordance with it if we refuse to act on particular maxims which are opposed to it. In such a case we might be said to act only on maxims which fall under the higher maxim of using the most efficient means to our ends. Needless to say we do not act on this higher maxim *in vacuo*—we must also desire a particular end and be aware of a particular means.

This account is far from adequate as a complete description of action —which, however, it does not profess to be. We might question the category of means and end altogether, since it may be doubted whether we will part of an action as a means and part as an end—the distinction seems rather a theoretical one applied to actions either already done or else contemplated. If we set this objection aside, we may still urge that the unity of an action, and still more of a policy, is not exhausted by conformity to any maxim, and in particular that it is not exhausted by conformity to the maxim of seeking the most effective means to our ends. The maxim is general, the action is individual. Because of this there must be more in the action than in the maxim, and the unity of an action or of a policy resembles in some ways the unity of a work of art rather than the unity of conforming to a concept. This, however, raises problems which cannot here be considered.[1]

---

[1] The Hegelians in particular charge Kant with considering only abstract universals and failing to take into account the individual, or what they call the 'concrete universal'. These charges are often exaggerated and are at times due to misunderstanding, but they are not without some element of truth.

Whatever be the deficiencies of Kant's doctrine, the distinction of means and end is commonly accepted, and he is dealing with a recognisable aspect of action which will be important for his later argument. Practical reason is manifested in maintaining the conscious unity of our actions and policies, and this unity may be described, although inadequately, as conformity to the concept of means and end.

§8. *The pursuit of happiness.*

It is not enough to maintain the unity of actions and policies in themselves, and practical reason manifests itself also in maintaining their unity in relation to one another in a whole organised life. We have many needs to meet, many desires to satisfy, many ends to attain, and all these must be fitted into a whole life or policy of life. This task Kant regards as the pursuit of happiness and as the principal function of practical reason below the level of morality.

His account of the pursuit of happiness is not altogether satisfactory, nor is it wholly consistent with itself. At times he takes a hedonistic view and seems to regard happiness as little more than the greatest possible amount of continuous or uninterrupted pleasure throughout the whole of life.[1] This he considers to be the final end which all men seek. He recognises indeed that reason, even on this level, must estimate happiness, not by the passing sensation, but by its influence on our whole existence and our contentment therewith.[2] Yet in the main the function of practical reason on this view is to will the appropriate means to this clearly envisaged end.

Here again the category of means and end seems inadequate for the description of action, and Kant himself combines this view inconsistently with another view, according to which we have no determinate and sure concept of happiness as an end which we seek.[3]

Happiness is then regarded as the total satisfaction of our needs and inclinations,[4] and what was formerly considered as a *means* to happiness is now considered as an *element* in happiness. Among such elements there appear to be reckoned such things as riches, knowledge and insight, long life, and health,[5] that is, objects which we desire and ends which we seek. Practical reason is no longer concerned primarily with the means to a known end—namely, happiness or continuous pleasure. Practical reason is above all concerned with what constitutes the happiness which we all seek as our end: it must aim at satisfying as many as possible of our needs in an organised life or (as Kant puts it) at bringing our natural inclinations into harmony with one another in a whole called happiness.[6] In so doing practical reason manifests itself as prudence or rational self-love, and it has the task of determining the constituents of happiness as well

---

[1] E.g. *K.p.V.*, 22 = 129 (= 40).
[2] *K.p.V.*, 61 = 181 (= 107).
[3] *Gr.*, 399 = 19.
[4] *Gr.*, 405 = 26.
[5] *Gr.*, 418 = 42-3.
[6] *Religion*, 58 (= 70).

as the task of prescribing means to the attainment of these constituents:[1] it is shown in a choice of ends as well as of means.[2]

This second view is much more satisfactory than the first, though it is not without its own difficulties. Rational beings seek to realise their multifarious ends within an organised and systematic life. This comprehensive rational end is perhaps unfortunately called 'happiness', but there seems to be no other more satisfactory word. It is absurd to suppose that the only object we desire and the only end we seek is continuous pleasure and the avoidance of pain. The principle of rational self-love is not so much a principle of using the means to continuous pleasant feeling, but is rather a principle of integrating our ends, of which pleasant feeling is only one, into a single comprehensive whole.

If we were writing a philosophy of action, this account would require a great deal of expansion and qualification. Because Kant is concerned primarily with the rational element in action, he makes no effort to consider the element of spontaneity or creativeness, and indeed of arbitrariness, which is present in our search for happiness and—to a lesser extent —even in our use of means towards particular ends. To suppose on this ground that he ignored or denied such an element would be completely unjustified. There are many indications that he distrusted a too nicely calculated method of life—see, for example, his obvious sympathy with the gouty man who risks his extra glass of port[3]—and in thinking as well as in art he is always on the side of creativeness and spontaneity. Indeed his whole philosophy may be described as one of spontaneity and freedom. At present, however, we are concerned only with the function of practical reason in controlling and organising the fulfilment of our desires.

The pursuit of happiness, if it were concerned only with the attainment of pleasure, might well be described as selfish; but if it is concerned with the fulfilment of our desires, it should be described as self-centred rather than as selfish, since, as Kant always recognises, we have other-regarding as well as self-regarding desires. The centre on this level is always the self, but the circumference, so to speak, may cover many things, including the happiness of others. So far from rejecting the life of prudence or self-love, Kant maintains consistently that every man has a right to pursue his own happiness so long as this does not conflict with the moral law. He even maintains that we may have an indirect duty to do so, since wretchedness may easily lead us into immoral action.

The maxim of prudence or rational self-love is: '*I will seek my own happiness.*' This is better interpreted, not as a maxim dealing with means and end ('*I will use the means to secure the maximum of pleasant feeling*'), but

---

[1] *Religion*, 45 n. = 52 n. (= 50 n.).

[2] *M.d.S., Tugendlehre, Einl.* III, 385 = 230. See also *K.r.V.*, A800 = B828, where Kant says that in the doctrine of self-love the whole task of reason consists in uniting all ends set us by our inclinations into the one end, happiness, and in harmonising the means for its attainment.

[3] *Gr.*, 399 = 19.

as a maxim of integration ('*I will aim at the satisfaction of my desires in a whole organised and systematic life*'). Indeed even the maxim of skill may be interpreted, not as concerned merely with the application of means to a particular end, but as concerned with the integration of an action or a policy as a limited whole.

However we interpret it, the maxim of prudence commonly overrides the maxims of skill, though it does not supersede them. We may reject the most effective means to a desired end, we may even reject a desired end itself, if such a means conflicts with our happiness as a whole. In this way the maxim of prudence may be our controlling maxim, and we may be said to act on particular maxims only as they fall under the maxim of prudence. But once again we do not act upon this controlling maxim *in vacuo*: it has its content only so far as we desire particular ends and seek to make use of particular means.

§9. *The denial of practical reason.*

To deny that practical reason plays this part in human life seems to me plainly false. The denial owes such plausibility as it possesses to an assumption of the following kind. Reason is purely theoretical; it reveals to us, although only in part, the situation in which we have to act; and we act differently in different situations. But what we call the will is itself a blind force, or even a combination of blind forces, which manifests itself differently in different situations as known to us. Reason affects action only in presenting to us the situation and, so to speak, the external stimulus to action.[1]

This assumption, though in one place it seems to receive a modified approval from Kant himself,[2] is surely mistaken. It is not the result of empirical observation, but of a dogmatic and even metaphysical prejudice, natural enough to those whose chief occupation is thinking. There are certainly occasions on which we think first and act afterwards, but far more often we think in acting: the action is not preceded by intellection, but is itself intelligent. How could a blind force, or combination of blind forces, even seem to respond differently and intelligently to each different known situation?[3] Reason is shown, not merely in understanding the situation or in recognising the quality of the completed action, but in willing the action as an action of a certain kind—as adjusted to the situation, as making use of the best means, and as contributing to the agent's happiness. The character of human volition is as different from animal behaviour as human apprehension of the situation is different from what we may suppose to be animal apprehension.

There is far more plausibility in the pragmatic contention that reason is always practical and is never merely theoretical. The truth is surely that

---

[1] See §4 above.   [2] *K.U.*, *Erste Einleitung*, I, 1–9.
[3] It may be objected that instinct seems to do something like this. Yet we know it is instinct and not reason only because of its lack of flexibility or intelligence.

reason is always both, although at one time the theoretical, and at another time the practical, aspect is the more prominent of the two.[1]

§10. *Morality*.

There is some ground for saying that men sometimes act, or at least believe themselves and others to act, on maxims of morality. Kant's view that the maxim of morality has a formal character has already been discussed.[2]

---

[1] For some points in this section I am indebted to a letter from Professor H. H. Price.
[2] See Chapter IV, especially §§3-4.

CHAPTER IX

PRACTICAL REASON
AND ITS OBJECTIVE PRINCIPLES

§1. *Subjective and objective principles.*

HITHERTO we have considered practical reason so far as its principles are in fact manifested in human conduct and can in that sense be called 'subjective'. Our contention has been that reason is practical since—even apart from morality—it does in fact influence human action: it is present in the material maxims of skill and self-love by which human action is very often determined. To deny that reason is practical is to assert that reason is never manifested either in the exercise of human skill or in the pursuit of happiness, and such an assertion is manifestly absurd.

On the other hand we know only too well that even on this level reason may fail to determine action. We may be led by some sudden passion into actions which may make the attainment of a desired end impossible and may even wreck the happiness of our whole life. Our human nature is far from being such that we must necessarily act in accordance with rational maxims of skill and self-love. In Kant's technical language these rational maxims are not 'subjectively necessary'; they are 'subjectively contingent'.[1] That is to say, we may act upon them, but equally we may not.

It must not be thought that in asserting this we are abandoning our previous contention that reason is manifested in *all* human action. When moved by passion we may still recognise the quality of our action, and we may will our action as an instance of yielding to fear or anger, as the case may be: if we ceased to do this, our action would become mere animal behaviour rather than human conduct. But in stupidly impulsive action the influence of reason is narrowed: we act on a maxim rational within its own limits, but irrational in relation to our wider view of the end we seek. We may be rational enough to recognise this irrationality, not merely afterwards, but even at the time, and only so do we impute folly to ourselves. If reason were not present as well as passion, our behaviour would be merely unfortunate and not foolish.

We can conceive a rational agent so rational that he would never act foolishly. In such an agent reason would have full control over the passions. He would never allow passion to distract him from acting in accordance with the principles of skill and self-love. To yield to passion in despite of reason would be contrary to his rational nature, and we can say that for him the maxims of skill and self-love would be subjectively

[1] *Gr.*, 413 = 36.

necessary and not—as in our own case—subjectively contingent. A fully rational agent could not but behave rationally.

Such a conception—even apart from the difficulties that may be felt about the freedom of rational agents—may appear to be valueless since we have no acquaintance with fully rational agents. The conception may, however, be useful if we are to consider the character of *objective* principles; for objective principles, as we saw above,[1] are principles on which a rational agent would necessarily act if reason had full control over his passions. Objective principles are valid for every rational agent, while subjective principles or maxims as such make no pretence to be valid for any one but the agent who is acting on them.

In the previous chapter we considered the principles of skill and of self-love merely as maxims on which rational agents sometimes act and in which practical reason is manifested. But on Kant's view they are more than mere maxims: even if they were never acted upon at all, they would still be objective principles, though of a special kind. Indeed—provided we are right in regarding them as manifestations of practical reason—it would be surprising if they had not some kind of validity for every rational agent.

Kant regards the principles of skill and self-love as principles on which any rational agent would necessarily act if reason had full control over the passions. To say this is to say that they are objective principles; and again, in Kant's language, that they are objectively necessary, even although they may be subjectively contingent.[2] What is peculiar about them is that although they are objective principles, they are so only *subject to a condition*. The meaning of this we must now examine.

§2. *The principle of skill.*

Let us consider first the principle of skill, and let us stick to Kant's terminology of means and end. A rational agent who seeks any particular end will—so far as reason controls his passions—necessarily make use of the most effective means in his power. Men indeed vary in power and consequently may have to use different means; but if we regard the agent's power as part of the situation in which he has to act, we can say that in the same situation every rational agent, *qua* rational, will necessarily act in accordance with the same maxim—that is, he will necessarily use the most effective means to this particular end, *if* he seeks the end.

It is possible to raise various objections which cannot here be considered in detail. Sometimes a rational agent may appear, quite rationally, to choose some means other than the most effective, as when a climber takes the most difficult way up a hill; but in such a case his end is something other than merely getting to the top. Sometimes he may dislike the means more than he likes the end and so may give up the whole project. Always the principle of skill may be rationally overridden by

---
[1] Chapter IV §2.
[2] For a fully rational agent they would be both objectively and subjectively necessary; for an imperfectly rational agent like man they are objectively necessary but subjectively contingent. *Gr.*, 412–13 = 36.

the higher principle of prudence, not to mention the still higher principle of morality. But within its own limits it is conditionally valid for every rational agent.

There must always be considerable 'latitude' or 'play-room' in the application of particular maxims of skill. An iron shot by Bobby Jones will differ in some ways from an iron shot by Harry Vardon even under the same conditions. This is still more obvious in the fine arts (which are not here in question save as regards technique): 'There are nine and sixty ways of constructing tribal lays, and every single one of them is right.' I see no ground for holding that Kant expects his principles to be applied mechanically and identically in every case. On the contrary, he speaks as if the essential character of a maxim were to require judgement in its application and to leave room for 'latitude'.[1] He asserts this primarily in regard to maxims of morality; but in the light of his treatment of art, and also in the light of his marked contempt for imitation as opposed to creation, we are justified in extending his view to cover maxims of skill.

In all action a rational agent not only has a maxim, but also sets before himself an end,[2] if we can interpret 'end' to cover actions done for their own sake and not merely for the results they produce.[3] The *general* principle of skill—the principle of using the most effective means—is objectively valid for any rational agent. *Particular* principles of skill (which are only applications of the general principle) are also objectively valid, but only subject to the condition that some particular end is sought. Their conditional character does not detract from their objectivity.

There is also another sense in which principles of skill are conditioned. No rational agent, even if he sought to attain a particular end, would necessarily, so far as he was rational, use means, however effective, which would destroy his happiness as a whole. Principles of skill are conditioned, not merely by the end sought, but also by their compatibility with the higher principle of prudence or self-love. This, however, in no way means that they cease to be objective principles.

§3. *The principle of self-love.*

The same considerations apply to the principle of rational self-love or prudence. According to Kant, a rational agent, so far as reason has full control over his passions, will necessarily seek his own happiness. Since man, as belonging to the sensible world, is a being with needs, reason has so far 'an office which it cannot refuse', the office of serving the interests of sensibility and of seeking happiness in this world and where possible in the next.[4] To seek one's own happiness is not merely a maxim on which many men act: it is also an objective principle of practical reason.

Although this principle is objectively necessary for a rational agent, it is not thereby also subjectively necessary for an imperfectly rational agent

---
[1] *M.d.S.*, *Tugendlehre*, Einl. VII, 390 = 235; *Einl.* XVIII, 411.

[2] *Gr.*, 427 = 55; *M.d.S.*, *Tugendlehre*, Einl. III, 385 = 229.

[3] This is assumed by Kant, although his language often suggests that an end is merely a product or result.

[4] *K.p.V.*, 61 = 181 (= 108).

such as man. Many men in fact wreck their own happiness through passion or weakness. To say this is not to deny that there is some rationality even in their imprudence. Imprudent actions have, however, a lower rationality, since in them reason, so to speak, takes account of less than all the facts which it has before itself.

As we saw in the previous chapter,[1] Kant interprets happiness in two ways. We shall find his view here also more convincing if we take happiness to be, not a maximum of pleasant feeling throughout life, but the maximum satisfaction of desires or the maximum integration of ends. We should not, however, take him to mean that the prudent agent will necessarily, so far as he is prudent, plan his whole life in advance. The part of prudence is not to destroy spontaneity, but to prevent one passing desire of the moment from thwarting many other desires permanently.

The philosophy of prudence might be elaborated indefinitely,[2] but it is not immediately relevant to our purpose. Probably for this reason Kant himself tends to neglect it. We must, however, recognise that maxims of prudence admit of great latitude in their application. While all rational agents will, so far as they are rational, necessarily seek their own happiness, they may find it in very different ways. The desires of the same individual vary within limits according to his circumstances and his experience; and an early decision, such as the choice of a career, may cause him to find his happiness in one way of life when he might equally well have found it in another.

The essential point for our present purpose is that *particular* principles of self-love, though objective, are still conditioned. They are conditioned first of all by the character and desires of the particular agent: we could not reasonably expect Mahatma Gandhi to find happiness in the same kind of life as Winston Churchill. In the second place—if Kant is right— the principles of self-love are conditioned by their compatibility with the principles of morality. On his view a rational agent, so far as reason had full control over his passions, would necessarily refuse to plunge a continent into war however much such a catastrophe might contribute to his own happiness.

It should be added that although (as we saw in the previous section) the principle of self-love may override principles of skill in particular cases, there is no general incompatibility between the two kinds of principle. So far as an agent is rational, he will seek to acquire and use the skill necessary for the realisation of those ends in which his happiness is to be found.[3]

[1] Chapter VIII §8.
[2] Much elaboration would be necessary to meet charges of over-simplification, but I must leave the reader to fill in the kind of qualifications which he may deem necessary. I tried to deal with some of these problems in *The Good Will*, especially Chapter VIII.
[3] This is, I think, brought out better by the German word '*Klugheit*', which I have translated as 'prudence' or 'self-love'. Kant defines it in *Gr.*, 416 n. = 41 n. as 'the sagacity to combine all one's purposes to one's own lasting advantage'. He recognises a second kind of '*Klugheit*'—namely, *Weltklugheit* (or worldly wisdom)—which is subordinate to the first and is more explicitly concerned with means; for it is described as skill in influencing others so as to use them for one's own purposes.

§4. *The principle of morality.*

So far we have recognised that while the principles of practical reason are objective, they are at the same time conditioned by the desires and character of particular agents. Many of us, perhaps most of us, may be content with such principles and may regard an enquiry into further principles as a mere waste of time. Nevertheless the question must arise whether there can be principles of practical reason which are objective without being conditioned. Such principles would be unconditioned or absolute; and on Kant's view the function of conceiving the unconditioned which appears to be implied by our knowledge of the conditioned is one which belongs to what he calls the power of reason in his special technical sense.

The technical name for such concepts of the unconditioned is 'Idea'—or more elaborately 'Idea of Reason'.[1] Kant always insists that we find it necessary to conceive such Ideas and that when properly understood they can play a useful part in our thinking. Nevertheless he holds—and this is the essential point—that, so far as speculative reason is concerned, they cannot give us knowledge of reality. Human beings can have knowledge only so far as their concepts refer to objects given to the senses. Since all objects given to sense are conditioned, and since the unconditioned is not given to sense, the Ideas of reason do not refer to possible objects of experience and cannot give us knowledge.

Our present concern, however, is not with speculative, but with practical, reason. We are discussing, not the ultimate nature of reality, but the principles on which a rational agent would necessarily act if reason had full control over his desires. The conditioned objective principles which we have hitherto examined have suggested to us the Idea of an unconditioned objective principle; and such a practical Idea might conceivably play in action a part similar to what Kant calls the 'regulative', as opposed to the 'constitutive', function of speculative Ideas in our thinking. It might set before us an ideal which we might continually strive to approach, even if it were beyond our attainment.

An unconditioned objective principle would omit all reference to the desires and character of particular agents: it would omit all reference to particular ends and even to the comprehensive end of the agent's own happiness. Such a principle, as we have seen,[2] could only be the form of a principle, or a formal principle—the principle, so to speak, of having an objective principle and so of being reasonable. Kant has described it as a principle of law-abidingness, a principle of acting in accordance with universal law as such.

Such a principle may appear completely empty, and we must be on our guard—as Kant himself well knows[3]—of omitting the conditions which

---

[1] I use the word 'Idea' with a capital 'I' as translation of the German word '*Idee*.' When 'idea' with a small 'i' is used, it is meant to be taken in the ordinary English sense —often as a translation of the German word '*Vorstellung*'.
[2] Chapter IV §3.   [3] *K.r.V.*, A674 = B702.

alone render a concept intelligible, and then imagining that what is left will be supremely intelligible and will give us some very special sort of insight. But where, as in this case, a principle is practical, and not theoretical, we may be able to fill up the empty form in action. If it is possible or even conceivable for a rational agent to act on such a principle in virtue of his rationality, then the principle itself will not be without meaning.

All this discussion would be completely in the air, were it not for our practical acquaintance with moral ideals and moral standards. Unless morality is an illusion, we must say that a morally good man is not merely ' one who is skilful in attaining his ends or prudent in co-ordinating a whole series of ends in an organised life. A morally good man is one who acts upon a law holding equally for himself and for other rational agents and who follows the principles of skill and of self-love only so far as these are compatible with such a universal law. For him the principles of skill and self-love are conditioned, not merely by reference to his desires, but also by reference to an absolute and unconditioned law.

No doubt there are many today who regard such moral beliefs as mere illusions to be explained away by various ingenious hypotheses. Apart from the extremer zealots who use their reason only to deny reason in action and even in thought, even a moderate man may feel considerable qualms. He may find no difficulty, since he is himself a rational agent, in understanding that a rational agent, so far as reason has full control over his passions, will necessarily act in accordance with conditioned principles of skill and self-love. But he may well ask what is our warrant for saying that a rational agent, so far as reason has full control over his passions, will necessarily act in accordance with the unconditioned principle of morality.

The difficulty arises, not only because the concept of an unconditioned principle is harder to understand, but also because in action we are conscious of acting more from motives of skill and self-love than from motives of morality. Nevertheless if we conceive a rational agent in a world of rational agents, and if we suppose that in him practical reason were not at the service merely of his own inclinations and his own happiness, what can we say of the principle on which he would necessarily act? I do not see that we can give any other answer than Kant has done—namely, that he would necessarily act on a principle or law valid for every rational agent as such. Admittedly this would have no meaning for us unless we were acquainted with what at least *seems* to be the ideal of moral action. It acquires a meaning because down the ages men have come more and more to recognise—no doubt amid much confusion—that a good man, whatever else he does, acts or endeavours to act on this principle, and only so is a good man.

Thus our analysis of practical reason brings us to the same result as our previous analysis of the implications of ordinary morality. We have been led to conceive a special kind of practical reason which Kant calls 'pure practical reason'—reason not simply functioning for the sake of satisfying desire, but determining action independently of desire. Such a pure practical reason would necessarily, if it had full control over desire, act in accordance with an unconditioned and objective principle such as appears to be manifested in moral action—a principle or law valid for every rational agent as, such irrespective of his particular desires for particular ends.

§5. *Conditioned and unconditioned principles.*

I have followed Kant in speaking of the principles of skill and self-love as conditioned and of the principle of morality as unconditioned, but it may be necessary to add certain qualifications. It is clear enough that *particular* principles of skill are objectively valid only *if* a certain end is desired, and that *particular* principles of self-love are valid only *if* the character of the agent is such that he will find happiness in acting according to these principles. But these particular principles are all applications of a general principle, of skill or of self-love as the case may be. The *general* principle of using the most effective means to a desired end is not itself conditioned by desire for a particular end: only its application is so conditioned. And the *general* principle of seeking the maximum satisfaction of desires or the maximum integration of ends is not itself conditioned by the particular character of the agent: only its application is so conditioned.

On the other hand the *general* principle of skill is, so to speak, taken up into the general principle of self-love. Self-love has in view a more comprehensive end, and in reference to that end it will use the most effective means. Here also it is rather *particular* principles of skill that are conditioned by the principle of self-love. The *general* principle of skill is similarly taken up into the principle of morality: a good man will use the most effective means to the attainment of his moral ends, and it is only *particular* principles of skill which are conditioned by the principle of morality.

Similarly *particular* principles of self-love are conditioned by the principle of morality, but it is harder to say whether the *general* principle of self-love is so also. Certainly on Kant's view the general principle is not opposed to morality: the good man has a right, and even at times an indirect duty, to seek his own happiness. At times, however, a good man, so far as he is good, will necessarily be prepared to sacrifice his whole happiness and his whole life, and this looks as if the general principle of self-love, and not merely its particular applications, is conditioned by the principle of morality.

Even if this is so, it seems clear that the general principles of skill and self-love (if we can distinguish these from their particular applications) are not conditioned by particular human desires,[1] although their application is so conditioned. So far both general principles seem to have an unconditioned character, and to have it in virtue of being objective principles.

When we turn to the unconditioned moral principle we find that its

[1] They are, however, conditioned by the fact that men, as finite beings, have desires.

applications are not conditioned by the agent's desire for any particular end or even for happiness. Nevertheless it would be a mistake to suppose that its applications were in no sense conditioned by human desires. Kant holds that the good man will necessarily act, for example, on the principle of seeking the happiness of others, and that the way in which he does this must depend, partly at least, on the desires of others. Kant may consider the different ways of making others happy to come within the 'play-room' or 'latitude', where prudence decides and not morality; but even so a good man, as a good man, will necessarily display such prudence.

I do not wish to obscure the clear difference, which it is Kant's great merit to have emphasised, between morality on the one hand and skill and self-love on the other; but if we are entitled to distinguish between principles and their application, the general principles of skill and prudence are in a sense unconditioned: and the application even of the unconditioned moral principle must be in a sense conditioned, although not conditioned by the agent's desires.[1]

It may be added that one principle is called higher than another because it takes a more comprehensive view. Self-love takes into account more ends than the one considered by mere skill; and morality takes into account other agents and their desires, not merely the desires and ends of the one agent considered by self-love. This may not be the whole difference, but it is a difference; and it helps us to understand how the lower principle may be conditioned by the higher.

APPENDIX

KANT'S VIEW OF REASON

§1. *Different senses of 'reason'.*

In Chapter VIII §2 two different traditional senses of 'reason' were mentioned, two senses which are accepted by Kant. But in addition he has a special usage of his own, and this must be grasped, at least in a simplified form, if we are to follow adequately his argument, and especially his argument in Chapter III of the *Groundwork*.

'Reason', as we saw, was traditionally used for the general power of thinking, as opposed to merely sensing or imagining. This general power of reason—which we may call *reason in general*[2]—was supposed to display itself in three main activities, and accordingly is given the name of three different powers. Firstly it conceives or entertains concepts, and is then called *understanding*. Secondly it applies concepts to given objects, and is

---
[1] On the other hand, even the general principles of skill and self-love rest on the supposition that we seek ends because of our sensuous desires, and they have no meaning apart from this supposition. The general principle of morality does not rest upon, nor is it conditioned by, such a supposition.

[2] Or 'reason as such'.

then called the power of *judgement*. Thirdly, it makes mediate inferences, and is then called *reason* in a narrower sense.

These activities may be described as the *logical* use of reason. Broadly speaking, concepts—so far as we ask after their origin—are supposed to be derived by abstraction from objects given to sense, and they are applied to objects given to sense. But in addition—and this is Kant's special doctrine—reason in general is alleged to produce certain concepts as a result of its own activity, or as a result of consciousness of its own activity, concepts which can in no way be derived from sense, or from objects considered merely as sensible. Such concepts are therefore *a priori*— that is, they are not derived from sense. They are products of what Kant calls generally '*pure reason*'.

So far as these concepts give us knowledge of objects, or claim to do so, we may describe their use as the *real* use of reason.

But here we get into terrible complications,[1] most of which must be passed over. It is enough to say that the power of entertaining these *a priori* concepts is called 'pure understanding', and these concepts themselves are called 'categories of the understanding'. Furthermore, by an activity of inference working on the categories, we arrive at another kind of *a priori* concept called 'Ideas of reason', and the reason which entertains these concepts is called 'pure reason' in a special and narrower sense than that used above. The application of all these concepts in judgement we may here ignore.

§2. *The category of cause and effect.*

We may perhaps follow this special Kantian doctrine more easily, if we consider a category which is of direct importance for his moral philosophy.

Reason in general—as is seen even in a hypothetical judgement as well as in a syllogism—necessarily makes inferences from grounds to consequents, and as it becomes explicitly or reflectively conscious of its own working, it conceives or entertains the concept of *ground and consequent*. The concept of ground and consequent is certainly not given to sense. It is therefore an *a priori* concept; it is entertained by pure understanding; and it may be called a *pure* category of the understanding.

Yet when we call it a pure category of the understanding, we imply, according to Kant, that the concept in question can be applied, or can be thought to be applied, to some sort of object. This is why we spoke above of a 'real' use as opposed to a merely 'logical' use. Can we apply the concept of ground and consequent, not to propositions, or parts of propositions, but to objects—that is, to individual things which can be given to sense (or given through sense)? Kant does not believe we can know any objects other than those that can be given to sense, and he maintains that when we apply the pure category of ground and consequent to objects, we use it no longer as the pure category of ground and consequent, but

---
[1] Some of these complications are necessary, but Kant also adds unnecessarily to our difficulties by using the word 'understanding' as if it were identical with 'reason'.

as the category (sometimes called by commentators the *schematised* category) of *cause and effect*.

The reasons behind this transition are so difficult that those of my readers who are unacquainted with the *Critique of Pure Reason* would be well advised to take this transition for granted, to skip my attempt at summary explanation, and to go straight on to §4. It is sufficient to see that a *cause* is a ground which necessarily precedes its consequent in time, and an *effect* is a consequent which necessarily succeeds its ground in time. We cannot understand cause and affect except by reference both to temporal succession and to the concept of ground and consequent. This is one reason why modern empiricists seek to abolish the concept of cause and effect or to reduce it to invariable succession.

§3. *The schema of regular succession.*

On Kant's view, if we are to apply the pure category of ground and consequent to sensible objects, we can do so only by supposing that where there is a regular succession of A followed by B, then A is to be taken as the ground and B as the consequent.[1] But it looks as if we had no more right to suppose that there must be regular succession in the sensible world than we have to suppose grounds and consequents in it. This is where Kant displays his greatest ingenuity, which, whether it is successful or not, is seldom adequately appreciated by modern thinkers. Kant argues that if we are to distinguish an objective succession of events in time from our own successive apprehensions[2]—and we all do this in practice—we can do so only on the supposition that in an objective succession each kind of succeeding event is always necessarily preceded by the same kind of preceding event.[3] More simply, there must be *regular succession* in events, if they are to be distinguished as objective events in time (and not merely as a succession in apprehension). We find our object for the category of ground and consequent in the regular successions whose necessity Kant believes he has proved. We then have a preceding event which is a ground, and a succeeding event which is a consequent; or in other words we have a cause and an effect.

All this is too summary to be convincing or even clear, and it cannot be precise, since it slurs over difficulties and complications. Furthermore, we cannot deal with one category in isolation—our statement really presupposes the category of substance. Nevertheless we may see—or at least assume—that necessary succession in accordance with a rule is what Kant calls the *schema* which justifies us in applying the pure category to objects,

[1] This statement requires qualification.
[2] In looking round a house we apprehend successively a series of what we believe to be simultaneous events or existents, while in watching a ship going down stream, what we successively apprehend—namely, the ship's changes of position—we believe to be also objectively successive. We always distinguish objective successions from merely subjective ones, and without this distinction there could be no human experience.
[3] This does not mean that in every objective succession of events the earlier event is necessarily the cause of the later: it may be or it may not, and the test, speaking roughly, is regularity or repetition. But every objective succession must be causally determined.

and which in combination with the pure category gives us the schematised category of cause and effect. The category of cause and effect necessarily applies to all objective events in time, if we can establish this schema (as Kant thinks he can) as necessary to experience of objective events in time.

I would add, since it will be highly relevant to later discussions, that if the mind thus imposes its own categories on the objects which it knows, it clearly can know reality only as it appears under human conditions, and not reality as it is in itself. This Kant regards as already established, since on his view time, and also space, are merely forms under which we must intuit reality, forms which our sensibility imposes upon what is given to our senses, and therefore forms which need have no counterpart in reality as it really is.

§4. *The Idea of freedom.*

If we are to follow Kant further, we must assume him to have proved, as he claims he has, that every event must have a cause. The category of cause and effect having been established, what does pure reason make out of it?

In its logical use reason not only infers consequents from grounds, but it also, according to Kant, seeks to find grounds for supposed consequents. The conclusion of a syllogism may follow from its premises; but reason is not satisfied thereby till it in turn finds the grounds for the premises, and the grounds for these grounds and so on. Reason must at least conceive the Idea of the totality of the grounds, a totality which, as a totality, could have no further ground, and so would be itself ungrounded, unconditioned, or absolute.

Something like this must happen to the category of cause and effect. Every event must have a cause, but the cause itself (or at any rate what Kant calls its 'causality', i.e. its causal action) is also an event which must have a further cause, and so on *ad infinitum*. Reason must therefore conceive the totality of causes for any given event, and this totality of causes, because it is a totality, cannot itself be caused. So we come to the necessary Idea of an unconditioned or uncaused cause, a spontaneous action which produces effects, but is not caused to do so by anything external to itself. The concept of such an unconditioned absolute spontaneity is the transcendental Idea of freedom, a concept not of pure understanding but of pure reason.

The Idea of freedom is a concept which pure reason cannot but entertain; yet if we suppose, as many do, that this Idea can give us knowledge of any reality, we fall into illusion. The supposedly real use of pure reason in this way is very natural, and even irresistible, but it does not thereby cease to be illusory. Our reason is discursive; that is, it can know objects by means of its concepts only if it can apply these concepts to objects given to sense. But the absolute spontaneity of a cause cannot be given to sense; and if it could be so given, it would itself be an event in time which would necessarily have a preceding cause, and so could not be spontaneous. Indeed since all objects of experience must be conditioned, and since all

Ideas of reason are concepts of the unconditioned, no Idea of reason can have any corresponding object of experience. We can even describe an Idea as a concept which can have no corresponding object.

It is, however, not unthinkable that such an Idea might refer to something in the world as it really is, though not to the world as we experience it, if it is true, as we have argued, that we cannot experience the world as it really is. But this is no help to us in the theoretical use of reason, since we have no knowledge of the world as it is, but only knowledge of the world as it appears to us in experience. The only use of the Idea of an absolute totality of causes is, for theoretical reason, a purely *regulative* one—that is, it does not help us to know objects (and so it is not what Kant calls '*constitutive*'), but it encourages us, when we have discovered a cause, to seek for a further cause, and so on indefinitely.

Nevertheless if practical reason necessarily acts on the supposition that it is free, and if it thereby acts in accordance with the Idea of freedom, it may turn out to be important that there is nothing self-contradictory in the Idea. As we have said, it is at least not unthinkable that the Idea might refer to something not in the world as we experience it, but in the world as it really is. For the purpose of action this might be enough.

Even from this imperfect attempt to summarise the *Critique of Pure Reason* in a few pages we can see at least that Kant is consistent in ascribing to *pure* practical reason the Idea of an unconditioned good, the Idea of an unconditioned principle (or law), and the Idea of an unconditioned or categorical imperative.

§5. *Different kinds of concept.*

It may be useful to add parenthetically a list of the different kinds of concept recognised by Kant:

1. *Empirical* concepts drawn from experience, such as the concepts of 'red' and 'cat'.
2. *Arbitrary* concepts, such as the concept of 'chimera'.
3. *Mathematical* concepts, such as the concept of 'triangle'. These he regards as a special kind of arbitrary concept.
4. *Categories* of the understanding, such as the concepts of 'substance' and of 'cause and effect', which must apply to all objects of experience.
5. *Ideas* of reason, such as the concepts of '*G*od', 'freedom', and 'immortality', which cannot apply to objects of experience.

§6. *Intuitive understanding.*

An Idea of reason is based on our knowledge of something conditioned and is a concept of the totality of its conditions. Such concepts are regarded by Kant as concepts of a systematic whole, or of a system as opposed to a mere aggregate. In a system the whole is the unconditioned condition of the parts, and the Idea of the whole is logically prior to the parts, while in an aggregate the parts are prior to the whole.[1]

We should not think of reason, in Kant's technical sense, as a mysterious faculty, or of Ideas as recondite concepts familiar only to philosophers. All human thinking has a natural tendency to pass from given parts to the conception of a wider whole, and ultimately of the widest possible whole in which the parts would become fully intelligible. In science, for example, the Idea of a complete system is at work in our thinking, like a kind of seed or germ, although science may have to proceed a very long way before the Idea can be seen in a clear light.[2] Once we have grasped the Idea, and with it the purpose and form of science as a whole, we should be able, according to Kant, to determine the necessary articulations of science into its various branches by *a priori* reasoning.

An Idea of reason, though it is the Idea of a complete systematic whole and so of something individual, is still a concept, and there is always less in a concept than in the individual object known by means of it. If by means of our Idea we are to *know*, and not merely to *conceive*, an individual object, this object must be given to sense, and in fact no complete and unconditioned individual whole can be given to sense. This suggests to Kant the thought of an intelligence different from ours, one in which there would not be this divorce between concepts and the individual reality as given to sensuous intuition. Such an intelligence would not require to await sensuous intuitions given to it from without. It would possess what Kant calls 'intellectual intuitions' or an 'intuitive understanding'; its thinking, if we can call it such, would be intuitive, not discursive like our own; and in its thinking it would know, without further aid from sense, an individual and intelligible reality. For such an intelligence there would no longer be a distinction between thought and sense: its universals would also be individuals, or in Hegelian language would be concrete and not abstract.[3] For it, so far as I can see, there would also be no difference between thought and action, since its thinking would be essentially creative of reality;[4] but this conclusion does not appear to be drawn explicitly by Kant himself.

We have no means of knowing whether an intelligence of this kind is even possible, let alone actual. Kant merely uses the concept of such an intelligence in order to bring out by contrast the limitations inseparable from our finite human understanding. Nevertheless he presumably believes that such an intelligence would have to be ascribed to an infinite being.

Speculations of this kind may appear to be merely fantastic. Yet surely there must be a curious limitation in my human understanding if I can know only a world in space and time 'whose margin fades for ever

[1] *Logik, Einl.* IX, 72; *K.r.V.*, A832–3 = B860–1.
[2] *K.r.V.*, A834–5 = B862–3.
[3] Kant does not use these terms but contrasts instead the 'analytically universal' with the 'synthetically universal'; *K.U.*, §77, 407 (= 348–9).
[4] This might also help to explain how God could act without sensuous desires besides knowing without sensuous intuitions.

and for ever when I move'; and it seems natural enough to conceive an infinite understanding which would grasp the whole of reality at once and would find it intelligible as it is not intelligible to us.

I mention this doctrine, however, only in order to suggest that on his own principles Kant appears at times to claim too much for human reason. He speaks of it as if it could go altogether beyond sensibility,[1] and gives us the impression that on his view what is absolutely good for human reason must be good even in the eyes of God.[2] Is he entitled to do this on his own premises? Our Ideas of reason are only the categories of the understanding pushed as far as the unconditioned; and the categories, even if they are not, in their pure form, bound up with space and time, are merely principles for combining given sensuous intuitions in accordance with certain rules and could have no significance in relation to the knowledge of an intuitive understanding.[3] What is more, so far as the Ideas of reason can be applied at all to individual objects, this can be done only through the medium of the categories.[4] In spite of all Kant's ingenuity it is hard to see how he can attain to the Idea of an absolute goodness which is not in some way relative to the limitations of human reason.

---

[1] *Gr.*, 452 = 85–6.   [2] *Gr.*, 439 = 70.   [3] *K.r.V.*, B145.
[4] *K.U.*, §76, 266 (= 338); *M.d.S., Rechtslehre*, §7, 253.

CHAPTER X

THE GOOD

§1. *The good in general.*[1]

PRACTICAL reason besides having principles has also objects, and these, according to Kant, are the good and the bad.[2] The good is defined as 'a necessary object of the power of appetition (*Begehrungsvermögen*) in accordance with a principle of reason'. To get a definition of the bad we have only to substitute 'the power of aversion' (*Verabscheuungsvermögen*) for 'the power of appetition'.

The principles of reason here mentioned are certainly objective principles, not mere maxims: otherwise the good and bad would be merely what we willed or rejected.[3] A power of appetition which is determined in accordance with a principle of reason is simply a rational will.[4] The good is therefore what a rational will, so far as it had complete control over the passions, would necessarily will, and the bad is what it would necessarily reject.[5] In more technical language we may say that the good is *a necessary object of a rational will in accordance with an objective principle of practical reason*.

It is all-important for Kant that the good falls under an objective principle and so under a concept. Because of this we can say that certain *kinds* of thing *must* be good: we are not left to judge each individual instance by immediate feeling, as we are in estimating the pleasant and even the beautiful. As Kant says in the *Critique of Judgement*,[6] 'What pleases by means of reason through the mere concept is good.' Our apprehension of the good is accompanied by an emotional satisfaction—of approval or esteem or even (in the case of moral goodness) of reverence—but this satisfaction is the result of our apprehension and not its ground; and the apprehension itself is by means of concepts or principles, principles

---

[1] I have discussed the subject of this chapter at greater length in *Kant's Idea of the Good* (*Proceedings of the Aristotelian Society*, 1944–5, pp. i–xxv).
[2] *K.p.V.*, 58 = 177 (= 101). In *K.p.V.*, 57 = 176 (= 100) Kant speaks, perhaps loosely, as if an object of practical reason were simply 'an effect which can be produced through freedom'.
[3] See also the definition of the practically good in *Gr.*,[1]413 = 37. The whole passage *Gr.*, 412–13 is presumably concerned with the good in general, although Kant may have in mind particularly the moral good. A maxim would at most give us only 'the seeming good'.
[4] *K.U.*, §4, 209 (= 13–14).
[5] The necessity in question is what Kant calls objective necessity: it is not in human beings also a subjective necessity.
[6] *K.U.*, §4, 207 (= 10).

[103]

of practical, not of theoretical, reason. Unless we had an internal acquaintance with action, the word 'good' would have no meaning for us; and every volition, perhaps every wish, is an implicit assertion of goodness or badness, which may, however, be mistaken.

Kant's definition is inadequate even from his own point of view. If we took seriously the suggestion that the object of a rational will is merely an effect which it produces (or endeavours to produce), this would deny goodness to actions, and still more to wills: goodness would be confined to the states of affairs which we were able to produce. This is not at all Kant's view. He is far more interested in the goodness of volitions and actions, and of the will itself, than in the goodness of mere products.

Clearly we must extend the meaning of 'object' to cover actions. This is reasonable, since an action may be regarded, though not without danger of error, as a change in the world produced by our will. But this would not be enough, since on Kant's view it is the will itself which above all must be esteemed as good. On his view a will which acts on objective principles is a good will; an action which is willed in accordance with objective principles is a good action; and what a good will would seek to produce or use in accordance with objective principles is a good state of affairs. Even this may be an over-simplification; and we must remember that in order to be good, or at any rate to be morally good, an action must not merely accord accidentally with objective principles: it must be *willed* in accordance with these principles. Nevertheless we may say that to be good is to be in accordance with objective principles of practical reason. To understand this fully we must see how Kant works out his principles in more detail.

In all this we must remember that we are so far concerned only with the concept of good in general. As we have already recognised three kinds of objective principle, there must be at least three different kinds of good or, perhaps better, different senses of good. To these we must now turn.

§2. *'Good for' and 'good at'*.

The objective principle of using the most effective means towards an end gives us the concept of the 'good as means' to something else.[1] Things which are good as means may be described as 'useful' or as 'good for' something, as a natural product like coal is good for burning, and an artificial product like a knife is good for cutting. Actions which are good as means may be described as 'skilful', though this term is rather too narrow, since it fails to cover such qualities as perseverance in action, which obviously are good as means. Actions may also, at least in some cases, be described as 'good for' something: for example, walking is good for health. When we turn to the will manifested in these actions or, better, to the man who wills these actions, we may describe him as 'skilful' or as 'good at' certain things. We may also say that he is good as a cricketer or good as a soldier, or more simply still that he is a good cricketer, or a good

---

[1] *Gr.*, 414 = 38.

soldier, or even a good poisoner. All these phrases indicate that the goodness in question holds only within a limited sphere. It is not an unconditioned, but a conditioned, goodness.

Although good in this sense is conditioned and relative,[1] it does not thereby cease to be objective. It is true that a knife may be no good to me, if I do not want to cut; but this does not alter the fact that it is good for cutting and that it would necessarily be so regarded by any rational agent who understood what is meant by 'cutting'.

Some means are clearly more effective than others, and so far means can be regarded as better or worse. There are thus degrees of goodness. But all this tells us nothing about the goodness of ends; although things (including actions and even men) have a limited goodness or badness merely as means, they have another quite different goodness or badness according as the ends to which they are means are themselves good or bad.

§3. *My good.*

We might expect that the objective principle of happiness would be concerned with the goodness of ends, or at least with the relative goodness of ends. Unhappily Kant's vague and varying views about happiness produce a corresponding vagueness on this side of his doctrine.

Kant certainly regards my happiness as my weal, my welfare, my well-being, and as a good which men naturally seek. So far as he takes happiness to be merely a state of continuously pleasant feeling, other things (including actions) are lumped together merely as means to this state. Their goodness is then merely goodness as means, and though happiness itself is clearly regarded as good, it may seem doubtful whether 'good' here means anything other than 'pleasant'. The only difference in the goodness of things as a means to happiness, rather than to other ends, is that happiness is an end which in fact all men seek, however much they may fail to get it because of ignorance or folly or passion.[2]

If we regard the pursuit of happiness as requiring a choice of ends as well as of means, and indeed as an attempt to integrate our different ends within a whole organised life, the position is different. This view becomes more prominent in Kant's later works, but it is not wholly absent even from the *Groundwork*. If it is true, as it surely is, that a rational agent, so far as reason has full control over his passions, will necessarily seek to integrate his various ends, then happiness as a comprehensive end is his good, and separate ends have their goodness as elements in this comprehensive end. They are not merely means to happiness, but elements in happiness, or as they are sometimes called 'constituent means'. The goodness of these ends is also reflected back, as it were, on the means to these ends, so that they

---
[1] *Gr.*, 438 = 68.
[2] Even on this view of happiness, however, Kant presumably regards continuous pleasant feeling as an end which a rational finite being—moral considerations apart—would necessarily pursue, if reason had full control over passion. If so, happiness is an objective good.

too can be judged with reference to the agent's good. They may still be abstractly good as a means to his particular ends, but they may be such that he may, or may not, be able to find his happiness or his good in making use of them.

In this way we arrive at the concept of 'my good' or 'the good for me'. This is not to be taken merely as what I happen to think good for me. I may be mistaken in what I think, and although this good is relative to my character and desires and needs, it does not thereby cease to be objective. On the other hand, what I think good for me is a factor in determining what is good for me. Apart from the fact that my thinking something to be good for me may arise from some unconscious need which I can hardly make clear to myself, I am on the whole unlikely to find my good and my happiness in things which other people, but not I, think will be good for me. Kant is always bitter against those who seek to make some one else happy in their way and not in his.

Many things may be described as good to me or for me, and in them I may in a sense find my good; but things proper (as opposed to actions) appear to be good only as means to the ends which constitute my happiness. This is particularly obvious in the case of things I do not really like: thus rice pudding may be good for me because it is a means to the health of my body; and even criticism may be good for me because it is a means to the health of my soul. In the case of gifts of fortune, like health and wealth, power and prestige, it is the possession or use of these things which constitutes my good; and the same is true of the gifts of nature, powers of mind like intelligence and judgement, or qualities of temperament like animal courage or natural moderation.[1] Broadly speaking, I find my good in activities rather than in things, in work and play, in love and affection, in philosophy and art. Different people will naturally find their good in different activities, and it is obvious that the same man may find different activities more or less good. Here too there are degrees of goodness.

Curiously enough, we are not in the habit of describing a man as good merely because he is good at integrating his ends or securing his own happiness. We describe him rather as sensible, competent, prudent, or even wise. There seems to be no precise word in English for this kind of goodness—perhaps it is covered better by the German word '*Klugheit*'—but there is no reason to doubt that a man of this character has a will which is 'in some sense good'.[2]

Happiness in the narrower sense of continuous pleasant feeling may be one of the ends which a rational agent, *qua* rational, must necessarily seek; but it is certainly not the only end, and experience tends to show that the less we deliberately pursue it, the more likely we are to attain it. On the other hand, if a man could attain in an organised life all the ends he set before himself and yet could experience no feeling of pleasure, we should not call him happy. Such a state of affairs may be impossible, and if it were possible it would surely indicate the presence of some desperate mental disease. In any case pleasure is not only one element in happiness,

[1] Compare *Gr.*, 393–4 = 11–12. [2] *Gr.*, 414 = 38.

it is a criterion of happiness, and this is one reason why it is so often mistaken for happiness itself.

Even at the cost of repetition I must emphasise that my happiness and the elements in my happiness are objective goods, although they are relative to the agent. My good is not merely what seems good to me. It is not even what would seem good to any rational agent who put himself dramatically in my place. In order to see my good another rational agent must indeed put himself dramatically in my place: he must make himself conscious in imagination of my needs and my desires and must judge in the light of such knowledge; he must also remember that in these matters there is great latitude for free and even arbitrary choice, and that the free choice of the individual is a potent factor in determining the possibility of happiness. But when all this is said, then, in spite of the uncertainty which shrouds these matters, it remains true that there are some activities which an agent of a particular type can combine in an organised life, and there are others which he cannot. I can find my good in some activities and not in others, in some kinds of life and not in others. Most important of all, although my good is relative to my needs and desires, and is in that sense conditioned, there is another sense in which my good and your good, my happiness and your happiness, must be regarded simply as *a good* by any impartial rational agent, and in that sense may be described as an unconditioned good.[1] This I believe to be fully accepted by Kant, but when we get to this point we are, I think, passing over to the moral point of view; and from this point of view my good may cease to be a good when it conflicts with the good of others. In that sense my good is still a conditioned good.

§4. *The moral good.*

The unconditioned objective principle of practical reason is concerned with the unconditioned or moral good, and indeed it was by an analysis of the moral good that we originally came to entertain this concept.

Hitherto we have considered an agent to be good in limited senses, (1) so far as he acted reasonably, i.e. skilfully, in satisfying his desires and so attaining his ends, and (2) so far as he acted reasonably, i.e. wisely or prudently, in pursuing his own happiness and so attaining the maximum satisfaction of his desires. In all this the prior condition of reasonable action has been the agent's own desires and needs. But nobody (unless he is momentarily corrupted by a false philosophy) pretends that such a reasonable agent is necessarily a good man. A good man is one who acts reasonably, not for the sake of satisfying his desires, but for the sake of

---

[1] This is the other side of the statement made in Chapter IX §5 that the *general* principle of self-love—like that of skill—is not conditioned by the desires of the particular agent, however much its applications may be so conditioned. Compare also the passage quoted in Chapter IX §3, in which it is said that reason has an office which it cannot refuse—the office of seeking happiness.

acting reasonably and so of satisfying his reason. This is why Kant—in his perhaps repellently technical way—speaks of the principle of goodness as a purely formal principle of following universal law as such: it leaves out reference to my desires and my needs as its prior condition. But in holding this Kant surely accords with ordinary moral judgement. To ask whether an action is morally good is not to ask whether it enables the agent to satisfy a desire or to realise his ideal of happiness; nor do we require to know the answer to the last questions before we can answer the first. Kant may put this view so strongly that to many it appears paradoxical, but this is the simple and obvious truth which he is endeavouring to teach.

Nevertheless it is impossible, at least for man, to act reasonably in a vacuum, and one of the commonest arguments against Kant is that it is useless to speak of moral goodness unless we suppose that other things are good besides the mere will to act well or to act reasonably. This is why I have had to insist so strongly, and with even more detail than Kant himself, that he does recognise the other objective, although conditioned, goods which we have discussed. Kant knows—no man better—that a good man will necessarily seek the happiness of others as well as of himself, but he is surely right in saying that he will not seek the happiness of others for the sake of his own. There are certain ends which reason must set before itself for its own sake or, as Kant puts it, for the sake of the law as such.[1] And a good will is not good merely because it produces or seeks to produce the happiness of the agent or even of other agents: it has a value far above that of mere happiness, and for the sake of that value even happiness and life itself may have to be sacrificed.

It is obvious that moral goodness does not characterise things, but actions and, above all, persons. Nor should it surprise us that an action is morally good only so far as the agent acts on a principle. The same thing is true even of skilful and prudent actions. We distinguish between a skilful action and a mere fluke; and if a man found happiness in a wife whom he had won in a lottery, we should count him fortunate, but not wise.

§5. *The teleological view of good.*

It may still be thought that it is not enough to recognise, besides the moral good, the good as the useful and the good as happiness or as an element in happiness (even if happiness is taken in a wide and Aristotelian sense). This may well be so, though Aristotle himself got on not so badly with no more. Certainly I do not pretend that Kant supplies an adequate philosophy of action or of the good, and he seems to me to rest too much on the category of means and ends. What I maintain is that he is not so inadequate as is commonly supposed.

[1] A morally good action is, on Kant's view, an action done for the sake of law as such, but it is not good merely as a means to an abstraction called the law: it is, on the contrary, good in itself, good in virtue of the objective and unconditioned principle embodied in it and not in virtue of the desires which it satisfies or the ends at which it aims. Moral interest, as we have seen in Chapter VII §3, is an immediate interest in the action itself.

It may well be the case that the value of things like philosophy, science, and art cannot properly be estimated in terms of human happiness, however widely this may be interpreted. These activities have standards of their own which are neither eudaemonistic nor moral, as Kant recognises. Nevertheless he might maintain that their goodness, as opposed to their validity or truth or beauty, must be relative to the objective principles of practical reason, and that they have their goodness as elements in a moral, and not merely in a happy, life. There is, however, in Kant a further strain which may be described as Aristotelian or teleological. We have already met this[1] in his view that reason in man must have a special function and a special end; and he appears to hold that the development and use of the powers which distinguish man from a mere animal have a value different from happiness inasmuch as they are realisations of distinctively human ends. This comes out clearly when he distinguishes between the perfection which the good man will seek for himself and the happiness which he will seek for others.[2] This special value or goodness is spoken of only in a moral context, but nevertheless its implications may be far-reaching.

Such a teleological view was too easily accepted in the Eighteenth Century. It is perhaps too easily rejected now, since Darwin propounded his doctrines of evolution. All we need note here is that although Kant may make an uncritical use of it in his moral philosophy, his doctrine of teleology is not to be interpreted in a crude way. Although we have to consider some things *as if* they had been made for a purpose, and although we are unable to understand them in any other way, this does not mean that we profess to know they have been made for a purpose, or even to think it. The concept of purposiveness in nature is what he calls 'regulative', not 'constitutive'.[3] Even modern mechanistic zoologists sometimes speak *as if* various organs had a purpose, although they would strenuously deny this to be the case.

Perhaps the assumption that practical reason has a function or purpose and that the fulfilment of this function or purpose must be good is the root assumption of Kant's whole moral philosophy, and indeed of almost all Western moral philosophy. Perhaps, when properly understood, this is a legitimate and even necessary assumption, like the assumption that in thinking we must trust our own reason. This is opposed, as I understand, to great Eastern philosophies which regard the only good as the complete annihilation of all activity. It would be ill to speak lightly of views of which one has little knowledge, but we may perhaps observe tentatively that when this view is maintained in the West, it seems to be often an expression of the natural desire for rest after toil, or at times even a reaction from an unsuccessful effort to use practical reason in the pursuit of enjoyment whether on the higher level of art or the lower level of sensuality. Kant himself believes that reason is a poor instrument for seeking happiness and that for this purpose it must inevitably fail; but he concludes from this

[1] Chapter II §8. See also Chapter XV §§4-6.
[2] M.d.S., *Tugendlehre*, Einl. IV, V, and IX, 385-94 = 230-40.
[3] K.U., §76, 404 (= 344).

that it must serve some higher purpose than the satisfaction of desire, not that we should abandon reason altogether in favour of instinct or even of unconsciousness.

It should be added that even if certain human activities have a goodness other than that of constituent elements in human happiness, and even if this goodness is not to be regarded as moral goodness (which may have been Kant's view), this in no way detracts from the supremacy of moral goodness. The goodness of specifically human activities is still a conditioned goodness in the sense that in a concrete situation they cannot be good unless they are compatible with moral law.[1]

§6. *The realistic view of good.*

Whatever may be thought as to the defects of Kant's account of goodness, there is a certain attractiveness in his attempt to see the different senses of good as constituting a developing series under a common concept. Nor is it difficult to understand how on his view the higher good must at times override the lower; for the principle of skill takes into account only the one desire and the one end; the principle of prudence takes into account all the desires and all the ends of one agent; the principle of morality, whatever else it does, takes into account the desires and ends of all agents, so far at least as they may be affected by the agent's action.

Views of this kind find little favour today, and we must recognise that even to those who do not reject reason in favour of sense or emotion Kant's whole attempt to define good in terms of practical reason and its principles seems a perverse effort to put the cart before the horse; and they take the plausible view that the good is not good because it is, or would be, willed by a rational agent, but that on the contrary it is, or would be, willed by a rational agent because it is good.

These are difficult matters, and for the appreciation of Kant's philosophy it may be sufficient to recognise there is a necessary and reciprocal connexion between goodness and a will, such that a rational will—if it had full control over the passions—would necessarily choose what is good, and what is good would necessarily be chosen by a rational will.[2] But such a view may be interpreted in various ways.

First of all there is the possibility that the good may be defined in terms of a rational will and its objective principles, and this I take to be the view of Kant, though he may not have been wholly clear about it. This view cannot, I think, be accused of what Professor Moore calls the 'naturalistic fallacy': at least it is not confusing the good with a natural object,[3] for an objective principle of practical reason is not a natural object. Furthermore, goodness in the subordinate senses is not arbitrary, but depends on the intrinsic properties of things (including the desires

[1] Compare Chapter II §§3 and 4.
[2] I omit the qualifications necessary, many of which are well brought out in *The Philosophy of G. E. Moore*, pp. 608–11 and 615 ff.
[3] See G. E. Moore, *Principia Ethica*, p. 13.

and needs of the agent). The main difficulties arise in regard to the moral and unconditioned good, if we take this to mean that such goodness has absolutely no reference to the intrinsic properties of things (including the desires and needs of rational agents). This I do not believe to be Kant's view, because, in spite of his insistence on the formal character of goodness and of the moral principle, he is well aware that every form must have a matter.[1] Nevertheless it may be thought by some that on this view goodness disappears altogether and is swallowed up in a so-called rational will which is merely arbitrary, if it is not completely empty.

A second possibility is that a rational will may be defined in terms of goodness.[2] This seems to me inadequate as an account of a rational will, and it is open to the same objections as the third possibility which we have to consider.

The third possibility is that a rational will and goodness can neither of them be defined in terms of the other, but that we can recognise a necessary and reciprocal connexion between them. This view has a great attractiveness and attempts, so to speak, to do justice to both sides of the equation. But can we understand the two factors separately, and above all can we make intelligible the possibility of understanding a necessary and reciprocal connexion between them? We can understand a rational will because we have, and indeed in a sense are, a rational will: if we cannot understand the principle of our own activity, how can we understand anything? In the case of goodness we must make up our mind as to the manner of its apprehension. If it is apprehended through sense or emotion, it is not easy to understand how our judgements about it can claim to be valid for any one but ourselves;[3] and it seems impossible to understand how we can be entitled to say that all things or all actions of *a certain kind* must be good, or again that the good would necessarily be chosen by a rational will. If on the other hand it is apprehended through a concept not derived from sense or emotion, how can we acquire such an *a priori* concept except from knowledge of the necessary working of our own minds or our own wills? If we set this question aside as improper, can we attach any meaning to a concept of some real quality which is not known by sense or emotion, a real quality of which we can say only that it is what it is and it is nothing other than it is? Above all, how in these circumstances can we be entitled to say that all things of a certain kind *must* have this quality, or again that a rational will, *qua* rational, *must* have this quality? On this view these judgements must be synthetic *a priori* judgements, not analytic ones;[4] and it is difficult to accept such judgements as true unless we can explain how such acceptance can be justified.

There may be a fourth possibility—that a rational will and goodness may be definable only in relation to one another, like 'right' and 'left', or

---

[1] See for example *Gr.*, 436 = 66 and 454 = 88.
[2] A view akin to this (substituting 'right' for 'goodness') seems to be suggested in *The Philosophy of G. E. Moore*, p. 616. But perhaps his view is more like that of the third possibility mentioned below.
[3] *Gr.*, 442 = 74.
[4] This distinction is discussed briefly in Chapter XII §§2–5.

'above' and 'below'. This view is clearly worthy of exploration, and it is less alien to Kant than the second and third views; but even this view he would probably consider a mistake since it treats goodness as co-ordinate with a rational will instead of subordinate to it and derived from it.

I have no wish to be dogmatic on this problem, the discussion of which has been greatly developed since Kant's time. But we can say at least that his view does not make goodness unreal or arbitrary, nor does it make goodness depend on the momentary attitude of the agent. What difficulties there are, arise, as I have said, chiefly in regard to the moral good or the absolute good. This is the most important sense of the word, and we are not really in a position to estimate Kant's doctrine until we have more knowledge of the way it works out in detail.

CHAPTER XI
IMPERATIVES

§1. *Imperatives in general.*

KANT'S account of imperatives can be seen in its proper perspective only when we have grasped his theory of the subjective and objective principles of practical reason and of their relation to different kinds of goodness. Otherwise imperatives will bulk far too large in our view of his philosophy, which will then become so distorted as to appear harsh and forbidding.

We have seen that the objective principles of practical reason need not also be subjective principles—that is, they need not be the maxims on which we act. This painful paradox of our practical experience arises from the fact that our inclinations may be 'obstacles and hindrances' to practical reason. This happens in regard to the objective principles of skill or self-love as well as in regard to the objective principles of morality. Many men are led by passion to act in a way which they know will interfere with the realisation of a desired end and will even be detrimental to their happiness. They are still more obviously led by passion to act in a way which they know to be morally bad. It is a plain fact that men do not always do what would necessarily be done by a rational agent if reason had full control over passion.

This fact makes all the objective principles of practical reason, which are always principles of some kind of goodness, appear to us as principles of obligation, and so as commands or imperatives. Instead of being the necessary laws of our inner rational nature, they seem to be something almost external or alien to us, something which constrains or compels or 'necessitates' our only partially rational will.

It is very important in this connexion to distinguish between 'necessity' and 'necessitation'.[1] A completely good or holy will would *necessarily*, although spontaneously, manifest itself in good actions. An imperfectly good will may, because of passion, feel reluctance and difficulty in following an objective principle of goodness, and the principle then seems to exercise pressure or constraint almost against our will. The principle, though recognised as objectively necessary, is not subjectively necessary; and the good action, even if we do it, seems to be, not necessary, but *necessitated*.

---

[1] *Gr.*, 413 = 36. The German for 'necessitation' is '*Nötigung*', and the Latin '*necessitatio*'. This term, as unfortunately are too many others, is obscured in the translation of Abbott, who renders it as 'obligation'.

This seemingly almost external necessitation[1] is brought out by saying that an objective principle appears as a command or imperative. No doubt this comparison is inexact (as comparisons always are); for a command is wholly external, whereas the objective principles of practical reason are manifestations of our own rational nature. No one has insisted on this more than Kant, who always rejects the view that morality can be mere obedience to the commands of the State or even of God. Nevertheless the affinity between obligation and command is shown by the common tendency to express moral and other obligations by using the imperative mood.

§2. *Definition of an imperative.*

Kant's definition of an imperative is as follows:

'*The conception of an objective principle, so far as it is necessitating for a will, is called a command (of reason), and the formula of the command is called an imperative.*'[2]

This definition should now offer little or no difficulty, but certain points may be noted.

(1) Kant seems to make no use of the distinction between a command and an imperative, and it can therefore be ignored.[3]

(2) Where a practical reason unhindered by desire would say simply 'I will', a practical reason hindered by desire has to say 'I ought'.

(3) The principles of goodness thus appear in our finite human condition as principles of obligation. This is true even where the principle in question is one of skill or rational self-love and not of morality. Men are not wholly rational in the pursuit of happiness or even in the adoption of means to ends.

§3. *Three kinds of imperative.*

We have recognised three kinds of objective principle in action and three corresponding kinds (or senses) of good: (1) the useful, or the good as means, (2) the good for me, or my good, and (3) the morally good. For an agent whose will does not necessarily conform to these objective principles, the three kinds of principle must appear as three kinds of imperative; and corresponding to the three kinds of good action there will be three kinds of action in some sense obligatory.[4]

---

[1] There is a passage in Mr. H. G. Wells's *Mr. Polly* which describes very well the seemingly external character of moral necessitation. The necessitation, as Kant says, is less marked in imperatives of skill or self-love; see *Gr.*, 416 = 41.

[2] *Gr.*, 413 = 36. Compare also *Gr.*, 414 = 38: 'Imperatives are only formulae for expressing the relation of objective laws of willing in general to the subjective imperfection of the will of this or that rational being, e.g., the human will.' The relation in question is that of necessitation or constraint.

[3] We may, if we choose, consider the imperative as the philosophical formula for what appears to the agent as a command.

[4] *Gr.*, 414 ff. = 38 ff.

Where the objective principle of practical reason is conditioned by an end, the imperative is *hypothetical*. It takes the form 'Every rational agent, *if* he wills a certain end, ought to will the action good as a means to this end.' The command of reason is here conditioned by the end; and as the ends vary, the action enjoined by reason will also vary.

Kant recognises two forms of hypothetical imperative. If the end is merely what one might will, the imperative is a *problematic* imperative, an imperative of skill. Where the end is what everyone naturally wills, namely happiness, the imperative is an *assertoric* imperative, an imperative of prudence or rational self-love, called also a 'pragmatic' imperative.

Where the objective principle of practical reason is not conditioned by any end, the action is enjoined for its own sake, as good in itself without reference to any further end. The imperative is then *categorical*: that is to say, it is not conditioned by the hypothesis that some particular end is desired. It takes the general form 'Every rational agent ought to will the action good in itself.'[1] This imperative Kant calls an *apodeictic* imperative, and it is the imperative of morality.[2]

Kant's terminology is not wholly satisfactory, and it is not unreasonable to say that he may have been unduly influenced by a supposed parallel with problematic, assertoric, and apodeictic judgements. Elsewhere[3] he himself suggests that a problematic imperative is a contradiction in terms, and that the proper expression is 'technical imperative' or 'imperative of skill'. The pragmatic imperative of self-love, he adds, is also a kind of technical imperative, but it requires a special name. The two reasons he gives for this are (1) the old reason—namely, that our own happiness cannot be accounted as a merely arbitrary end like the ends of skill; and (2) a new reason—namely, that self-love is concerned, not merely with the method of attaining an end already presupposed, but also with determining what constitutes the end itself.

§4. *Rules, counsels, and laws.*

The different kinds of imperative exercise different kinds of necessitation or constraint.[4] Kant marks this difference by his terminology. He opposes '*the rules of skill*' and '*the counsels of prudence*' to '*the commands (or laws) of morality*'.

The rules of skill may be clear and definite, but we are bound by them only so far as we wish to attain a particular end. The counsels of prudence or self-love are in some ways more uncertain, yet they are also more binding. They are more uncertain because different counsels may hold for different individuals: it is difficult or even impossible to be sure wherein a particular individual will find his happiness, and this will depend

---

[1] We must not forget that an action which is good in itself is one which is done for the sake of universal law as such. Compare Chapter VII §3.
[2] Note also that Kant sometimes opposes the word 'practical' in the sense of 'moral' to 'pragmatic' in the sense of 'prudent'.
[3] *K.U., Erste Einleitung*, I, 8 n. [4] *Gr.*, 416 = 41.

partly on what the individual believes to be necessary for his happiness. Kant tends to be pessimistic about the chances of attaining happiness by nicely calculated conduct. Indeed temperamentally he seems almost to dislike the calculations of prudence when compared with the spontaneity of inclination. Yet in spite of their uncertainty the counsels of prudence are more binding than the rules of skill, since it is mere folly to wreck one's happiness, an end which is very far from being arbitrarily chosen.

Both rules of skill and counsels of prudence are opposed to the commands of morality, which alone are strictly entitled to be called 'laws'.[1] The word 'command' serves to show that moral obligation does not depend on our inclinations and may even be opposed to them: there is no question here of cajolery or persuasion. The word 'law', it must be remembered, does not necessarily carry with it the idea of 'command';[2] it expresses here, as Kant says, an unconditioned necessity (not necessitation) valid for every rational agent as such. A holy will would act necessarily and spontaneously in accordance with moral law, though in this there would be no consciousness of obligation. To imperfectly rational agents the moral law appears as an obligation or command because of their imperfection; and this obligation is still unconditioned: the obligation in no way depends on the fact that we happen to seek a particular end or even on the fact that by acting in accordance with the law we are likely to attain happiness. On the contrary, the law will still hold even if it is opposed to our inclination and even if it is detrimental to our happiness.

To deny this is to deny morality altogether. If we consider that morality as ordinarily understood is an illusion, by all means let us say so; but at least let us avoid the muddled thinking which retains the ordinary terms of morality, but interprets them as referring only to self-interest or even to mere passing and personal emotions.

§5. *Obligation and goodness.*

Kant's three kinds of imperative enjoin three kinds (or senses) of good action.[3] For him obligation is inseparable from some kind of goodness, though there may be goodness where there is no obligation, as in the case of a holy will. Thus goodness is more fundamental than obligation, which arises only because of our human imperfection. Apart from some kind of goodness there is no kind of obligation.

This general principle holds in the case of moral obligation. The moral imperative enjoins moral goodness: it bids us to act morally—that is, as we have seen, to act for the sake of the law or for the sake of duty.

---

[1] *Gr.*, 416 = 41. Earlier—in *Gr.*, 413 = 36—Kant speaks of *all* imperatives both as laws and as commands. This may be defended so far as the *general* principles of skill and self-love (though not their application) are unconditioned. See Chapter IX §5.
[2] See Chapter VI §2.   [3] *Gr.*, 413 = 37; 414 = 38.

The universal ethical command is 'Act in accordance with duty for the sake of duty'.[1]

If we take the universal moral imperative to enjoin action for the sake of duty, we must recognise that as it is applied to particular situations, it enjoins also some particular kind of action, such as the paying of debts where money is owed. How such application is possible, we are not here concerned to ask. Granted the possibility of such application, Kant insists that the moral imperative bids us pay our debts for the sake of duty; that is, it enjoins not merely a kind of action, but the doing of this kind of action from the moral motive of duty. Indeed on his view this is what differentiates mere law—that is, State law—from morality.

If we do an action of the kind enjoined but do it without the moral motive, we can call it an action 'done in accordance with duty' (*pflichtmässig*). We have no precise adjective for this in English,[2] but we might call it the action 'due'. When the action is done for the sake of duty we describe it not merely as 'due', but also as 'dutiful' (*pflichtvoll*); and only so is it a morally good action. Thus on Kant's view the moral imperative enjoins actions which are not only due, but also dutiful.

It is merely a matter of verbal convenience whether or not we say that a man who has done the action which is due has done his duty. He has done his duty in one sense, even if the moral motive is not present; but in another sense he has not done his duty, for his action is not dutiful and so has not fulfilled the moral imperative.

We come, however, to a profound philosophical difference when the view that we ought to act for the sake of duty is explicitly rejected.[3] This doctrine is so strongly maintained today that it can hardly be passed over in silence.

§6. *The duty to act morally.*

It is impossible to deal adequately with this question here, but there are two main objections to Kant's view.

The first objection is that since we cannot summon up motives at will, it cannot be our duty to act on them. On this view motives are regarded as feelings, and it is true that we cannot summon up feelings

---

[1] *M.d.S., Tugendlehre, Einl.* VII, 391 = 236: '*Handle pflichtmässig aus Pflicht*'. Kant even accepts the commands 'Be holy' and 'Be perfect', though he recognises with his usual common sense that this is an ideal to which we can only approximate progressively: the duty is one of imperfect obligation. See *M.d.S., Tugendlehre*, §§21 and 22, 446-7.

[2] The word 'right' is sometimes used for this, but (1) the original meaning of 'right' seems to be 'fitting' rather than 'obligatory'; (2) in its ordinary usage it means 'permissible' rather than 'obligatory'; and (3) it is not without the suggestion of some kind of value, which ought here to be excluded.

[3] See Sir David Ross, *The Right and the Good*, pp. 4-6.

of benevolence or affection, which are sometimes regarded as moral motives. Kant himself (so far as he takes a motive to be a feeling) regards the feeling of reverence as the only moral motive in man, but for him it is the necessary emotional accompaniment or consequence of my recognition of duty. Hence it does not need to be 'summoned up'; if it were absent, I should recognise no duties, and I should be neither moral nor immoral, a mere animal and not a man. As he himself says of moral feeling, 'no man is wholly destitute of moral feeling; for if he were totally unsusceptible to this sensation, he would be morally dead'.[1]

There is, however, a more subtle objection. We are told that to do act A from a sense of duty is to do act A from a sense that it is our duty to do act A. The moral imperative therefore, if it bids me to do act A from a sense of duty, asserts that it is my duty to do act A from the sense that it is my duty to do act A. But in this there is a contradiction. The contradiction lies in the fact that while the whole assertion affirms that it is my duty to do act A from a certain motive, the final clause affirms that it is my duty to do act A simply, that is, altogether apart from any motive. If I try to amend the final clause so as to make it harmonise with the whole assertion, I merely repeat the contradiction in a different form equally requiring amendment, and so fall into an infinite regress. It becomes my duty to do act A from a sense that it is my duty to do act A from a sense that it is my duty to do act A from a sense . . . and so on *ad infinitum*.

From a Kantian point of view the use of the phrase 'sense of duty' is unfortunate, not only because he firmly denies that there is any such sense, but also because it suggests, not merely a feeling, but a judgement;[2] and since in morally good action we must have judged act A to be our duty, it is easy to suppose from this that the moral motive must be concerned with this particular duty. But surely while our *intention* is to do the particular duty which we have called act A, our *motive* is to do our duty as such. To say that we ought to do act A for the sake of duty is a completely different thing from saying that we ought to do act A for the sake of this duty.[3] To act for the sake of this duty would seem to indicate a personal preference among duties which is distinct from, if not opposed to, the motive of morality.

It is in any case clear that the objection based on an alleged infinite regress assumes that we cannot act for the sake of duty as such. This assumption seems to me erroneous,[4] and it results in the paradox that we have no duty to act morally. It would be hard to believe this even if the

---

[1] *M.d.S.*, *Tugendlehre*, Einl. XIIa, 400 = 247. If we take the moral motive to be the law itself or duty itself—see Chapter V, Appendix—it is still more clear that we can always act on the motive of duty: we have only to act on the principle of doing nothing which we recognise to be incompatible with moral law.

[2] *M.d.S.*, *Tugendlehre*, Einl. XIIa, 400 = 247.

[3] Similarly to say that we ought to kill this German soldier because he is *a* German soldier is a completely different thing from saying that we ought to kill him because he is *this* German soldier.

[4] If we cannot act for the sake of duty as such, why should we even ask what our duty is?

objections were stronger than they are. At any rate, if we are to understand Kant, we must recognise that for him the one supreme duty is to act for the sake of law as such or duty as such, not for the sake of a particular law or a particular duty. In other words our supreme duty is to act morally, and if this were not so, we should have no particular duties at all.

CHAPTER XII

HOW ARE IMPERATIVES POSSIBLE?

§1. *The meaning of the question.*

THE next question to be considered is 'How are the different kinds of imperative possible?'[1] This question should not be misunderstood, as it sometimes is. The question is not a psychological one: it is not concerned with the way in which consciousness of obligation gradually develops in the individual or in the race; it is not even concerned with the way in which imperatives give rise to emotion and so affect action, though Kant elsewhere discusses at some length the way in which reverence is aroused by the categorical imperative.[2] Nor is the question a metaphysical one: it does not ask how reason, and especially pure reason, can be the cause of events in the phenomenal world of experience. Such a question Kant expressly declares to be unanswerable, at least as regards the categorical imperative.[3]

The question may be described as logical or epistemological, though even these terms are not wholly suitable. Imperatives are propositions, although they are practical and not theoretical. Our task is to show how these propositions can be justified or how they can be valid. The question and its answer find their parallels in the *Critique of Pure Reason*, where Kant attempts to answer the questions 'How is pure mathematics possible?', 'How is pure physics possible?', and 'How is metaphysics possible?'.

In order to understand Kant's answer we must first get clear about the logical difference between analytic and synthetic propositions, and especially about the logical character of what Kant calls 'synthetic *a priori* propositions'.[4]

§2. *Analytic propositions.*

In an analytic proposition the predicate is contained in the subject-concept and can be derived by analysis of the subject-concept.

---

[1] *Gr.*, 417 = 41.   [2] See Chapter V §2.
[3] *Gr.*, 458–9 = 94; 461 = 98. He also says, in *Gr.*, 417 = 41, that the question is not how it is possible to conceive the accomplishment of the action enjoined by the imperative: the question is how it is possible to conceive that necessitation (or obligation) of the will which is expressed in the imperative.
[4] See *K.r.V.*, A6 ff. = B10 ff. I here follow Kant in using the terms 'proposition' and 'judgement' as equivalent. Some philosophers deny that there are such things as judgements, while others deny that there are such things as propositions; but Kant is dealing with a real problem which may be expressed in other terms but cannot be ignored save at our peril.

[120]

An example of an analytic proposition is 'All bodies are extended.' 'Being extended' not merely characterises all bodies, but is contained in the concept of body as such. You cannot conceive a body except as extended.

It is all-important in this connexion to guard against a too common error. The *subject-concept*—that is, the concept or notion of the subject—should on no account be confused with the *subject*, which is usually not a concept but a thing or class of things. Manifestly in every true proposition (whether analytic or synthetic) the predicate must be contained in the *subject*—in the sense that it must characterise the subject. It by no means follows from this that in every true proposition the predicate must be contained in the *subject-concept*. The concept, as universal, contains in itself much less than do the particulars which fall under it. Thus when I truly say 'This body is made of gold', 'being made of gold' may—not too happily—be said to inhere in this body. But it is ridiculous to suppose that 'being made of gold' is contained in the concept of 'body', which is here on Kant's view the subject-concept, as indeed it must be if concepts are always general.

In spite of this obvious distinction the subject-concept is often confused with the subject, not only by beginners, but also by masters, in philosophy (including interpreters of Kant). Indeed according to Kant the whole intellectual system of Leibniz rests on this elementary error.[1]

All analytic propositions are necessary and universal and therefore *a priori*. This is true even where the subject-concept is an empirical concept, e.g., the concept of 'body'. To know what a body is, is to know that it is extended, and there is no need of any further appeal to experience. Nor, granted that we possess complex concepts, is there any difficulty in explaining how analytic propositions are possible.

We may of course be challenged to show that there are real objects corresponding to any particular concept which we have used in a particular analytic proposition. An analytic proposition, though this is not always recognised, professes to be a statement about objects, and not merely about a concept, as is obvious in the example I have given.

Kant was the first to make the distinction between analytic and synthetic propositions, and if we are to understand him, we must take the distinction as he made it. The view sometimes held that analytic propositions are about concepts or even about the meaning of words is a distortion of his doctrine. A statement that a concept has certain parts would be for him no more analytic than a statement that a fiddle has certain parts: all that has happened is that a possible subject-concept has been turned into a subject. A statement that a word is, or will be, used by me or by others to mean a particular kind of thing, or as an equivalent for certain other words, is quite obviously not an analytic statement in

---

[1] See *K.r.V.*, A281 = B337. This is well brought out by the late Mr. Joseph in lectures which I hope will be published. On Leibniz' theory to say that the predicate is in the *subject* of a true proposition (*praedicatum inesse subjecto verae propositionis*) is to say that it is contained in some way in the *notion* of the subject. It is easy to see how this must result in a theory of monads.

his sense at all; and indeed such a usage seems extraordinarily far-fetched. It is of course open to his successors to say that the propositions which he dubbed analytic in a precise sense have in fact a quite different character; but if they continue to apply to them the term 'analytic', presumably on historical grounds, this can lead to nothing but confusion, so far at least as the interpretation of Kant is concerned.

It should be added that analytic propositions need not be confined to those which assert a relation of subject and predicate. As we shall see, hypothetical imperatives are for Kant analytic propositions, although they are most naturally expressed by an 'if' clause. In order, however, to bring out their analytic character he translates them into the subject-predicate form.

§3. *Synthetic propositions*.

In a synthetic proposition the predicate is not contained in the subject-concept and cannot be derived by analysis of the subject-concept. It may be, and it often is, derived by an analysis of the subject—that is, of a thing or things conceived in the subject-concept and experienced by us through the senses.

An example of a synthetic proposition is 'All bodies are heavy.' 'Being heavy' is on Kant's view no part of the concept of body. There is no contradiction in supposing that an astral body so-called or a resurrected body should be without weight.

Most synthetic propositions are empirical.[1] They are known through experience of the thing conceived in the subject-concept. We are aware that bodies are heavy because we have experience of bodies. And if we do not enquire too closely into the nature of experience, there is no difficulty in understanding how such synthetic propositions are possible.

§4. *Synthetic* a priori *propositions*.

Some synthetic propositions, according to Kant, are necessary and universal and are therefore *a priori* — that is, they cannot be derived from experience.[2] For example, the proposition 'Every event must have a cause' is not empirical; and it is also not analytic, for the concept 'event' does not contain in itself the concept 'being caused'. As it stands, it is a synthetic *a priori* proposition.

The most difficult, and also the most important, task of philosophy is to explain how synthetic *a priori* propositions are possible—that is, how they can be valid or how they can be justified. Kant holds, not only that

---

[1] Mr. Ayer, in *Language, Truth and Logic* (first edition), p. 103, avoids difficulties by *defining* synthetic propositions as empirical. 'A proposition ... is synthetic when its validity is determined by the facts of experience.' But this begs important philosophical questions.

[2] See Chapter I §3.

e know certain synthetic *a priori* propositions to be valid, but also that if no such propositions were valid, we could understand neither how experience is possible nor how empirical synthetic propositions are possible.

§5. *Difficulties.*

That there are many difficulties in Kant's distinctions should not be ignored—particularly the difficulty of determining precisely what is contained in a subject-concept.[1] Modern logicians may reject some or all of Kant's examples and may seek to state his problem in other terms. Nevertheless these distinctions are far from dead in modern philosophy.[2]

Purely logical difficulties are beyond the scope of this discussion, but some readers may feel a special difficulty in understanding the difference between an analytic proposition and a synthetic *a priori* proposition; for in both cases there is asserted a necessary connexion between the subject and the predicate. The difference is roughly that in the case of an analytic proposition you cannot conceive the subject without also conceiving the predicate, however obscurely; while in the case of a synthetic *a priori* proposition you *can* conceive the subject without conceiving the predicate. This may be grasped most easily from an example. In the analytic proposition 'Every *effect* must have a cause', you cannot conceive an effect without conceiving that it has a cause; for an effect is simply an event that has a cause. In the synthetic *a priori* proposition 'Every *event* must have a cause', you *can* conceive an event without conceiving that it has a cause; for an event is merely a changing of something in time or a coming to be of something in time, and whether or not this must necessarily have a cause is a matter for further consideration. In the case of analytic propositions a necessary connexion can be established by a mere analysis of the subject-concept by itself. In the case of synthetic *a priori* propositions, as indeed in all synthetic propositions, we require some further evidence, some 'third term', to establish the connexion between the subject and the predicate.

§6. *Imperatives of skill are analytic propositions.*

We can now return to the question 'How are the different kinds of imperative possible?' It must be admitted that Kant's treatment of hypothetical imperatives is over-simplified and would be much too summary for a philosophy of action. All he is doing is to clear them out of the way and so get on to the moral problem.

According to Kant the possibility of imperatives of skill requires no

---
[1] Compare *K.M.E.*, I, 82 ff.
[2] It is instructive to see how very similar problems arouse the interest of Professor G. E. Moore and are sometimes expressed by him in very similar terms. See *The Philosophy of G. E. Moore*, pp. 660 ff., especially pp. 663 and 667.

special explanation, since they are all analytic propositions.[1] He seems to assume that the end is always an object or result, that there is only one means to the end, and that this means is always some possible action of the agent. We could then say that in the concept of willing an end (as opposed to merely desiring it or wishing it) there is contained the concept of willing the means to the end. Hence the proposition 'to will the end is to will the means' is a theoretical analytic proposition.[2]

Kant himself is sketchy about the way in which this theoretical analytic proposition becomes a hypothetical imperative and so a practical analytic proposition. We must try to fill up the gaps. First of all we have the objective principle of practical reason, 'Any rational agent who wills the end will necessarily—so far as reason has a decisive influence over his actions—will the means which are in his power.' This proposition, which is still analytic, appears as an imperative to us because reason, though present in us, has no such decisive influence. It then takes the form 'If any rational agent wills the end, he *ought* to will the means.' All this must be taken within its own limits, wider considerations of prudence or morality being excluded.

It may be objected to this slightly tidier version of Kant's argument that there is in it a contradiction. If to will the end is to will the means, how can it be said that a rational agent *ought* to will the means? Does not the latter statement imply that in fact it is possible to will the end and yet not to will the means?

Perhaps we should meet this by speaking, as Kant himself does almost immediately afterwards, of willing the end 'completely' and not just of willing the end. Perhaps, however, it is better to keep the statement as it stands; for it at least serves to bring out what Kant calls, in another connexion, the 'contradiction' in imperfectly rational wills, a contradiction which is analogous to a contradiction in thought but is better called an 'antagonism'. It arises from the fact that, as we have seen, a principle which is objectively necessary is not thereby also subjectively necessary.[3] And it is surely only too true to experience that we can both will and yet not will an end, e.g., when our attention is distracted in a greater or less degree.

The assumption of all this appears to be that we actually possess a rational will, but that in action this rational will may be opposed by what Kant calls 'inclination'. Perhaps it would be better to say, at least where the inclination prevails, that a rational volition is overcome by a less rational volition. It is the possibility of such defeat that gives rise to imperatives, and unless both types of volition were present in us, or at least possible in us, there would be no imperatives.

Into the difficulties of this we cannot enter. Kant's fundamental

---

[1] *Gr.*, 417 = 42.
[2] Kant himself does not begin with this proposition; but a more elaborate proposition to the same effect is given subsequently as the reason why the objective principle of practical reason is analytic.
[3] See *Gr.*, 424 = 51. Compare IX §1.

assumption clearly is that practical reason, like theoretical, cannot contradict itself.[1] A rational agent, so far as he is rational, will necessarily act, as he will necessarily think, coherently; and he ought so to act if he is irrational enough to be tempted to do otherwise.

§7. *Synthetic propositions are presupposed.*

We have so far considered only the *general* principle of imperatives of skill. Even this, it should be observed, already presupposes knowledge of synthetic propositions; it presupposes knowledge that events have causes and that we may have power to cause events; for to will the means to an end is to will the cause of a desired event. These synthetic propositions are theoretical; and many more synthetic theoretical propositions are needed if we are to apply the general principle to particular cases. They are needed, as Kant says,[2] to determine the means to a proposed end. Take, for example, the *particular* imperative 'If I want to see properly, I ought to wear glasses.' No such imperative could be formulated without knowledge that the wearing of glasses will counteract my defects of sight; and to know this is to apprehend a synthetic proposition. Nevertheless, Kant insists, the imperative itself remains an analytic proposition *so far as willing is concerned.*

I take him to mean something like this. All sorts of synthetic propositions are required if we are to know the possible causes of events that we desire. These propositions are purely theoretical. But once we have this theoretical knowledge, the principle governing rational action, and so the principle of hypothetical imperatives of skill, is simply the proposition that to will the end—so far as reason has decisive influence on action—is to will the means. This is an analytic proposition; and so far as action is concerned it remains so, no matter how many synthetic propositions are necessary in order to specify what are the particular means to a particular end proposed in a particular situation.[3]

In the *Critique of Judgement* Kant speaks of all technical rules as being mere corollaries or consequences of purely theoretical knowledge. They differ from theoretical knowledge only in their formulation, not in their content.[4] It is not clear how far he regards this view as modifying the view of the *Groundwork*; but we have still to explain the difference in formulation, and it is hard to see how this could be done without bringing in the analytic proposition that to will the end is to will the means.

---

[1] That is, it cannot do so 'objectively' or *qua* reason. Subjectively—that is, as influenced by feeling and desire—it can contradict itself or at least oppose itself.
[2] Gr., 417 = 42.
[3] Though the necessary means are not contained in the concept of an end, willing whatever means are necessary is contained in the concept of willing an end.
[4] *K.U., Erste Einl.* I, 4; also *Einl.* I, 172 (= xiii).

§8. *Imperatives of prudence are analytic propositions.*

For imperatives of prudence or self-love the same explanation holds as for principles of skill.[1] The only new difficulty is that here our concept of the end is so vague and imprecise. Everybody wants happiness, but no one knows, or can know, exactly what it is that he wants. Nevertheless when, so far as we can, we have determined, in synthetic theoretical propositions, the means to our own happiness, we can infer the corresponding imperatives of prudence or self-love on the supposition that practical reason, like theoretical, is necessarily coherent with itself. The general principle of the imperatives of prudence is the same as the principle of the imperatives of skill, namely, that a rational agent who wills the end must, so far as he is rational, necessarily will the means, and ought to do so if he is irrational enough to be tempted to do otherwise. This practical principle remains analytic however many synthetic propositions may be required in order to determine theoretically the means to our happiness.

This sounds simple enough, but even if our end were happiness considered as the maximum possible amount of pleasant feeling, there would still be a new problem—the problem of combining the various means in an organised life. This problem did not arise in our oversimplified account of the imperative of skill. Furthermore, although Kant persists in regarding the problem merely as one of means and ends, his language, as we have seen, betrays another view, which becomes fully explicit only in his later writings—the view that the problem is concerned also with the constituents of the end itself. What other ground could there be for saying that the concept of the end is vague and 'indeterminate'?

Manifestly the imperatives of prudence must be grounded on another principle, if we are concerned with a choice of ends as well as of means. Perhaps we might say that any rational agent who wills a total end will necessarily—so far as reason has a decisive influence over his actions—will the constituents of that end as well as the means to it. This proposition would be merely analytic. We should still have to consider how the total end is determined. The problem of determining the total end may be regarded as a theoretical problem—the problem of satisfying the maximum possible of the agent's desires or of realising the maximum possible of the agent's powers. It remains theoretical, even if it can be solved, however imperfectly, only by experiment, and even perhaps if it must take into account as an important factor choices that are to a large extent arbitrary. There is, however, a further practical assumption—that since man, as belonging to the sensible world, is a being with needs, reason has so far 'an office which it cannot refuse', the office of serving the interests of sensibility and of seeking happiness in this world and where possible in the next.[2] Kant's imperatives of self-love are not derived merely from the fact that all men happen to seek happiness. They are derived

[1] *Gr.*, 417–19 = 42–4.   [2] *K.p.V.*, 61 = 152 (= 108).

from the assumption that this is what a finite rational agent, *qua* rational, would necessarily do. Only so can the principle be an unconditioned principle (except in so far as it may be overridden by a higher); and only so can happiness on Kant's theory be an objective and genuine good. It is, however, by no means obvious that this principle is an analytic proposition.

In spite of his waverings and even confusions in regard to this topic Kant is sound in his insistence that happiness is an uncertain Ideal of the imagination, the ideal of a whole of satisfaction which can never be determined by reason with precision. He is very far from the crudely 'scientific' principles of hedonists and utilitarians. He is also sound in insisting that for this reason prudence can give us only counsels and not commands, mere rough generalisations about the average ways in which men can be happy. Incidentally it is interesting to observe that he personally thinks, as an oldish man, that happiness is most likely to be found in diet, frugality, politeness, and reserve! This rather pathetic conclusion suggests that he is perhaps sound in thinking reason to be but a poor instrument for the attaining of happiness as our only end.

§9. *Categorical imperatives are synthetic* a priori *propositions.*

The main point of Kant's discussion has been to provide a sharp contrast with the categorical imperative. Categorical imperatives do not bid us will the means to an end, and so are not conditioned by will for an end already presupposed: this is why we say that they are unconditioned, absolute, and categorical. A categorical imperative says simply and unconditionally 'Every rational agent ought to will thus and thus.' Hence the explanation given of hypothetical imperatives can in no way apply to it.[1]

The very concept of a categorical imperative might appear fantastic were we not acquainted with the seemingly unconditioned claims of morality. Kant, however, insists that we can in no way establish the categorical imperative by an appeal to experience. He knows too well that seemingly categorical imperatives may conceal a motive of personal interest. So-called moral action may have some secret self-interest as its basis, as many philosophers maintain today. We have the difficult task of establishing the possibility of a categorical imperative, not merely the task of explaining a possibility which we already take to be established.[2] Even the latter task, needless to say, could not be completed by an appeal to experience, since experience cannot tell us what ought to be, but only what is. A categorical imperative is not an empirical, but an *a priori*, practical proposition.

The special difficulty of dealing with the categorical imperative arises from the fact that although it is an *a priori* proposition, it is not analytic.

[1] *Gr.*, 419 = 44.
[2] *Gr.*, 420 = 45. Thus in the *Groundwork* our question about the categorical imperative is more akin to the question 'How is metaphysics possible?' than it is to the question 'How is mathematics possible?'

By merely analysing the concept of 'rational will' or 'rational agent' we cannot, Kant always insists,[1] arrive at the obligation to will in a certain way. The paradox is that we connect the obligation *directly* or *immediately* with the concept of a rational will as such (that is to say, we do not connect it mediately through the supposition that some end is already sought); and yet this obligation is not contained in the concept of 'rational will'.[2] A categorical imperative is a practical synthetic *a priori* proposition,[3] and to explain how synthetic *a priori* propositions are possible is always an undertaking of the greatest difficulty. As in all synthetic *a priori* propositions we shall require some 'third term' to establish a necessary connexion between a subject and a predicate which is not contained in the concept of the subject. This 'third term' we shall find to be the Idea of freedom.

This problem must be reserved till later. For the present we must be content to determine the character of the categorical imperative more precisely and to examine its various formulations.

---

[1] Compare *Gr.*, 426 = 54 and 440 = 71.
[2] Compare *Gr.*, 420 n. = 46 n. For a closer adherence to Kant's actual words see Chapter VIII §3.
[3] *Gr.*, 420 = 45–6.

BOOK III

THE FORMULATION OF THE CATEGORICAL IMPERATIVE

CHAPTER XIII

THE FIVE FORMULAE

§1. *The five formulae.*

We might have expected Kant to be content with one formulation of the categorical imperative. Instead he embarrasses us with no less than five different formulae, though, curiously enough, he tends to speak as if there were only three.[1] If we are to see where we are going, it may be well to set forth all five formulae at the outset. For ease of reference I propose to give each formula a number (or a number + a letter), and also a title based on its key words. The system of numeration adopted is intended to bring out the special connexions between different formulae and to conform, as far as possible, to the view that there are three main formulae.

Formula I or the Formula of Universal Law:
Act only on that maxim through which you can at the same time will that it should become a universal law.[2]

Formula Ia or the Formula of the Law of Nature:
Act as if the maxim of your action were to become through your will a UNIVERSAL LAW OF NATURE.[3]

Formula II or the Formula of the End in Itself:
So act as to use humanity, both in your own person and in the person of every other, always at the same time as an end, never simply as a means.[4]

Formula III or the Formula of Autonomy:
So act that your will can regard itself at the same time as making universal law through its maxim.[5]

Formula IIIa or the Formula of the Kingdom of Ends:
So act as if you were always through your maxims a law-making member in a universal kingdom of ends.[6]

[1] *Gr.*, 436 = 66 and 437 = 67.   [2] *Gr.*, 421 = 47.
[3] *Gr.*, 421 = 47.   [4] *Gr.*, 429 = 57.
[5] *Gr.*, 434 = 63. It is worth noting that alike in Formula I and Formula II and Formula III the phrase 'at the same time' cannot properly be ignored.
[6] *Gr.*, 438 = 69.

[129]

§2. *The relations between the five formulae.*

We can follow the relations between these formulae only as we study both them and the arguments by which Kant passes from one to another. It is, however, obvious that there is a close connexion between Formula I and Formula Ia, and again between Formula III and Formula IIIa, though Formula IIIa is also closely connected with Formula II. The system of numeration adopted, together with the classification which it implies, does not profess to be more than a convenience.

It may also be observed there is at first sight a close resemblance between Formula I and Formula III, so much so that the difference between them is sometimes ignored. If to ignore this difference were not clearly contrary to Kant's intention, we might identify Formula III with Formula I and take Formula I as occupying a special position above all the others. We could then take Formula Ia, Formula II, and Formula IIIa as subordinate formulae, intended to help us in the application of Formula I by bringing the general and supreme principle of morality (Formula I) nearer to intuition and so to feeling. There is at least some warrant in Kant himself for treating Formula Ia, II, and IIIa along these lines,[1] but we must not carry this so far as to ignore Formula III altogether. In the *Critique of Practical Reason* it is Formula III, and not Formula I, which takes pride of place.[2]

§3. *The purpose and structure of the argument.*

On the face of it Kant's examination of the five formulae is carried on for its own sake, and the task of articulating the different aspects and implications of the categorical imperative he regards as appropriate to a metaphysic of morals.[3] Nevertheless we must not suppose that he is losing sight of his argument as a whole. On the contrary, by leading us up to the principle of autonomy and the principle of a kingdom of ends he is preparing the ground for the argument in the last part of the book: he is establishing principles which will be connected later with the concept of freedom and the concept of an intelligible world. From this point of view Formula III and Formula IIIa are the most important. They constitute, as it were, the main hinge on which the argument of the *Groundwork* turns.

It will be remembered that Kant regards his argument at the present stage as analytic or regressive—that is, as an argument from the conditioned to its condition.[4] This must not, however, be taken too literally: it can hardly apply precisely to every step in the argument. Thus in moving

---

[1] *Gr.*, 436–7 = 66–7.
[2] *K.p.V.*, §7, 30 = 141 (= 54): 'So act that the maxim of your will can always at the same time be valid as a principle making universal law.'
[3] See Chapter I §10 and Appendix.
[4] See *Gr.*, 392 = 9.

XIII §4]   THE FIVE FORMULAE   131

from Formula I to Formula II we are moving from the form to the matter of moral action, while Formula IIIa combines both form and matter.[1]. Such a movement cannot be merely from the conditioned to its condition. Furthermore, Kant is prepared to pass directly from the essence of a categorical imperative to Formula II[2] and also to Formula III,[3] just as he does in the case of Formula I.[4] Hence we cannot say that each successive formula stands to its predecessor in the relation of condition to conditioned.[5] What we can say is that throughout Kant is accepting the concept of duty as implied in our moral judgements and is attempting to analyse its conditions and implications.

§4. *The application of the formulae.*

The aim of the present discussion is to formulate precisely the supreme principle of morality. We are not endeavouring to justify this principle: all attempt at justification is reserved till later. Above all, we are not seeking to work out a system of morality or to show how the supreme principle articulates itself in a moral code. This task is expressly rejected by Kant[6] and belongs, not to the *Groundwork*, but to his later *Metaphysic of Morals*.

Nevertheless Kant has always in mind the actual concrete moral judgements of the good man, and he attempts to throw light on his supreme principle by giving a few examples of its application. This is a natural and reasonable thing to do; but if we concentrate on this aspect of his exposition, we shall get a very misleading impression. His formulae might be completely sound, even if his method of application were totally fallacious. Moreover, even his method of application cannot be judged on the basis of a few examples given only for the sake of illustration. In actual fact his systematic application of the categorical imperative in the *Metaphysics of Morals* differs greatly from the sketchy illustrations given in the *Groundwork*. To reject Kant's principles merely on the ground that they do not give us some easy and infallible criterion for moral judgement is an absurd method of criticism and one which we should never dream of applying to any other philosopher.

This type of criticism, it must be admitted, is encouraged by some of Kant's own expressions.[7] His great strength as a philosopher is his persistence in seeking higher and more general principles behind any accepted doctrine. His weakness is a tendency to pass too quickly from his higher principles to the empirical doctrines which fall under them—witness, for example, his passage from general principles which underlie all experience and all physics to the special doctrines of Newton.[8] In spite of

---

[1] *Gr.*, 436 = 66.
[2] *Gr.*, 431–2 = 60.
[3] See Chapter I §§7–8.
[4] E.g., *Gr.*, 403–4 = 24–5.
[5] *Gr.*, 428–9 = 56–7.
[6] *Gr.*, 420–1 = 46–7.
[7] *Gr.*, 392 = 9.
[8] See, for example, *K.r.V.*, B225.

showing a caution and common sense which is not always the most conspicuous feature of German philosophers, and which a Scotsman may be pardoned for attributing to his paternal ancestry, Kant exhibits this tendency to a too hurried application in some of his moral utterances. Nevertheless the value of his formulae is one thing, and the method of their application is another.

CHAPTER XIV

THE FORMULA OF UNIVERSAL LAW

§1. *Formula I.*

'*Act only on that maxim through which you can at the same time will that it should become a universal law.*'[1]

This injunction is already familiar to us. We found it, though in a negative form, as the result of analysing the implications of ordinary moral judgements.[2] On a higher philosophical level we found it again—though we did not make it fully explicit—in analysing the objective principles and imperatives of practical reason, and in particular of pure practical reason.[3] In this analysis we were concerned only with the question 'What is an unconditioned objective principle and what is a categorical imperative?'—we did not ask expressly 'What is it that a categorical imperative enjoins?' Nevertheless the answer to this last question was implicit in our discussion; for, as Kant tells us,[4] in discovering what a categorical imperative is we have also discovered what it enjoins.

An unconditioned objective principle is one which every rational agent irrespective of his particular desires for particular ends would necessarily obey if reason had complete control over his passions, and one which he ought to obey if he is irrational enough to be tempted to do otherwise. The categorical imperative formulates the obligation or command to obey this unconditioned principle; and a principle excluding reference to particular ends can be only the form of a principle, or a formal principle, or universal law as such. What the categorical imperative bids us do is to act for the sake of law as such; and this means that the maxim of our action (whatever else it may be) should be to obey universal law as such.[5] There is thus only one categorical imperative; and we may call it '*the* categorical imperative'.

This formulation will now seem a little less jejune if we remember that, according to Kant, the categorical imperative also bids us perform actions which are good, not as a means to some further end, or to the satisfaction of some particular desire, but in themselves; for an action good in itself is one which every rational agent as such would perform if reason had complete control over his passions. The unconditioned principle of pure practical reason is the principle of action good in itself, although the categorical imperative expresses it as a principle of obligation—that is, as one which in our imperfect rationality we *ought* to obey. And we must

[1] *Gr.*, 421 = 47.
[2] Chapter VI §5.
[3] See especially Chapter IX §4.
[4] *Gr.*, 420-1 = 46-7.
[5] Compare Chapters IV §4 and VI §4.

[133]

not think of universal law as a principle *outside* the action or as a further end for the sake of which the action ought to be done. On the contrary, it is the principle *of* the action, the formal principle which is embodied in the action and in virtue of which the action is good.[1]

§2. *The one categorical imperative.*

When Kant speaks of '*the* categorical imperative' and asserts that there is only one, he has in mind the *principle* of all particular categorical imperatives; just as *the* hypothetical imperative 'If you will any end, you ought to will the means' is the *principle* of all hypothetical imperatives.[2] Particular hypothetical imperatives are applications of *the* hypothetical imperative; and particular categorical imperatives, like 'Thou shalt not kill', are applications of *the* categorical imperative. In Kant's language, they are 'derived' (*abgeleitet*) from it as from their principle, but this need not mean, and in fact does not mean, that they are 'deduced'.[3]

Kant holds that to conceive a categorical imperative is to know what it enjoins, but that to conceive a hypothetical imperative is not to know what it enjoins.[4] This view requires some qualification.

To conceive the principle of all hypothetical imperatives—'If you will any end, you ought to will the means'—is to know what it enjoins: Kant himself holds that it is an analytic practical proposition. What we do not know is the particular hypothetical imperatives in which it is applied. To know these we require to know something else—namely, what end we seek and what are the means to it. If we have this knowledge, we know all that is necessary to establish a particular hypothetical imperative.

As regards the principle of all categorical imperatives, to conceive this is to know what it enjoins, but it is not to know the particular categorical imperatives in which it is applied. So far there is no difference between the categorical imperative and the hypothetical imperative. The difference lies in this—that in the case of the categorical imperative knowledge of the end we seek and of the means to this end does not determine how the imperative is to be applied.[5] The categorical imperative, unlke the hypothetical, can and must be applied independently of our particular desire for a particular end.

---

[1] Compare Chapters VII §3 and X §4.

[2] Strictly speaking, the principle need not be expressed in the form of an imperative. The imperative rests ultimately on the principle that a rational agent who wills an end will necessarily, *qua* rational, will the means.

[3] *Gr.*, 421 = 47. Abbott actually translates it as 'deduced', although an examination of Kant's usage will show that it seldom or never means this, and although it is not the ordinary German word for 'deduced'. Kant habitually opposes the derived or derivatory (*abgeleitet*) to the original (*ursprünglich*) without any suggestion that one is deduced from the other. For this usage as applied to *intuition* see *K.r.V.*, B72; as applied to *good* see *K.p.V.*, 125 = 267 (= 226); as applied to *possession* see *M.d.S., Rechtslehre*, §6, 251.

[4] *Gr.*, 420 = 46.

[5] This knowledge is indeed embodied in the material maxim whose conformity with the categorical imperative has to be judged; but our moral judgement must not be determined by the known fact that we seek or desire a particular end. See §5 below.

Kant may perhaps think that by an act of will we can decide to live a life of obedience to moral law as opposed to one of self-interest and can thereby already obey the categorical imperative. But we could equally decide to live a life of prudence rather than one of impulse, so that there seems to be no real difference here.

§3. *Universal law.*

Kant's insistence on the duty to act for the sake of universal law as such is repugnant to many people; but when we remember that he is here concerned only with the *form* of moral obligation, we shall see that a great deal of what he says is common to most, if not to all, moral philosophy which does not regard duty as purely subjective, or as a matter of self-interest. He is assuming, as we all must, that there are, or at least may be, other rational agents besides ourselves, and he is saying that the principle of moral action must be the same for every rational agent. No rational agent is entitled to make arbitrary exceptions to moral law in favour of himself or even in favour of his friends. To say that the ultimate moral law must be universal is to say that every particular moral law must be objective and impersonal, that it cannot be determined merely by my desires, and that it must be impartial as between one person and another. In this there is surely nothing to cavil at, even if we believe that we have a direct intuition of an unanalysable quality of goodness (or obligation) and a direct intuition of the kinds of action in which such an unanalysable quality is necessarily manifested.

Perhaps we may add that the universality of moral law already implies reciprocity of obligation between person and person.[1] It implies that I am not morally entitled to treat you on one principle and yet to claim that you should treat me on another; or again that if I can claim to be treated by you in one way, I must be prepared to treat you in the same way. The importance of this for morality can hardly be exaggerated. It is made more explicit by Kant in his later formulae.

We need not further insist on Kant's view that the moral law holds for every rational agent, and that it appears as a command to finite human beings only because they are not completely rational.[2]

§4. *Maxims.*

A more distinctive feature of Kant's doctrine is his introduction of maxims as intermediaries between the abstract universal moral law and the concrete individual action. So far from embarking on a futile attempt to deduce particular moral laws from the bare form of law as such he bids us begin with an action done or contemplated and consider what is the principle actually manifested in it. The principle or maxim in question is the *material* maxim of the action,[3] as, for example, 'When I am in need

[1] Compare *M.d.S.*, *Rechtslehre*, §8, 256. [2] Chapter VI §2.
[3] Chapter IV §§2-4.

of money, I will borrow it on a promise of repayment which I do not intend to keep'.[1] We must then ask whether we can will the action, not merely as falling under a principle upon which we propose to act, but also as falling at the same time under a principle valid for every rational agent. More simply, is our maxim merely a principle on which we choose to act or is it one which we can at the same time regard as valid for a rational agent as such? If we adopt or reject the maxim according as the answer to the second alternative is 'Yes' or 'No', we are acting on the *formal* moral maxim 'I will obey universal law as such'.[2]

Such a procedure is surely in conformity with common sense. The formal maxim of morality does not act in a vacuum, but it selects from among our proposed material maxims in the same kind of way as does the general maxim of prudence.[3] In judging any particular case it is always well to consider the concrete action, to formulate the principle manifested in it, and then to ask whether this principle can be regarded as a moral law or a moral rule. This is wiser than approaching each situation with a set of ready-made rules. The latter procedure may indeed serve well enough when the moral situation is simple, but we cannot always be sure beforehand that the moral situation will be simple. And it is important to remember that in judging the validity of moral laws, such as 'Thou shalt not kill', or of moral rules, such as 'It may be the duty of a soldier to kill',[4] we shall judge best if we have concrete instances before our mind.[5]

We need not further labour the point that in dutiful action the material maxim, which may embody both consequences aimed at and motives for arriving at them, is present *at the same time* as the formal maxim.[6] The formal maxim is present if we would have rejected the material maxim had we thought it incompatible with universal law. Perhaps Kant wishes to emphasise the interpenetration, as it were, of the formal and the material maxim, when he uses the rather curious preposition—'Act only on that maxim *through* which you can at the same time will that it should become a universal law.'

Obviously it will not always be easy to say whether or not an action has its sufficient determining ground in the formal maxim of morality. It may not even be easy to say what is the material maxim of an action, and in this there lie great possibilities of self-deception, which the genuinely good man will necessarily seek to eliminate. This question belongs to a discussion of the way in which Kant's formula is to be applied in detail. It is, however, important to observe that for different purposes it is legitimate and necessary to consider different maxims for the same action.

What I mean by this is that if we take a narrow view of duty and wish to consider only what is 'due',[7] we shall omit from the maxim all

[1] *Gr.*, 422 = 48. [2] Compare Chapter IV §4.
[3] Chapter VIII §8 at end, and Chapter III §4.   [4] Chapter I §5.
[5] Moral judgement has certain resemblances to what is called 'intuitive induction' such as is found in mathematics, although there are also great differences between them.
[6] See Chapter III, Appendix.   [7] Chapter XI §5.

questions of motive. This is perfectly legitimate, but the truly conscientious man in judging his own actions will take his maxim as generalising the motive as well as the action. He will regard it as right to pay his debts, but wrong to do so from the motive of spiting his children; and he will endeavour to diminish any feeling of bitterness in his heart and to prevent it from influencing his actions.

§5. *Material maxims.*

It is by the way of material maxims that *circumstances* are considered in our moral judgements. Material maxims are of the form 'When life offers me more pain than pleasure, I will commit suicide', 'When I am in a difficulty, I will tell a lie', and so on. These examples might indeed be intended to indicate the motive rather than the circumstances of the action, but even in the most moral action it may be necessary to specify the circumstances. Thus a thoroughly moral maxim might be 'When I see a person drowning, I will pull him out of the water.' If my maxim were 'Whenever I see any one in the water, I will pull him out', this would be a maxim, not of duty, but of insanity.

Similarly it is by the way of material maxims that *ends* and *consequences* are considered in our moral judgements. 'When I can cause any one pain, I will do so' is a thoroughly immoral maxim. 'When I can cause anyone pleasure, I will do so' is a moral maxim if it is accompanied by the proviso that the pleasure caused must not be incompatible with moral law, as would be, for example, pleasure in the pain of others. Kant is surely right in saying that an action is not good or obligatory merely because it aims at so-called good consequences like pleasure or even the pleasure of others: we have to take into account the whole context in which so-called goods may be real evils. And he is also right in saying that there may in principle be some cases in which remote good consequences must be ignored. It is wrong to refuse to pay your debt to a rich man on the ground that the money would more profitably be spent on the education of your children. All this does not alter the fact that a material maxim is concerned with ends and consequences, and so alone can it be judged.

A further advantage arising from the introduction of material maxims is that the maxim, however specific, is abstract and general, while the action is individual and concrete. This means that there is a latitude or 'play-room' in the application of the maxim. There is indeed no such latitude where the maxim has to be rejected as immoral; but where the maxim is accepted as moral, it is important to recognise, as Kant does, that there is still some place for common sense.

§6. *The canon of moral judgement.*

It may be objected that even if all this be true, it does nothing to explain how some material maxims can be regarded as fitted to be

[1] Chapter IV §2 towards the end.

universal laws and others not. We may be bidden to do what every rational agent as such would do, and this may sound very fine indeed; but how are we to find out *what* every rational agent as such would do?

From a logical or theoretical standpoint this objection is sound. We cannot extract theoretical propositions from the mere form of law or universality. If we are given a series of theoretical propositions, we can indeed say which are universal in form and which are not. The logical form of universality could not, however, tell us which universal propositions were true and which false, though we might be able to decide this without further ado in the case of analytic propositions. Is Kant asserting that, given the two propositions 'All rational beings ought to tell the truth' and 'All rational beings ought to tell lies', we can say by mere inspection that one is false and the other true? He himself holds that these are not analytic propositions.

From this standpoint it seems as if we shall have to fall back on a direct intuition that telling the truth is good or obligatory or is what every rational agent as such would do.

On this point Kant gives us no very clear light beyond saying on occasion that certain moral principles 'leap to the eye';[1] and it may be that he would not be altogether averse from admitting some element of what may be called direct intuition. But attention must be called to another distinctive feature in his doctrine—namely, that the propositions in question are not theoretical, but practical, propositions and must be treated as such. There is a special 'canon' for practical moral propositions: we must be *able to will* that a maxim of our action should become a universal law.[2]

From the standpoint of action Kant's principle takes on a very different colour. In actual practice the value of the principle can hardly be exaggerated. The attempt to stand outside our personal maxims and estimate impartially and impersonally their fitness to be principles of action for others than ourselves is the necessary condition of all moral judgement and may throw a most unwelcome light upon our own actions and our own character. It must also be remembered that all of us, even very young children and—it may be conjectured—even sceptical philosophers, have a very acute and precise sense of what is unfair or unjust in regard to ourselves. If men were willing to take these principles, to universalise them, to apply them to others, and above all to act upon them when so universalised, the world would be a much better place than it is. Even bad men have this clear conviction of justice and injustice, though they fail to universalise it. Hitler himself was probably genuinely shocked at any injustice inflicted upon his country or compatriots by foreigners.

We may explain away all such convictions in philosophy; we may show that they are mere illusions; but we cannot get rid of them in practice. Yet in making claims on our own behalf to standards which we implicitly assert to be objective, we are appealing to Kant's principle of

[1] E.g. *M.d.S., Tugendlehre*, §8, 427. Compare also *Gr.*, 423–4 = 50.
[2] *Gr.*, 424 = 50.

a universal law. A truly rational will must surely, as Kant maintains, will coherently, as a rational mind must think coherently. We cannot without contradiction claim that all rational agents as such should treat us in accordance with certain universal principles, and claim at the same time that we are not bound by these principles ourselves.

§7. *Contradiction in the will.*

The phrase 'able to will' is manifestly the main clue to the understanding of Kant's doctrine, but it is unfortunately very hard to interpret. It appears to mean 'able to will without contradiction'. We have already found that a contradiction arises in imperfectly rational wills which act contrary to their own hypothetical imperatives.[1] We are now told that a contradiction arises also in regard to categorical imperatives.[2] So far Kant is a supporter of the coherence theory of goodness, a theory which has had wide support from Plato onwards but is difficult to make sufficiently precise.

There is clearly a contradiction in willing that a maxim should be a universal law and willing at the same time that we should make arbitrary exceptions to it in our own favour. According to Kant we shall find that this is what happens in our actual infringements of the law. We do not—and on his view we cannot—will that our immoral maxim should be universal law. On the contrary, we recognise that the law stands; but we say to ourselves 'This is a very special occasion' or 'I am a very special person', and so proceed to establish an exception to our own advantage. He adds that although from the point of view of reason there is a *contradiction* in this, in action it is rather an *antagonism* between reason and inclination, an antagonism in virtue of which we sophistically take the moral law to be general rather than truly universal. Nevertheless, he maintains, we recognise the validity of the categorical imperative, and only permit ourselves, as we pretend, some inconsiderable exceptions to it.

All this is sound enough practically, though we may add that the antagonism would be better described as one between a rational volition and a less rational volition. But it supposes—as I supposed in the case of injustice to ourselves—that we know what the law is: it does not explain *how* it is possible to know it. If we can assume certain maxims to embody the law, it is not too difficult to judge our consistency or inconsistency in their application. The difficulty is to see how the universalisation of certain maxims immediately brings out their self-contradictory character. In the next chapter we shall have to consider Kant's further attempts to explain this.

§8. *The coherence of rational wills.*

There is, however, already another side to Kant's doctrine, although it is made more explicit in his later formulae. The form of law is a form

[1] Chapter XII §6. [2] *Gr.*, 424 = 51.

which requires a matter, and this matter consists of the inclinations and ends of rational agents. There is a suggestion that some matter can, and some cannot, be adjusted to this form. The Idea of our pure rational will stands to our will as affected by sensuous desires in roughly the same relation as the categories stand to our sensuous intuitions.[1] This doctrine is already expressed in the statement that we must be able to will our *material* maxims as universal laws.

Kant brings out this side of his doctrine most clearly in the *Critique of Practical Reason*.[2] There he maintains that only if our actions are determined by a formal principle can there be a harmony or coherence (*Einstimmigkeit*) of rational wills. He expresses astonishment that intelligent men should have imagined maxims of self-interest, because they are universally acted on, to be therefore suitable to constitute a universal practical law. The result of adopting such maxims would produce only the greatest disharmony; for in that case the will of all has not one and the same object, but every one has his own, and any harmony between them is purely accidental. The harmony of self-seekers is really a disharmony, as when Francis I remarked 'What my brother Charles wants (Milan), I want too.'

Kant's view is clearly that coherence of rational wills can be based only on obedience to one and the same universal law as such, and that without this there can be no genuine coherence.[3] This principle applies more obviously to external legislation, but according to Kant it applies equally to internal legislation and presumably to our duty to ourselves as well as to our duty to others.

If this is so, in seeking to obey universal law as such we are seeking to realise the condition of coherence among rational wills. It is not yet clear how far Kant is taking into account the possible coherence of rational wills in determining what maxim is or is not suited to be a universal law. This question belongs to the discussion of our maxims as possible laws of nature.

§9. *The rational will as arbiter.*

Whatever the difficulties in Kant's view—and they are many—his fundamental assumption is that the will is as rational in action as intelligence is in thinking. We know what is good or obligatory, not in abstract thinking, but in virtue of actual or imagined willing. If we abandon mere self-seeking and adopt the standpoint of universal law, the will with no great difficulty will decide in a concrete situation what it ought to do. He is not attempting to introduce any new principles of morality but merely to formulate with precision the principle actually at work in the moral actions of ordinary men.[4]

[1] *Gr.*, 454 = 88. More will be said about this in the Appendix to this chapter.
[2] *K.p.V.*, §4, 27 ff. = 137 ff (= 49 ff.); see also *K.r.V.*, A811 = B839.
[3] See also Ernst Cassirer, *Kants Leben und Lehre*, pp. 256 ff.
[4] *K.p.V.*, 8 n. = 111 n. (= 14 n.).

Kant may exaggerate the ease and certainty with which the rational will decides upon its course of action, but it seems unfair to charge him with offering us a mechanical criterion of moral action and unreasonable to complain that he has failed to do so.[1] He himself compares his principle to a compass;[2] but possession of a compass does not absolve us from the necessity of finding out where we are in relation to our destination, nor even from the necessity of adjusting ourselves to the lie of the land as we proceed in that direction. We cannot base a great deal on a mere metaphor, but it looks as if we ought to be told more about the best way to use the compass we have been offered.

To some extent the information required is supplied by Kant's other formulae. What is surprising is that he speaks as if the present formula by itself were sufficient and as if in using it we were following the strictest method.[3] One would rather have imagined that by itself it was incomplete.

§10. *The permissible and the obligatory.*

There is a further point of interpretation which demands attention. Kant's doctrine is commonly supposed to be that where we can will a maxim to be a universal law, we ought to act on that maxim. That is to say, the possible universality of a maxim imposes on us a positive duty. Yet it seems not too difficult to will that the maxim of playing games in one's spare time should be universal law, although few would suggest that every one ought to play games in his spare time even if he feels that he can get more satisfaction or more relaxation in other ways.

It is quite clear that on Kant's view to act on maxims which will not meet the requirements of universality is to act wrongly. It is also clear that it is permissible (and in that sense 'right') to act on maxims which meet this requirement. But what is the ground for saying that he regards it as a positive duty to act on every such maxim?

It will be noted that in the *Groundwork* Kant is prepared to express the first formula of the categorical imperative negatively.[4] Even in the variant we have given[5] the phrase used is 'Act *only* on that maxim through which . . .' The word 'only' has a rather negative flavour which may be intended primarily to exclude maxims which do not satisfy this demand. It is true that the word 'only' is sometimes omitted;[6] but against this it may be observed that while a good man has the duty at all times of acting on maxims which can be willed as universal laws, it does not follow that in any particular situation he is obliged to act on a particular maxim which may meet this test—not if there are other suitable maxims which will meet it equally well.

It should also be noted how Kant says expressly[7] that the universal validity of our maxim as a law must be *the limiting condition* of our actions. This phrase, which is more commonly used of the Formula of the End

---

[1] Compare his rejection of a universal criterion of truth in *K.r.V.*, A58 ff. = B82 ff.
[2] *Gr.*, 404 = 24–5.
[3] *Gr.*, 436–7 = 67.
[4] *Gr.*, 402 = 22; 440 = 71.
[5] *Gr.*, 421 = 47.
[6] *Gr.*, 436–7 = 67.
[7] *Gr.*, 449 = 92.

in itself,[1] indicates a limiting condition of freedom and is clearly a negative condition. It entirely fits in with the doctrine that every man has a right (but not a duty) to pursue his own happiness except in so far as this is incompatible with universal law.[2]

If this interpretation is correct, it puts an entirely different complexion on Kant's doctrine. The categorical imperative, so far, prohibits certain actions; but where actions are not prohibited, we have every right to go forward as we please in accordance with our inclinations. The young man, so often quoted, who is in love with a young woman, can go ahead and marry her without asking whether it is his duty to do so. All he has to consider is whether there is any just impediment in the way.

It may be objected that nevertheless Kant manages to extract from this formula positive duties, like the duty of developing talents and of helping others. My reply is that even here Kant at least professes to establish these duties by showing that to will the opposite is to fall into self-contradiction.[3] Furthermore, in such cases our duty is not to perform certain definite actions but rather to adopt certain maxims of action which must be applied with prudence.

So far as I can see, the *Metaphysic of Morals* bears out my interpretation. There we are told that according to categorical imperatives some actions are permissible or non-permissible, while others or their opposites are obligatory.[4] The positive duties which are not merely the other side of a prohibition seem to depend on something more than mere form, on ends which are also duties, and so on matter.[5] All this is connected with the difference between perfect and imperfect duties, and also with the difference between legal and ethical duties. It is not easy to find one's way through the complications of Kant's doctrine, but without doing so no one is entitled to be dogmatic in his interpretations.

APPENDIX

THE SPONTANEITY OF MIND

§1. *Intellectual spontaneity.*

KANT's ethical doctrine maintains that pure practical reason can spontaneously order and regulate, in accordance with its own principle, the human maxims and actions which are based ultimately on desire.

---

[1] *Gr.*, 431 = 59.
[2] See also the use of the word 'permitted' (*erlaubt*) in *Gr.*, 439 = 70.
[3] *Gr.*, 424 = 50.   [4] *M.d.S., Rechtslehre, Einl.* IV, 221-22.
[5] *M.d.S., Tugendlehre, Einl.* II, 382 ff. = 226 ff.; §4, 419.

This doctrine can best be understood when we have grasped similar doctrines which he propounds in regard to the spontaneity of mind as manifested in other spheres of activity.

In the sphere of knowledge we should, according to Kant, know nothing either of objects or of ourselves apart from the spontaneous activity of imagination and understanding. Mere sensations as passively received, and in that sense given, have in themselves no reference either to objects or to a self; nor could knowledge either of self or of objects ever arise from any loose association of images or even from memory of successive sensations. The imagination must spontaneously combine sensations in one time and space and in so doing give rise to transcendental schemata corresponding to certain principles of combination inherent in the understanding.[1] These principles, in accordance with which the understanding works—as, for example, the principle of ground and consequent—when they are consciously conceived and applied through the schemata to sensations are the categories; and through them we experience a world of objects, a world of permanent substances, the succession of whose accidents is causally determined. Without the spontaneous activity of mind working in accordance with its own principles there could be no knowledge of an objective world nor could there be any knowledge of the knowing self.

Thus in knowledge the mind must function in accordance with its own principles just as the will must function in accordance with its own principles in moral action.[2] There is, however, a fundamental difference between the two. In knowledge the mind is applying more than the mere concept of law or universality as such.[3] According to Kant, in the ordering of given sensations it has at its disposal a whole series of specific categories, and it has also before it the forms of time and space, through which these categories can be applied. In action the will works only with the form of law or universality, and it is consequently much more difficult to understand how its principle can be applied in the ordering of actions based on given desires.[4]

There is a further difference between the two cases. The categories are concepts of the understanding; they refer to sensible objects, apart from which they have no objects at all; and they are, so to speak, confirmed by their actual use in experience. The supreme moral principle is an Idea of reason which can have no object in sensuous experience and so cannot be confirmed by experience: it belongs—and this is Kant's view—to another world than the world of experience, though we can give it a kind of object so far as we act in accordance with it.

[1] Chapter IX, Appendix §3.
[2] *Gr.*, 454 = 88. Kant indicates that the parallel is only a rough one by using the word '*ungefähr*' (roughly), which Abbott perversely translates as 'precisely'.
[3] Kant himself rather slurs over the difference by saying that the categories by themselves mean nothing other than the form of law in general; but surely they mean specific forms of law.
[4] Kant himself, however, develops his categories also into categories of freedom, and he seems to consider the absence of reference to space and time to be a positive advantage; *K.p.V.*, 65–6 = 186–8 (= 115–17).

§2. *Aesthetic spontaneity.*

Kant recognises also a further kind of spontaneity—the spontaneity of imagination in the experience of beauty.

In knowledge imagination is at the service of concepts: its business is to exhibit concrete instances falling under concepts. Just as imagination produces transcendental schemata corresponding to the categories when it combines sensations in one time and space, so it produces schemata on a humbler level in making pictures or images—which might be tactual as well as visual—corresponding to the empirical concept of dog or the mathematical concept of triangle.[1] These schemata are sometimes spoken of as themselves wavering diagrams,[2] but they seem more correctly to be the imaginative apprehension of the method necessary to construct such images and in this way to be kinaesthetic quite as much as visual. In all this we have a co-operation or harmony between understanding and imagination, the work of imagination always corresponding to concepts entertained by the understanding.

In aesthetic experience Kant recognises a further activity of imagination not directed to the construction of instances falling under a concept. Here the concept is irrelevant: a picture is not necessarily beautiful because it is the picture of a madonna. The distinctive feature of Kant's aesthetic theory is that he considers successful aesthetic activity to be still a kind of co-operation between imagination and understanding, although without a specific concept. Presumably the work of imagination possesses that kind of unity in difference which might be necessary for the 'exhibition' of a concept, but is here produced independently of a concept, the individual image being portrayed for its own sake. The success of this co-operation between imagination and understanding is judged, not by reference to any concept, but by a special kind of feeling, the aesthetic feeling or the feeling of beauty.

Here too we have a kind of parallel between the free activity of imagination in harmony with understanding and the free activity of the rational will in harmony with the Idea of law. On this ground Kant himself speaks of beauty as a symbol of morality. The freedom of the imagination is 'represented'—here presumably meaning 'felt'—in the appreciation of the beautiful as harmonious with the law-abidingness of the understanding; and the freedom of the will is conceived in moral judgement as an agreement of the will with itself in accordance with universal laws of reason.[3] The moral feeling of satisfaction in the performance of duty corresponds in some ways with the aesthetic feeling of beauty.

[1] *K.r.V.*, A140-2 = B180-1. See also *K.U.*, §57, *Anmerkung* I, 341 ff. (= 239 ff.), and §59, 351 ff. (= 254 ff.)

[2] *K.r.V.*, A570 = B598.

[3] *K.U.*, §59, 354 (= 259). In the previous paragraph Kant, in speaking of aesthetic judgement, says that it gives itself *the law* in regard to objects of so pure a satisfaction, just as reason does in regard to the faculty of desire (*Begehrungsvermögen.*) This, however, is only one of the many ways in which beauty is a symbol of morality.

Nevertheless here also there are fundamental differences between the two cases. The aesthetic judgement is based on feeling, but to Kant it is anathema to say that the moral judgement is based on feeling: the precise contrary is true, for the moral feeling must be based on the moral judgement, and the moral judgement rests on the concept of universal law as such, while the aesthetic judgement rests on no concepts whatsoever.[1]

Hence there are difficulties in regard to moral judgement which do not arise in regard to aesthetic judgement.

---

[1] This is why in aesthetic judgement the harmony is 'represented' or 'felt', while in the moral judgement it is 'conceived' or 'thought'.

CHAPTER XV

THE FORMULA OF THE LAW OF NATURE

§1. *Formula Ia.*

'*Act as if the maxim of your action were to become through your will a UNIVERSAL LAW OF NATURE.*'[1]

The difference between this formula and the previous one is sharp, and should not be slurred over. Up till now we have been concerned with a universal law of *freedom*—one on which any rational being would act so far as reason had full control over passion. The best, if not the only, way to make such a law vivid in our imagination is to picture to ourselves a world in which everybody in fact acted in accordance with it. This is the eminently sensible procedure which Kant now commends to us. It is one which is commonly followed by ordinary men.[2] The duty of fire-watching, for example, was sometimes pressed home by the question 'What would happen if everybody refused to do it?' To ask questions of this kind is to consider a maxim as if it were to become through our will a universal law of *nature*. Here, as so often, Kant is close to the logic of action, which must be distinguished from the logic of abstract speculation.

We can will that the maxim of our action should become at the same time a universal law of freedom—in the sense that we can will our action as an instance of a principle valid for all rational agents and not merely adopted arbitrarily for ourselves. We cannot, however, will that our maxim should become a universal law of nature: that is a project far beyond our power.[3] Hence in this new formula Kant very properly says 'Act *as if* . . .'

In using this formula we put ourselves imaginatively in the position of the Creator and suppose that we are making a world of nature of which we ourselves are a part.[4] In the *Critique of Practical Reason*[5] Kant puts his formula in a more elaborate way: '*Ask yourself whether you could regard your proposed action as a possible object of your will if it were to take place in accordance with a law of nature in a system of nature of which you were yourself a part.*'

From the illustrations given in the *Groundwork*[6] it is clear that in applying this formula we assume empirical knowledge of nature (par-

---

[1] *Gr.*, 421 = 47.   [2] *K.p.V.*, 69 = 192 (= 122–3).
[3] I believe this to be Kant's view—see also *Gr.*, 436 = 66 and *K.r.V.*, A807 = B835 —though at times he speaks loosely as if we could will maxims to have the universality of a law of nature; e.g., *Gr.*, 424 = 50.
[4] *Religion, Vorrede*, 5 (= VIII).   [5] *K.p.V.*, 69 = 192 (= 122).
[6] *Gr.*, 421 ff. = 48 ff.

ticularly of human nature) and its general laws. This shows again the absurdity of the view that Kant proposed to apply the moral law without taking into account any empirical facts. The moral law remains *a priori* even when applied to men, but if we are to bring particular cases under it and enable it to affect human wills, we must have judgement sharpened by experience.[1]

The illustrations in the *Groundwork* all apply Formula I by means of Formula Ia, though Kant speaks as if Formula I could be even better applied by itself.[2] In the *Critique of Practical Reason*[3] he asserts that Formula I can be applied only through Formula Ia—just as a pure category can be applied only through a transcendental schema.[4]

If Kant had regarded the Formula of the Law of Nature merely as a useful, or even as a necessary, practical device in estimating the suitability of our maxims to be moral laws, there would be little or nothing to boggle at. The weakness of his position is the apparent suggestion that by this means we can reach a purely intellectual and non-moral criterion of moral law—at least in the case of what he calls 'perfect duties'.

§2. *Perfect and imperfect duties.*

Kant attaches great importance to the distinction between perfect and imperfect duties, but he seems nowhere to define the distinction clearly, although he admits that he is not following the ordinary usage of the schools.[5] The ordinary usage regarded duties as perfect if they could be enforced by external law, and as imperfect if they could not be so enforced.[6] This would presumably mean that perfect duties could be only duties to others. Kant holds that we can have perfect duties also to ourselves.

Perfect duties, he here informs us, admit of no exception in favour of inclination, and this would suggest that imperfect duties do admit of such exceptions. Such a suggestion is surprising from Kant, and he is probably speaking more precisely in the *Metaphysic of Morals*,[7] when he indicates that the exceptions in question are rather the limitation of one maxim of duty by another—as when the duty of benevolence to a neighbour is limited by a similar duty to one's parents. Kant's view is apparently that some duties, as, for example, the paying of debts, are not so limited: we are not entitled to refuse payment of a debt on the ground that we need the money to assist our parents; and the payment of a debt must be regarded as a perfect duty.

[1] *Gr.*, 389 = 6. See also *Gr.*, 412 = 35; 410 n. = 33 n.; *M.d.S.*, *Rechtslehre*, *Einl.* II, 216–17 = 16. The first passage cited shows signs of Kant's confusion between moral law and moral laws. Compare Chapter I §5.
[2] *Gr.*, 436–7 = 67.   [3] *K.p.V.*, 70 = 193 (= 123).
[4] See Chapter IX, Appendix §3; Chapter XIV, Appendix; and also the Appendix to the present chapter.
[5] *Gr.*, 421 n. = 47 n.
[6] Mellin, *Wörterbuch der Kritischen Philosophie*, IV, 562.
[7] *M.d.S.*, *Tugendlehre*, *Einl.* VII, 390 = 235–6.

That there is an important distinction between such duties as the payment of debts on the one hand and such duties as benevolence on the other must be readily admitted; but we may doubt whether even the duty of paying a debt is—to employ a term Kant uses elsewhere[1]—an unconditioned duty in the sense that it cannot be overridden by any other. As Plato pointed out long ago, it would not be a duty to return a weapon to a man who had become a homicidal maniac.[2]

Kant marks his distinction also in another way. In the case of perfect duties we are obliged to perform a definite *act*—for example, to pay precisely the £5 9s. 6d. which we owe. In the case of imperfect duties we are bound to act only on a *maxim*: although we ought to act on the maxim of benevolence, it is left to our discretion to decide whom we ought to help, and to what extent we ought to help. There is thus a 'latitude' or 'play-room' in the case of imperfect duties, which are also called 'broad' or 'meritorious', as opposed to 'narrow' or 'strict' or 'rigorous', duties [3] The last three adjectives appear to be equivalent to 'perfect' when they are applied to duties.

If we have perfect and imperfect duties both to ourselves and to others, duties are thereby classified into four main kinds. The object of Kant's illustrations is to show that each *kind* of duty falls under the Formula of the Law of Nature. Maxims opposed to perfect duties cannot even be *conceived* as laws of nature without contradiction. Maxims opposed to imperfect duties can be conceived as laws of nature, but could not be *willed* as such without contradiction.

§3. *The causal law of nature.*

In its strictest sense Kant usually takes a law of nature to be a causal law, and it is essential to such a law that it should have no exceptions: the same cause must always produce the same effects. Hence it may be thought that if we are to find contradiction in a maxim when it is conceived as a law of nature, this must be because it would assert that the same cause could produce different effects.

It is perhaps possible to interpret Kant's discussion of suicide on this basis. Here the maxim is supposed to be 'I will commit suicide, if life offers me more pain than pleasure'.[4] This is a principle of self-love, and we assume empirical knowledge that self-love—described here oddly as a sensation—has the 'determination' (*Bestimmung*) to work for the further- ance of life. Hence if we universalise this maxim of a law of nature, we are supposing that self-love, which is the cause of life, should in cer- tain circumstances be the cause of death. We are, in short, conceiving a law of nature to admit of arbitrary exceptions, and so we are falling into a contradiction. From this the inference is made that the maxim must be contrary to moral law: it is a breach of a perfect duty to oneself.

[1] *Das mag in der Theorie richtig sein; Ak.* VIII, 300 n.
[2] *Rep.* 331 c.   [3] *Gr.*, 424 = 50–1.   [4] *Gr.*, 421–2 = 48.

Kant is right in saying that there can be no arbitrary exceptions either to a moral law or to a law of nature: but it is manifestly impossible to find, by this method, breaches of a law of nature from which we are entitled to infer breaches of a moral law. We assert no breach of a law of nature if we say that food, which ordinarily causes life, may in special circumstances—for example, in certain kinds of illness—cause death. Nor need there be any breach of causal law if self-love, which ordinarily causes life, should in special circumstances cause death.[1] Indeed we may say generally that any attempt to make the causal law of nature a test of moral law is foredoomed to failure.

It is, however, abundantly clear, if we look at the discussion of the other kinds of duty, that this is not the correct interpretation of the argument. Kant is not concerned with causal laws nor with finding breaches in them: his arguments, if interpreted in this way, are completely broken-backed. In every case he appeals to teleological considerations; and there is no possibility of even beginning to understand his doctrine, unless we realise that the laws of nature he has in mind are not causal, but teleological.

§4. *Teleological law in nature.*

Nature is the totality of phenomena governed by law. Phenomena are the matter of nature; but the form in virtue of which they constitute nature—and not mere chaos—is the form of law. This law is primarily causal law, which covers not only the mechanical causation of physical bodies, but also the instinctive behaviour of animals, and even—from one point of view—all human action and experience. Nevertheless in nature causal law is not the only kind of law recognised by Kant.

Even in the understanding of physical nature we may have to use another concept besides that of causal law—the concept, namely, of purpose or end. This concept seems to be necessary for the study of organisms. To say this is not to say either that organisms and their organs are the product of conscious purpose or that they themselves have a conscious purpose: it is rather to say that we must consider them *as if* they had a purpose and see whether in this way we can understand them better.[2] For the understanding of human nature the concept of purpose or end is still more necessary; for it is an essential characteristic of human nature to set purposes before itself. As we shall see later,[3] morality even seems to demand that we should act *as if* nature itself were purposive and had a final end.

Teleological laws, it is true, do not constitute nature in the same

---

[1] Incidentally it would be interesting to discover what ingenious gentleman first interpreted this passage as meaning that suicide could not be a law of nature because, if it were, there would be nobody left to commit suicide! This interpretation is repeated so frequently as to be almost orthodox; yet it has no justification in this passage nor, so far as I know, in any other.

[2] They seem to have what Kant calls 'purposiveness without a purpose'—that is, without a conscious purpose.

[3] See Chapter XVIII §8.

sense as do causal laws: it is perhaps even stretching a point to speak of them as laws of nature. Nevertheless in using the law of nature as a means of applying the moral law Kant is going behind causal law to the more fundamental abstract idea of law as such, which constitutes the form of nature. Why he then proceeds to take teleological laws to embody law as such we shall consider in a moment.

§5. *The perfection of nature.*

To understand the background of Kant's doctrine we must remember that for him the teleological view of an organism is not only that as a whole it is adapted to a purpose or end, but that every organ is also adapted to a purpose or end which is an element in the total purpose or end.[1] In the *Critique of Pure Reason*[2] he declares that reason in considering living beings must necessarily accept the principle that no organ, no faculty, no impulse, indeed nothing whatsoever, is either superfluous or disproportionate to its use, but that everything is exactly adapted to its purpose (*Bestimmung*) in life. That he was deeply affected emotionally by this view is brought out by a story which, according to Wasianski,[3] he used himself to tell as an old man. In a cool summer, when there were few insects, he discovered that the swallows themselves were casting some of the young ones out of the nest so that there should be sufficient food for the others. At first, Kant said, he could not believe his eyes; and added with strong emotion 'My mind stood still—there was nothing to do but fall down and worship.'

Whether or not his observations were correct, his whole attitude may seem strange today. Eighteenth-Century optimism about nature was shattered by the advent of Darwinism, and we tend to regard nature as 'red in tooth and claw', careless of the race as she is careless of the individual. The correctness or incorrectness of Kant's biological presuppositions, however, is not here in question. What is important is this —that on Kant's view to conceive human nature as governed by teleological law is to suppose a complete harmony of ends both within the race and within the individual. We can consider human nature *as if* there were such a systematic harmony of ends in accordance with a law of nature; and we can ask whether any proposed maxim, if it were made a law of nature, would fit into such a systematic harmony. Some maxims would destroy such a systematic harmony, while others would merely fail to foster it, and this seems to be the basis of the distinction between perfect and imperfect duties.

§6. *The appeal to teleological law.*

Kant's appeal to a teleological, rather than to a causal, law of nature may at first sight seem arbitrary, but this is far from being the case.

[1] See Chapter II §8.   [2] *K.r.V.*, B425.
[3] *Immanuel Kant in seinen letzen Lebensjahren*, p. 411, in *Immanuel Kant*, by Alfons Hoffmann, which also contains the accounts of Kant by Jachmann and Borowski.

When we are asked to conceive a proposed maxim as a law of nature, we must conceive it as a teleological law of nature; for it is a maxim of *action*, and action as such (quite apart from moral considerations) is essentially purposive. Furthermore, we are asked to conceive it primarily as a law of *human* nature, even if we are setting it against the background of nature as a whole; and human nature must be regarded as essentially purposive. All this was apparently so much taken for granted by Kant that he fails to state it explicitly, and so tends to mislead his readers.

When we ask whether we can *will* a proposed maxim as if it were to become thereby a law of nature, we are asking whether a will which aimed at a systematic harmony of purposes in human nature could consistently will this particular maxim as a law of human nature. Clearly we cannot do this without empirical knowledge of the needs, desires, and powers of men, but it is no part of Kant's doctrine that the moral law can be applied without any regard to empirical knowledge of the facts of human life.

In all this we must be clear what Kant is doing. He is putting forward the doctrine that the ideal coherence of human purposes and human wills is the test or criterion, but not the essence, of moral action. This is why the moral law must be distinguished from the law of nature.

This distinction may be seen most clearly as regards the duty of kindness or benevolence. Here we are aiming at the happiness of other men. The happiness of the individual may be regarded as the systematic satisfaction of his desires and the systematic harmonisation of his ends. In normal action it is our duty to promote this happiness in individuals so far as it is not inconsistent with similar happiness in others.[1] No doubt in each case our duty is towards one individual or a group of individuals, but this must be subject to the controlling maxim of promoting the general happiness; and in this sense we may be said to be aiming at the systematic harmonisation of human ends. But this we may do for various reasons. We may do it for the purely selfish reason that in this way we may contribute most to our own comfort. We may do it because we happen to be good-hearted people whose generous emotions happen to be peculiarly strong. Such conduct may be prudent; it may even be admirable and praiseworthy and amiable; and it would be chimerical to ignore these auxiliaries to morality.[2] Nevertheless a man is not morally good merely in virtue of the fact that he is pursuing the systematic harmonisation of human ends. For moral goodness something more is necessary. A good man is not moved merely by an emotion, however amiable: he is seeking to obey a law valid for rational agents as such, binding upon him and upon others even in the absence of generous emotions, and indeed even in the presence of natural dislike. Nevertheless, since such obedience is the only way in which the purposes of men can be fully harmonised, we may take it that when a maxim universalised as a law of nature could lead to such a harmony of human purpose, that maxim is fit to be adopted also as a moral law. When it is so adopted, we perform benevolent actions

[1] I here omit further qualifications.   [2] Compare *Ak.* XIX, Nr. 6560.

because they are in themselves good and because they are our duty, not merely because of a desire for their results.

By the help of the law of nature we can decide what we ought to do; but the law of nature tells us nothing about the spirit in which we ought to do it. Hence, as I have said, we have here a test of moral action, but not its essence.

§7. *Kindness.*

We shall see Kant's doctrine more clearly if we look at his illustrations.

As regards the duty of kindness or benevolence,[1] Kant assumes empirical knowledge that men, because of their weakness, at times need and desire each other's help. He does not argue from this prudentially that we must help others if we wish to be helped ourselves; nor does he make the improbable suggestion that if we refuse help to others, nobody will ever help us. He admits further that men could go about their purposes even if nobody ever helped any one else: mutual refusal of help could perfectly well be conceived as a law of nature. There would, however, be inconsistency in a will which willed this to be a universal law; for since each of us at some time is bound to seek help for himself, he would thereby will an exception to this law, and consequently he could not will it to be a law.

This way of putting the matter stresses too much the need of the individual agent for help and so gives rise to the mistaken view that Kant is concerned merely with self-interest. It is, however, true to say that our kindness will be less mixed with condescension if we remember that we also are subject to human needs; and it is important to emphasise that we can reasonably claim help from others only if we are willing to regard the principle of helping others without thought of reward as a law which is binding equally upon ourselves. Nevertheless, as Kant shows in another discussion of kindness,[2] the argument does not turn on the fact of my own needs: it holds even if I am strong enough to do without the help of others. The argument turns rather on the fact that human beings are in need of mutual help, and that only by means of mutual help can the systematic harmony of their purposes be attained.[3]

§8. *Promises to repay loans.*

As regards the keeping of promises to repay borrowed money,[4] Kant assumes empirical knowledge that the purpose of such promises is to produce trust and so to get out of financial difficulties; and further that the universal breaking of such promises would make the attainment of

---

[1] *Gr.*, 423 = 49–50.   [2] *Gr.*, 398–9 = 17–18.
[3] Compare *M.d.S.*, *Tugendlehre*, §30, 453. There Kant himself says helping those in need is a duty because we must regard each other as fellow men subject to needs and as united by nature in one dwelling for purposes of mutual help.
[4] *Gr.*, 422 = 48–9.

this purpose impossible. Here again Kant does not proceed to argue prudentially that I ought to keep my promises if I want to be believed,[1] nor does he make the improbable assumption that if I break this promise, the result will be that I shall never be believed again. What he argues is this—that if my maxim were to be a universal law of nature, so that everyone in financial difficulties made similar false promises, this would defeat the very purpose of such false promises. The law would cancel itself out and could not even be conceived, let alone willed, as a law of nature. Here again, it must be remembered, a teleological law of nature, on Kant's view, must assert the adequacy of every organ for its purpose and could not admit of purposes which defeated themselves.

What Kant says is true enough so far as it goes, but it does not offer a satisfactory basis for moral judgement unless we make the further assumption that the keeping of such promises and the mutual confidence thereby aroused are essential factors in the systematic harmony of human purposes. That this is an assumption which Kant makes is shown by his later discussion,[2] and we must, I think, read it into the present argument if we are to find it other than artificial. Furthermore, without assumptions of this kind we might find ourselves compelled to regard honour among thieves simply as a virtue.

It may be said that when we talk about mutual confidence we are simply judging the action by its results, and that the action is still wrong, even if it does not disturb mutual confidence. This might very well happen if the lender were to die suddenly without leaving any record of the loan.

In one sense we are not judging the action by its results—firstly, because Kant does not pretend that universal disturbance of confidence will be the result of my action, and secondly, because Kant is not arguing that because I happen to want the prevalence of confidence among men, therefore I ought not to break a promise. Such an argument would be prudential and not moral. What he is doing is to take the principle of our action and to ask whether if universalised it is compatible with a systematic harmony of purposes in society. The answer is clearly 'No', and this answer remains, even if in this particular action I might be able to escape discovery.

In another sense he *is* taking into account the consequences. He is endeavouring to see the action as it fundamentally and essentially is—that is, as an action destructive of mutual confidence and of any systematic harmony of purposes in a particular sphere (and ultimately in every sphere); just as in considering murder one must take into account that it is the killing of a human being. This seems legitimate, although it might be said that he lays too much stress on the destruction of confidence, and too little on the fact that the breaking of such a promise is in itself the treacherous disruption of a systematic harmony of wills,

---

[1] *Gr.*, 402 = 22–3.
[2] *Gr.*, 429–30 = 58. He also makes the further assumption—see *M.d.S.*, *Tugendlehre*, §9, 429—that the power of communicating our thoughts has as its essential and natural end the telling of the truth; but this assumption belongs to the discussion of lying as a sin against oneself, not as a breach of our duty to others.

whether it is discovered or undiscovered. The second point he makes clear when he deals with men as ends in themselves. Perhaps his emphasis on the relatively external side of the action is due to the fact that he has in mind a contract which can be enforced by State law, since perfect duties to others were traditionally regarded as falling under the law of the State, and the State must necessarily take an external view of action.

§9. *Suicide.*

When Kant considers duties towards oneself, he does not test maxims by their fitness to produce a systematic harmony of purposes among men if they were to become universal laws of nature. He does, however, test them by reference to harmony of purpose, a harmony between the ends proposed by the maxim, when universalised as a law of nature, and what he calls 'purposes of nature'.[1]

In the case of suicide, when Kant says that the 'determination' (*Bestimmung*) of self-love is the furtherance of life,[2] he means that this is its purpose or function and not merely its effect. If I conceive myself as having created man and given him self-love with this end in view, can I will, or even conceive, it to be a law of nature that this self-love should in certain circumstances aim at producing death? Kant's answer is 'No'; but it may be conjectured that he gives the answer because he already assumes suicide to be wrong. Why should it not be a merciful dispensation of Providence that the same instinct which ordinarily leads to life might lead to death when life offered nothing but continuous pain?

This is the weakest of Kant's arguments. It might be maintained as against him that the principle of self-love, which he usually regards as a rational principle of reason at the service of desire, would be in contradiction with itself if it did not vary in its effects according as pleasure exceeded pain or *vice versa*. Kant here calls it a 'sensation', meaning by that presumably some sort of instinct of self-preservation.[3] But this is not one of the powers which distinguish man from the brutes, where Kant's method of argument is more plausible; and unless we have an exaggerated idea of the perfection of teleology in nature, unless indeed we commit ourselves to some theory of the working of divine Providence, this argument can carry little conviction except to those already convinced.

The argument would be more plausible if we were to maintain that to commit suicide only because life offered more pain than pleasure is at variance with the function of reason as aiming at absolute good; for it is to withdraw oneself in the interests of comfort from the duty of leading the moral life.[4] The essential thing for our present purposes is, however,

---

[1] E.g., *Gr.*, 430 = 59. Compare the phrase 'the essential ends of humanity' in his *Lectures on Ethics*; see, for example, *Vorlesung*, Menzer, 161; Infield, 136.

[2] *Gr.*, 422 = 48.

[3] The rational principle of self-love, when considered not as a law of freedom but as a law of nature, is reduced to the level of instinct.

[4] Compare *Gr.*, 429 = 57; *M.d.S.*, *Tugendlehre*, §6, 422–3. See also Chapter XVI §7.

not the plausibility of the particular argument, but rather the general principle on which the argument is based.

§10. *Culture.*

In the case of developing talents—particularly those talents which distinguish man from the brutes—Kant is on stronger ground. Here his teleology is more explicit, and he even puts it almost in the language of religion; for he says that a rational being must necessarily will the development of his powers, not only because they serve, but also—in the second edition—because they have been *given*, for all sorts of possible purposes. This, he holds, remains true, although there is no contradiction in conceiving (as opposed to willing) a law of nature such that all men live the life of lotus-eaters. Apart from the theological language, if I conceive myself as having created men with all sorts of talents, I should certainly feel myself to be willing inconsistently if I willed it to be a law of nature that these talents should never be developed or used. This argument is miles apart from the argument that I ought to develop my talents because I shall find this profitable or advantageous to myself.

The powers which Kant has in mind include the powers of the body, but they concern primarily the powers which distinguish men from the brutes—the power of scientific thinking, the power of aesthetic appreciation, and above all the power of leading a rational or moral life.[1]

In all his discussions of duty to oneself there is a marked strain of teleological or Aristotelian ethics, but this holds especially as regards the development and exercise of powers whereby men are distinguished from animals. Here we cannot start, as in the case of duty to others, merely with the purposes which men naturally have and proceed to ask how they can be combined in a systematic harmony. We have to argue that man has a duty to himself as a man to use his powers for the purpose inherent in themselves, and above all to develop and use the powers in virtue of which alone he is a man. This is a doctrine not fashionable today, and if it is to be reinstated it will have to be reformulated in the light of modern evolutionary theory; but to sweep it aside as silly, or—still worse —as silly against an Eighteenth-Century background, is to show a lack of historical and philosophical insight.

§11. *Practical reason and purpose.*

Kant's doctrine becomes intelligible only when his law of nature is interpreted teleologically as concerned with the harmony of human purposes. Behind all he says there is a fundamental assumption that practical reason, and indeed that pure practical reason, is concerned with the realisation of human purposes and of a systematic harmony among them. Kant puts this very clearly in the *Metaphysic of Morals*:[2]

[1] *M.d.S., Tugendlehre, Einl.*, VA, 386–7 = 231–2; §19, 444–6.
[2] *M.d.S., Tugendlehre, Einl.* IX, 395 = 242.

'What in the relation of men to themselves and others *can* be an end, that *is* an end for pure practical reason; for it (that is, reason) is a power of ends as such; to be indifferent in regard to these, that is, to take no interest in them, is therefore a contradiction.' And he drives this home by adding that if practical reason were indifferent to ends, it would not determine maxims for actions (since these always involve an end); and therefore it would not be practical reason at all.

For Kant the view that practical reason ought to aim at complete detachment and ultimate oblivion would be self-contradictory and immoral—a breach of the logic of action. And it is perhaps fair to say that if there is anything in his doctrine that willing is as rational as thinking, then for the understanding of his doctrine we must adopt the standpoint, not of mere observers, but of agents; or in his own language we must be, not world-observers, but world citizens.[1] You can no more judge moral action without at least trying to act morally yourself than you can judge thought without thinking yourself.

§12. *The principles of moral action.*

We may now see more clearly the way in which the two Formulae of Universal Law and of the Law of Nature may together be a guide to actions.

First of all the good man must set aside the principle of self-interest as the sole guide to conduct and must subordinate it to a wider impersonal and impartial principle—the principle of acting reasonably and objectively, or, as Kant puts it, acting on a law valid for all rational agents. This is a fundamental change of attitude in the will, the adoption of a new spirit, the very essence and principle of the moral life. It is expressed in the Formula of Universal Law.

Kant may hold, perhaps too easily, that a will which adopts this attitude can by its own nature find its way clear before it in actual living —in somewhat the same way as does the artist who gives himself to art or the thinker who sets aside prejudice and gives himself unreservedly to the dispassionate and free working of his own thought. Nevertheless Kant recognises that the empty form of law must be filled, and that the purposive actions of men must be brought under the law by a consideration of the principles or maxims at work in them.

In order to do this we must imagine these maxims to become laws of nature as a result of our volition. We can test them so far as they affect others, by considering how far the universal adoption of these maxims would further, or fail to further, or would actually destroy, a systematic harmony of purposes among men. We can test them so far as they affect ourselves by considering whether as universal laws of nature they would further, or fail to further, or would actually destroy, a systematic harmony of purpose in the individual, it being assumed that his powers have a natural purpose which can be recognised and that these powers, and especially the powers which are the differentia of man,

[1] *Ak.* XV, ii, Nr. 1170.

must be furthered and not destroyed, if this systematic harmony of purpose is to be realised.

All this is the mere bare bones of Kant's view; but unless we grasp this elementary anatomy, we shall never begin to understand the body of his doctrine.

The test of the maxims is thus—speaking broadly—a systematic harmony of purpose such as might accord with a law of nature. But this is only a test of moral action, not its essence. You might have such a harmony in a colony of ants, but there would be no morality there. You might conceivably have it, or something like it, in a society governed entirely by self-love as a result of action and reaction, but there would be no morality there. Nor would there be morality even if everybody in such a society aimed at this harmony of purposes on the ground that he happened to like it or that it would make things more comfortable for himself. Morality would be embodied in such a systematic harmony of purpose only so far as each member of the society sought to further this harmony, not merely because of his own desires, however generous, but because he was at the same time endeavouring to obey a law valid for all rational agents. This must be, not his only, but his controlling and overruling, motive. If the moral law is included in the concept of the systematic harmony of purposes, then—it goes without saying—this concept and the idea that we can help to bring about the existence of such a harmony is at the same time the determining ground of a pure moral will.[1]

It may be added that not even in the case of perfect duties is Kant applying a purely intellectual test. The reason why certain maxims cannot be conceived as laws of nature is that to will in accordance with such maxims is not merely to fail in furthering a systematic harmony of purposes, but it is to disrupt and destroy that systematic harmony which not only is essential to the concept of a teleological law of nature, but is also the outward, if ideal, manifestation of obedience to the moral law.

APPENDIX

THE LAW OF NATURE AS A TYPE OF THE MORAL LAW

§1. *The form of law.*

IN the *Groundwork* Kant gives us hardly any explanation of his reasons for introducing Formula Ia as a supplement to Formula I. In Formula I we are told that our maxims ought to conform to the universality of law as such. Kant then informs us that the universality of law constitutes the form of nature. Nature, whatever be its matter, is characterised essentially

[1] Compare *K.p.V.*, 109-10 = 244-5 (= 196-7).

by the fact that in it all events take place in accordance with universal law—particularly the law of cause and effect. Nature and moral action thus in a sense have the same form—the form, namely, of universal law—however much the laws of nature and the laws of freedom differ. On this ground Kant apparently assumes that the universal law imposed by the categorical imperative can be translated in terms of a universal law of nature; and we thus pass from Formula I to Formula Ia.[1]

This appears to mean that there is some sort of *analogy* between the universal law of freedom (to which all actions ought to conform) and the universal law of nature (in accordance with which all phenomena are determined). It is in virtue of this analogy that we can substitute 'universal law of nature' for 'universal law' in our formula. This analogy is explicitly mentioned in the useful summary of the argument provided towards the end of Chapter II of the *Groundwork*.[2]

A view of this kind manifestly requires considerable expansion, which Kant avoids in the *Groundwork*, perhaps as being too technical.

§2. *The problem of 'exhibition'.*

Kant's problem is expressed more technically in the *Critique of Practical Reason*.[3] It is the problem of applying a concept to individual objects or of 'exhibiting'[4] an object corresponding to a concept. By means of our concepts we can know objects only if we can exhibit the corresponding objects in some sort of sensuous intuition. When we exhibit the objects of a concept, we are often said to exhibit the concept itself.

There is no difficulty in exhibiting objects for our empirical concepts. These concepts are abstracted from sensuous experience, and we can reconstruct objects for them in imagination—the imagination in so doing follows very much the same procedure as it follows in combining sensations when we are actually seeing the object. Imagination can also construct objects for our arbitrary mathematical concepts in pure intuition, that is, to speak roughly—the expression is not Kant's—we can in imagination carve them out of space.[5] In being aware of the imaginative procedure necessary for each concept we have what Kant calls a 'schema' of the concept.[6] If a sensed or imagined object fits the schema, it falls under the concept.

There is more difficulty in exhibiting objects for a pure category of the understanding, like ground and consequent. Nevertheless, since in order to have knowledge of empirical objects we must combine them in one consciousness, we have in knowing objects to combine them

---

[1] *Gr.*, 421 = 47. The same transition is apparently made also in *Gr.*, 436 = 66.
[2] *Gr.*, 437 = 67. Compare also *Gr.*, 431 = 60, where the conformity of moral actions to universal law is said to be *similar* to an order of nature.
[3] *K.p.V.*, 67 ff. = 189 ff. (= 119 ff.).
[4] '*Darlegen*' or '*darstellen*'—in Latin '*exhibere*'.
[5] In *K.U.*, §62, 365 (= 276), a mathematical object is said to be possible only by 'determining' space.
[6] See also Chapter XIV, Appendix §2.

imaginatively in one time and space. This means, according to Kant, that we must combine—or at least seek to combine—sensuous intuitions in certain ways, and the necessary procedure of imagination here gives us what are called 'transcendental schemata' corresponding to the different pure categories. In particular it gives us the transcendental schema of necessary succession in accordance with a rule; and where this is present, as it must be if we are to be aware of objective change, we are entitled to apply the pure category of ground and consequent, which thus becomes the category of cause and effect. Necessary succession in accordance with a rule is the transcendental schema in virtue of which we can exhibit objects falling under the category of the understanding.[1]

The difficulty about our concept of the unconditioned and absolute law of morality is that it is an Idea of reason: and therefore *ex hypothesi* it can have no corresponding object in sensuous experience.[2] The actions which we wish to bring under the moral law are—from one point of view —mere events subject to the law of nature and not to the law of freedom. They cannot be adequate to the Idea of an unconditioned law, and we have no schema, transcendental or otherwise, whereby we can exhibit an object for such an Idea of reason.[3]

§3. *Symbolic exhibition.*

There is, however, a second kind of exhibition possible, exhibition, not directly by means of *schemata*, but indirectly by means of *symbols*, and this is the method by which we supply sensuous intuitions for Ideas of reason, although no sensuous intuition can be adequate. Symbols are not objects falling directly under a concept, but they are objects which we use in order to attach some sort of meaning to a concept. They do so in virtue of an analogy.[4] In this they differ from mere arbitrary signs, such as the letters of the alphabet.

An analogy, according to Kant, expresses, not an imperfect likeness of two things, but a perfect likeness of two relations between things wholly unlike. Thus A (promotion of a child's happiness) is to B (a father's love) as C (human welfare) is to X, where X is the unknown something in God which we call love, although it cannot be like any human inclination. A father's love for his child is therefore a symbol whereby through an analogy we can represent to ourselves God's love for human beings.[5]

Kant holds all our knowledge of God—or at least our way of conceiving God—to be symbolic in this sense. If we ascribe to Him human inclinations, or even human understanding and human will, we are falling into anthropomorphism. Nevertheless by using these human characteristics as symbols, although we cannot know God as He is, we can conceive His relations to us in terms of relations with which we are

---
[1] See also Chapter IX, Appendix §3.   [2] See Chapter IX, Appendix §5.
[3] Compare *K.r.V.*, A665 = B693.
[4] *K.U.*, §59, 351 ff. (= 255 ff.). Compare also *K.r.V.*, A678 = B706 and A696 ff. = B724 ff.
[5] *Prol.*, §58, 357.

familiar; and this may be sufficient for purposes of action.[1] For man the invisible must be represented by something visible or sensible; and indeed for purposes of action it must, as it were, be made sensible by means of an analogy.[2] Religious rites and sacraments can be justified as such symbols. When they are practised as having value in themselves, they become mere superstitions.[3]

Is it possible for us to exhibit actions as objects falling under the Idea of moral law, if we make use of the symbolic or indirect method of exhibition by means of an analogy?

§4. *The 'type' of moral law.*

I have already pointed out[4] that there is an analogy between the universal moral law and the universal law of nature. The preceding section suggests that it would be more correct to speak of an analogy between the two sets of objects conceived to fall under the two laws, moral wills on the one hand and temporal events on the other; and this is confirmed to this extent—that Kant speaks of an analogy between the kingdom of ends and the kingdom of nature.[5] We need not, however, spend time on subtleties, though we could wish that Kant had articulated his doctrine more fully. The two types of law play similar parts in two different systems, and we may say that there is a kind of analogy between them. This relation between the two laws Kant expresses by saying that the law of nature can be called a 'type' of the moral law.[6]

The word 'type' is commonly used in theology in more or less the same way as Kant uses the word 'symbol': it is that by which something is symbolised or figured. Thus the people of Israel are said to be a type of *God*'s people, and the Paschal lamb is said to be a type of Christ. Kant's application of the word to the law of nature is a natural extension of this usage.

The law of nature, as a concept of the understanding, has always a schema or schemata in virtue of which it applies to sensible objects, the schema of causal law in particular being necessary succession in accordance with a rule. The law of freedom, as an Idea of reason, can have no schema whereby we can exhibit objects for it directly in intuition. Kant's suggestion is that we can exhibit objects for it indirectly or symbolically: in virtue of the analogy between the moral law and the law of nature,

---

[1] *K.U.*, §59, 352–3 (= 257–8); *Prol.*, §58, 358; *Religion*, 65 n. (= 82 n.). For beauty as a symbol of morality see also Chapter XIV, Appendix §2.
[2] *Religion*, 192 (= 299).   [3] *Religion*, 192 ff. (= 299 ff.)   [4] §1 above.
[5] *Gr.*, 439 = 69. His earlier statement of the analogy in *Gr.*, 437 = 67 is extremely elaborate, but it is nearer asserting an analogy between the two laws than between the sets of objects conceived to fall under them.
[6] *K.p.V.*, 69 = 192 (= 122). He also says, *K.p.V.*, 70 = 193 (= 124), that we can use the *nature* of the *sensible world* as the *type* of an *intelligent nature*, but he means here *natura formaliter spectata*, which in turn is the form of law as such. It may also be relevant that he speaks of 'exhibition' as a *hypotyposis*; *K.U.*, §59, 352 (= 255). ὑποτύπωσις—Latin, *adumbratio*—is a kind of sketch or outline. Compare Aristotle, *Eth. Nic.* 1098 a 21 and Plato, *Timaeus*, 76 E.

which share the common form of universality, we can treat events governed by the law of nature as symbols for objects conceived to fall under the law of freedom.¹ If we can do this, we use the law of nature as a type of the moral law.

It must be remembered that in all this Kant has in mind a contrast between the sensible world and the intelligible world, the world of phenomena and the world of noumena, the world of appearances and the world of things-in-themselves. Furthermore, it is no accident that the Idea of the moral law has to be applied through the law of nature and the categories of the understanding. While understanding with its concepts is always directed through schemata to sensible objects, reason, alike in its logical and in its transcendental use, is always directed to the concepts of the understanding, and only through them to sensible objects.² There is always more in Kant's proceedings than meets the eye; but without going into the full implications of his doctrine it is possible to see that events in nature might be used to symbolise moral actions, and that the order in nature might be used to symbolise the moral order, in somewhat the same way as the love of a parent for his child might be used to symbolise the love of God for men.

§5. *The natural order.*

In modern times we may feel more compunction in using the natural order as a symbol of the moral order. This is not only, as I suggested above,³ because the impact of Darwinism dealt a shattering blow to Eighteenth-Century optimism: it is also because modern physics leaves a different emotional impression on the modern mind than that conveyed by the discoveries of Newton to his contemporaries and successors. We have become acutely conscious—especially since the famous Romanes lecture of T. H. Huxley—that the order of nature is compatible with the wildest convulsions, with the collision of stars and the annihilation of worlds. We believe that our own planet must some day become destitute of life and mind, and that the very universe as a whole may be gradually running down. All this has made us less ready to see in nature the working of a divine purpose or any concern for the ideals of men. It is put personally and bitterly by a modern poet:

> 'For nature, heartless, witless nature,
>   Will neither care nor know
> What stranger's feet may find the meadow
>   And trespass there and go,
> Nor ask amid the dews of morning
>   If they are mine or no.'

In contrast with this the discoveries of Newton seem to have left men with a feeling of the order and harmony of the universe as the

---
¹ *K.p.V.*, 69 = 192 (= 122). ² See *K.r.V.*, A302 = B359; A664–6 =B692–4.
³ Chapter XV §5.

manifestation of a divine wisdom. This is expressed in the well-known hymn of Addison—'The spacious firmament on high'—with its interesting denial of the music of the spheres, perhaps on the ground of the unreality of secondary qualities:

> 'What though in solemn silence all
>   Move round the dark terrestrial ball?
> What though no real voice, nor sound,
>   Amidst their radiant orbs be found?
> In Reason's ear they all rejoice,
>   And utter forth a glorious voice;
> For ever singing, as they shine,
>   "The hand that made us is divine." '

We have only to turn to the too much quoted passage about the starry heavens and the moral law in order to see that Kant, in spite of his ruthless insistence upon causal law as the only constitutive law of nature, was deeply affected by this view of the physical universe; and indeed that the two laws, the natural and the moral, however much he might insist on their difference, were closely connected in his emotional experience. This is brought out by the way he couples together Newton and Rousseau—Rousseau who had first opened his eyes to the true nature of moral value. 'Newton was the first to see order and regularity combined with simplicity... and since then comets move in geometrical paths. Rousseau was the first to discover... the deeply hidden nature of man and the concealed law in accordance with which Providence is justified through his observations... since Newton and Rousseau God is justified.'[1]

It is in the light of this attitude, common to Kant and to many of his contemporaries, that the use of the natural order as a symbol for the moral order is to be understood. In the light of this attitude we can also understand more easily how Kant can pass, without any statement of his grounds, from the formal law of nature to teleological laws of human nature as a basis for the rightness or wrongness of our maxims. He is justified in doing this, as I have suggested, because he is dealing with human maxims and human character, which must be regarded as purposive. But this legitimate appeal to a systematic harmony of human purposes he may have found all the easier because he tends to regard the order of nature as itself a systematic harmony, and perhaps even a systematic harmony of purpose, however much he may reject the claim of such beliefs to be treated as scientific knowledge.[2]

§6. *Practical exhibition:*

The theory of the use of symbols as an indirect method of exhibiting concepts and the emotional attitude of the period to the law of nature must be taken into account in understanding Kant's doctrine. But in

---

[1] *Fragmente*, Phil. Bib., VIII, p. 329. This note is probably rather early.
[2] See, for example, *K.r.V.*, A620 ff. = B649 ff.; A691–2 = B719–20.

dealing with the categorical imperative we are not concerned with the theoretical use of symbols, and still less are we concerned with the symbolic expression of emotion. Our concern is with action: 'Act *as if* the maxim of your action were to become *through your will* a universal law of nature.' This is the test of the maxims to be adopted or rejected by a man whose motive is always, at the same time, to obey a universal moral law valid for all rational agents. The problem is to determine for purposes of action which maxims are to be regarded as moral or immoral: indeed it is to exhibit in action itself, and not merely in theory, examples or instances of obedience to the moral law. The problem is one of practical, and not theoretical, exhibition.[1]

Kant's solution is that the actions which can and ought to be willed in obedience to moral law (or 'exhibited' symbolically in practice as instances of such obedience) are those whose maxims, if conceived as a law of nature, would further a systematic harmony of purposes among men, or at least would do nothing to destroy such a systematic harmony. This is a very broad statement: it omits the different ways in which systematic harmony is to be understood according as we are dealing with duties to self or duties to others; it obviously requires a great deal of working out in detail in order to carry full conviction; but in itself it is at least not unreasonable, and it is very far from being the kind of nonsense commonly attributed to Kant. Indeed it may well be doubted whether it is possible to work out a systematic moral philosophy on any other basis, even although we may hold that Kant's own attempt to work it out is in many respects faulty.

Furthermore, Kant is right in saying that an action aiming at a systematic harmony of purposes is not thereby necessarily moral. In his technical language such actions are symbols, not examples, of the moral law; and so far as empirical or scientific knowledge is concerned, they can be nothing more. In order to have genuine goodness these actions must be willed, at the same time, for the sake of the moral law itself. When this motive is present—and we cannot be sure that it is—we can in action produce examples which are, at least approximately, examples of obedience to the moral law and so objects which—in this case alone—can be said to be concrete manifestations, however inadequate, of an Idea of reason.

In this way, according to Kant, we avoid empirical theories of moral philosophy, which suppose, falsely, that actions are good merely according to what is done. The morally good man must have another motive than merely the desire to produce certain results, even such a desirable result as general happiness or a systematic harmony of purpose among men. We also get rid of mystical theories which take as a schema what is merely a symbol and suppose that the moral motive springs from non-sensuous intuitions of an invisible kingdom of God. The danger from mystical theories is less, partly because these are compatible with the purity of the moral law, and partly because they are contrary to the natural thinking of mankind. Empirical theories, on the other hand, destroy

[1] *K.p.V.*, 71 = 194 (= 125).

morality at its roots; for they substitute for duty a merely empirical interest based ultimately upon inclination.[1]

It should be noted further that for Kant, here as always, obligation is derivative and goodness original. He starts from the notion of a good will seeking to obey the moral law as such, and he tells us the kinds of action which would necessarily be performed by such a good and rational will. If we are so irrational as to be tempted to act otherwise, these kinds of action must appear to us as duties, but this is possible only because of the presence of a good will in us; and we cannot say we are acting morally except in so far as we can say that we have performed our duties for the sake of duty or for the sake of moral law as such.

---

[1] $K.p.V.$, 70-1 = 193-4 (= 124-6).

CHAPTER XVI

THE FORMULA OF THE END IN ITSELF

§1. *Formula II.*

'So act as to use humanity, both in your own person and in the person of every other, always at the same time as an end, never simply as a means.'[1]

This new formula may be said to enjoin respect for personality as such. This is necessary to supplement the first formula, which forbids us to be respecters of persons—in the sense of discriminating arbitrarily and unfairly between them. The new formula, like the old, should, once it is understood, receive the immediate approval of ordinary moral judgement.

Strictly speaking, this formula, like all others, should cover rational beings as such; but since the only rational beings with whom we are acquainted are men, we are bidden to respect men as men, or men as rational beings. This is implied in the use of the term 'humanity'—the essential human characteristic of possessing reason, and in particular of possessing a rational will. It is in virtue of this characteristic that we are bound to treat ourselves and others, never simply as a means, but always at the same time as ends.

The words 'at the same time' and 'simply' must not be overlooked: they are absolutely necessary to Kant's statement. Every time we post a letter, we use post-office officials as a means, but we do not use them simply as a means. What we expect of them we believe to be in accordance with their own will, and indeed to be in accordance with their duty. Considerations of this kind do not arise in regard to the stamp which we stick on our letter or the post-box to which we entrust it: they arise only in regard to persons and not to things. So far as we limit our actions by such considerations, we are treating persons 'at the same time' as an end, though we may also be using them as a means.

The formula applies to the agent's treatment of himself as well as of others. Some thinkers hold that all duties are social, and that even our duties to ourselves are duties to a society of which we are members. There are others who hold that all duties are personal, and that if only we respect our own personality, our duties to others will immediately follow. Kant takes the middle path between these one-sided views, but he holds that we could have no duty to others unless we had a duty to ourselves.[2]

It should be added that by 'using persons merely as means' Kant has in mind the using of them as means to the satisfaction of inclination or

[1] *Gr.*, 429 = 57.   [2] *M.d.S.*, *Tugendlehre*, §2, 417–18.

to the attainment of ends based on inclination.¹ To sacrifice one's life in the performance of duty is not to use oneself merely as a means. As we have seen,² it is an error to regard even a good action as a means to the realisation of the law: it *is* a realisation of the law. It would be a still greater error to suppose that in dying for the sake of duty I was using my rational will as a means to a further and merely relative end. Moral sacrifice is a problem not to be dealt with lightly, but at least we can say that sacrifice in the way of duty is not the use of my rational will as a means to the satisfaction of inclination: it is rather the subordination of my inclinations, and even of my life, to an end whose value is incomparable with that of any sensuous satisfaction—the manifestation of a good will as an end in itself.³

§2. *The nature of ends.*

If we are to understand Kant's formula, we must consider what is meant by an end; and in so doing we must look more closely at an aspect of the will hitherto taken for granted. One essential characteristic of a will we have already discussed at length: a rational agent wills—or sets himself to act—in accordance with his conception of laws—that is, in accordance with principles.⁴ There is, however, another essential characteristic to be considered—namely, that the willing of a rational agent is always directed towards an end which he sets before himself.⁵ All willing has an end or purpose as well as a principle.

The concept of 'end' is familiar to us, but it is not altogether easy to define precisely. An end is ordinarily taken to be an effect which the will seeks to produce, but it must be said further that the idea of this effect, or the idea of producing this effect, determines the will: it does so most obviously in inducing us to adopt certain means towards the production of the end. On this level we may with Kant define an end as an object of a free will (*Willkür*), the idea of which determines the free will to an action whereby the object is produced.⁶

The 'idea' of an object must here be a concept: it is more than a mere image or sensum, as when the smell or sight of a rabbit induces a dog to pursue and kill. Man knows what he is doing in purposive action, and this means that we must have a concept of the object to be produced, although naturally images may, and perhaps must, be present as well. Hence Kant says also that an end is the object of a concept so far as the concept is regarded as the cause of the object (the real ground of its possibility).⁷ Perhaps we may put this otherwise by saying that here, as always, our

[1] This is expressly stated in *Gr.*, 436 = 66.
[2] Chapter VII §3.
[3] I have discussed this problem in *The Good Will*, pp. 397 ff.
[4] *Gr.*, 427 = 55 and 412 = 36. See also Chapter VIII §5.
[5] *Gr.*, 437 = 67; *K.p.V.*, 58–9 = 178 (= 103); *M.d.S., Tugendlehre, Einl.* III, 385 = 229; *Einl.* VIII, 392 = 238.
[6] *M.d.S., Tugendlehre, Einl.* I, 381 = 224; *Einl.* III, 384 = 229.
[7] *K.U.*, §10, 220 (= 32); *Einl.* IV, 180 (= xxviii).

action has a maxim or principle, the principle of producing an object conceived as being of a certain kind. As Kant says elsewhere, ends are always 'determining grounds of the will in accordance with principles'.[1] Needless to say this does not exclude either images of the objects or desires for the object.

Kant tends to speak of an end as if it could only be an effect of the action, like a house or picture, but clearly it may also be the action itself, as in the case of playing games.[2] Furthermore, where the sight or thought of an apple is the starting point of a purposive action, the end of the action is the eating of the apple, not the apple itself, so that here too it looks as if the action itself is our end. Even where our action aims at producing something, as in the building of a house, it may be that our end is not the house itself, but rather the possession of the house. But complications of this kind must here be ignored.

For our present purposes, the important point is the connexion between ends and principles. We will the end freely, but in willing this particular end we must will in accordance with a particular maxim, so that the end may be said to be the ground of our maxim, and thus to be the ground which determines our will in accordance with a principle. So far we have spoken only of maxims or subjective principles; but we must add—and this is the absolutely essential point—that our chosen ends are the ground also of objective principles, the ground of hypothetical imperatives. A rational agent, if he wills the end, ought to will the means; and in this sense ends are grounds which determine our rational wills in accordance with principles which are objective, although hypothetical.[3]

This may be part of what Kant means when he defines an end—most obscurely—as that which serves as an objective ground for the self-determination of the will.[4] At any rate he goes on to point out that ends —material ends—which are arbitrary products of our will are only relative; that their worth is relative to the special constitution of the agent (or, as I should say, they are 'good for' him); and finally that they can be the ground only of hypothetical imperatives. They cannot be the ground of categorical imperatives since these are not conditioned by the fact that we happen to desire the production of a particular effect.

§3. *Ends in themselves.*

So far we are on comparatively familiar territory. The new problem we have to face is the relation between ends and categorical imperatives: There must be such a relation, since every categorical imperative enjoins action and every action must have an end.[5]

---

[1] *K.p.V.*, 59 = 178 (= 103).
[2] Compare also Chapter X §1.
[3] See Chapter IX, especially §§1-2.
[4] *Gr.*, 427 = 55. By 'objective ground' he may possibly mean here merely 'a ground in objects'.
[5] *M.d.S.*, *Tugendlehre*, Einl. I, 381 = 224; Einl. III, 385 = 229.

If this is so, there must be ends given us by mere reason itself, not by reason at the service of inclination. These ends must be valid for every rational being; they must be objective ends, not merely subjective ones; they must be absolute and not relative; they must have an absolute and not a relative worth, being good in themselves and not merely good for a particular kind of agent. To say this is to say that they must be ends in themselves.[1]

It may be thought that we know the solution to this problem already. It is open to Kant to say that the ends enjoined by the categorical imperative are simply moral actions willed for the sake of duty, which he recognises to be good in themselves. It is also open to him to say that the effects which such actions seek to produce—such as one's own natural and moral perfection and the happiness of others—must by extension be regarded as objective ends, at least in those contexts where it is our duty to pursue them. In his own terminology these are ends which are also duties.[2]

All this is sound Kantian doctrine, but in his eyes it is apparently not enough. This may be partly because the products of moral action are not absolutely good, good in any and every context; and because even morally good actions, though good in themselves, are not absolutely good, good in every respect and the supreme condition of all good, such absolute goodness belonging only to a good will.[3]

An action is morally good because it is the manifestation of a good will, and the categorical imperative in enjoining morally good action in accordance with a universal law is enjoining that a good will as such should be manifested and not thwarted by mere inclination. A good will manifesting itself in action is the end enjoined by the categorical imperative; and it must follow from the very nature of a categorical imperative that I ought to respect the rational wills of all moral agents including myself and not subordinate them to mere inclination.

Another reason for Kant's view appears to be that he is looking for an absolute end which can itself be the *ground* of categorical imperatives in somewhat the same way as relative ends are the ground of hypothetical imperatives. If anything could be the ground of categorical imperatives, it would fall under Kant's definition of an end; for it would be 'a ground determining our will in accordance with principles', which in this case would be not only objective principles, but also categorical principles valid for every rational agent as such.[4]

In using this language Kant is manifestly extending the meaning of the word 'end'. An objective and absolute end could not be a product of our will; for no mere product of our will can have absolute value. An end in itself must therefore be a self-existent end, not something to be produced by us. Since it has absolute value, we know already what it

---

[1] *Gr.*, 427–8 = 55.
[2] *M.d.S.*, *Tugendlehre*, *Einl.* III–IV, 384 ff. = 229 ff.
[3] *K.p.V.*, 62 = 182 (= 109).
[4] It would presumably also serve as an objective ground for the self-determination of the will, according to the obscure definition in *Gr.*, 427 = 55.

must be—namely, a good will.[1] This good or rational will Kant takes to be present in every rational agent, and so in every man, however much it may be overlaid by irrationality. Hence man, and indeed every rational agent as such, must be said to exist as an end in itself, one which should never be used simply as a means to the realisation of some end whose value is merely relative.

It may seem arbitrary to speak of existent things as ends, yet it is true that the existence of persons does determine a rational will, *qua* rational, in a way analogous to the way in which the adoption of an end determines a rational will. Furthermore, since the existent things in question have rational wills, it is possible to further, or at least to refrain from overriding, their rational volitions. When we do this, not from mere inclination only, but also at the command of reason, we are treating rational agents, not as mere means, but also as ends in themselves, and the phrase 'end in itself' becomes less inappropriate than at first sight it seems. No doubt it is difficult to make this conception theoretically precise, but we may say provisionally with Kant that the will of a rational person is not to be subjected to any purpose which cannot accord with a law which could arise from the will of the person affected himself.[2]

We must distinguish sharply between this duty to respect the will of others and a mere prudential adjustment to them. We may further the inclinations and happiness of others because this satisfies our own inclinations or administers to our own happiness: to do this is to use them as a means. We may also yield prudentially to their pressure or threats, and in this we are treating them like any other obstacle which we have to overcome or avoid. There is no difference in principle between running away from a bandit out of concern for our own safety and running away from an avalanche or a man-eating tiger. In prudential adjustment to others we treat them as means or as obstacles to our satisfaction, as we may treat inanimate objects and animals. This is something quite different from treating them as ends in themselves.

§4. *Grounds and ends.*

It may still seem puzzling that Kant should regard rational agents both as the objective ends enjoined by categorical imperatives and also as the grounds of such imperatives.

There is no difficulty in seeing that the end of an action is also its ground and so the ground of the maxim embodied in the action. Nor is there any difficulty in seeing that in hypothetical imperatives of skill the end chosen is the ground of these imperatives, though these imperatives enjoin only the means to the end and not the end itself. In the case of hypothetical imperatives of self-love their ground is the happiness of the agent, and it is also the end enjoined—so far as we take these imperatives

---

[1] Kant establishes this afresh by eliminating the claims of objects of inclination, inclinations themselves, and mere irrational things whose existence is a product of nature; *Gr.*, 428 = 56. Compare *Gr.*, 400 = 20.
[2] *K.p.V.*, 87 = 215 (= 156).

to be concerned, not with the means to happiness in the sense of continuous pleasure, but with the harmonisation of the ends set before us by inclination.[1]

Granted that a categorical imperative enjoins the treatment of rational agents as ends-in-themselves, in what sense can we say that rational agents are also the grounds of a categorical imperative?

There seem to be three senses in which this can be said. Firstly, it is because rational agents exist that a categorical imperative must enjoin respect for their rational wills. Secondly, it is because rational agents exist with wills which can be thwarted or furthered in different ways that we must recognise particular categorical imperatives: we ought not to thwart their wills by fraud or violence, and we ought to further their happiness. Thirdly, it is only because rational agents exist that there can be such a thing as a categorical imperative at all. Because agents are rational, their will necessarily manifests itself in universal laws. Because they are imperfectly rational, these universal laws must appear as categorical imperatives. The categorical imperative has its ground in the will of rational agents who are not completely rational.[2]

It is the first two senses that Kant presumably has in mind when he speaks of man as the ground of a possible categorical imperative and of particular categorical imperatives. But the ultimate reason why man can be such a ground is because he is a ground in the third sense: it is because the categorical imperative has its origin in his rational will that his rational will ought not to be subordinated to any meaner end but is itself an end which the categorical imperative must bid us to further and not to thwart.

§5. *The approach to Formula II.*

Kant's approach to Formula II is over-subtle, and there are four main strands to be distinguished in his argument. There is first of all the argument from the essence of a categorical imperative, the ends which it imposes, and the grounds on which it rests. This is the argument we have just considered. It is supplemented by a second argument based on the way in which rational agents as such must conceive themselves—namely, as agents capable of acting in accordance with rational laws of freedom and therefore not to be subjected as a mere means to the satisfaction of inclination.[3] In the final summary we have a third argument starting from the conception of an absolutely good will and its objects, instead of from the essence of a categorical imperative, but otherwise following in

---

[1] See Chapter VIII §8. They contain 'the rule of prudence in the choice of ends'; *M.d.S., Tugendlehre, Einl.* III, 385 = 230.
[2] This accords with Kant's general view that while *a priori* principles cannot have their ground in objects, they can have their ground and origin in reason; *K.r.V.*, A148–9 = B188. Similarly categorical imperatives cannot, like hypothetical ones, have their ground in objects, but they can have their ground and origin in practical reason. An imperative so grounded must enjoin respect for rational wills as ends, and rational wills thereby become grounds in a derivative sense.
[3] *Gr.*, 429 = 57 as supplemented by *Gr.*, 447–8 = 80–1.

brief the same line as the first argument.[1] This is followed by a fourth argument—perhaps the easiest of all—which maintains that Formula II is already implicit in Formula I, if we consider action on its purposive side.[2]

This multiplicity of arguments is typical of Kant's method, but, as they are somewhat complicated, I reserve them for treatment in an appendix. At the risk of over-simplification we may say that they all rest on one principle, the principle that a good will has a unique and absolute value. Granted that this is so, it must be wrong to subordinate it as a mere means to any end of lesser value, such as the satisfaction of personal inclinations. It must indeed be a duty, not merely to refrain from thwarting its manifestations in action, but also to further these manifestations so far as it is in our power to do so. This is a principle on which any rational agent, whose reason had full control over passion, would necessarily act, and it is one on which he ought to act if he is irrational enough to be tempted to do otherwise.

There is a further point. As Kant well knows, men are not saints, and for this reason it may at times be necessary to refrain from furthering their ends and even to thwart their wills. This must introduce qualifications into applications of our principle, especially when we have to consider the function of the State. Nevertheless—and this is a fundamental conviction of Kant—a good will is present in every man, however much it may be overlaid by selfishness, and however little it may be manifested in action.[3] Because of this he is still entitled to respect and is not to be treated as a mere instrument or a mere thing.[4] As a being capable of moral action, a man, however degraded, has still an infinite potential value; and his freedom to work out his own salvation in his own way must not be restricted except in so far as it impinges on the like freedom of others. We shall never understand Kant aright unless we see him as the apostle of human freedom and the champion of the common man.

§6. *Kinds of duty.*

Like Formula I, Formula II is a supreme practical principle from which all other laws of the will may be derived.[5]

In the light of our discussion it is easy to see how this principle gives rise to the distinction between perfect and imperfect duties. So far as we take the principle negatively it forbids us to use rational agents merely as a means and so to override the rational wills of moral agents in order merely to satisfy our own inclinations. This is the basis of perfect duties, and it forbids such wrongs as murder, violence, and fraud, as also suicide and lying. It lies at the root of Kant's philosophy of legal obligation. But

---

[1] *Gr.*, 437 = 67–8.   [2] *Gr.*, 437–8 = 68. See also *Gr.*, 431 = 59.
[3] See also Chapter XXV, §§2, 10, and 11.
[4] *M.d.S.*, *Tugendlehre*, §39, 463. For this reason, Kant holds, men should never be subjected to shameful punishments.
[5] *Gr.*, 429 = 57.

we must also take our principle positively: it bids us to act on the maxim of furthering the ends of rational agents. Here, it must be remembered, there is a place or 'play-room' for discretion. This positive interpretation is for Kant the basis of positive and ethical, as opposed to legal, obligations.

We transgress perfect duties by treating any person merely as a means. We transgress imperfect duties by failing to treat a person as an end, even though we do not actively treat him merely as a means.

The difference between duties to self and duties to others is commonly recognised, though in some respects it is not easy to account for such a difference. Kant pushes this difference very far in regard to imperfect duties by insisting that our duty to ourselves is to seek as an end our own natural and moral perfection but not our happiness; and that our duty to others is to seek as an end their happiness but not their perfection. It may, however, be our duty to seek our own happiness as a means to our moral welfare; and it may be our duty to seek the moral welfare of others in a negative sense. We ought not to tempt them to courses of action which might be likely to cause them pangs of remorse.[1]

§7. *Kant's illustrations.*

As might be expected in the case of a formula dealing specifically with ends, Kant's illustrations[2] bring out more clearly—and in some cases more satisfactorily—the teleological implications which we saw in the previous chapter to be involved in his appeal to a universal law of nature.

1. *Suicide.* The man who commits suicide because the disagreeable prospects of life seem to overbalance the agreeable ones is making pleasure and the avoidance of pain his final end; and in him practical reason, which is capable of realising absolute moral worth, is being subordinated as a mere means to the relative end of avoiding discomfort. If—apart from all questions of duty to others—there can be a right to commit suicide, this can be justified only on the ground that there is no longer any possibility of living a moral life and manifesting moral worth. Such cases may arise when pain is unendurable or insanity certain. Suicide cannot be justified lightly on the ground of mere discomfort, however gently we may judge those whose misfortunes have brought them to so desperate a state of mind. Kant's principle is fundamentally sound even if he may—and I do not say that he does—interpret it with undue rigidity.

2. *Promises to repay loans.* In extracting money from others by false promises it is obvious that we are using them as mere means and not as ends. As Kant says, this is still more obvious in crimes of violence. What is interesting is Kant's view that to treat others as ends in themselves is to treat them in such a way that their rational wills can be in agreement with ours and that they must be able 'to contain in themselves' the end of our action towards them.

---

[1] *M.d.S., Tugendlehre, Einl.* VIII, 394 = 240.   [2] *Gr.*, 429–30 = 57–9.

3. *Culture.* As to the imperfect duty of developing one's talents, failure to do this is not actively to use oneself only as a means: we are still maintaining humanity in ourselves, and not destroying it, but we are failing actively to further humanity in ourselves as an end. Here again Kant bids us assume that it is the purpose of nature to develop humanity in us—that is, to develop in us especially those powers which distinguish us from the brutes.[1] In this argument 'humanity' covers, not only our rational will, but all our rational powers as manifested in art and science, and indeed our bodily powers so far as these are necessary for the leading of a human life.[2]

4. *Kindness.* In the case of imperfect duties towards others—here the duties primarily of kindness or benevolence—Kant recognises that the natural end of man (which is to be distinguished from the end or purpose of nature)[3] is happiness. If we are to harmonise positively, and not merely negatively, with humanity in others, as an end in itself—that is, if we are to further it actively, and not merely to refrain from violating it—we must make this natural end of others, as far as possible, our own. This means that we must, as far as possible, further the relative ends of others. To treat other men as ends in themselves, if this idea is to have its full effect, must be to make their ends, their relative and personal ends, as far as possible our own.

The phrase 'as far as possible' presumably indicates two things: (1) that it is not within our powers to further the ends of all men equally, and all that is enjoined is the adoption of a maxim which must be applied with discretion; and (2) that we ought to further the ends of others only so far as they are not manifestly foolish or incompatible with the moral law.

§8. *The soundness of Kant's view.*

It may be objected to Kant's principle that having first of all told us that a rational agent ought to act on the principles on which every rational agent would act (if reason had full control over passion), he is now telling us that every rational agent ought to be treated in the way every rational agent would will to be treated (if reason had full control over our passion). To tell us this is to tell us precisely nothing.

Such a view in the first place complains that when Kant sets out to state the *form* of moral action, he does state the form of moral action, and not its matter. It is hard to see why he alone among philosophers should be blamed for being consistent. If we are not interested in the form of moral action, there is no reason why we should study Kant's moral philosophy.

In the second place such a view forgets that Kant is trying to state

[1] Compare also *Gr.*, 438–9 = 58–9.
[2] *M.d.S., Tugendlehre, Einl.* VIII, 391–2 = 237–8; §19, 444–5.
[3] *K.U.*, §67, 378 (= 299).

the form of moral *action*, the supreme principle of a rational *will*. He is trying to formulate clearly the principle upon which, however vaguely envisaged, good men have acted, and upon which we ought to act. If we consider his principle from the point of view of agents, and not of logicians, we shall find that it throws a flood of light upon what we ought to do and what we ought not to do. The difference between the good man and the average sensual man is surely that the former recognises the infinite and unique value of all moral agents and treats them in accordance with this value, while the latter does not. The adoption of this principle in action constitutes a moral revolution in the soul of man, as does the adoption of the Formula of Universal Law.[1]

It may be said that this is a mere excuse for vagueness of thought, the substitution of an emotional attitude for the clear analysis incumbent on a philosopher. What is the use of telling us to adopt an attitude, a spirit, a principle of action, if you don't know and can't say what the principle is?

The answer is that we do know what the principle is, although, like many other things which we know, it may be extremely difficult to formulate with precision. Kant has done his best to formulate it, and it may be doubted whether anyone has formulated it better. If the complaint about lack of precision means that his formulation does not contain in itself the criterion of its own application, this is a perfectly outrageous demand to make. There are no moral principles, there are not even moral laws or moral rules, which can be applied mechanically or by any method of logical deduction without practical judgement and moral insight. If Kant thought that there were—and I do not believe he did—he may be blamed for so thinking; but we cannot both blame him and at the same time accept this thought as the basis of our own criticisms.

What we can say is that there is a vast field open for discussion as to the way in which Kant himself applies his principles. This, however, cannot be done without a careful examination of his *Metaphysic of Morals*. In the *Groundwork* he attempts no more than to show by way of illustration how certain types of accepted virtues and vices fall under his principle. In this he succeeds—so far as it is possible to succeed without entering into an elaborate discussion of various kinds of circumstances which might form the context of action. And once more he has shown clearly enough that the natural desires and powers and purposes of men constitute, on his view, the matter which has to be organised within the framework of moral principle.

We must indeed recognise that the systematic application of Kant's principles will offer more difficulty than he anticipates,[2] and that it may not be easy to formulate, let alone to justify, the further presuppositions on which his exposition rests. But these considerations belong to another enquiry.

---

[1] See Chapter XV §12.   [2] *Gr.*, 392 = 9.

§9. *Special characteristics of Formula II.*

It should be observed that the Formula of the End in Itself has no subordinate formula to be used in its application, whereas the Formula of Universal Law has a subordinate formula (Formula Ia), in which the law of nature is used as a 'type' for the application of the moral law. This difference is more apparent than real. The Idea of 'humanity'—which, strictly speaking, ought to be the Idea of 'personality' or of a 'rational will'—is applied through the concept of 'man' as a rational animal with distinctive powers and personal desires and needs; and the ideal systematic harmony of human purposes is the test of moral action even more clearly than it was before.

In this connexion it should also be noted that Kant speaks of the possibility that those affected by my action should themselves 'contain' the end of my action; and says also that I should make the ends of other rational agents, as far as possible, also my own. Here too we have a conception which requires a lot of working out. There is clearly more in question than mere approval; but it is not easy to express precisely the sense in which different agents may have the same ends so far as their actions are willed in accordance with the same universal law.

The Formula of the End in Itself is in Kant's mind closely connected with freedom. Men can compel me to perform actions which are directed towards certain ends, but they cannot compel me to adopt any end as my own.[1] This is why ethics proper is concerned with purposes (and so with motives), while the theory of law is concerned only with external actions. This is also one reason why Kant can pass from this present formula to the Formula of Autonomy (Formula III).

If Formula I is supposed to deal with maxims in relative isolation—though this may be doubted—Formula II marks a real step forward in bidding us consider individual persons as wholes. It must, however, be itself inadequate, unless we consider the individual agent more explicitly as a member of society. This Kant proceeds to do in Formula IIIa, but he does so by first passing through Formula III.

APPENDIX

ARGUMENTS IN SUPPORT OF FORMULA II

The main strands of Kant's argument may be worked out as follows:

§1. *Argument from the essence of the categorical imperative.*

First of all there is an argument from the essence of the categorical imperative itself, the argument examined in Chapter XVI, §§3-4 above. We may put it here summarily for the sake of completeness.

[1] *M.d.S., Tugendlehre, Einl.* I. 381 = 224.

If there is a categorical imperative, it must enjoin upon us objective and absolute ends. Since these ends must have absolute worth, they cannot be the relative ends which we seek to produce: they must be rational agents or, for practical purposes, men. Without this there could be no absolute worth and so no categorical imperative. Hence the categorical imperative must bid us treat men as absolute ends or as ends in themselves.[1]

Worked in with this conclusion is the view that men, considered as ends in themselves, are the *ground*, both of a possible categorical imperative (that is, of Formula II), and also of particular categorical imperatives.[2]

§2. *Argument from the nature of rational agents.*

In a different sense of 'ground' the ground of our present formula is said to be 'Rational nature exists as an end in itself.'[3] Kant seems to take this as an independent starting point; and it is supported by a new and obscure argument, which may be called the argument from the nature of rational agents as such.

Every man, he says, necessarily regards his own existence as an end in itself; and since every other man does the same as regards *his* existence on the same rational ground which is valid also for me, this is not merely a subjective principle, but also an objective principle valid for every one: it is, in fact, the basis or ground of our present formula.

This is too brief to be intelligible, and it looks like a fallacy worthy of John Stuart Mill himself. Kant might be taken as arguing that because each man takes a self-centred interest in his own welfare, therefore all men ought to take an interest in the welfare of all. We must, however, note Kant's assertion that the ground of the judgement which other men make about their own existence is 'the same rational ground which is valid also for me'. For the justification of this assertion we are referred, rather vaguely, to Chapter III of the *Groundwork*. I take him to mean by this the section on the necessary presupposition of freedom, which begins by saying that it is not enough to ascribe freedom to our own rational will on whatever ground: we must show it to be presupposed by every rational agent as such.[4]

If the passage about freedom is the key to the present passage, Kant means that when I regard myself as an end in myself, I am regarding myself as a moral agent subject to moral law and so of infinite value. I must do this in virtue of my nature as a rational agent, and so must every other man. Hence this principle is an objective principle valid for all rational agents as such and applying to all rational agents as such. In

---

[1] *Gr.*, 428–9 = 55–7. [2] *Gr.*, 427–8 = 55 and 428–9 = 56–7.
[3] *Gr.*, 429 = 57. See also *Gr.*, 428 = 56. [4] *Gr.*, 447–8 = 80–1.

virtue of my rational nature as such I must regard—and treat—all persons (including myself) as moral agents.[1]

If this is the correct interpretation, it is similar to Kant's insistence that every man regards himself as subject to moral law, even in transgressing it.[2] Perhaps there is also the suggestion that what is an end *to* itself must also be an end *in* itself, and therefore necessarily an end for every man.[3]

§3. *Argument from the character of a good will.*

In the final summary of his argument[4] Kant—as is his habit—seems to break new ground. Here he starts neither from the essence of a categorical imperative nor from the essential nature of a rational agent, but from an absolutely good will, which is the fundamental basis of his whole moral philosophy.

Every rational will must in its actions set before itself an end; but in considering a good will we have to abstract from the ends it seeks to produce, since a good will, as we have seen, cannot derive its absolute goodness from the attainment of such ends. Kant assumes, however, that even thus considered in abstraction a good will must still have an end—in a sense an abstract end—and that this end must therefore be an already existent end. This means that it is an end only in a negative sense, something against which a good will must never act, and therefore something never to be treated merely as a means.[5] He adds, as before, that this end must be the subject of all possible ends—that is, a good or rational will itself. The fundamental contention—which one might have thought could stand by itself without all this preparation—is that an absolutely good will, and even the human being capable of manifesting such a will, cannot be subordinated as a means to any object of merely relative worth without contradiction—that is, without a breach of rational and coherent willing.

§4. *Argument from the Formula of Universal Law.*

Kant's final and most obvious argument[6] is that Formula II is already implicit in Formula I, if we take into account the purposive as well as the formal side of human action. This argument may also be regarded as following from the essence of the categorical imperative; for Formula I merely states the essence of the categorical imperative.[7]

---

[1] Compare also the statement, in *Gr.*, 428 = 56, that the nature of persons as rational beings marks them out already as ends in themselves—that is, as something which ought not to be used merely as a means.
[2] *Gr.*, 424 = 51.   [3] Compare *Gr.*, 428 = 57.
[4] *Gr.*, 437–8 = 67–8.
[5] In this negative statement he appears to forget imperfect duties.
[6] *Gr.*, 437–8 = 68.   [7] *Gr.*, 420–1 = 46–7.

My material maxims are always maxims of using means to some end. Formula I bids me act on these maxims subject to a limiting condition—that they can be valid as laws for every rational agent. Since these laws are laws of freedom, laws in accordance with which every rational agent as such can *will*, this means that the will of every rational agent is a limiting condition in my use of means to an end; and this means in turn that my adoption of maxims is subject to a limiting condition, that of not using rational agents merely as means.

I will try to put this less technically. Formula I bids me act only on maxims which can be universal laws for all men. Since these laws are laws of freedom, this means that in determining my actions I have to take into account the rational wills of other men: I ought to act only in such a way that as rational beings they can act on the same law as I. Hence their rational wills limit my actions and must not be arbitrarily overridden by me. That is to say, I ought not to use them merely as means to the satisfaction of my desires. Similarly I ought not to use my own rational will merely as a means to the satisfaction of my desires.

In this argument Kant concentrates both on the law, and on the existence of rational agents, as *limiting* conditions of my arbitrary will. But the fact that we also have imperfect duties, which are positive, shows this treatment to be unduly negative. If the aim of a good man is the realisation of an objective and universal moral law for its own sake, then as a rational agent he must be concerned, not only to refrain from thwarting, but also positively to further, all actions of others as well as of himself so far as these actions accord with the moral law. No doubt we are more immediately concerned with the realisation of our own maxims; but from a moral, and so impersonal, point of view, this is not because they happen to be *our* maxims, but because their realisation is more under our control. The good man is concerned with the realisation of good as such, whether it is realised through himself or through another; and if this is so, he can no more subordinate the rational will of others to his own inclinations than he can subordinate his own rational will to his inclinations.

§5. *Summary*.

The multiplicity of Kant's arguments and the subtlety of his thought tend to weaken the force of a doctrine which can be stated with comparative simplicity. Morality can be regarded in various ways—as obedience to a categorical imperative, as the manifestation of a good will, and as the expression of our rational nature in action; and Kant complicates his argument by bringing in all these different ways. But his essential point may be expressed thus: if morality, however regarded, is the control of inclination by a rational will obedient to universal law, it cannot but be immoral to use a rational will in ourselves or others merely as a means to the satisfaction of inclination (or to the attainment of ends set up by reason solely at the service of inclination). This does not exclude the pursuit of relative ends which satisfy the inclinations of ourselves and others; indeed under certain conditions it positively enjoins the pursuit of such ends;[1] but it does mean that these relative ends must be limited by, and subordinate to, an ultimate end—the realisation of a good will in myself and in others.

---

[1] Compare *Gr.*, 433 = 62.

CHAPTER XVII

THE FORMULA OF AUTONOMY

§1. *Formula III.*

'*So act that your will can regard itself at the same time as making universal law through its maxim.*'[1]

This formula is based on the principle that a rational will makes, or gives itself, the laws which it obeys—the principle of autonomy. In the *Critique of Practical Reason*[2] it is described as the fundamental law of pure practical reason. It is there expressed as follows: '*So act that the maxim of your will can always at the same time be valid as a principle making universal law.*'

At first sight this new formula seems to add nothing to Formula I. In bidding us act only on a maxim through which we can at the same time *will* that it should become a universal law, Formula I is already suggesting that a rational will is its own law-maker or law-giver. Nevertheless in Formula I the emphasis is on the objectivity of the moral law and the necessitation or compulsion which it exercises on an imperfectly rational will. Formula III brings out what is only implicit in Formula I. It does not indeed deny necessitation or compulsion; for it is a formula of duty. But it insists that the necessitation or compulsion is exercised by our own rational will. We make the law which we obey. The will is not merely subject to law: it is so subject that it must also be regarded as making the law, and as subject to the law only because it makes the law.[3] Autonomy is the source of the unconditioned or absolute worth which belongs to moral persons as making laws and not merely obeying them.[4]

It should be noted that where I speak of 'making universal law', translators and others often speak of 'universal legislation'. This means nothing at all. 'Universal law-making'—or more literally 'universal law-giving'—does not mean 'universal legislation'. The word 'universal' qualifies the law, not the making—just as in English an antique furniture dealer is not an antique gentleman who deals in furniture but a gentleman who deals in antique furniture.

---

[1] *Gr.*, 434 = 63.
[2] *K.p.V.*, 30 = 141 (= 54). In *Gr.*, 440 = 71 the autonomy of the will is described as 'the supreme principle of morality'.
[3] *Gr.*, 431 = 60.   [4] *Gr.*, 439–40 = 71

§2. The approach to Formula III.

As is his wont, Kant arrives at Formula III in a number of ways which he does not sharply distinguish from one another. He suggests that Formula III follows from combining Formula I and Formula II.[1] But he also suggests, as I have already done, that Formula III can be derived directly from Formula I;[2] and again that it can come out of Formula II.[3] In yet another passage he speaks as if the inference were from Formula I to Formula II, and from Formula II to Formula III.[4] Finally, as in other cases, he proposes to derive Formula III from the essence of a categorical imperative as such.

Kant would have helped the reader considerably if he had been more methodical in setting forth his arguments. Nevertheless we must remember that he is writing a treatise on moral philosophy, not on mathematics. Any clever man who adopts the modern practice of taking words as if they were mathematical symbols which can be substituted for one another in accordance with grammatical rules without any regard to what is being said can make nonsense of any kind of moral philosophy. What we must remember is that Kant always has his eye very closely on what he is talking about, and that he is endeavouring to bring out the different aspects essentially involved in moral action as such.

The really important point is to see why Kant lays such stress on Formula II in his passage to Formula III.

The main reason is clearly this. In enjoining respect for rational wills as such Formula II already suggests that the moral law must originate in rational wills: as he says, they are the *ground* both of a categorical imperative and of particular categorical imperatives.[5] But there is perhaps also a further reason: the setting of ends before oneself is the essential mark of freedom. By force or threats I can be compelled to actions which are directed as means to certain ends; but I can never be compelled by others to make anything my end.[6] If I make anything my end, I do so of my own free will; and if duty or the law enjoins, as it does, the adoption of certain ends, and in particular if it enjoins the treating of all rational persons as ends in themselves, then the compulsion or necessitation always present in duty must spring from my own free and rational will. I must be the source and author of the law to which I am subjected.

Hence Formula II, in enjoining the pursuit of ends, implicitly asserts the autonomy of the will in making the laws which it ought to obey. Or, if we prefer it, we may say that it is the combination of the Idea of law (as expressed in Formula I) and the Idea of an end in itself (as expressed in Formula II) which gives rise to the Idea of autonomy—the making of universal laws whereby I impose ends on myself.

---

[1] *Gr.*, 431 = 60. Compare also *Gr.*, 436 = 66, though there he passes directly to the kingdom of ends.
[2] *Gr.*, 434 = 63.
[3] *Gr.*, 434 = 64 and *Gr.*, 435 = 65.
[4] *Gr.*, 438 = 68.
[5] See Chapter XVI §4.
[6] *M.d.S.*, *Tugendlehre*, Einl. I., 381 = 224.

§3. *The exclusion of pathological interest.*

There is a further strand of argument in Kant's attempt to derive Formula III directly from the essence of a categorical imperative as such.[1]

Because the moral imperative is categorical and unconditioned, every formulation of it must *implicitly* exclude interest, that is, pathological interest: it is not, like a hypothetical imperative, conditioned by the presence of a pathological interest in us. Formula III *explicitly* excludes interest; for to say that a moral will is autonomous, that it makes its own law, is to say that it is not determined by any interest. To be determined by interest, and so by desire and inclination, is to be heteronomous, to be subject to a law not of our own making, and so ultimately to a law of nature, which here must be a law of empirical psychology, the law of our own needs.[2]

Hence we can say 'If there is a categorical imperative, the moral will which obeys it must not be determined by interest, and therefore must itself make the universal laws which it is unconditionally bound to obey.' This is the principle set forth explicitly in Formula III.

It should be noted that while the principle of autonomy can thus be established by analysis of the concept of morality and the concept of a categorical imperative, it cannot, according to Kant, be established by analysis of the concept of 'rational being' or 'rational will'. It remains a synthetic, and not an analytic, practical proposition.[3]

§4. *Legislating through maxims.*

There is another side of Kant's doctrine which is apt to be overlooked. Kant is not saying merely that in every man there is present, however obscurely, a pure practical reason which necessarily wills in accordance with law as such and imposes this as an ideal by reference to which the maxims of action are to be selected and rejected. He is saying that a rational agent ought to act in such a way that he can regard himself at the same time as making universal law *through his maxims*.[4]

This serves to bring out Kant's view of spontaneity or freedom. On the one hand he insists—in a way which leads almost inevitably to misunderstanding—that the free and autonomous and moral will must be influenced by no needs, no desires, no pathological interests, in determining its duty.[5] On the other hand he does not forget that our sensuous motives must be 'taken up' into our maxim, if they are to influence action;[6] nor does he forget that if we are to have moral action, our

---

[1] *Gr.*, 431–2 = 60–1.
[2] *Gr.*, 439 = 70. But see also Chapter XX §8. [3] *Gr.*, 440 = 71–2.
[4] Compare the curious use of the preposition 'through' even in Formula I; *Gr.*, 421 = 47. See also *Gr.*, 439 = 70 and 432 = 61.
[5] See, for example, *Gr.*, 441 = 72–3.
[6] *Religion*, 23–4 = 24–5 (= 12). See also Chapters IV §2 and VIII §5.

maxims must in turn be taken up into our rational volition of law as such. Because of this it is possible for moral men to make, or to give, particular moral laws *through their maxims*. The Idea of law as such has its origin in pure practical reason, but the making of particular moral laws constitutes the dignity and prerogative of *man* as a rational animal; for the maxims *through* which he legislates are based upon his sensuous nature and not only upon pure reason.[1]

The common criticisms of Kant—that his ethics are purely formal, that he forgets the need for every form to have a matter, that he ignores the sensuous and empirical element in morality—all spring from a curious blindness to this side of his doctrine. Even when it is observed that in practice Kant always brings in sensuous and material considerations, there is a tendency to say 'You see how inconsistent he is, and how impossible it is to work out a purely formal ethics!' But on this point Kant is not inconsistent. The alleged inconsistency arises only because first of all a one-sided view is imposed on Kant by the critic, and then all deviations from this view are regarded as mere lapses. As a consequence Kant's views are made to appear doubly ridiculous. Once we adopt the hypothesis that Kant means what he says, and that he is engaged in analysing the formal side of moral actions which have always both a form and a matter, his whole doctrine becomes reasonable and intelligible, and a vast mass of traditional difficulties begin to disappear. His theory will still have difficulties, as all theories have; but we shall no longer have to face the difficulty of explaining why Kant came to hold moral beliefs which could not conceivably have been held by any man of moderate intelligence and ordinary common sense.

§5. *The application of Formula III.*

All this is very important if we are to understand Kant's view of the application of the categorical imperative. It must be applied not by thinking in abstraction, but by action.

Since human reason is discursive, every Idea, every principle, and indeed every concept, must be abstract: it must contain less than the instances which fall under it.[2] In the case of theoretical principles, where they can have concrete instances, we are able to apply them by the observation of nature. Thus while we can say *a priori* that every event must have some cause, we cannot say *a priori* what the cause will be; but we can, as it were, fill up our abstract formula by the study of regular sequences in the phenomenal world. This method of procedure is not open to us where we are dealing with Ideas, including practical Ideas; for *ex hypothesi* Ideas can have no instances which it is possible to observe. Yet, as Kant explicitly recognises, *the particular cannot be derived (abgeleitet) from the universal by itself.*[3]

[1] *Gr.*, 438 = 68–9. A kingdom of ends is possible *only* in accordance with maxims or self-imposed rules.
[2] *K.U.*, §77, 407 (= 348–9).   [3] *K.U.*, §77, 406 (= 348).

In Kant's technical language we cannot directly 'exhibit' an instance or instances of the categorical imperative, but we can exhibit such instances 'symbolically' in action so far as we act upon maxims through which we may regard ourselves at the same time as making universal laws.[1] These maxims, provided we can act *as if* they were to become through our action teleological laws of nature, can be regarded as what he calls 'types' of the moral law. As we freely and spontaneously adopt such maxims in action on the ground of their fitness to be universal laws, we thereby make them to be particular moral laws for ourselves and others. These particular laws are not derived by deduction from an empty formula: they are rather enacted in the living of a good life.

We can understand this best if we compare it with the activity of the artist who creates beauty, which, like goodness, cannot be deduced from any empty formula.[2] Yet we must not forget that the good man, unlike the artist, is willing in accordance with concepts—the concepts of universal law and of a universal and teleological law of nature.

Apart from the metaphysical problem of freedom, which we must face in due course, there is here no difficulty other than those we have already met; and Kant thinks it unnecessary to illustrate this principle with further examples.[3]

Formula III, like Formula I, must be applied by reference to teleological laws of nature; and when we pass to the next principle, the principle of the Kingdom of Ends and its analogy with the Kingdom of Nature, we shall find that these laws are concerned with a complete system of ends. It is therefore natural to regard our next formula as the means through which Formula III is applied. For this reason I call it Formula IIIa and not Formula IV. This fits in with Kant's own final summary of the different formulae, where the concept of law-making and that of a kingdom of ends as a kingdom of nature are combined in one formula, which he himself describes as his third.[4]

---

[1] See Chapter XV, Appendix, especially §6.
[2] See Chapter XIV, Appendix §2.
[3] *Gr.*, 432 n. = 61 n.
[4] *Gr.*, 436 = 66.

CHAPTER XVIII

THE FORMULA OF THE KINGDOM OF ENDS

§1. *Formula IIIa.*

'So act as if you were through your maxims a law-making member of a kingdom of ends.'[1]

This is perhaps the simplest of the many versions of Formula IIIa. It is, however, incomplete in so far as it makes no mention of the 'kingdom of nature', which Kant, in his arbitrary way, does not bring in till he comes to his final summary. We must supplement it as follows:

'*All maxims which spring from your own making of laws ought to accord with a possible kingdom of ends as a kingdom of nature.*'[2]

In this second version the kingdom of ends is parallel to the 'universal law' of Formula I (with the addition of the 'ends in themselves' of Formula II), while the kingdom of nature is parallel to the 'universal law of nature' of Formula Ia. The use of the word 'kingdom' makes it clear that the laws in question are not to be considered in isolation but as part of a system of laws in both cases.

Formula IIIa is thus the most comprehensive of all Kant's formulae. It expressly mentions both the form (universal law) and the matter (ends in themselves) of moral action. It shows that we are dealing, not with isolated laws or isolated ends, but with a system of laws and a system of ends. It correlates the law of freedom with the law of nature; and—like the Formula of Autonomy—it renders explicit the freedom with which the morally good man makes his own laws through his maxims.

Kant puts some of these points more technically—some may think more pedantically—with reference to the categories of unity, multiplicity, and totality. Formula IIIa is said to be a 'complete determination' of the maxims of moral action.[3] In Formula I we recognised that moral action has *one* form (the form of universal law). In Formula II we recognised that it has for its matter *many* objects—or ends. Finally in Formula IIIa we have reached the conception of *all* rational beings as ends in themselves united in one complete system under one universal law.[4] This formula combines the other two in itself.[5]

In these circumstances it may seem odd that Kant should regard Formula IIIa as in some sense inferior to Formula I (and presumably

---
[1] *Gr.*, 438 = 69. See also *Gr.*, 434 = 63 and 439 = 69.
[2] *Gr.*, 436 = 66.
[3] *Ibid.* To say this is to say that it combines form and matter.
[4] *Gr.*, 436 = 67. For a similar treatment of the categories see *K.r.V.*, B111 and B114.
[5] *Gr.*, 436 = 66.

to Formula III). He appears to adopt this view precisely because Formula IIIa does not restrict itself to the form of morality, but brings in the matter as well—namely, persons as ends in themselves and as having at the same time their own subjective ends. In so doing it presents us with the attractive prospect of a world where, as a result of moral action, the ends of all free agents are realised (so far as they are compatible with freedom under universal law), and where in consequence happiness is proportionate to virtue. This supplies a strong motive for morality,[1] but therein lies its danger; for we may be tempted to seek the realisation of such a world only because we believe that in it our many interests might more easily find their satisfaction. The actions enjoined by morality must be done for their own sake as embodiments of the law and not as a means to the furtherance of our own interests. The superiority of Formula I—and still more perhaps of Formula III—lies in its insistence that action is morally good in virtue of its *motive*, not in virtue of its objects or results. Kant has by now made it plain that the moral law enjoins the pursuit of certain ends; but he still maintains that a man is not morally good merely in virtue of pursuing these ends: if he is to be morally good he must have a motive other than self-interest or the satisfaction of natural impulses.

In the formalism of Kant, even when it seems pushed to the verge of paradox, there is almost always a core of common sense.

Kant does not fail to recognise the advantages of bringing in also the matter of moral action—the persons whose happiness we seek and the order of society which it is our purpose to establish. It is necessary to do this in order to bring our Idea of the moral law nearer to intuition and so to feeling 'by means of a certain analogy'.[2] But we must not blind ourselves to the truth that in moral action there must be a moral motive and not merely the pursuit of a right end.

§2. *The approach to Formula IIIa.*

The approach to our new formula is comparatively easy. We could establish it from any of Kant's previous formulae, but the simplest way is to start from Formula III.

In Formula III every rational agent is enjoined to look upon himself as the maker of universal laws through his maxims, and to adopt this standpoint[3] for the purpose of criticising himself and his actions. This leads straight to the concept of a kingdom—that is, of a self-governing society, a connected system of rational agents under common, self-imposed, and yet objective, laws. It leads to the concept of a kingdom of

---

[1] *Gr.*, 439 = 70.
[2] *Gr.*, 436 = 66 and 437 = 67. See the appendix to Chapter XV for the question of analogy. The Formula of the Law of Nature seems also to fall under this assertion—indeed there primarily we get our analogy—though it is given in *Gr.*, 436 = 66 under the head of 'form', not 'matter'.
[3] *Gr.*, 433 = 62; also *Gr.*, 438 = 68-9. This is the 'standpoint' from which we regard ourselves as free; *Gr.*, 450 = 83.

ends because, as stated in Formula II, the laws enjoin that every member should treat himself and all others, never merely as means, but at the same time as an end.

If we combine the principle of universal law with the principle of ends in themselves, we must conceive a kingdom of ends; and a kingdom of ends is said to be 'possible'—that is, conceivable—in accordance with our previous principles.[1] Such a kingdom is very unlike our actual society, and it is admittedly only an Ideal.

§3. *The kingdom of ends.*

An Ideal is a whole or system conceived by an Idea of reason,[2] and the kingdom of ends is a whole or system of all the ends which we ought to seek. These ends are not only rational agents as ends in themselves, but are also *the individual ends which each rational agent may set before himself.*[3] This latter assertion may seem at first sight inconsistent with what Kant also says at the same time (and indeed in the same sentence)—namely, that we must abstract from the personal differences of rational beings and from all the content of their private ends. By this, however, he presumably means that, when we act as law-giving members of a kingdom of ends, our actions cannot be determined by personal differences or private ends as such: the kingdom of ends is concerned with private ends only so far as they are compatible with universal law.[4]

The system of a kingdom of ends governed by self-imposed, objective laws is the framework within which the private ends of ourselves and others ought to be realised. Such a framework by its apparent emptiness leaves room for the creativeness, in a sense the arbitrary creativeness, of human will.

§4. *Kingdom or realm.*

There is one point of terminology to be noted. For a time I was persuaded by an Oxford colleague[5] to abandon the phrase 'kingdom of ends'. This was on the ground that the German word '*Reich*' does not strictly mean a 'kingdom' but a 'realm.'[6] A '*Reich*' may be a kingdom (*Königreich*) or an empire (*Kaiserreich*) or a mere tyranny like the so-called 'Third Reich', now fortunately deceased.

These are strong arguments, and in some ways the word 'realm' is a more exact translation. On the other hand it is not always possible

---

[1] *Gr.*, 433 = 62.   [2] *K.r.V.*, A574 = B602.   [3] *Gr.*, 433 = 62.
[4] His statements avoid inconsistency because they are based on the premise that 'laws determine our ends by reference to their universal validity'. That is to say, the good man seeks ends which are universally valid because permitted or enjoined by universal laws. This must be so, if maxims are the maxims of actions aiming at ends, and if the good man acts only on maxims which he can at the same time will to be universal laws.
[5] Mr. W. D. Falk.   [6] Or perhaps a 'commonwealth'.

to get precise equivalents in different languages. The word 'realm', when taken strictly, is a trifle pompous and archaic, whereas the word '*Reich*' is neither. What is worse, the word 'realm', like the word 'sphere', is apt to be taken colourlessly, as when we speak of 'the realm of fancy' or 'the sphere of industry'. The conclusive consideration is, however, this—that the word '*Reich*' is here manifestly reminiscent of '*Das Reich Gottes*' (The Kingdom of God). If the Germans use the word '*Reich*' as a translation of the Greek Βασιλεία (kingdom), it cannot be wrong for us to speak of a 'kingdom of ends'.

§5. *The supreme head.*

Kant assumes that the kingdom or realm of ends would have a supreme head.[1] Such a supreme head would be the author of the law, but he would not be subject to the law, as are the members of the kingdom of ends. This is possible only in the case of a being who is holy: a holy being is not indeed above the moral law, for in virtue of his rational nature he would necessarily act rationally; but he is above a law limiting his will, and so is above duty and obligation, and in this sense is not subject to the law.[2] Hence he must be a being who is completely (and not just partly) rational. Such a being could have no needs, since these may give rise to desires opposed to a moral will; and this means that he must be a completely independent, and so presumably infinite, being. The power of such a being would be adequate to his holy will.

Kant adds that the supreme head would *not* be subject to the will of any other, thereby implying that a law-giving member of the kingdom of ends *would* be subject to the will of others. Perhaps he has in mind the external compulsion which is justly imposed on finite members of human society so far as they attempt to interfere with the freedom of others.

The doctrine of a supreme head is here introduced without any argument or defence. The argument for it belongs to the *Critique of Practical Reason*,[3] though its metaphysical background is adumbrated in the last part of the *Groundwork*. On Kant's view the existence of God is a postulate of pure practical reason, and moral law must lead to religion—that is, to the recognition of all duties as divine commands. He presumably brings in this doctrine here because without it the concept of a kingdom of nature would not be intelligible.

§6. *Dignity and price.*

Although the members, as distinct from the supreme head, of the kingdom of ends are subject to the law, they are nevertheless subject

[1] *Gr.*, 433–4 = 63.
[3] *K.p.V.*, 124 ff. = 265 ff. (= 223 ff.).
[2] *K.p.V.*, 32 = 144 (= 58).

to laws imposed by their own rational will. The kingdom of ends is possible only through the autonomy, or the freedom of will, of its members.[1] This autonomy is the ground of their absolute value, their 'dignity' or 'prerogative', their inner value or worth or worthiness.

'Dignity' or 'worthiness' is a technical term borrowed from the Stoics and is opposed to 'price'.[2] The fact that everything in the kingdom of ends has either a price or a dignity shows how concretely, indeed how prosaically, Kant is at times prepared to interpret his kingdom of ends.

Price is value in exchange: a thing has a price if we can put something else in its place as an equivalent. Dignity or worthiness is above all price and has no equivalent or substitute.[3]

The interesting thing about this doctrine (which apart from the terminology is already familiar to us) is that Kant distinguishes between a 'market price' and what, in spite of misleading associations, we may perhaps call a 'fancy price' (*Affektionspreis*), meaning thereby a value for fancy or imagination. The market price, according to Kant, is determined by the universal inclinations and needs of men: the fancy price depends on taste and not on any previous need.

If both these are properly called 'price', and if the things which have such a price can have an equivalent, then the price is in both cases determined by supply and demand, and there is no real difference between them. But Kant appears to be feeling his way towards a distinction between the economic value of a thing, which alone has an equivalent even in the case of works of art, and its aesthetic value, which strictly has no equivalent and yet is here regarded by Kant as 'relative'. Perhaps he means that music has no value for a deaf man, nor painting for a blind one; nor indeed has any work of art any value for a philistine. A distinction of this kind would place aesthetic value somewhere between economic value and moral value, which is absolute and unique, valid for all rational agents as such, and incomparable with any other value.

It is only through morality that a rational being can be a law-making member of a kingdom of ends and consequently can be an end in himself. From this Kant concludes that only morality, and humanity so far as it is *capable* of morality, can have dignity or worthiness or inner worth,[4] and so can be an object of reverence.[5] All other things, even our aesthetic activities, are only conditionally good—that is, good under the condition that their employment is not contrary to the moral law.[6]

It is worth noting that throughout his discussion Kant is concerned with the value of human activities. As examples of what has a market price he mentions skill and industry, presumably having in mind the doctrine

---

[1] *Gr.*, 434 = 63.
[2] For *dignitas* as opposed to *pretium* see Seneca, *Ep.*, 71, 37.
[3] *Gr.*, 434 = 64.
[4] *Gr.*, 435 = 64 and 440 = 71. See also *M.d.S.*, *Tugendlehre*, §11, 434 ff.; and §§38–9, 462 ff.
[5] *Gr.*, 436 = 66.
[6] *Religion*, *Vorrede*, 4 n. (= IV–V n.). Compare Chapters II §6 and IX §5.

of Adam Smith that labour is the real measure of exchangeable value.[1] The examples of what has a fancy price are wit and humour and imagination.

§7. The kingdom of nature.

Up to this point I have treated the kingdom of ends on a common-sense level, as I believe Kant expects us to treat it at this stage. The ideal set before us is a community of rational persons, obeying the same moral law for its own sake, respecting each other's freedom, and in this way striving to realise a harmonious system of ends such as can be realised in no other way. The duty of a good man is to act as a law-making member of such an ideal community. When Kant, rather late in the day,[2] tells us that the maxims of a good man ought to accord with such a possible kingdom of ends *as a kingdom of nature,*, he in a way corroborates this common-sense treatment; yet at the same time the distinction between a kingdom of ends and a kingdom of nature offers us a glimpse of his own metaphysical doctrines and gives rise to metaphysical problems which go beyond the limits of moral philosophy in its ordinary sense and belong strictly to the final section of the *Groundwork* so far as they can be considered at all in a book whose range is deliberately restricted.[3]

When we think of a world of rational agents which is completely in accord with moral laws, as from the moral point of view it can and ought to be, we are thinking of a moral world very different from the world of nature and of men as we know it in experience. Kant describes it therefore as *an intelligible world* in conceiving which we abstract from the hindrances to morality and even from all ends considered as conditions of obligation. The concept of such a world is a *practical Idea* which can and ought to influence the world of sense or experience: we must not take it as giving knowledge of some supersensible object.[4]

This concept Kant identifies with the concept of a kingdom of ends, which then appears to be taken in abstraction from its manifestations in action. He tells us that in virtue of the autonomy of rational wills a world of rational agents, described for the first time as an intelligible world (*mundus intelligibilis*), is 'possible'—in the sense of 'conceivable'[5]—as a kingdom of ends. If it is to be possible in another sense—that is, if it is to be capable of realisation—this can be so only through an *analogy* with a kingdom of nature.[6]

We have already met with a similar analogy between the universal moral law and the universal law of nature.[7] There, however, we were concerned primarily with the problem of 'practical exhibition', the problem of discovering in what kinds of action obedience to the moral law would be manifested. Kant's answer was—speaking broadly—that

---

[1] See *M.d.S., Rechtslehre*, §31, I, 289.
[2] *Gr.*, 436 = 66.
[3] *Gr.*, 391 = 8–9.
[4] *K.r.V.*, A808 = B836.
[5] Compare *Gr.*, 433 = 62 and §2 above.
[6] *Gr.*, 438 = 69.
[7] See Chapter XV, Appendix, especially §6.

the actions in question were those whose maxims, if conceived as laws of nature, would further a systematic harmony of purposes among men, or at least would do nothing to destroy such a systematic harmony. This continues to hold when we are dealing with the kingdom of ends and the kingdom of nature. But in his discussion of the two kingdoms Kant seems to be concerned with a different, though allied, problem: even if we know what kinds of action are obligatory on one who seeks to realise a kingdom of ends as a kingdom of nature, what are the conditions under which alone it is possible for this ideal to be realised?

Before we consider Kant's answer we must observe that he emphasises the sharp difference between the moral laws of the kingdom of ends and the mechanical laws of nature. The kingdom of ends is possible only as governed throughout by the self-imposed laws of its members, while nature as such is governed by external and mechanical laws, above all by the laws of cause and effect. Nevertheless nature as a whole, although regarded as a machine, can also be called a kingdom of nature *so far as it is directed to rational beings as its end*. The analogy between the kingdom of ends and the kingdom of nature holds only in so far as nature can be regarded as purposive, and indeed as directed to a final end. This corroborates our contention that the laws of nature provide a useful analogy with the moral law only so far as they are taken to be teleological.

It would be extremely arbitrary to regard nature and its laws as teleological unless we had some basis for this in human experience. I have already pointed out[1] that to Kant and his contemporaries the discoveries of Newton seemed to come as the revelation of a divine purpose in the universe; and even apart from this it is one of Kant's essential doctrines in the *Critique of Judgement* that we must presuppose a *logical* purposiveness in nature;[2] that is to say, the scientist must presuppose that the empirical laws of nature constitute an intelligible system, and he must proceed *as if* nature were in this sense adapted to human understanding. But Kant's fundamental point is that when we examine *organic life* in nature, we must make use of the theoretical Idea of a kingdom of ends in order to explain what actually exists. The moralist, on the other hand, is using the practical Idea of a kingdom of ends as a kingdom of nature in order to bring into existence something which does not exist but can to some extent be made real as a result of our efforts.[3] The concept of teleology in nature offers us a bridge between a natural world where everything is mechanical and a moral world where everything is free.

§8. *The realisation of the kingdom of ends.*

We are concerned, however, not with the completeness of Kant's system nor with the subtleties of his teleological doctrines, but with the possibility of realising the kingdom of ends in moral action. Such a

[1] Chapter XV, Appendix §5.   [2] *K.U.*, *Erste Einleitung*, V, 23.
[3] *Gr.*, 436 n. = 66 n.

kingdom could become actual only if the maxims prescribed to rational agents by the categorical imperative were universally followed.[1] Obviously it could become actual only if *all* rational agents always acted in accordance with such maxims and in this sense constituted, as it were, a kingdom of human nature; but even this would not be enough. A kingdom of ends could become actual only if nature itself were a kingdom governed by teleological law and were so constituted as to promote or guarantee the success of our moral volitions. In spite of his insistence that a good will is good in itself, Kant recognises that the effective manifestation of good will in the world depends, not only on the co-operation of other men, but also on the co-operation of nature itself. This is inconceivable unless nature can be regarded as manifesting a divine purpose and so as a kingdom of nature under a divine head. A good man in endeavouring to realise a kingdom of ends in this world is acting *as if* nature were created and governed by an all-wise and beneficent ruler for the ultimate purpose of realising the whole or perfect good (*bonum consummatum*) in which virtue is triumphant and is rewarded with the happiness of which it is worthy.[2]

The paradox of morality is the absolute obligation to aim at an ideal which can be realised only if the kingdom of ends and the kingdom of nature are united under one divine head.[3] On Kant's view it is far beyond the powers of human reason to prove that such a condition can be fulfilled. The utmost that theoretical reason can do is to show that such a supposition is neither self-contradictory nor excluded by the character of our experience. Nevertheless this supposition is a necessary 'postulate' of pure practical reason and is inseparable from an unconditionally binding moral law.[4]

It may perhaps be thought that Kant puts his point too crudely, after the fashion of the Eighteenth Century, by speaking as if the main function of the deity were to add a purely external happiness to the human achievement of virtue; but however we may express it, the fact remains that the state of affairs at whose realisation the good man holds himself obliged to aim cannot be brought about by his own efforts. In this struggle to attain an ideal which is beyond his unaided powers and yet is imposed on a good man by the law of his own reason lies, according to Kant, the 'sublimity' of the moral life. A good will retains its unique and absolute value whether or not its efforts are crowned with success.

§9. *The application of Formula IIIa.*

As in the case of the other formulae the Formula of the Kingdom of Ends is useless for those who seek to determine moral duties by a process of theoretical demonstration, but it is illuminating to those who are willing to adopt it as a principle of action. In some ways, as Kant recog-

---

[1] *Gr.*, 438 = 69.   [2] See Chapter II §7.
[3] *Gr.*, 439 = 70.   [4] *K.p.V.*, 122 = 263 (= 220).

nises, it is the most human and the most moving of all his principles. One thing that war brings home even to the most unreflective is that men are greatly moved and uplifted by playing their part, without thought of self-interest, in a great common enterprise under a great leader. It is in the light of such an experience, and not as a problem of purely logical analysis, that Kant's doctrine has to be judged.

This is true, but it does not exempt the philosopher from the duty of endeavouring to articulate his practical ideal in theory, difficult though such a task must be. He must always remember how hard it is to explain in words even such simple actions as swinging a golf-club or playing a game, and how meaningless such explanations are unless we have direct experience of such actions. This is still more true of attempts to describe the moral life or the moral ideal, and it may be that Kant should have given more attention to this question on the highest abstract level. Nevertheless he does give us some guidance. He speaks of a *corpus mysticum* of rational beings in the world so far as their free will (*Willkür*) under moral laws has thorough-going systematic unity both with itself and with the freedom of every other.[1] Such a systematic unity of purposes or ends has to be understood, on his view, in the light of our experience of systematic unity of purpose in an individual will: we must conceive all actions of rational beings so to happen *as if* they sprang from one supreme will which grasped all private willings (*Willkür*) in itself or under itself.[2] And indeed, as we have seen, the moral ideal of the kingdom of ends cannot be realised, unless there is such a single and supreme will. If there is to be complete unity of purpose among different wills, the supreme will must be all-powerful, all-knowing, omnipresent, and eternal.[3]

With the theological implications of this we are not here concerned, but it is surely obvious that the systematic unity of different wills can be adequately described only when we have first described the systematic unity of one individual will. This task is unfortunately neglected by Kant, perhaps because he fails to recognise the need for a philosophy of action as such.[4] On the whole we can say that his analysis of what is meant by the systematic unity of different individual wills is incomplete. Attempts, whether satisfactory or not, to carry further this analysis have been made by various philosophers belonging to what is sometimes called the idealistic school.

In spite of this limitation it is abundantly clear that on Kant's view this abstract framework of systematic unity has to be filled up by reference to the actual needs, desires, powers, and purposes of men. The common assertions to the contrary rest only on misunderstandings which have now become traditional and ingrained. We have already seen in connexion with the Formula of the Law of Nature how actions must be judged according as they further, or at least do nothing to destroy, such a systematic harmony of purposes among men; and we have also seen that an action aiming at such a systematic harmony of purposes is not thereby

[1] *K.r.V.*, A808 = B836. [2] *K.r.V.*, A810 = B838.
[3] *K.r.V.*, A815 = B843. [4] See Chapter I, Appendix, at end.

necessarily moral.[1] Coherence is the test, but not the essence, of moral action.

There is, however, a further question which Kant has not adequately treated, the question how far in action a good man has to modify his conduct to meet the conditions of an imperfect world. This question arises in regard to all his formulae, but it arises most conspicuously in regard to the Formula of the Kingdom of Ends.

At times his language suggests that a good man should in no way modify his conduct to meet the actual evil present in the world, and very often his doctrine is interpreted in this rigoristic sense. Such a doctrine would be manifestly absurd, and any one who has taken the trouble to study the applications of Kant's theory in detail ought to be aware that in practice Kant is very far from such extreme crudeness, very noticeably indeed in his philosophy of politics.[2] What Kant's view is in this matter requires much more careful consideration than it receives— it really demands a book for itself alone; but we may say with confidence that it is far more humane and sensible than is commonly believed. In particular we should never forget that for him there is in ethics what he calls latitude or play-room in the application of our moral maxims, and that he is always antagonistic to those who think otherwise. Nevertheless it may well be said that this is a problem which ought to be tackled fairly and squarely on the highest level, and that on this level Kant's treatment is inadequate and perhaps at times even misleading.

§10. *Moral progress.*

However inadequate in certain respects Kant's analysis may be, we must recognise—provided we are willing to refrain from impossible demands such as are made on no other philosopher—that he has succeeded in setting forth supreme principles of morality which are on quite a different level from a mere classification of particular duties. Without such supreme principles morality must be reduced to a hard and dogmatic legalism, when it is not dissolved into mere prejudice or emotion. One great merit of Kant's system is that it puts into a true perspective the spirit, as opposed to the letter, of the moral law.

If we ask ourselves whether there is still something lacking in Kant's moral doctrines, the answer at first sight might be that—as so often in

[1] See Chapter XV, especially the Appendix §6.
[2] Apart from Kant's insistence on punishment, which would have no place in a community of saints, we may note the following points. He recognises that what is abstractly right in itself may, for reasons of subjective convenience, not be right in the eyes of the law. He expressly asserts that where there is no organised civil society, we are not obliged to act in the same way as if there were such a society. He declares that an institution, such as a hereditary nobility, may be permissible for a certain age and may even be necessary according to circumstances. See *M.d.S.*, *Rechtslehre*, §§36–40, 296 ff.; §42, 307 ff.; and *Anhang*, 8 c., 369. In his lectures on P*hysical Geography—Einleitung* §5 —he goes so far as to say that while the first principle of civil society is a universal law, particular laws are relative to the soil and inhabitants of a particular region.

Eighteenth-Century philosophy—they are too rigid and static and fail to give an account both of moral progress and of the empirical conditions under which such progress must take place.

It is true enough that in his ethical writings Kant devotes little attention to these matters, though even here the short sections on methodology both in the *Critique of Practical Reason* and in the *Metaphysic of Morals* give us some inkling of his doctrines. He has a habit of dealing with one subject at a time, and it should not be assumed from this that he fails to see the relation between one subject and another. So far from being uninterested in history and moral progress he is miles ahead of his time in these matters as in so many others—the late Professor Collingwood, a good authority and no Kantian, used to assure me that Kant's views on the philosophy of history were the soundest he knew on that subject. Kant's observations on moral progress are scattered throughout his writings, but the simplest, clearest, and shortest account of them is to be found in his *Idea for a Universal History*, published in 1784—that is, in the year *before* the publication of the *Groundwork* itself.[1] Here we need note only a couple of points.

In the first place Kant is well aware that what he calls 'culture', in which morality must be included, evolves in the first instance, not on the basis of *a priori* thinking, but as a result of give and take. This evolution he ascribes chiefly to the conflict of men in society, to what he calls their 'unsocial sociability'. In this way the first real steps are taken from barbarism to culture: all talents are gradually developed, taste is formed, and through progressive enlightenment the beginning is made in forming an attitude of mind which can in time change the rough natural disposition for making moral distinctions into determinate practical principles and can thus in the end transform a pathologically extorted harmony into a *moral* whole.[2]

In the second place Kant is equally aware that even when men have risen to the apprehension of moral principles, progress in moral insight is neither mechanical nor the result of purely intellectual ratiocination. Reason, he says, does not work instinctively, but requires experiment, practice, and instruction in order to progress gradually from one level of insight to another.[3]

We may think that he ought to have developed his views on such points at greater length, but we must not imagine that he was blind to these fundamental truths.

§11. *Kant's historical background.*

If, as Kant holds, the moral philosopher formulates, clarifies, and systematizes the moral principles already presupposed in moral judgements and moral actions, we may ask what is the historical background with reference to which Kant's own doctrines are to be understood.

---

[1] It is contained in the eighth volume of the edition of the Prussian Academy.
[2] *Idee zu einer allgemeinen Geschichte*, Satz 4, 20–1.   [3] *Op. cit.*, Satz 2, 19.

This is a further question deserving detailed study, but perhaps we can say simply that the two greatest factors in Kant's historical background are, firstly, the Christian religion in its Protestant form, and, secondly, the influences which made for the American and French Revolutions.

The whole of Kant's moral philosophy might almost be described under the title of one of his last books as 'religion within the bounds of reason alone'. For him religion is primarily the Christian religion purified, not only from the dogmas of an authoritarian church, but also from miracles and mysteries and from what he regards as the substitution of historical beliefs for rational ones. His Formula of Universal Law, insisting as it does on the spirit as opposed to the letter of the moral law, is his version of the Christian doctrine that we are saved by faith and not by works. His Formula of the End in Itself is his way of expressing the Christian view that every individual human being has a unique and infinite value and should be treated as such. His Formula of the Kingdom of Ends as a Kingdom of Nature is quite explicitly his rational form of recognising a church invisible and visible, the Kingdom of God which has to be made manifest on earth.

The influences behind the American and French Revolutions, which can be summed up as the 'Enlightenment', may be regarded as a continuation of the Reformation, though the French Revolution was more bloody, and more violent against religion, because there the Reformation had been defeated. These influences are shown most markedly in Kant's passionate insistence upon freedom as the basis of all progress and all morality. The more direct and obvious influences come out, as is natural, in his political philosophy and especially in his hatred of despotism in any shape or form.

It may perhaps be objected to what I have said about religion that Christianity is a religion of love and that in this respect Kant misses its very essence. Even if this were wholly true, it would in no way alter the fact that other central doctrines of Christianity find in Kant their philosophical expression. But without denying that there is here some partial truth, it may be conjectured that the sickly, unmanly, and almost meaningless sentimentality which, in Kant's day as in our own,[1] is sometimes preached to us under the sacred name of love, is very far removed from the original doctrine of ἀγάπη; and indeed it may be suggested that Kant is very much nearer to that original doctrine than is commonly supposed.

There are many nowadays who will think that such historical facts invalidate Kant's doctrines from the start, since they are thereby shown to be a mere 'rationalisation' of something arrived at on wholly other grounds. Even on a higher level there are many distinguished thinkers whose interest in the history and background of philosophy has led them to the view that the philosophy of any period sets forth merely the presuppositions consciously or unconsciously accepted at that period and has no bearing on other periods nor any claim to express what is rather contemptuously called 'eternal' truth. We may indeed rightly be modest

[1] Compare $K.p.V.$, 157 = 307 (= 280).

about claiming truths to be eternal, and we must recognise that philosophy is more intimately bound up with its background than is such a study as pure mathematics. This gives rise to difficult problems which cannot be considered here. But it is a monstrous perversion of the truth to condemn or depreciate philosophical doctrines on the ground that, besides being the product of an unusually able individual mind, they also, as it were, bring into focus the thought and experience of an age or even of many ages. Such a view is too absurd to merit discussion. Unless we are complete sceptics—in which case we can say nothing about anything—we must to the best of our ability judge every philosophy on its own merits. What we judge to be its errors we may properly seek to explain as the result of merely contingent circumstances. But it is a far cry from this to the doctrine that a theory must be false if it has a historical background.

This is particularly true as regards the moral doctrines of Christianity. One of the disadvantages of asserting that these doctrines must be true because they are given by divine revelation is that those who deny revelation often infer—by an obvious *non sequitur*—that the doctrines must be false. If these doctrines are, as is contended, the result of merely human thought and experience and endeavour through many ages, this in itself warrants a strong presupposition that they contain at least a core of truth. No doubt the moral and religious thought of different ages (including our own) tends to be cluttered up with a lot of extraneous and accidental nonsense; but it is the mark of the great thinker to set aside the nonsense, to get at the core of truth underneath, and from this starting point to develop further the moral insight of men. This is what Kant has attempted to do; and it would be completely unreasonable to dismiss his efforts as foredoomed to failure on the purely *a priori* ground that doctrines which are the fruit of a long and laborious historical evolution must be unworthy of serious consideration.

§12. *Kant's personality.*

Men are apt to judge a philosophy by the personality of its creator, and alongside the popular caricature of Kant's doctrines there has grown up a similar travesty of his character. Unfortunately, though we know a great deal—perhaps too much—of his life as an old and even a dying man, we know very little of his youth and not very much of his middle age. Hence a picture of him has become popularly accepted in which he is a figure of fun, the traditional philosopher, unable to think when the trees begin to obscure the face of the town clock, determined at all costs to avoid the slightest perspiration, governed at every moment of the day by a punctual and unvarying routine, the slave of what he called 'maxims', without spontaneity or heart, an intellectual machine, and not a man. Like all caricatures this has some slight basis in reality, at least in his old age;[1] and indeed without a fixed routine it would have been quite impossible for him to get through the immense amount of teaching and writing, let alone thinking, which he did when he was already elderly, if not old.

But we must remember that there was a time when Kant was young, when in spite of his pocket stature and his pigeon breast he was known as '*der schöne Magister*'.[2] He was outstandingly good at cards, but he had to give them up because he could not bear the slowness with which his partners played. He was fond of the society of ladies as they were fond of his; and he enlivened every party at which he was present by his graceful, though dry, and at times caustic, but never pedantic, wit. Until he was a very old man he never dreamed of dining alone, but had guests at his own table, 'never less than the number of the graces or more than the number of the muses'. In his lectures he could enthral the rough youth of Königsberg, and could apparently at will excite them to laughter and even, it is said, to tears. And when, in later middle age, he had been appointed to a full professorship, the wiseacres could still shake their heads and say that he was too much of a dilettante to be much good at philosophy.

Even when he was old and withered, he did not lose his simple and kindly and courteous character. When he was so weak that he fell in the street and could not rise till two unknown ladies helped him up, he presented one of them with the rose which he happened to be carrying. Perhaps the most illuminating story is of a visit paid him by his doctor nine days before his death. The old man, already almost blind and incapable of speaking clearly, so feeble that he could hardly stand, struggled to his feet and with a great effort remained standing, mumbling some unintelligible words about 'posts', 'kindness', and 'gratitude'. The doctor was unable to understand, but Kant's friend Wasianski explained that he was trying to thank the doctor for coming in spite of many other claims upon him, and that he would not sit down till his guest was seated. At first the doctor doubted this, but was soon convinced and moved almost to tears, when Kant, gathering together all his forces, said with a supreme effort 'The feeling for humanity has not yet left me.'

These are little things, but they help to reveal character; and they should be set beside the little things which show Kant in an absurd, or even an unpleasing, light. A truer view of Kant's life will show him as essentially a humane and kindly man in spite of his single-minded devotion to philosophy. And a truer view of Kant's ethics will show him as the philosopher, not of rigorism, but of humanity.

---

[1] For some of it I have not been able to discover any evidence. Thus it is commonly repeated that he ate too many cakes at tea, and that his only moral problems arose in regard to this matter. I know no evidence for this, and the whole story is most surprising, as it is well known that he took only one meal a day, and this meal was certainly not tea.

[2] Perhaps this can be best rendered in the Scottish tongue as 'the bonny M.A.'

BOOK IV

THE JUSTIFICATION OF THE CATEGORICAL IMPERATIVE

CHAPTER XIX

THE PROBLEM

§1. *The question to be answered.*

IF we are to understand Kant's attempt to justify the categorical imperative, we must keep in mind its place in the whole argument. In Chapter I of the *Groundwork* Kant started from an analysis of ordinary moral beliefs, and he argued from them that the condition of moral action—at least for finite human beings—is obedience to law for its own sake or obedience to a categorical imperative. In Chapter II he formulated the categorical imperative in five different ways. For our present purpose, and for the *Critique of Practical Reason*, the Formula of Autonomy is the most important: '*So act that your will can regard itself at the same time as making universal law through its maxim.*' Autonomy, or the making of the universal laws which we are bound to obey, is thus the principle behind ordinary moral beliefs and purports to be the condition of moral action. The question we have now to face in Chapter III of the *Groundwork* is 'Can this principle be justified?'

Though Kant does not always keep the distinction clear, we should not forget that the principle of autonomy need not take the form of a categorical imperative: it expresses the essence of moral law—that is, it is the principle on which a rational agent as such would necessarily act if reason had full control over passion. As we shall see,[1] Kant attempts to justify the principle *as a moral law* and only thereby to justify it *as a categorical imperative*: if it is a principle on which a fully rational agent would necessarily act, it must also be—on his view—a principle on which an imperfectly rational agent *ought* to act, if he is tempted to do otherwise. We can pass without difficulty from an unconditioned objective principle of action to a categorical imperative.

Since the Formula of Autonomy sets forth the essence of the categorical imperative, our question may be put in the form 'How is a categorical imperative possible?' This question we have hitherto burked on the ground of its difficulty, a difficulty arising from the fact that a categorical

[1] See Chapter XXIV §7.

imperative, unlike a hypothetical one, is a synthetic *a priori* practical proposition.[1]

The possibility of hypothetical imperatives could easily be made intelligible because it rested on the purely analytic proposition that to will the end is to will the means. Hence any rational agent, so far as reason had decisive influence over his inclinations, would necessarily will the means to his chosen end, and ought to do so if he is sufficiently irrational to be tempted to do otherwise. But according to Kant no analysis of the concept of 'rational being' or 'rational agent' can give us a categorical imperative affirming that every rational agent ought to act in accordance with the principle of autonomy.[2] Here we have an *a priori* proposition which cannot be derived from mere analysis of the subject-concept and is consequently synthetic. As in the case of all synthetic *a priori* propositions we require some 'third term' to establish a necessary connexion between the subject and the predicate. This 'third term' we shall find—speaking broadly—to be the Idea of freedom.

The problem which we have here to face is therefore a special form of the general problem which is always for Kant the fundamental question of philosophy, namely, 'How are synthetic *a priori* propositions possible?' Kant's answer varies greatly in dealing with special problems—he is never satisfied with merely mechanical solutions—but it may be said that in every case it has one common characteristic: it seeks to justify a synthetic *a priori* proposition by tracing its origin to the nature of mind as such and in particular to the activity of reason itself. Such a justification is what Kant calls a 'transcendental deduction'; and it belongs to a critique or criticism of reason by itself.

Since the synthetic *a priori* propositions with which we are at present concerned are practical propositions, stating not what must be, but what ought to be, our argument belongs to a critique of practical reason.[3] It does not, however, profess to be a full critique, but aims only at setting forth the main features of such a critique so far as these are necessary for our present purpose.[4] Such a summary treatment, taken by itself, is bound to over-simplify and so give rise to difficulties. For an adequate understanding of Kant's doctrine we require knowledge of his other works.

It is clear from all this that Chapter III of the *Groundwork* is on quite a different footing from the first two chapters. Chapters I and II may be influenced by Kant's doctrines, but they at least profess to offer an analysis of the implications of our ordinary moral judgements: this analysis might stand, and I suggest does stand, whatever we think of the Critical Philosophy as a whole. In Chapter III we have to make an incursion into Kant's own metaphysical doctrines, his views of freedom and necessity, and his distinction between the phenomenal and the noumenal world. Nevertheless it would be a mistake to suppose even here that the questions raised and the difficulties involved are

---

[1] See Chapter XII §9.   [2] *Gr.*, 440 = 71–2; 420 n. = 45–6 n.; 449 = 82.
[3] *Gr.*, 440 = 72.   [4] *Gr.*, 445 = 77; 391 = 8–9.

peculiar to Kant's philosophy. His way of stating—and of solving—problems may be peculiar to himself, but this should not blind us to the fact that he is dealing with real problems, not artificial ones.

§2. *An alternative question.*

Can we justify the proposition that *a rational agent* as such ought to act in accordance with the principle of autonomy? This is the question which Kant has asked and the question which in fact he attempts to answer in his argument. Unfortunately, however, he puzzles us by propounding also what seems to be a quite different question, though he shows little sign that he is conscious of the difference. His second question is 'Can we justify the synthetic *a priori* proposition that an *absolutely good will* must be one which acts in accordance with the principle of autonomy?'[1]

It must not be thought that an absolutely good will is here one which is holy, and so one which is not under a categorical imperative, although it necessarily acts in accordance with self-imposed laws; for in this connexion Kant has said—rather loosely—that the principle of an absolutely good will must be a categorical imperative.[2] Neither an absolutely good will nor a rational agent as such need be under a categorical imperative; but both of them alike under human conditions, where they have to meet the resistance of passion, are under a categorical imperative; and Kant is still concerned with them under such human conditions, although this qualification is not continually repeated. Otherwise his question could not be 'How is a categorical imperative possible?'

Curiously enough, Kant has already said that analysis of the concepts of morality can perfectly well show that the principle of autonomy is the only principle of morality.[3] If so, presumably analysis of the concept of a moral will must equally be able to establish the principle of autonomy; and this suggests a distinction in connotation, if not in denotation, between an absolutely good will and a moral will. There are also further complications into which we need not enter.[4]

The simplest way out of these complications is to assume that a rational will and an absolutely good will are regarded by Kant as identical, and this might be maintained on the basis of his definition of goodness, provided it were suitably amended.[5] Certainly it seems reasonable to maintain that a good will can be only a will which acts rationally; but here again we have to ask whether this is an analytic or a synthetic proposition. If it is a synthetic proposition, how is it to be justified? If

---

[1] *Gr.*, 447 = 79; 444 = 77. The two questions seem to be connected in *Gr.*, 449-50 = 82.
[2] *Gr.*, 444 = 77.   [3] *Gr.*, 440 = 72.
[4] In *Gr.*, 397 = 16, for example, the concept of duty is said to contain in itself the concept of a good will, although under certain subjective limitations and hindrances.
[5] See Chapter X §1

it is an analytic proposition, it must surely rest, not on an arbitrary definition, but on some kind of direct insight.

In spite of the importance of the connexion between an absolutely good will and the principle of autonomy, we must take Kant's main question to be concerned with the relation between a rational agent as such and the principle of autonomy. His position appears to be that if this main question can be answered satisfactorily, the question about an absolutely good will offers no further difficulties.

Kant's insistence that the Idea of freedom is necessary to connect an absolutely good will with the principle of autonomy[1] shows clearly his own emotional attitude: it is in freedom that he finds the unique worth and sublimity of finite human beings. We must not assume that this necessarily introduces an irrational and merely subjective element into his argument, but it is reasonable to say that in this respect his argument requires careful scrutiny.

§3. *The purpose of a transcendental deduction.*

In some cases a transcendental deduction is necessary only to *justify* the known possibility of a synthetic *a priori* proposition, whereas in other cases it is necessary also to *establish* it. Thus, according to Kant, the synthetic *a priori* propositions of mathematics and physics are already known to be possible because of the success of these sciences: our only task is to consider *how* they are possible. In the case of metaphysics, however, we are offered so many contradictory statements that we have to ask *whether* its synthetic *a priori* propositions are possible before we begin to ask *how* they are possible.

In the *Groundwork* Kant treats the synthetic *a priori* principles of moral philosophy as more akin to those of metaphysics than to those of mathematics or physics. Over and over again he insists that he is not maintaining their truth, still less pretending that he has a proof of them.[2] All he has done is to determine by a regressive or analytic argument the ultimate conditions or presuppositions of accepted moral beliefs. If this is so, we cannot without a vicious circle proceed to justify ordinary moral beliefs progressively from these ultimate conditions, unless we can in some way establish these ultimate conditions independently by a transcendental deduction.[3] Hence we require a transcendental deduction of the principle of autonomy. Its purpose is to *establish* the possibility that moral judgements may be valid, and not merely to *justify* a possibility taken as already established. At present it is an open question whether moral beliefs, and with them the presuppositions on which they are grounded, may not be illusions.

Kant certainly regards the *Groundwork* as offering us such a transcendental deduction. Thus he talks about the rightness of his deduction;[4]

---
[1] *Gr.*, 447 = 79.   [2] See, for example, *Gr.*, 444–5 = 77.
[3] *Gr.*, 450 = 83; 453 = 86–7. See also Chapter I §9.
[4] *Gr.*, 454 = 88.

about the deduction of the concept of freedom from pure practical reason;[1] and about his deduction of the supreme principle of morality.[2]

§4. A different view.

We must remember that by a 'deduction' Kant does not mean a deduction in the ordinary sense, but rather a 'justification' based on the insight of reason into its own rational activity. Nevertheless the view of the *Groundwork* is open to grave objections. In the first place, the moral law may seem to be more certain than its alleged justification: we have at least as much assurance of being under moral obligations as of being free. In the second place, even if this were not so, it is surely inconceivable that the moral law could be justified by anything other than itself.

Kant seems to have become aware of both these objections. There are traces of such an awareness even in the *Groundwork*, though the obvious interpretation is the one I have given: but it is in the *Critique of Practical Reason* that there emerges a view which is fundamentally different.

The difference between his two views may be put roughly as follows. In the *Groundwork* he seems to think that the moral law is both justified and established by an independent and necessary presupposition of freedom. In the *Critique*, on the contrary, it is our consciousness of the moral law which leads to the concept of freedom; and in such consciousness Kant no longer finds difficulty. 'We can become conscious of pure practical laws just as we are conscious of pure theoretical principles.'[3] The moral law is, as it were, a 'fact of pure reason', of which we have *a priori* knowledge and which is apodeictically certain.[4] Only on the basis of the moral law can we justify the presupposition that the rational will must be free; and the moral law is even described as a principle for the deduction of freedom. We are expressly said to seek in vain for a deduction of the moral law, which requires no deduction.[5]

We need not, however, exaggerate the difference between the two views or suppose that the argument of the *Groundwork* is a mere waste of breath. Even if we hold the moral law and the categorical imperative to be apodeictically certain, there still remains the problem of freedom; and if freedom were merely an illusion, this could not but suggest that our belief in moral obligation and moral responsibility must also be an illusion. Hence both the *Groundwork* and the *Critique of Practical Reason* have at least to show *how* a categorical imperative is possible by refuting the dogmatic determinism which affects to prove that freedom is

---

[1] *Gr.*, 447 = 79.   [2] *Gr.*, 463 = 100.
[3] *K.p.V.*, 30 = 140 (= 53).   [4] *K.p.V.*, 47 = 163 (= 81).
[5] *K.p.V.*, 47–8 = 163–4 (= 82–3). The moral law does, however, receive some sort of 'credentials' (*Kreditiv*)—that is, apparently, some additional and purely theoretical ground for being accepted—from the fact that it gives positive content to the Idea of freedom which pure theoretical reason can and must conceive only negatively.

impossible. This problem lies behind the whole of the argument we are about to consider, though Kant does not make it explicit till he is within sight of the end.[1] We must keep an open mind and continue to judge the argument on its merits.

It may, however, seem disappointing if we are no longer to expect proof of the validity of the moral law or of our obligation to obey it. But this disappointment, as Kant recognises even in the *Groundwork*,[2] may spring from false expectations and from complete misunderstanding of the moral law itself. The metaphysician cannot prove the validity of the moral law from some principle which is not itself moral. If Kant ever thought that he could, he was mistaken; but it is doubtful how far he regards freedom in the *Groundwork* as a non-moral principle.[3]

§5. *Possible misunderstandings*.

We must be clear at the outset as to the meaning of the question 'How is a categorical imperative possible?' There are various ways in which this question may be misunderstood.

What we are asking is whether a proposition is or is not valid. Ordinary moral judgements affirm that we ought—or ought not—to do certain actions (or kinds of action). We are not now concerned with the truth or falsehood of these judgements in particular cases. The point is that, so far as they are moral and not prudential, they do not assert that we ought to do something *if* we happen to want something else: what they assert is that we ought—or ought not—to do something, whatever we may happen to want. Thus every moral judgement presupposes the possibility of asserting a simple, unqualified, or categorical 'ought'. If Kant's analysis of this assertion is sound, all moral judgements presuppose the ultimate proposition that every rational agent as such ought to act in accordance with the principle of autonomy. What we must now ask is whether we are justified as rational agents in accepting and acting on this proposition. Is the proposition the result of mere prejudice or is it valid for every rational agent as such? If the proposition is not valid, then all our moral judgements without exception are illusory: we cannot say, for example, that the sadists of Belsen acted wrongly, but only that we happen to dislike their conduct—especially if it is directed towards ourselves.

To many people it may seem that Kant's proposition is already justified if the rejection of it means the denial of all moral judgements: it is as much justified as a theoretical proposition of which it can be truly asserted that unless you think this, you cannot think at all nor can there be any such thing as truth. But even if this were so, even if on this ground we did not doubt that Kant's proposition is valid and in that sense 'possible', we might still ask '*How* is it possible?' We do not doubt the propositions of

---
[1] *Gr.*, 455 ff. = 89 ff.   [2] *Gr.*, 463 = 99–100.
[3] In *K.p.V.*, 29 = 140 (= 52) he hints that an unconditioned moral law and the positive concept of freedom may be the same thing, but his language is careless. The word '*diese*' in line 27, p. 29, of the Academy Edition ought surely to be '*dieses*'.

mathematics, but we may still ask *how* these propositions are possible and give an answer. It would, for example, be an answer—though on Kant's view a false answer—if we could show that the propositions of mathematics are all analytic.

The question we are asking in no way concerns the historical development of moral ideas. For enquiries of this kind Kant always shows the greatest respect; but although they might explain how we came to entertain certain concepts, they would do nothing to justify our acceptance of them.[1] There is even a tendency nowadays to assume without further ado that they would show our concepts to be illusory.

We are concerned solely with the validity of propositions, just as we are when we ask how pure mathematics is possible. No doubt there are important differences between theoretical and practical propositions as regards validity: but if we turn back to Kant's discussion of the possibility of hypothetical imperatives,[2] we shall see that there too he deals with the validity of a proposition and indicates clearly enough that the question about the possibility of a categorical imperative is of the same kind as the question about the possibility of hypothetical imperatives.

Hence it is a mistake to suppose we are concerned with psychological questions. We are not asking how a categorical imperative can manifest itself in action by giving rise to some emotion which can act as a motive. It is true that in the *Critique of Practical Reason*[3] Kant does attempt to explain how consciousness of our subjection to moral law can arouse the feeling of respect or reverence which is the emotional side of moral action and may be regarded as its motive; but this explanation is not concerned with the possibility of categorical imperatives. It is true also that in his present argument Kant speaks of the 'interest' attaching to moral Ideas; but he takes a different view from that in the *Critique* and maintains that moral interest is totally inexplicable.

It is a still greater mistake to suppose that Kant is trying to propound a speculative theory about the way in which a categorical imperative can have effects in the phenomenal world. He has, it is true, to deal with metaphysical questions in order to show that the possibility of freedom is not excluded by the very nature of our experience. But this is subsidiary to his main task, which is to justify a synthetic *a priori* proposition by showing that we are entitled to affirm a necessary connexion between subject and predicate in virtue of a 'third term'—namely, the Idea of freedom.[4]

It is sheer error to suggest that Kant is trying to explain how pure reason can be practical or how freedom can be possible.[5] These questions Kant has not only refrained from answering: he roundly asserts that they are beyond the power of human reason to answer.[6]

[1] Compare *K.r.V.*, A86–7 = B118–19.   [2] Chapter XII §§6 and 8.
[3] *K.p.V.*, 71 ff. = 196 ff. (= 128 ff.). See also Chapter V §2.
[4] *Gr.*, 447 = 79.
[5] It seems to me that even the criticisms made by so good a scholar as the late Professor Hoernlé in the *Personalist* (October 1939) rest upon this error.
[6] *Gr.*, 461 = 97–8; 458–9 = 94.

§6. *Kant's method.*

In this important discussion, as in so many others, Kant's arguments are repeated more than once and are apt to be modified in the process. This is almost inevitable since of the 5 Sections into which Chapter III of the *Groundwork* is divided, the first three are preparatory; the fourth gives a summary outline of the whole argument; while the fifth both clarifies what has gone before and adds a variety of new points. We shall have in so difficult a matter to follow Kant's divisions pretty closely, while trying to avoid some of the repetition. His method, we must remember, is deliberate: he expects us to get fuller insight as we proceed. Though this is not without its advantages, it offers considerable difficulty to the reader, at least if he is mathematically minded and expects a quite different kind of argument.

CHAPTER XX

FREEDOM AND AUTONOMY

§1. *Kant as a pioneer.*

IN the discussion of freedom Kant's work is that of a pioneer. The Greeks never really came to grips with the subject and did little to carry it beyond limited questions of legal responsibility. In mediaeval philosophy there was a real advance, but the problem was considered in theological terms: how was human freedom to be reconciled with divine omnipotence and omniscience? Kant separated the problem of freedom from its legal and theological setting and asked simply how freedom can be compatible with the causal law which prevails throughout nature, and apparently also throughout human nature.

As Kant is breaking new ground, we need not be surprised if we find a certain roughness and obscurity, perhaps even inconsistency, in his doctrines. This will not deprive him of the credit of having posed the question so sharply that thereafter it can no longer be neglected. It seems probable that there was a considerable development, not only in Kant's terminology, but in his views: we have already noted[1] a fundamental difference between the *Groundwork* and the *Critique of Practical Reason* in this respect. A full discussion of Kant's theory of freedom demands a book to itself: here we can attempt only to understand the argument of the *Groundwork* in the light of his other writings.

§2. *Freedom as the key to the moral problem.*

Kant begins his discussion by suggesting that the concept of freedom is the key to the explanation—he should rather have said 'justification'—of the principle of autonomy. If we could justify the concept of freedom by tracing it to its origin in practical reason, we should then be able to show how a categorical imperative, as expressed in the Formula of Autonomy, is possible. Our first task, however, is merely to show that a free will is equivalent to an autonomous will and so to a will under moral law. This equivalence must be established by stating what freedom is; that is, by giving an acceptable definition of freedom or of a free will.

Granted that we can define a free will correctly, the proposition that a free will is equivalent to an autonomous will is on Kant's view an analytic proposition.[2] It can be established by analysis of the concept of a free will, though in our analytic proposition we make explicit what was only implicit before.

[1] Chapter XIX §4.   [2] *Gr.*, 447 = 79; *K.p.V.*, 28–9 = 138–40 (= 51–2).

Although a free will is equivalent to an autonomous will, we apparently arrive at these two concepts by different routes. Our concept of an autonomous will was obtained by an analysis of the conditions or presuppositions of morality. Our concept of a free will is to be obtained by a definition which presumably must be based on insight into the nature of something other than moral beliefs. This last view appears to be explicitly rejected in the *Critique of Practical Reason*,[1] yet it is not altogether without interest and plausibility.

§3. *Will as causality.*

Assuming that freedom, if it characterises anything, must characterise a will, Kant begins with a new definition of 'will'. Hitherto we have known 'will' as 'the power of a rational being to act in accordance with its conception of laws, i.e. in accordance with principles'.[2] We are now told[3] that 'the will is a kind of causality belonging to living beings so far as they are rational'. Will is regarded as the power of a rational being to produce effects in the phenomenal world, and primarily in the physical world. The power to act would commonly be regarded as a power to produce such effects.

Our will, however, may also produce changes in our own mental world, the world of inner sense—as when we decide, for example, to think about a particular topic. A rational being capable of doing this might be considered to possess a will even if he were unable to influence physical events. The point is of some importance, for, as we shall find later, Kant regards our judgements, and not merely actions in the ordinary sense, as taking place under the Idea of freedom.[4]

Kant has also indicated the possibility that we might will (not merely wish) and yet through some special disfavour of fate might produce no external result or at least not the result intended.[5] He may have in mind some sudden misfortune, such as a stroke of paralysis; but quite apart from this it is only too common an experience to find that what we do is in fact different from what we willed to do—every missed stroke at tennis is an example of this. Perhaps it was with reference to some such distinction between willing and doing that Kant defined the will as 'a power to *determine* oneself to action in accordance with our conception of certain laws'.[6] Problems of this type are, however, generally passed over by Kant. They belong not to moral philosophy but to the philosophy of action. For purposes of moral philosophy we are perhaps entitled to consider only what may be described as the normal case—namely, that we produce the effect which we will to produce.

If the will is a power to act—or to set oneself to act—in accordance with one's conception of laws, willing must be a conscious, and indeed in some degree a self-conscious, activity. To think of rational beings as

---

[1] *K.p.V.*, 29–30 = 140 (= 53).
[2] *Gr.*, 412 = 36.
[3] *Gr.*, 446 = 78.
[4] *Gr.*, 448 = 81; 452 = 86.
[5] *Gr.*, 394 = 12.
[6] *Gr.*, 427 = 55.

endowed with a will is to think of them as possessing 'consciousness of their causality in regard to action '.[1]

One last point should be noted. The word 'causality' is commonly used by Kant in two senses. (1) It may mean 'a power to produce effects'; and (2) it may mean 'causal action'. When he says that the will is a kind of causality, he means that it is a *power* to produce effects. When he speaks of an efficient cause as being 'determined to causality' by something else,[2] he means that it is determined to causal *action*—that it is itself caused to act causally. Willing may be described as causal action, but 'the will' is merely the power to act causally—that is, to produce effects. We may fail to understand Kant if we neglect to notice this ambiguity.

§4. *Freedom and natural necessity.*

If we conceive the will to be free, we must mean in the first place that the will is a power to produce effects without being *determined*—or caused —to do so by anything other than itself. Freedom is a quality belonging to a special kind of causality. Perhaps it would be simpler to say that it characterises a special kind of causal action. It is opposed to 'natural necessity' or 'the necessity of nature', a quality characterising all causal action in nature.[3] We may for brevity state the contrast simply as one between freedom and necessity, but we must remember that there may be other kinds of necessity—for example, logical necessity.

What is meant by this 'necessity' which characterises causal action in nature? Let us take a crude example. If a billiard ball strikes against a billiard ball which is at rest, it will cause the second ball to move. But the first ball does not spontaneously cause the second ball to move: it causes the second ball to move only because it was itself driven against the second ball by a billiard cue. It does produce an effect—namely, the movement of the second ball; but its causal action in so doing was itself caused by something other than itself—namely, by a blow from a cue. In Kant's more technical language its causal action was necessary—we might almost have said necessitated—and not free.

If to act is to produce effects, then all action is causal action. Hence we can omit the qualification 'causal' and say that all action in nature is necessary. In nature there is no spontaneity and no freedom—only an endless chain of causes and effects. The necessity of nature is causal: it is a necessity in accordance with which every event must be caused by a preceding event.

The necessity of nature is not confined to inorganic objects. It is because of an external influence that moths fly into a light. Even on the level of the higher animals Kant conceives of a dog as moved to pursuit by the sight or smell of a rabbit. To say this is not to say that a dog is merely a material machine. We may with Leibniz call it a spiritual, and

---

[1] *Gr.*, 449 = 81. [2] *Gr.*, 446 = 79.
[3] *Gr.*, 446 = 78. The word 'action' is here used widely and not restricted to distinctively human action.

not a material, automaton, for it is moved by ideas; but it falls under the mechanism of nature, which may cover psychological as well as purely physical laws.[1]

If the will of a rational agent is conceived as free, this must mean that we regard his causal actions, or more precisely his volitions, as *not determined* by causes external or alien to himself. Under external causes we must here include, not merely physical forces, but also the sensa given us from without, the images suggested by these sensa, the emotions aroused by sensa and images, and the desires stimulated by emotions. It must never be forgotten that on Kant's view the whole succession of events in inner sense, and in particular the succession of sensa, images, emotions, and desires, is as much governed by natural necessity as is the movement of stocks and stones.[2]

This does not mean that Kant recognises no differences between men and animals any more than it means he recognises no differences between animals and things. If we look at the question purely from a psychological point of view, animals differ from things in being moved by ideas as well as by physical forces, and men differ from animals in being moved by reason as well as by ideas of sense and imagination. It is an empirical fact that men have a power to rise above immediate sensuous impressions and impulses through concepts of what is useful or harmful in a remoter way. This remains an empirical fact even if the reason which thus prescribes laws for action is itself determined in turn through influences from elsewhere. Hence Kant ascribes to animals an *arbitrium brutum* and to men an *arbitrium liberum*, terms which unfortunately have no satisfactory English equivalent.[3] We may dislike the terminology, we may even suspect confusion of thought to lie behind it, but there is no doubt whatever that this is Kant's doctrine, and that in it he is at least recognising empirical facts which it would be stupid to ignore.

This empirical characteristic of man by which reason plays some part in determining his actions—a fact recognised equally by Hume[4]—Kant sometimes calls, not too happily perhaps, 'psychological' or 'comparative' freedom; but he knows perfectly well that it may all fall under the head of 'natural necessity'. Man might still be a spiritual automaton, even if he were moved, not by instinct, but by a reason which revealed to him remoter objects of desire and the means to attain them: his so-called freedom might be rather like that of a turnspit which moves of itself once it is wound up.[5] The freedom which we have conceived as belonging to a will is something quite different: it can be present only if the will is a power to produce effects without being determined by anything other than itself.

As so described the freedom which is opposed to necessity is a negative

[1] *K.p.V.*, 96–7 = 227–8 (= 172–4).
[2] *K.r.V.*, A549–50 = B578–9; *K.p.V.*, 95–7 = 226–8 (= 171–4).
[3] *K.r.V.*, A802–3 = B830–1; A534 = B562. The nearest we can get to an English expression for *arbitrium* (*Willkür*) is perhaps 'choice', or 'free choice' where the *arbitrium* is *liberum*. See also §8 below.
[4] Compare Mrs. R. M. Kydd, *Reason and Conduct in Hume's Treatise*, p. 115.
[5] *K.p.V.*, 96–7 = 227–8 (= 172–4).

concept, an Idea of reason derived from reflection upon necessity itself. We may call it the 'transcendental Idea' of freedom, a purely theoretical concept not based upon any moral considerations and in itself empty.[1] Yet if we totally reject this negative concept, it will be impossible to justify a positive concept of freedom. Kant claims to have proved in the *Critique of Pure Reason*, not that there corresponds to this negative concept any actual, or even possible, object, but only that the concept is neither self-contradictory nor necessarily excluded by the nature of our experience.[2]

§5. *The positive concept of freedom.*

Kant has to go beyond the negative sense of freedom to a positive one if he is to show that freedom is equivalent to autonomy. He attempts to do this by means of the concept of causality, having defined will as free causality, that is, as a power of free causal action. The concept of causality, he asserts, implies the concept of law; and this must hold whether causality—here used presumably in the sense of causal action—is determined by natural necessity or is free.[3]

The grounds alleged for this crucial assertion are curiously inadequate. The concept of causality, we are told, implies the concept of laws (*Gesetze*) in accordance with which through something which we call 'cause' something else—namely, the effect—must be posited (*gesetzt*). Hence a causality characterised, not by necessity, but by freedom, cannot be lawless, but must accord with unchanging laws of a special kind. Otherwise a free will would be a logical absurdity (*ein Unding*).

The word 'posited' in English is always obscure, and with us there is no magic in the connexion between '*Gesetz*' (law) and '*gesetzt*' (posited). The law of which Kant speaks appears, by his own account, to be a law connecting cause and effect so that like causes necessarily have like effects. But this applies only to natural necessity. It is hard to see how we can be entitled to pass from this to a law of freedom, which—so far from connecting causes and effects—is a law for causal action considered in itself.[4] The law or principle of autonomy, as we have seen it hitherto, in no way asserts a necessary connexion between causes and effects.

There is rather more force in the contention that a lawless free will would be an absurdity. Such a view, however, is not derived from any necessary connexion between causality and law. It arises because a lawless free will would be governed merely by chance and so could not properly be described as free.

If Kant's doctrine turned merely on the present argument, we should have to dismiss it as fallacious. The curious thing is that the argument is as superfluous as it is weak. There is no need whatever to make the connexion between free will and law depend on the concept of causality.

[1] See Chapter IX, Appendix §4. [2] *K.r.V.*, A557–8 = B585–6.
[3] *Gr.*, 447 = 78. See also *K.p.V.*, 89 = 218 (= 160); *Religion*, 35 = 39 (= 32).
[4] Perhaps Kant has in mind the account of what he calls 'character' in the *Critique of Pure Reason* (see especially A539 = B567 and A549 ff. = B577 ff.). But I cannot see that it justifies his present assertion.

The very definition of will as previously given was 'the power of a rational being to act in accordance with its conception of laws, i.e. in accordance with principles'.[1] If so, a lawless free will would not be a will at all: it would be a contradiction in terms (a mere *Unding*).

As we shall see, Kant's doctrine rests on insight into the necessary activity of reason, and in particular of practical reason. The present statement puts forward a rough account of what he hopes to justify, and supports it by an unconvincing argument, which were better omitted. He is not trying to prove that the will is free, but merely showing how a free will—if there were such a thing—would have to be conceived. We need not labour the point that a will governed by the laws of natural necessity would not be free; for by such laws, whether physical or psychological, causal action must itself be caused in the long run by something other than the agent, and no one would regard this as freedom. If a free will cannot be lawless, its laws must be of a different kind from the laws of nature.

§6. *Freedom and autonomy*.

How are we to distinguish the laws of nature from what we may now call the laws of freedom? In nature the causal action of an efficient cause is itself caused by something else: it is not spontaneous. This means, according to Kant, that the law governing causal action in nature is not self-imposed but is imposed by something else. This is what he calls 'heteronomy'. Hence if we are to distinguish the laws of freedom from the laws of nature, we can do so only by supposing that the laws of freedom are self-imposed. The spontaneous causal action of a free will must therefore take place in accordance with self-imposed law. But this is just what we mean by 'autonomy'; and a free will must be conceived as acting under the principle of autonomy—that is, as capable of acting on maxims which can at the same time be willed as universal laws. Since we have discovered this to be the principle of moral action, we can say that a free will and a will under moral laws are one and the same thing.[2]

The argument, to say the least, is hurried. We have to make several assumptions, each of which demands careful consideration. We have to assume (1) that free willing must have its own special kind of law; (2) that since all law must be either self-imposed or other-imposed, the law of freedom must be self-imposed; and (3) that self-imposed law can be only the law of following law as such. In spite of some help from previous discussions, these assumptions are not to be lightly made.

The argument might be more hopeful if it could be tackled, so to speak, from the other end. If we could show that practical reason must assume itself to be capable of acting in accordance with its own rational principles, we might be justified in holding that it must be free and also autonomous in the sense required.[3] This, as we shall see, is much more like the argument which Kant actually uses, though in it the Idea of

---

[1] *Gr.*, 412 = 36.   [2] *Gr.*, 447 = 79.   [3] See Chapter IX §4.

XX §7]   FREEDOM AND AUTONOMY   213

freedom becomes less prominent as the link connecting the subject and predicate of the categorical imperative. We must take the present argument as one of the preliminary and incomplete discussions with which Kant is wont to preface his central arguments.

Incidentally, it is not wholly clear, even in the present passage, whether the positive concept of freedom is itself the 'third term' necessary for Kant's purpose. Freedom, we are told, furnishes (*schafft*) this 'third term', but it is also said to 'point' to this 'third term' (*worauf uns die Freiheit weiset*). Sometimes Kant speaks as if the 'third term' were not freedom but membership of the intelligible world. On the whole, however, these two concepts are so closely interconnected that he may not have been conscious of any sharp difference between them.

§7. *Is only a good will free?*

There are further difficulties about the meaning of Kant's doctrine. Is he maintaining that a morally good will alone is free, while a morally bad will is determined?

It may be thought that the answer must be in the affirmative, since Kant has just said that a free will and a will under moral laws are one and the same thing. This, however, would be a mistake. Kant expressly distinguishes between a will 'under moral laws' and a will which always obeys moral laws.[1] To be under-moral laws is to recognise the categorical imperative, but not necessarily to obey it.

Apart from the merely linguistic question there is no doubt that Kant believes us to assume freedom in the mere recognition of the categorical imperative: 'I ought' implies 'I can'. Indeed the examples by which he illustrates his doctrine of freedom are nearly always examples of bad moral action, such as lying and thieving.[2] The bad man could have acted otherwise. Unless this is so, there is no meaning in saying that he ought to have acted otherwise, and there is no justification in blaming him for what he has done. Whatever may be the case with other philosophers, it is not Kant's view that we are responsible for our good actions and not for our bad ones: we are responsible for both alike. In the *Groundwork* itself, while he declares very sensibly that we are not responsible for our inclinations and impulses, we *are* responsible for the indulgence which enables them to influence our maxims to the prejudice of moral law.[3]

In his later works Kant sets forth what seems to be a development of his present position. There he makes a distinction between will (*Wille*) and *arbitrium* (*Willkür*). Will in this technical sense is concerned only with the law and so seems to be equivalent to pure practical reason: it is said to be neither free nor unfree.[4] *Arbitrium*, on the other hand, is the source

[1] *K.U.*, §87, 448 n. (= 422 n.).
[2] *K.r.V.*, A554 = B582; *K.p.V.*, 95 = 226 (= 171).   [3] *Gr.*, 458 = 93.
[4] *M.d.S.*, *Rechtslehre, Einl.*, IV, 226 = 27. In this he may perhaps be forgetting that such a will may be creative, but perhaps he considers that in man it is so only in conjunction with *arbitrium*. God's will is free because spontaneous and not predetermined (there being no temporal succession in God); *Religion*, 50 n. = 57 n. (= 58–9 n.).

only of maxims, and so far may be identified with practical reason on its subjective side: it alone is free. We are free in adopting maxims, and behind our maxims it is useless to seek further determining grounds of our actions.[1]

It must not be thought from this that Kant is deliberately falling back on the liberty of indifference. He insists that we cannot define freedom merely as a power of choosing to act for or against the law, although experience gives us many examples of the latter.[2] The power of choosing to act against the law is not a *necessary* characteristic of freedom. He apparently thinks that such a power in a rational being is unintelligible, as indeed it is; and he even declares it not a power, but rather an incapacity. Freedom in relation to the inner law-making of reason is alone properly a power.

All this is highly abstract and difficult, and it may be confused: but it all serves to show that for Kant we are free so far as we are capable of obeying the moral law; and this on his view is a characteristic not merely of saints, but of all men, and indeed of all rational agents; for apart from this there could be no recognition of duty and no moral responsibility for failure.

§8. *Two kinds of heteronomy.*

It may be objected that Kant has identified natural necessity with heteronomy,[3] and he has also asserted that heteronomy is present wherever the motive of action is other than purely moral.[4] If non-moral, and still more if immoral, actions are instances of heteronomy, can it be denied that they must fall under natural necessity? How can we maintain that they may be free?

To answer this we must anticipate a little. According to Kant there are two points of view from which actions may be regarded. We may call these provisionally the point of view of the observer and the point of view of the agent. From the point of view of the observer all actions, moral and immoral alike, are instances of natural necessity. From the point of view of the agent these same actions, both moral and immoral, must be regarded as free, since he recognises, even in doing immoral actions, that he could obey the moral law and ought to do so.

Kant does not hold that the very few morally good actions—if there are such—are wholly free, whereas all other actions are wholly determined. Nor could there be much to recommend such a theory.

To this it may be replied that even if all actions from one point of view may be regarded as determined and so as heteronomous, there must be some sense in which from one and the same point of view— presumably the point of view of the agent—non-moral actions are heteronomous, while moral actions are not.

---

[1] *Religion*, 21 n. = 22 n. (= 7 n.).
[2] *M.d.S., Rechtslehre, Einl.* IV, 226–7 = 28–9.
[3] *Gr.*, 446 = 79. [4] *Gr.*, 441 = 72.

Such an observation is just, but it means that Kant, whether consciously or not, is using 'heteronomy' in two senses. Heteronomy in the case of inanimate objects means that their causal action is wholly determined from without. This is not the case as regards human action from the point of view of the agent. In all human action will is active and spontaneous: it does not indeed act for the sake of law as such, except in the case of morally good actions; but it is said to go beyond itself and seek the law which is to determine it in the character of some object or other.[1] If we look at Kant carefully, we shall see that human *arbitrium* or choice is never pathologically determined[2] or necessitated by sensuous motives: it is always merely affected or influenced, and this is the main reason why it is called *arbitrium liberum* or free choice.[3]

Arbitrium is attributed to animals, presumably because they are moved by sensuous impressions and not merely by physical forces. Their *arbitrium*, however, is not *liberum* but *brutum*, because their action is determined or necessitated, and not merely influenced or affected.

There are indeed grave difficulties in supposing that from one point of view human action may be wholly free, and from another wholly determined. But these difficulties are not here in question. We are trying to discover only what Kant's doctrine is; and there is no doubt whatever that for him—at least from one point of view—the heteronomy of non-moral actions is compatible with freedom.[4] Human action, whether moral or immoral, is worlds apart from the motions of inanimate bodies or even the behaviour of animals; and this difference is due to the presence in man of practical reason.

§9. *Degrees of freedom.*

Even if we decline to attribute to Kant the absurd view that moral action is wholly free and all other action wholly determined, there is still the question whether in all our actions we are equally free. Are there degrees of freedom?

On this point Kant does not appear to have a clear and consistent view. At times he adopts a rigidity of moral attitude such as is fitting, if at all, in judging ourselves and not in judging others. We may judge from one point of view that the telling of a wicked lie is completely determined by a man's unhappy nature, wretched circumstances, and past life. Yet from another point of view we none the less blame the agent: we judge him on the supposition that the past can be wholly set aside; that in performing the action, reason is completely free and self-sufficient,

---

[1] *Gr.*, 441 = 72.   [2] Compare *Gr.*, 458 = 93.
[3] *K.r.V.*, A534 = B562; A802 = B830; *K.p.V.*, 32 = 144 (= 57); *M.d.S., Rechtslehre, Einl.* I, 213 = 12; *Anthr.* §9, 144; *Religion*, 49 n. = 56–7 n. (= 58 n.). This freedom is different from the so-called psychological freedom in which reason affects actions by its concepts of what is remotely useful or harmful. See §4 above.
[4] Presumably we must freely allow ourselves to be influenced by heteronomous laws.

whatever be the sensuous obstacles; and that in the moment of lying the guilt is entirely his.[1]

Here apparently there are no degrees of freedom: as soon as we attain the age of discretion, we are all completely free. But quite a different, and much more human, view stands cheek by jowl with this.[2] According to this view the genuine morality of actions, their merit or guilt, is entirely concealed from us. We can judge only what Kant calls a man's empirical character; but how much of this is the pure effect of freedom, and how much has to be ascribed to mere nature, to a fortunate or defective temperament, no man can fathom; and consequently no man can judge with complete justice.[3]

Here surely there is a possibility of degrees of freedom. It is far too common to look at the rigid side of Kant and to ignore the humaner side, which is equally compatible with his central doctrine. He always differs consciously from the doctrine of the Stoics and allows much both for human ignorance and for human weakness. It is true that for him the command of duty is 'Be perfect' and even 'Be holy'; but we must remember that although the ideal is absolute, yet as regards degree this can only be an imperfect obligation because of the frailty of human nature. It is our duty to strive after this ideal, but not (in this life) to attain it.[4] If we could progress continuously towards our ideal, we should have done our duty.

---

[1] K.r.V., A554–5 = B582–3. See also K.p.V., 99–100 = 231 (= 178–9).
[2] K.r.V., A551 n. = B579 n.   [3] See also M.d.S., Tugendlehre, §48, 474.
[4] M.d.S., Tugendlehre, §§21–2, 446–7.

CHAPTER XXI

FREEDOM AS A NECESSARY PRESUPPOSITION

§1. *Freedom and rational agents.*

IF freedom as we have now described it could be established, then, according to Kant, the principle of autonomy, and so the supreme principle of morality, would follow by a mere analysis of the concept of freedom. If, however, we are to justify the moral principle, it is not enough merely to define freedom or to describe the characteristics which must necessarily be present in a will if it is to be regarded as free. It looks as if we have to show that every rational agent is, and indeed must be, free in the sense we have explained;[1] and this task certainly cannot be regarded as an easy one. Apparently anything short of this would fail to give us that justification of moral principle for which we seek; for we have seen that the moral law must be valid for all rational agents, and for all men only in virtue of the fact that they are rational agents.[2]

It is useless to appeal to any alleged experience of human nature; for experience of freedom, if it were possible (which it is not), would give us only a fact and not a necessary connexion of the kind which we seek. The plain man may indeed say that he feels himself to be free in action, and especially in moral action. But we are not entitled to derive from mere feeling a necessary connexion between being human and being free, and still less to extend our observation so as to cover all rational agents as such. Furthermore, on Kant's view, what is revealed to us by experience of our own successive states of mind is not freedom but necessity. Here as elsewhere a transcendental deduction must rest, not on experience, but on the insight of reason into its own necessary activity.[3]

§2. *The presupposition of freedom.*

Kant makes no claim to prove that a rational agent as such must be free. Such a claim to theoretical knowledge he regards as far beyond our human limitations. We might, however, be able to show that a rational agent as such can act only on the *presupposition* that he is free (only under the Idea of freedom). From the practical point of view of the agent, not the observer, this would be sufficient; *for the laws which would hold for a being known theoretically to be free must—for purposes of action—hold also for a being who must act on the presupposition that he is free.*[4] The establishment of such a necessary presupposition would be enough to justify the moral

[1] *Gr.*, 447 = 80.   [2] *Gr.*, 408 = 30–1; 411–12 = 35.
[3] Compare *K.p.V.*, 29 = 143 (= 52–3).   [4] *Gr.*, 448 = 80 and footnote.

law and so to complete our task as moral philosophers. If a rational agent must act on the presupposition that he is free, he must act on the presupposition that he is under the principle of autonomy.

In all this Kant is following out his doctrine that no Idea can give us knowledge of an actual or even possible reality. What it does is to prescribe a rule which reason by its very nature must obey and to set forth an ideal at which it must aim.

§3. *Theoretical reason and its presupposition.*

At this point the argument takes a surprising turn. Kant bases his case, not merely on the nature of practical reason, but on the nature of theoretical reason.

'We cannot possibly conceive of a reason as being consciously directed from outside in regard to its *judgements*.'[1] If a rational being were conscious of any such external influence, he would regard his judgements as determined, not by reason, but by impulse. Reason must—if it is to be reason at all—regard itself as the author of its own principles independently of external influences.

This is a strong argument, though it is seldom used in discussions about freedom.[2] It applies most obviously to a judgement which is the conclusion of an argument. If every judgement is determined solely by previous mental events and not by rational insight into a nexus between premises and conclusion independent of temporal succession, there can be no difference between valid and invalid inference, between reasoning and mere association, and ultimately there can be no truth. In that case determinism itself could not be accepted as true, nor could the arguments in its defence be accepted as valid.

Kant seems to be correct in saying that any reason which is conscious of itself as reason must regard itself as reasoning (or as forming its own conclusions) in accordance with its own rational and objective laws or principles, and not by the influence of any external cause or bias. This remains true even although it may be reasoning about something given it from without, as, for example, so-called sense-data. That is to say, reason must regard itself as the author of its own principles and as capable of functioning according to these principles independently of external influences. This means, in Kant's terminology, that reason must regard itself as free, both negatively and positively, in the act of reasoning.

§4. *Practical reason and its presupposition.*

If Kant's argument holds of theoretical reason, it holds equally of practical reason—that is, of a rational will or of reason as exercising

---

[1] *Gr.*, 448 = 81. The italics are mine.
[2] Compare A. E. Taylor, *Freedom and Personality*, Philosophy, XIV, 55; and *Freedom and Personality Again*, Philosophy, XVII, 65.

causality. Here too a rational agent as such must in action presuppose his rational will to be the source of its own principles of action and to be capable of functioning in accordance with these principles. In other words he must in action presuppose his rational will to be free both negatively and positively—that is, to be free from determination by desire and free to obey its own rational principles. To say this is to say that a rational agent can act only on the presupposition that he is free: he must act under the Idea of freedom. This is the doctrine which we set out to establish and from which the principle of autonomy is said to follow analytically.

This doctrine need not be based merely on an inference from theoretical to practical reason—though Kant may think that it is. It may rest also on the same kind of rational self-consciousness as does the previous argument. We may perhaps say that our insight into theoretical reason is also an insight into reason as such and consequently must cover practical reason as well; but the same insight into reason as such is surely found again in our insight into practical reason, and indeed *must* be found again if our conclusion is to be justified.

I do not want to make too much of this, but I believe Kant to be saying more than that in acting we necessarily conceive ourselves to be free. Action is not a blind something which is preceded and succeeded, or even accompanied, by thought. Action is as intelligent and as rational as thinking. What distinguishes human action from animal behaviour, and still more from physiological functioning or physical movement, is that we *will* in accordance with principles. I take Kant to be saying that a rational agent can act, just as he can think, only on the presupposition of freedom: he must think and act *as if* he were free. The presupposition of freedom is as implicit in his acting as in his thinking; and unless we can act on this presupposition there is no such thing as action, and there is no such thing as will. As Kant himself puts it, 'The will of a rational being cannot be a will of his own except under the Idea of freedom'.[1] Human action cannot differ from animal behaviour merely in being accompanied by a conception of freedom: if it differs at all, it must differ by being itself rational. A rational agent must will his actions under the Idea of freedom, just as he must will his actions as instances of a particular principle or maxim.[2]

No doubt there are many today who will be content to deny that there is any such thing as action or as will, if by this is meant rational action and rational will. This view can be reasonably held, as Kant recognises, if we take up the standpoint of observers. But if we regard thinking from the same external point of view—and it is arbitrary not to do so—we shall equally be compelled to deny that there is any such thing as thinking. There are some who are willing to accept even this conclusion; but if they do, it seems foolish to try to convince others of it by argument.

Kant makes a point of considerable value by his appeal to the self-consciousness of theoretical, as well as of practical, reason; for we cannot lightly accept its verdict in the one case and reject it in the other.

[1] *Gr.*, 448 = 81.   [2] See Chapter VIII §5.

§5. *The self-consciousness of reason.*

Kant's argument turns on what may be called the self-consciousness of reason in its own activities. Such self-consciousness is for him no mystical insight into the nature of some mysterious pure ego, as it is sometimes called, which can be known apart from its activity. It rests rather on a rational understanding of the *principles* manifested in the activity of reason as such. These principles are manifested, however imperfectly, in our every-day thoughts and actions; but we are able, on Kant's view, (1) to conceive them in abstraction from their empirical concomitants, and (2) to understand both their internal necessity and their necessity as conditions of the whole activity from which they are abstracted. That is to say, we can, in virtue of our own rationality, understand both how these principles are necessary manifestations of reason as such, and also how they are necessary to our theoretical and practical judgements.

In the case of theoretical reason these principles may for the present be regarded as what Kant calls the Principles of the Understanding—especially the three Analogies of Experience;[1] but behind these, and behind the categories applied in them, there is the more ultimate concept of universal law as such.[2] This is the concept bound up with, and correlative to, that ultimate self-consciousness of reason which Kant calls the transcendental unity of apperception.

If the self-consciousness of reason is inseparable from consciousness of the rational principles manifested in its own activity, what are these principles in the case of practical reason? The principles in question must obviously be what we have called 'objective principles of practical reason',[3] principles in accordance with which a rational agent, *qua* rational agent, would necessarily act, if reason had full control over passion. For the present purpose Kant ignores the objective principles of skill and self-love, whether because they are irrelevant to his argument or because they are regarded as merely hypothetical and as subordinate to desire. We are left with the unconditioned objective principle of morality, the principle of acting for the sake of universal law as such. To agents only partially rational this principle must appear as a categorical imperative and in particular as the imperative of autonomy.

If this is so—and in the *Critique of Practical Reason* Kant recognises that it is so—we cannot ascribe to rational agents a necessary presupposition of freedom independently of their recognition of the categorical imperative. If the Ideas of freedom and of moral autonomy are really distinct, the inference is not from freedom to autonomy but *vice versa*. 'I ought' implies 'I can.' Duty implies freedom.

---

[1] The principles of Formal Logic and the Ideas of reason have to be considered as well. See Chapter XXIV §8.

[2] *Gr.*, 454 = 88. This is identical with what may be called the principle of objectivity in knowledge or the concept of an object in general.

[3] See Chapter IX. Yet we must also remember that for Kant—at least in his later works—freedom is manifested in acting upon maxims.

Kant may indeed be right in asserting that reason as such, and in particular theoretical reason, must ascribe to itself freedom to function in accordance with its own principles independently of necessitation from without. This may give us ground for suspecting that practical reason must ascribe to itself a similar freedom; but the nature of this freedom is not intelligible without grasping the unconditioned objective principle of action—that is, the principle of morality. It is a mistake to suppose—as Kant may have supposed in the *Groundwork*—that morality could be justified by a non-moral concept of freedom established without regard to any moral considerations. Our consciousness of the fundamental principle of moral autonomy can—according to the *Critique of Practical Reason*—be called a 'fact of reason': it cannot be extracted by subtle argument from antecedent data of reason, such as consciousness of freedom; for this is not antecedently given.[1]

§6. *The position of the argument.*

If on these grounds we must abandon the attempt to derive freedom directly from the self-consciousness of reason as such and thereby to produce a transcendental deduction of the categorical imperative, how do we stand? Are we simply to say that Kant's moral philosophy, in spite of all its ingenuity, has ended in failure?

It seems unnecessary to take up so pessimistic an attitude. If, as Kant claims,[2] he has given a correct analysis of the implications of all moral judgements, if apart from the categorical imperative and the principle of autonomy we must abandon all belief in moral goodness and in binding obligations, this in itself would justify us in accepting—and in acting upon—his doctrine. However much we may disagree with particular moral judgements, it is almost as hard for us to set aside the fact of moral judgement as it is to set aside the fact of theoretical judgement. A philosophy which can show that you must accept its principles if you think at all, is on strong ground; and a philosophy which can show that you must accept its principles if you make moral judgements at all, is on almost equally strong ground.

Kant does not, however, rest his case merely on the fact that his philosophy gives the correct account of the implications or conditions of ordinary moral judgement. In the regress which he has made, every step seems to involve insight not merely into the relation between the conditioned and the condition, but also into the truth of the judgement which expresses the condition.[3] In particular he holds that as rational agents we have direct insight into the truth that a rational agent as such would necessarily act in accordance with a universal principle valid for

---

[1] *K.p.V.*, 31 = 143 (= 55–6). Kant still insists that the principle of autonomy is a synthetic *a priori* proposition, grounded neither on pure nor on empirical intuition. It would be analytic—presumably in the sense that it would follow analytically—if we could presuppose the freedom of the will. For this, however, as a positive concept we should require an intellectual intuition such as we cannot presume to have.

[2] Compare *K.p.V.*, 32 = 143 (= 56). [3] See Chapter I §9.

all rational agents.[1] This doctrine still turns on what I have called the self-consciousness of reason, and to this topic we shall have to return later.

The presupposition of freedom remains a necessary presupposition for rational agents, although it is now based on recognition of the categorical imperative. It is possible to act on presuppositions which we do not know to be true; but it is not possible to act on presuppositions which we know not to be true. Hence the presupposition of freedom is in need of defence; we must show at least that it is neither self-contradictory nor excluded by experience. This is the task to which Kant now sets himself, although he complicates it by bringing in a variety of considerations whose relevance is not altogether clear.

---

[1] See Chapter IX §4.

CHAPTER XXII

THE INTELLIGIBLE WORLD

§1. *Side issues.*

WE have now to concern ourselves with Kant's distinction between the sensible (or phenomenal) world and the intelligible (or noumenal) world. The main reason why we must do so is that without this distinction we shall be compelled, on Kant's view, to deny the possibility of freedom and therefore to reject, not only his own ethical doctrine, but also the very possibility of morality. This seems to be the view of the *Critique of Practical Reason*. In the *Groundwork*, curiously enough, he does not make this explicit till after he has completed his arguments; and, perhaps because he is seeking—mistakenly—to derive the imperative of autonomy from the presupposition of freedom, he approaches the problem of the intelligible world in quite a different way. He raises two apparently interconnected difficulties: (1) the question of what he calls 'moral interest'; and (2) the question of the vicious circle. These seem to be side issues at the best.

§2. *Moral interest.*

His first question is 'Why should I be moral?' Granted that as a rational agent I must act on the presupposition of freedom, and granted that from the presupposition of freedom there follows, for finite creatures like men, the principle of autonomy as a categorical imperative, why should I subject myself as a rational agent to this principle? Why should I limit my actions to those whose maxims can be willed at the same time as universal laws? And why should I attach so supreme a value to conduct of this kind that in comparison the claims of pleasure become negligible?[1]

It may be said that to these questions Kant has given no sufficient answer. This objection he recognises, but his language does not make it clear whether he regards it as a sound criticism or not. He indicates once more that it would be no answer to say I was driven by some pathological interest: pathological interest cannot give us a categorical imperative. Nevertheless I must *take* an interest, a moral interest, in duty, and I must be able to understand how this can happen; for 'I ought' is equivalent to 'I will' for a rational agent as such, and appears as 'I ought' only because of the hindrances of passion.[2] He adds that it is no answer to say that in fact I do take such a moral interest, since this interest, which he has else-

---

[1] *Gr.*, 449 = 82. [2] See also *Gr.*, 414 = 38.

where equated with reverence,[1] itself follows from the supposition that the moral law is binding.

How far Kant takes this objection seriously cannot be easily determined by the subsequent course of the argument. He does not return later to this argument explicitly, except at the very end of the book; and there he seems to say that these questions are really due to misunderstanding. The only answer to the question 'Why ought I to do my duty'? must be 'Because it is your duty.' To expect any other answer is to deny the essence of duty and to suppose that we ought to do our so-called duty for some other reason, presumably from self-interest.

We can indeed say that a rational agent as such will necessarily act in accordance with a universal law equally valid for all rational agents, and that he ought so to act if he is irrational enough to be tempted to do otherwise. But this is the answer Kant has already given, and it rests on the ultimate insight of reason into its own principles, beyond which we cannot go either as regards thinking or as regards action. Kant may believe he is going to add to this answer by saying that in so acting a rational agent is being his real and intelligible self, or at least is acting in accordance with his Idea of his real and intelligible self. This line of thought, however, though familiar to us in later idealism, is at least not conspicuous in Kant. It is in any case more satisfactory to regard his doctrine of our membership in the intelligible world as a metaphysical defence of the ethical doctrine already expounded and not as an attempt to prove an ethical doctrine on purely metaphysical grounds.

§3. *The alleged vicious circle.*

There is a second objection interwoven with the previous one. The objection is that in appealing to the presupposition of freedom we have fallen into a vicious circle. We have argued that we must be free because we are subject to a categorical imperative; and we have then proceeded to argue that we must be subject to a categorical imperative because we are free.[2]

This circle is of the kind which inevitably arises if we follow up a regressive argument by the same argument stated progressively.[3] In the present case the argument, as Kant indicates, may establish a necessary and reciprocal connexion between the concept of being under the categorical imperative and the concept of being free; but it does nothing to establish either the validity of the categorical imperative or the necessity of presupposing freedom. Why should we not reject both?

We need not suppose that Kant takes this criticism too seriously: it is the kind of objection which may be thought to arise.[4] Nevertheless it is strange that he should not only mention it, but should make so much

---

[1] See *Gr.*, 401 n. = 22 n.   [2] *Gr.*, 449 = 82; 450 = 83; and 453 = 86–7.
[3] See Chapter I §9.
[4] The use of the phrase '*es scheint*' ('it appears') often indicates in Kant the illusory character of what is being said.

of it, and should apparently admit that only by an appeal to the doctrine of an intelligible world can he succeed in escaping from the circle. In plain fact the objection totally misrepresents his argument. He never argued from the categorical imperative to freedom, but at least professed, however mistakenly, to establish the presupposition of freedom by an insight into the nature of self-conscious reason quite independently of moral considerations. Perhaps when he came to the objection he was beginning to see dimly that the presupposition of freedom of the will did really rest on moral considerations; but it is surely unusual for a man to answer the sound argument which he has failed to put and to overlook the fact that this is irrelevant to the unsound argument which alone has been explicitly stated.

§4. *The way of escape.*

We are now introduced to the doctrine of the two standpoints as a way out of our alleged vicious circle. In order to escape from this we must ask 'Do we take *one point of view* of ourselves when we think of ourselves as free causes working according to our own laws, and *another point of view* when we think of our actions as observed events in the sensible world?'[1]

The suggestion here is that there may be two equally legitimate points of view from which we may regard ourselves. From one point of view we may regard ourselves as belonging to an intelligible world and so as free, while from another point of view we may regard ourselves and our actions as belonging to the world of nature. This may be a way of reconciling moral freedom with causal necessity, but how is it going to help us get out of our circle?

There is clearly no hope of escape unless we can claim an independent insight into our membership of the intelligible world. The insight claimed must rest neither on the presupposition of freedom nor on the presupposition of morality; for otherwise we shall merely have added another link to the alleged circle, which will remain incorrigibly vicious. As we shall see, Kant does to some extent appear to escape from the circle by concentrating his attention on the *theoretical* function of reason and thereby attempting to establish a necessary characteristic of reason as such. But this is exactly what he had already in fact done in justifying the presupposition of freedom. Furthermore, it is by no means clear that he deliberately wishes to rest his case on insight into the activity of theoretical reason. At the end of his argument[2] he does suggest that a rational being must consider himself *as intelligence* (presumably theoretical intelligence) to belong to the intelligible world, and therefore to act under the Idea of freedom, and therefore to be subject to the categorical imperative of autonomy. Yet immediately thereafter,[3] in claiming to have escaped from the circle, he does so on the ground that *when we think of ourselves as free*, we transfer ourselves as members to the intelligible world.

[1] *Gr.*, 450 = 83–4.   [2] *Gr.*, 452 = 86.   [3] *Gr.*, 453 = 87.

In the section which follows and purports to give the answer to the question 'How is a categorical imperative possible?' we find the same appearance of hesitation. He begins again by maintaining that a rational being must *as intelligence* count himself as belonging to the intelligible world, and seems to infer that only so can he consider himself to exercise causality and manifest a free will.[1] Yet at the end of his whole argument he sums it up by saying that categorical imperatives are possible since the *Idea of freedom* makes me a member of the intelligible world.[2] Is he arguing from membership of the intelligible world to freedom or *vice versa*? Or is he merely establishing a universal and reciprocal connexion between the concept of membership in the intelligible world and the concept of freedom, a connexion which would do nothing whatever to break the alleged circle.[3]

This is not merely a technical point which it is a waste of time to consider. On the contrary, it raises a fundamental issue of principle. If Kant really supposes that he can start from theoretical reason and infer from this to membership of the intelligible world, and from this to freedom, and from this to a justification of the binding character of the moral law, then—however much he may be escaping a vicious circle—he is falling into a fundamental error. It is manifestly impossible to deduce moral obligation from purely metaphysical or epistemological considerations which have nothing to do with morality.

Metaphysical considerations about freedom and about membership of the intelligible world may be absolutely necessary to *defend* a moral principle taken to be independently established, but they cannot by themselves *establish* it. Whatever be his view in the *Groundwork*, Kant himself was well aware of this when he came to write the *Critique of Practical Reason*. Our main task must therefore be to consider how far his argument is successful as a defence of freedom and so of morality.

§5. *The two standpoints.*

The doctrine of the two standpoints takes us for the first time into the heart of the Critical Philosophy. Here we must face the difficulty that knowledge of the *Critique of Pure Reason* is necessary for a full understanding of what Kant is now trying to say. The main doctrines of that work and the arguments without which they are barely intelligible cannot be expounded in a short book devoted to ethics. On the other hand it cannot be assumed that readers interested in ethics have a detailed grasp of the *Critique of Pure Reason*. Hence Kant—and any commentator who tries to follow him—has to give a semi-popular and admittedly inadequate exposition of his metaphysical doctrines.[4] He does so partly by making dogmatic statements based on his previous work and partly by offering some rather simple arguments in support of his position. The result cannot be wholly satisfactory and must be taken only as an introduction

[1] *Gr.*, 453 = 87.
[3] Compare §3 above.
[2] *Gr.*, 453 = 88.
[4] *Gr.*, 451 = 84.

to the whole philosophy, in the light of which the argument for freedom must be judged.

Broadly speaking, Kant's fundamental doctrine, his Copernican revolution, is the result of an attempt to work out a view commonly held in the Eighteenth Century and present in such diverse thinkers as Leibniz and even Hume,[1] though Kant alone made a serious and sustained effort to think out its ramifications in detail. This view is that the human mind *contributes* something to the world as known to it. If this were so, and if the human mind were simpler and more easily known than the world, then a philosophical study of it would enable us to discover certain fundamental characteristics which the world as known to us must necessarily have.

It would at once follow, although this consequence was not clearly grasped before Kant, that we should have no reason to consider the world as known to us to be identical with the world as it is in itself. On the one hand we should have the world as it appears to limited and human finite minds, the world which may be described as the world of appearance or the phenomenal world. Since this world is revealed to us only through our senses, we may also call it the sensible world. This, *ex hypothesi*, is the only world we could know; but we should have to conceive, as it were behind it as its ground, the world as it really is in itself, the world of things as they are in themselves. This world may be described as the world of things-in-themselves or again as the intelligible or noumenal world. This last description clearly requires further justification, but at least it is not inappropriate so far as we may be said to conceive such a world in our thought, though it can never be known to us through our senses. Indeed, since on Kant's view all knowledge depends on a combination of thought and sense, we must say that the world of things-in-themselves, though it can and must be conceived, cannot be known by us at all.

Such a view assumes both that human minds function in the same sort of way and that the world which appears to them is one and the same world, however differently it may appear to different persons.

The first assumption, however hard to justify, is one which every philosopher must make in the act of communicating his thought. But why should we assume that the different phenomena which appear to different observers are grounded in one and the same real world, even if it can never appear to them as it really is?

The doctrine of the thing-in-itself is impatiently swept aside both by those who hold that there is no reality other than sensa (and perhaps sensibilia) and by those who hold that the human mind must know reality as it really is. Kant's whole philosophy is a continuous argument against the latter view, which he calls transcendental realism. As against the phenomenalists, who are content to regard sensa as the only reality, he is an empirical realist: that is, he believes with Newton and common sense that space is filled with permanent substances which act causally upon one

---

[1] Compare Price, *Hume's Theory of the External World*, p. 9.

another; and indeed one of his main aims is to demonstrate that this must be so. But while he holds that the world as it appears to human observers who possess both sense and intelligence must appear as a world of bodies in space and time, he regards this world of bodies as itself only an appearance: and he seems to take for granted rather than to argue explicitly that it could not appear to us as one common world unless, in addition to there being minds which functioned in the same sort of way, there were also one and the same real world which appeared to them all, the world as it is in itself and not as it appears under the limitations of finite minds. Without assuming a world as it is in itself, even if it cannot be known by us, it is at least difficult for the phenomenalist to justify his rejection of solipsism—if he does reject it; and if he is prepared to accept the existence, in some sense, of individual minds, it at least looks as if for him each individual mind must have its own private world, out of which it can never escape to a common or public world.

The sensible world is better called the phenomenal world, since for Kant it is an appearance, not to sense alone, but to sense and thought; and if we are speaking Greek, we should contrast it with the noumenal world. But if we prefer to speak English, we may contrast the sensible with the intelligible world, so long as we remember that the sensible world is not merely sensible.

This terminology should not lead us into the error of thinking that on Kant's view there are two worlds. For him there is only one world: though we can know the world only as it appears to us, what we know is the one real world as it appears to us. We must indeed *conceive* this one world (1) as it appears to our sensuous experience and (2) as it is in itself.[1] This is the reason why Kant speaks of two standpoints or points of view: (1) the point of view from which we regard things as phenomena, and (2) the point of view from which we conceive things as noumena or things-in-themselves. The phrase 'point of view' is not intended, as is sometimes thought, to indicate that either phenomena or noumena or both are unreal: it is used only to guard against the supposition that there are two distinct and separate worlds. There is only one world, but it can be looked at from two different points of view.

§6. *The argument from the passivity of sense.*

In order to render this doctrine intelligible to uninstructed readers Kant supports it by an argument which he thinks likely to find acceptance on the level of common sense or at least common judgement.[2] This argument is not used in the *Critique of Pure Reason*, and by itself it is, at most, persuasive rather than convincing. It fails to do justice, not only to the arguments for his doctrine, but also to the doctrine itself. We may call it the argument from the passivity of sense.

[1] *Gr.*, 457 = 92; *K.r.V.*, B xxvi; A38 = B55.
[2] *Gr.*, 450-1 = 84-5

On Kant's view our knowledge of an objective world depends on the co-operation of two cognitive powers:[1] (1) an active power of thinking by means of concepts; and (2) a passive capacity of sensibility—that is, a capacity to receive what are today called sensa or sense-data. Kant himself calls them 'sensations' (*Empfindungen*) to indicate that they are neutral:[2] apart from thinking, they reveal to us neither the characteristics of physical objects nor the states of our own mind. Though there are objections to this usage, it is perhaps no more question-begging than any other. He also calls them ideas or representations or presentations (*Vorstellungen*), though this is a term of wider application.

We know physical objects only through sensations. Thus we think—for without thinking we can know no physical object—that the brown which we sense is the quality of a penny; and similarly with its other qualities. However active we may be in thinking, we do not make our sensations: they are passively received and in that sense given. As naive realists we find no difficulty in assuming that the qualities of objects are thus given to us directly; but a little reflection and a very little physiology is apt to disturb this assurance. Our sensations, we discover, are the result of a chain of causes emanating from the physical object and effecting changes in our nerve-endings and ultimately in our brain. As soon as we realise this, it seems as if there is no reason for supposing our sensations to give us qualities of the object, or even to be like the object in any respect. Yet since we know objects only through sensations, it looks as if we cannot know objects at all. What we call physical objects in space (including our own brain) become mere mental constructions based on sensations; and with this result the science of physiology seems to commit suicide.

It may be objected that physiology cannot legitimately destroy the fundamental assumptions on which it itself is based. Nevertheless this is what it seems to do, and some philosophical solution of the difficulty is demanded. There may be different solutions. Kant's solution is that the world of bodies extending through infinite time and space is in fact a mental construction based on our sensations, but that these sensations must themselves be grounded on a reality which we can never know. Only on this supposition, and on the supposition that different minds function on the same principles, can we have before us one phenomenal world of physical bodies (including our own brain) in causal interaction with one another.

Kant himself puts the position much more simply. He merely urges that since sensations come to us in ways we cannot control, they can give us knowledge of objects only as the objects *affect* us, and not as they are

---

[1] I pass over the power of imagination which is also essential both for 'taking up' or 'apprehending' sensations and for combining them with images. Those who argue against Kant that sensation must be also active forget that the active side of sensation, the taking up of the given into consciousness, is recognised by him, but is attributed to imagination.

[2] Strictly speaking, we have no adequate translation for the neutral word '*Empfindung*'. Kant equates it with '*Sensation*' only when it at the same time attracts attention to the state of the subject. See *Anthr.* §15, 153.

in themselves.[1] This argument, however, is telescoped, unless we distinguish clearly between (1) the sensations, (2) the physical object revealed by the sensations and supposed to cause them, and (3) the thing as it is in itself, which is the ground of the sensations and so of the physical object revealed by them. The physical object affects our brain, and both the physical object and our brain are phenomenal objects. The thing-in-itself —if it affects anything—affects our mind; but this is not a causal relation. The thing-in-itself is the ground, and not the cause, of our sensations; or, better, it is the unknown reality which, because of our human limitations, appears to us as a hard, brown, circular object in a particular region of space-time, the physical object which we call a penny.[2]

It is not by itself a convincing argument to maintain that our sensations, because they are passively received apart from any activity or choice of ours, must be given from some other source, and must reveal the way in which we are affected by something which can never be known by finite minds whose knowledge is necessarily dependent on sensations.

On the other hand it seems reasonable to assume, at least as a hypothesis, that there is some reality which is other than the individual self and is what it is independently of our knowing it. It is difficult, if not impossible, to believe that this reality is composed only of sensa, or even of sensa and sensibilia. If Kant can also show, as he claims, that bodies (or physical energy) occupying space-time cannot be such an independent reality, it at least looks as if reality as it is in itself cannot be known by finite human minds; nor does there appear to be anything antecedently improbable in such a supposition.

§7. *Other arguments.*

If we are to understand Kant's doctrine properly, we must have in mind the three lines of argument used to support it in the *Critique of Pure Reason*. The first two rest on the contention that the human mind must *contribute* something to reality as known to it.

The first concerns space and time. Space cannot, as Newton supposed, be a real thing in its own right independently of what is in it. But equally it cannot be a mere quality of physical things, as Leibniz held (though with considerable qualifications). The only alternative is that it must be a form of our sensibility—that is, a form under which alone our sensations, and consequently physical objects revealed by these sensations, can be given to our human minds. Our mind imposes space on what we sense in somewhat the same way that blue spectacles impose blue colour on what we see. Similar considerations apply to time.

It is strange that Kant regards this argument as absolutely conclusive. If, however, he is right in holding that these are the only three possibilities, the plausibility of his argument is very great.

[1] *Gr.*, 451 = 84.
[2] This does not mean that there must be a separate thing-in-itself for everything that we choose to regard as a distinguishable physical object.

The second line of argument rests on the necessity of thinking, if we are to know not mere sensa, but real objects, especially physical objects. In order to do this we must make use of certain categories, such as substance and accident or cause and effect. These categories are certainly not given to our senses and cannot be derived by abstraction from what is so given. They are imposed by the nature of our thinking on objects as known to us.[1]

If both these lines of argument are sound, and if we assume that in knowing we are concerned with a reality other than ourselves which is not of our creating, then clearly we have no reason whatever for assuming that reality as it is in itself is characterised either as spatial or as temporal or as subject to such categories as cause and effect. On the other hand reality as it appears to us must be so characterised, and a reality not so characterised we can never know.

The third line of argument goes farther and sets forth reasons for denying that reality as it is in itself can be so characterised. For if we suppose that the world which we know as spatial and temporal and governed by causal law is reality as it is in itself, then we fall inevitably into a series of contradictions called by Kant '*Antinomies*'. These contradictions disappear only if we suppose that the world which we know by means of our categories is not reality as it is in itself, but is only reality as it must appear to human minds.

This third line of argument should certainly be received with caution, though many of the so-called refutations of it are based on misunderstandings of what Kant's doctrine is. If this argument were sound, it would really clinch Kant's case; and it is, as we shall see later, very especially concerned with the defence of freedom.

Incidentally this last type of argument clearly assumes that reality as it is in itself cannot be self-contradictory: contradictions can characterise only appearance. Perhaps Kant even assumes positively that reality must be some sort of coherent system. He never denies that we must conceive reality as it is in itself and must do so by means of the pure categories which have no reference to time:[2] we have indeed no other means of thinking at all. But for us there is no *knowledge* without sense as well as thought, and it is impossible for us to sense a reality which is non-temporal and non-spatial. Hence we cannot know that there is, or even that there can be, such a reality. Though we must conceive such a reality by an Idea of reason, our conception cannot be elevated to the dignity of knowledge.

§8. *Conclusion.*

In the light of these arguments we can understand better what Kant means by his two standpoints.

Suppose we are asked 'Is the world governed throughout by causal

[1] For a fuller statement see Chapter IX, Appendix.
[2] See Chapter IX, Appendix §3.

law?' The answer is 'Yes, certainly'—if we are interested in a point of view concerned only with the world as it must appear to human minds. If, however, we are interested in a point of view concerned with the world as it is in itself independently of human knowing, the answer must be 'Certainly not'—or at the very least that we have no reason for thinking so, and every reason for thinking the opposite. The two answers cease to be contradictory only when it is understood that they are given from different points of view. There is at least no contradiction in supposing that both answers may be true.

It may be hard to give an exact parallel for such differences in point of view, and so far as I know Kant does not give any. But it may be supposed that the physicist, the chemist, and the biologist might give seemingly contradictory answers to a question about living organisms, and yet the contradiction would disappear if we took into account the differences in their point of view. Similarly, if we were asked whether bodies were or were not solid, we might give one answer from a macroscopic, and quite another from a microscopic, point of view, and do so without any contradiction.

CHAPTER XXIII

MEMBERSHIP OF THE INTELLIGIBLE WORLD

§1. *Inner sense and mental states.*

WE have now to consider Kant's suggestion that from one point of view we may regard ourselves as belonging to the intelligible world and so as under the law of freedom, while from another point of view we may regard ourselves as belonging to the sensible world and so as under the causal law of nature. Unfortunately Kant's doctrine of self-knowledge is the most obscure and difficult part of his philosophy, and for the present purpose it has to be treated very summarily.

Since all knowledge requires a combination of thought and sense, our knowledge of self must be based on what Kant calls 'inner sense'[1] in order to distinguish it from the outer senses, through which we become aware of physical objects, including our own body. Inner sense may be identified with the power of introspection, as it is sometimes called today. At every moment we are directly and immediately aware of our own states of mind. These states of mind may be, and perhaps always are, both cognitive and affective and conative. Our thoughts, our feelings, our inclinations, our desires, our resolutions, and also, quite explicitly, our ideas of physical objects—all these belong to inner sense.[2]

Inner sense is appropriately described as a kind of sense (though unlike the outer senses it has no special sense-organ); for it is always an immediate awareness of something individual given here and now. Starting from what is given to inner sense, we are able in thought to reconstruct our whole mental history in somewhat the same way as, starting from what is given to outer sense, we can in thought reconstruct the history of the physical universe. Our knowledge of ourselves is as empirical as our knowledge of the world, and it is equally based on what is directly given and passively received, not made by our knowing of it.

If we accept Kant's previous argument from the passivity of sense, it follows that we can know ourselves only as we appear to human minds, and not as we are in ourselves. And since we know our mental states only as succeeding one another in time, the same conclusion follows if we accept the argument that time can be only a form of our sensibility.[3]

---
[1] *Gr.*, 451 = 85.
[2] *K.r.V.*, A357–8; B67; B xxxix n.; A34 = B50; *M.d.S., Rechtslehre,* **Einl. I,** 214 = 13.
[3] See Chapter XXII §§6 and 7.

[233]

The succession of mental states which is all we are aware of through inner sense may be called the phenomenal self, the self as it appears. It must, however, be remembered that such a succession cannot be known through inner sense in itself; for this we require also imagination, memory, and thought. Since thought, on Kant's view, must work by means of its own categories, the phenomenal self as an object of knowledge must fall under the categories, particularly the category of cause and effect, which is concerned with objective succession in time.[1]

Hence from one point of view we must regard ourselves—that is, our phenomenal selves—as belonging to the sensible world and so as subject to the causal law of nature.

§2. *The noumenal self.*

So far we know ourselves through inner sense only as a succession of appearances. Kant holds, as he did in regard to outer experience, that we must assume something else to be the ground of these appearances. That something else must be the I-as-it-is-in-itself.[2] This must be conceived; but since on his principles it cannot be sensed, it can no more be known than can the thing-in-itself. We may call it the intelligible or noumenal self, and we must regard it as belonging to the non-sensible, and in that sense to the intelligible, or noumenal, world.

At this point the difficulties become acute, and we can almost hear the positivists shouting 'Take away that bauble.' This is not the place to expound, and still less to defend, Kant's doctrine in detail; but here also, it may be observed, Kant's view, if strangely expressed, bears some resemblance to what may be described as the assumptions—or prejudices—of common sense. Besides the long mental history of ideas, feelings, desires, and volitions which is known as my phenomenal self, must there not be an I which knows this history, and which has these ideas, these feelings, and these desires? If this be a superstition, it is one which is at least difficult to avoid.

We must, however, admit that Kant's treatment of this subject is necessarily inadequate in the *Groundwork*, and also that it is far from clear even in his other writings. All we can attempt is to clarify, if possible, some of the statements in the passage we are now considering.

---

[1] See Chapter XXII §7. There is some doubt as to the way in which Kant conceived the category of substance to apply to the self. We are not, he says, adequately informed either through experience or through inferences of reason whether man has a soul (in the sense of a spiritual substance dwelling in him distinct from the body and capable of thinking independently of it) or whether life may not rather be a quality of matter. 'Life' here is 'the power of a being to act in accordance with its own ideas'. And again he says that reason as a theoretical power could quite well be the quality of a living corporeal being. See *M.d.S., Tugendlehre,* §§3–4, 418 = 19, and *Rechtslehre, Einl.*, 211 = 9. See also *K.p.V.*, 9 n. = 112 n. (= 16 n.) for 'life'. If there is nothing permanent in mental life, as Kant holds, and if the phenomenal self is to be known under the category of substance and accident, it is hard to see how he can regard mental states as other than qualities of a permanent material body. Compare *K.r.V.*, B275 ff.

[2] *Gr.*, 451 = 85.

§3. *The mind affects itself.*

According to Kant if man knows himself through inner sense, he knows himself only 'through the way in which his consciousness is affected'. Here again we have the assumption that since mind is passive in sense, it must be affected by something. In dealing with the objects of outer sense we supposed that our mind must be affected by a thing-in-itself which is other than our self. In self-knowledge we come up against the strange paradox that the mind must somehow be affected by itself.

Kant's efforts to explain this paradox are difficult to follow.[1] He gives ordinary 'attention' as an example of what he means;[2] and it is easy to see that attending to something does affect our mental consciousness and brings a different content into the phenomenal self. Indeed all our thinking and all our willing may be said to do the same.

It may be objected that we are now passing from the realm of paradox into that of downright contradiction. We have said that all our thoughts and volitions are states of mind which we know through inner sense. How can we also regard them as activities which by affecting consciousness make the phenomenal self what it is?

There is certainly a difficulty here, but is it arbitrarily created by Kant? If we consider, for example, a historian, it looks—from one point of view—as if he stood above the battle as a timeless observer assigning to each historical event its place in a causal series which he understands. Yet when we turn to consider what he has done in composing his history, this too appears as an historical event in the same causal series, and in no way different from any other historical event. But in saying this we seem again to be ourselves above the battle—only to find on reflection that our judgement is in turn something to be judged as on the same level with its object. Every man is, as it were, the historian of his own life, and it looks as if Kant were right in saying that we must regard ourselves from two different points of view.

What we know as an object is always the phenomenal self, but the knowing of it seems to be something different; and when in turn we regard this knowing as an event at a particular time, we do so in virtue of a fresh knowing which seems, as it were, to be above events and above time. And so it goes on through some infinite regress in which we can never get rid of the knowing which is itself not known as an event, although it makes a change in our consciousness, a change which can be known to further reflection as a mental state.

This curious contrast runs through all our thinking, which can always be considered from two different points of view. The scientist contemplates nature almost as if he were a god; yet from another point of view all his science is only a part of nature. The psychologist contemplates human

---

[1] Compare *K.r.V.*, B155 ff.
[2] *K.r.V.*, B156–7 n. Attention may be directed either to outer objects or to states of mind. One of the difficulties about introspection is that the effort of attention present in it tends to alter the consciousness which we seek to introspect.

nature and human thought as if he alone were a divine judge; yet from another point of view all his psychology is just another piece of human thought.

The strange thing is that although we can turn back and contemplate our own thinking, it then ceases to be thinking, and becomes merely thought. It is no longer thinking, but an object thought about and different from the thinking which thinks about it. In the terminology of Gentile it has ceased to be *pensiero pensante* and has become *pensiero pensato*.

Hence our thinking appears to be an activity which affects our consciousness and is thereby the ground of a state of mind which can be known through inner sense (together with fresh thinking); but as known through inner sense it has become a state of mind which is no longer an activity—an object known, rather than itself an act of thinking.

Perhaps this is not so surprising as it seems. We can see everything within the range of our vision except the place from which we see. If we step back a little, we can see this place also, but we do so again from another place which we cannot see.

§4. *Knowledge of mental activity.*

It may well be felt that there must be something wrong about all this. Kant's view, it may be said, is perhaps just intelligible as regards knowledge of outer things, but as regards self-knowledge it is merely fantastic. Let us try to put the matter by means of a rather crude analogy.

According to him we have before us in outer sense some sort of semi-transparent screen on which images are thrown from the other side and can be seen by us. We must suppose that something throws these images on to the screen, perhaps some kind of cinematograph; but as we cannot get to the other side of the screen, it is reasonable enough to maintain that we can never know what this something really is. In the case of self-knowledge the situation is quite different; for there the cinematograph (or whatever it is) is on the same side of the screen as I am, and indeed I am supposed to be the person who is turning the handle. How then can it be maintained that I still know only what appears on the screen and can have no knowledge of the reality which is its ground?[1]

We may put the same point without the aid of analogy. If my activity 'affects' my consciousness and thereby is the ground of a state of mind which is known through inner sense, surely I must know something of my own activity as well as of the resulting state of mind.

Kant does not overlook this point. He says that *pure* activity in a rational agent comes into consciousness *immediately* and *not* through affecting the senses.[2] This looks a little like what Professor Alexander called 'enjoyment' as opposed to 'contemplation'. It seems to be a special

[1] Perhaps to complete the analogy we should add that what is thrown on the screen from the far side is not visible till something is done from my side. But this is doubtful, since Kant holds that it is possible—as in the case of animals—to have outer sense without inner sense (and consequently without consciousness of time).
[2] *Gr.*, 451 = 85.

XXIII §4] MEMBERSHIP OF THE INTELLIGIBLE WORLD 237

kind of self-evidence of which we should like to have a much fuller account.[1] The name which Kant gives to this kind of awareness is 'pure apperception'.[2]

Kant does not believe that this pure apperception can by itself give us knowledge of ourselves. In all knowledge of objects, including knowledge of ourselves as objects, there must be present both sense and thought, both passivity and activity. Thought is the source of conceptions, and sense of intuitions. The self-consciousness of thinking is only a consciousness of the principles (or conceptions) in accordance with which it functions. We can separate out by abstraction these principles of thinking, but what we have then is logic and not psychology, an awareness of the timeless principles in accordance with which thinking as such must necessarily function. If we seek to know anything individual, we must bring in the empirical element always present in actual thinking; but as soon as we do this we bring in sense, and in particular inner sense; and consequently knowledge of ourselves as individuals, and of our thinkings as individual events, is always consciousness of the self as it appears to us in time, and not as it is in itself.

It looks as if the knowing self is in a curious way different from the self as known to be a succession of mental states in time. Although they are the same self regarded from different points of view, the first self seems to be the reality in which the second self is grounded.[3] Yet, when we seek to know the knowing self, we seek in vain, and always apprehend only some new mental states instead. Similarly if we seek to see our own eyes, we do so in vain, and always see something else instead. Nevertheless we must conceive our self as a power of binding together given sensa and images in accordance with certain principles whose necessity we understand. This is why Kant speaks of the synthetic unity of apperception as the highest point to which all use of the understanding must be attached.[4]

In all this we must remember that Kant is concerned with the kind of unity or identity the self must have *in order to know*—that is to experience —the physical world and its own mental history. This problem should not be confused with another and quite different problem—that of discovering the kind of unity or identity which the self must have *in order to be known* as a self.[5]

The knowing self Kant does not conceive of as an eternal substance but as an activity, a pure activity[6] of synthesis in accordance with certain necessary principles. One difficulty of this is that pure activity, as merely conceived in abstraction from all its sensible accompaniments, must be conceived as timeless and must be manifested only in (or even identified

[1] See Chapter I §9.   [2] *K.r.V.*, A115–16; B153; *Anthr.* §7, 141–2.
[3] The contents of the phenomenal self are also partly grounded in a reality, a thing-in-itself, other than the self.
[4] *K.r.V.*, B134 n. The central defect of Caird's interpretation is that he always assumes the *analytic* unity of apperception to be the highest point and—equally groundlessly—identifies this analytic unity with the tautological proposition 'I am I'.
[5] Compare my paper on *Self-Identity*; *Mind*, Vol. XXXVIII, N.S. No. 151, especially pp. 328–9.
[6] By a pure activity Kant means one unmixed with sense.

with) timeless principles of synthesis whose necessity we understand. The proposal that we should conceive of an activity as timeless is one which is not unnaturally nowadays accepted with some reluctance.[1]

On the other hand our actual empirical thinking is successive and is known to be successive—as Kant recognises;[2] it appears to us as a succession of mental states in time. But on Kant's view there are present in all empirical thinking certain necessary principles of unity which are themselves timeless, although they are successively manifested in time because they are, as it were, embedded in empirical data. The difficulty, if we approach the problem from this angle, is that it is hard to see why such principles (together with the fundamental principle that there must be one necessary synthetic unity in all our thinking) should be regarded as themselves timeless activities.

To this paradox we must return later.[3]

§5. *The activity of reason.*

In virtue of whatever pure activity may come *immediately* into consciousness man must account himself as belonging to a world which Kant here describes, not merely as the intelligible world, but as the 'intellectual' world—one, that is to say, which is intelligent as well as intelligible, perhaps one which is intelligible because it is intelligent.[4] This is a big step forward; but before we consider it, we must be clear about the particular pure activity which Kant has in mind. The pure activity on which he lays stress is the *theoretical* activity of reason, as it was in his previous discussion of freedom;[5] but this time theoretical reason is taken in its special Critical sense as a power of Ideas.[6]

Why does Kant single out this special function of theoretical reason as concerned with Ideas of the unconditioned?

Reason in its most general sense as the higher faculty of cognition[7] has its own principles, which Kant seems to find in the forms of judgement and of syllogism recognised by the traditional logic, but which might be described in a more convincing way.[8] In this general sense reason must regard itself as the author of its own principles and as functioning in accordance with these principles, and this was our ground for saying that it must function on the presupposition of freedom.[9]

On Kant's view these principles (as manifested in the forms of judgement) determine certain necessary characteristics which all objects must have if they are to be known as objects.[10] They are then called the categories of the understanding, the word 'understanding' being here used in its

---
[1] Compare *K.r.V.*, A37 = B54.   [2] *K.r.V.*, A210 = B255.
[3] Chapter XXVI §8.   [4] *Gr.*, 451 = 85. See also Chapter XXV §4.
[5] Chapter XXI §3.   [6] Chapter IX, Appendix §§4 and 5.
[7] Chapter VIII §2.
[8] See *K.M.E.*, I, 553–4, and especially Reich, *Die Vollständigkeit der kantischen Urteilstafel.*
[9] *Gr.*, 448 = 81.
[10] Chapter IX, Appendix §2, and Chapter XXII §7.

special Critical sense. Understanding must conceive its activity to be spontaneous, and consequently must function under the presupposition of freedom; but although its categories are the product of pure rational activity and are not derived by abstraction from what is given to sense, they seem in Kant's eyes to suffer from some defect for purposes of the present argument. This defect concerns, not their origin, but their application: they serve only *to bring sensuous ideas* under rules and thereby to unite them in one consciousness.[1] As an example of the rules in question we may take the principle that every event must have a cause, a principle which applies, and applies only, to sensible events in time.

All this is familiar to students of the *Critique of Pure Reason* and must here be stated dogmatically.

Thus understanding, however active or spontaneous, and however distinct from sense, which is passive, is nevertheless closely bound up with sense and is directed to the knowing of sensible objects. Reason suffers from no such limitation. In its special Critical sense reason shows a spontaneity so pure that by means of its Ideas it goes far beyond anything which sensibility can offer it as an object. It conceives the unconditioned and is able to show that if we think of the sensible world as unconditioned, we are bound to fall into contradictions. These contradictions it resolves by treating the sensible world as conditioned and ascribing the unconditioned to the intelligible world; and thereby it confirms the distinction, which we must make on the level of understanding, between the sensible and intelligible worlds. In so doing it performs its highest office and is able to set limits for the understanding.[2]

It is not quite clear what Kant gains by his concentration on this special function of pure reason: indeed he himself goes on immediately to speak as if his argument were based on reason in its most general sense, in which it is opposed to our lower powers, certainly those of sense and perhaps also those of imagination. Perhaps he is influenced by the fact that the Idea of the unconditioned forces us beyond the limits of experience and compels us to suppose that the unconditioned must be found in things-in-themselves.[3] Perhaps in this respect reason is shown most conspicuously to be an activity wholly distinct from sense.[4] Perhaps a further ground may be that theoretical reason as a power of Ideas is the closest approximation to pure practical reason and so makes the passage from the theoretical to the practical more easy to follow. But in spite of all this the argument seems to hold, if it holds at all, for theoretical reason in all its forms; for all reason must assume itself to be a power of spontaneous activity in accordance with its own principles, whatever be the objects to which it is directed.

---

[1] *Gr.*, 452 = 85.
[2] *Gr.*, 452 = 86; *K.r.V.*, B xx–xxi (including the footnote). See also Chapter IX, Appendix §4, and Chapter XXII §7.
[3] *K.r.V.*, B xxi.
[4] But see Chapter IX, Appendix §6.

§6. *Membership of the intelligible world.*

Kant's conclusion is that a rational being must regard himself *qua intelligence* as belonging, not to the sensible, but to the intelligible, world.[1] This, it must be remembered, is only a necessary presupposition of thinking, not a claim to knowledge. It should also be noted that the self, both here and elsewhere,[2] seems to be regarded as belonging to the sensible world, not only so far as it is known through inner sense, but also so far as it is capable of receiving sensations passively.

Hence a rational being has two standpoints from which to consider himself. From both standpoints he can know the laws—this emphasis on laws should be noted—of the use of his own powers and consequently the laws of all his actions.[3] So far as he regards himself as belonging to the sensible world, these laws are the causal laws of nature. So far as he presupposes himself to belong to the intelligible world, these laws are principles of reason which are not empirical and are independent of nature.

If we confine ourselves to laws or principles, Kant's contention seems to be wholly sound. The difficulty lies in the alleged membership of the intelligible world, if this is conceived as something more than being under the principles of reason. From this membership he goes on, whether by inference or by further insight, to maintain that his doctrine applies equally to a rational being assumed to exercise causality in virtue of his reason. Man as a rational being must conceive himself to will, as well as to think, in accordance with independent principles of reason. This means, as we have seen already, that he must conceive himself as acting under the laws of freedom and so under the principle of autonomy and the categorical imperative of morality.

We need only add that it is as belonging to both the sensible and the intelligible worlds that the principles on which as rational beings we should necessarily act appear to us as imperatives on which we ought to act. Here again the self seems to be reckoned as belonging to the sensible world, not only as an object of inner experience, but also as possessed of lower capacities—in this case the capacity for feeling and desire as opposed to a rational will.

§7. *The principles of reason.*

Kant has still some further points to add to his argument, and we must consider these before we can attempt to assess its value. But whatever we may think about the argument as a whole, he is on very strong ground in maintaining that a rational being must suppose himself able both to think and to act in accordance with principles of reason which are other

---
[1] *Gr.*, 452 = 86.   [2] *Gr.*, 451 = 85.
[3] Here Kant seems to pass already from theoretical to practical activity, apparently by way of inference.

than laws of cause and effect. It would indeed be a mistake to suppose that we could, as it were, infer the principles of morality from the principles of logical thinking; and if Kant's doctrine is to be upheld, there must be as sure an insight into the principles of action as into those of thought. Nevertheless the presuppositions of moral action receive strong confirmation if similar presuppositions are present in all thinking as such.

In particular we are given a possible answer to the scientist or psychologist who asserts that all this talk of rational moral principles must be nonsense since the conduct of man is determined by causal law just as much as the movement of the planets. Kant's answer is that from one point of view this contention is correct, but that there is another point of view; and furthermore that this other point of view is necessarily taken by the scientist himself even in asserting the truth of determinism. For the determinist is himself assuming that his own assertion is made in accordance with principles of reason and not merely as a result following from a causal series of sensa and feelings and desires. It is only on this supposition that his assertions have any claim to be true; and if a supposition of this kind is legitimate for the thinker, it cannot be dogmatically set aside as necessarily illegitimate for the moral agent.

CHAPTER XXIV

HOW IS A CATEGORICAL IMPERATIVE POSSIBLE?

§1. *The deduction.*

WE have now come to the end of Kant's preparatory exposition, and we naturally expect to be given his transcendental deduction of the categorical imperative. We are confirmed in this expectation by the heading given to the section we are about to study. It is entitled 'How is a categorical imperative possible?'[1]

When Kant, as is his habit, gives us a preparatory exposition and follows it up by what may be called an authoritative exposition, he expects us to read the authoritative exposition in the light of the preparatory one; and at times the authoritative exposition would be hardly intelligible if it stood by itself.[2] This is what happens in the present case. He gives such a brief and almost perfunctory summary of his previous argument that one can hardly avoid a feeling of anti-climax. He does, however, add one seemingly new point, and he follows up his whole argument, as usual, by an appeal to ordinary moral judgement for confirmation.

§2. *The additional argument.*

His new contention is obscurely expressed,[3] but its aim is apparently to clamp together his previous arguments. Having defined freedom in such a way as to identify it with autonomy, he has maintained that a rational being must think and act under the presupposition of freedom. This presupposition, he has insisted, is neither self-contradictory nor excluded by experience once we grasp the necessity of considering reality from two different points of view. A rational agent must from one point of view regard himself as belonging to the intelligible world and as acting under the Idea of freedom. From another point of view he must regard his actions as belonging to the sensible world and as subject to the causal laws of nature. If I were merely a member of the intelligible world, my actions would conform to the principle of autonomy. If I were merely a member of the sensible world, my actions would conform to the heteronomy of nature.

---

[1] *Gr.*, 453 = 87.
[2] An example of this is the second and authoritative exposition of the transcendental deduction of the categories in the first edition of the *Critique of Pure Reason;* A115 ff.
[3] The obscurities are dealt with in an appendix.

If the two points of view were equal and co-ordinate, it is hard to see where this would take us. Kant's new argument seems intended to show that one point of view must be subordinate to the other. *The intelligible world is the ground of the sensible world and of its laws.*[1] Hence my free will acting under the principle of autonomy can, as belonging to the intelligible world, be none the less the ground of actions which, as belonging to the sensible world, are under the causal laws of nature. The relation between my free will and my determined actions is in no way unique, but is only a special case of the generic relation which must be conceived to hold between the intelligible and the sensible world.

§3. *The conclusion.*

The rest of Kant's argument follows the beaten track.[2]

In spite of the fact that I must recognise myself as a being belonging to the sensible world, I must also recognise myself, *qua* intelligence, as 'subject to the law of the intelligible world, that is, to the law of[3] reason, which in the Idea of freedom contains the law of the intelligible world'. This law is identical with the principle of autonomy, and all my actions would necessarily conform to it, if I were only a member of the intelligible world. I must, however, regard myself as also a member of the sensible world and so as affected and hampered by desires and inclinations. It follows that I must regard the principle of autonomy as an imperative for me and must consider actions which accord with this principle to be duties.

This doctrine is not new to us,[4] but I believe—though with some hesitation—that Kant holds it to be fully intelligible only when we have seen that the intelligible world is the ground of the sensible world and of its laws, and consequently that a rational will can be the ground of actions which—from one point of view—are causally determined.

Kant might seem to make a new point in so far as he appears in this passage to identify the law of the intelligible world with the law of reason or of freedom. But he must not be thought to claim knowledge that the intelligible world is necessarily characterised by freedom in the positive sense. He is not arguing that since we conceive ourselves as belonging to the intelligible world and consequently as subject to its known laws, we must therefore conceive ourselves to be under the law of freedom. We know nothing of the law of the intelligible world apart from our knowledge of the necessary principles of our own reason.[5] The most we can be said to know—or at least to think—of the intelligible world is that it cannot

---
[1] *Gr.*, 453 = 87. See also *Gr.*, 461 = 97, where it is said that appearances must be subordinated to the character of the thing-in-itself.
[2] *Gr.*, 453 = 88.
[3] It is possible to omit the words 'the law of' as some translators do.
[4] See *Gr.*, 414 = 37–8 and compare also *Gr.*, 455 = 89.
[5] In regard to his pure activity a rational agent must account himself as belonging to the intellectual world, *of which, however, he has no further knowledge; Gr.*, 451 = 85. See also *K.p.V.*, 43 = 157–8 (= 74).

be under the law of nature, and this conception is purely negative. Kant may indeed hold we are justified in *believing* that the intelligible world is also an intellectual world, but this is based, mainly at least, on our moral insight and so cannot be used to justify an ethical doctrine.

§4. *The failure of the deduction.*

It seems clear enough that Kant's argument has failed as a deduction of the supreme principle of morality. Certainly there can be no question of a deduction in the common meaning of that word: we cannot by inference derive morality from the presupposition of freedom, and still less can we by inference derive the necessity of presupposing freedom—in the positive sense—from the presupposition that we are members of an intelligible world. Even in Kant's sense of a 'justification', we cannot justify morality by anything other than itself: there can be no higher principle in the functioning of a rational agent than the principle of morality.

This objection by itself is fatal, but in any case we have no independent insight into the alleged necessity for presupposing freedom. Kant is indeed ingenious and, I think, sound in suggesting that freedom (in the sense of a power to accord with the principles of reason) is a necessary presupposition of all thinking. This may serve as a *defence* of the presupposition of a similar freedom in action, but it is not sufficient to *justify* this presupposition. The justification for presupposing freedom of the will can rest only on our insight into the principle of moral action, which therefore cannot be derived from the presupposition of the freedom of the will.

Even if the presupposition of freedom could be established independently of moral insight, our difficulties would not be over. What we are trying to show is that a rational agent as such would necessarily act in accordance with the principle of autonomy, and ought so to act if he is irrational enough to be tempted to do otherwise. This is a synthetic *a priori* proposition, and we therefore require a 'third term' to justify our statement that there must be a necessary and universal connexion between being a rational agent and acting only on maxims which can at the same time be willed as universal laws. If it is surprising that a mere Idea, like the Idea of freedom, should function satisfactorily as a 'third term' for this purpose, Kant is perhaps justified in asserting that from a practical point of view the same law must be valid for a being who acts under the Idea of freedom as would be valid for a being known to be in fact free. But even if this is so, his attempt to establish the requisite connexion between the Idea of freedom and action in accordance with a self-imposed universal law suffered, as we saw,[1] from very obvious weaknesses. If we are to defend him, we should have to show that these weaknesses could be overcome, and it may be doubted whether this is possible.

The chief difficulty, however, concerns the very assertion that a

---
[1] Chapter XX §5.

rational being must as such think and act under the presupposition of freedom. Even if we do not doubt—and I see no reason to doubt—the truth of this assertion, we must still ask what is its logical character. Have we here a new synthetic *a priori* proposition? If so, our original difficulty is merely postponed, and we have to look for yet another 'third term' to connect the subject and predicate of this new proposition. This, for reasons already given, we are hardly likely to find in our Idea of membership in the intelligible world; and even if we could find it there, should we not merely have provided yet a fresh synthetic *a priori* proposition, and should we not be obliged to seek still another 'third term' in order to connect a rational being with the Idea of membership in the intelligible world? It looks as if this process would go on indefinitely, unless we can come, at some stage, to direct insight into the necessary activity of a rational being as such; and in that case we should have ultimately to rely on a proposition which in some sense is self-evident.[1]

§5. *Direct insight into the principle of autonomy.*

If we admit the possibility of direct insight into the necessary activity of a rational being as such, do we really require Kant's elaborate machinery in order to establish the principle of autonomy? As he himself says,[2] the human mind does not always at first find the shortest way towards its goal. May we not have direct insight into the principle of autonomy itself? And is not this really assumed by Kant's argument?

If we consider theoretical reason, a rational being must have direct insight into the principles of rational thought and must conceive himself to be capable of thinking in accordance with these principles. Furthermore, he must conceive these principles to be valid for all rational beings as such: whatever these principles may be in detail, they must be conceived as having universal validity. Unless we accept this, there is an end to all rational discourse and indeed to anything that can properly be called thinking.[3]

The same doctrine applies equally to practical reason. A rational agent must have direct insight into the principles of rational action and must conceive himself to be capable of acting in accordance with these principles. Furthermore, he must conceive these practical principles to be valid for all rational beings as such: they too must be conceived as having universal validity. Yet to say this is to say that a rational agent as such will necessarily act on a principle universally and unconditionally valid for all rational agents as such. This proposition is identical with the principle of autonomy which Kant has discovered by analysing the implications of ordinary moral judgement; for the principles of rational action, like those of rational thought, are not imposed on a rational being

---

[1] See Chapter I §9.   [2] *M.A.d.N.*, 476 n.
[3] We may on Kant's theory conceive an intuitive understanding different from our own, but at least we must suppose the principles of rational thought to be valid for all human rational beings, if not also for all finite rational beings. See Chapter IX, Appendix §6.

from without but are the necessary principles of his own rational activity and in that sense are self-imposed.

If this contention is admitted as regards theoretical reason and denied as regards practical reason, the onus of proof surely lies on those who at least appear to be making an arbitrary distinction.

We might well be content with Kant's principle of autonomy, if it could be shown to be the necessary condition of all moral judgements and so of all moral actions. Nevertheless the principle becomes greatly strengthened if we can legitimately claim that as beings who are themselves rational agents we have a direct insight into the necessity of the principle when considered in itself.

§6. *Is the principle of autonomy analytic?*

Even if we claim as rational agents to have direct insight into the principle of autonomy, we have still to face the question whether the principle itself is synthetic or analytic.

In spite of Kant's repeated assertions to the contrary we should not reject without consideration the possibility that the principle of autonomy may be an analytic proposition. Certainly the proposition that a rational agent as such will necessarily act rationally seems to be analytic. It is perhaps not so clear whether we must regard as analytic the proposition that to act rationally is to act in accordance with a principle unconditionally valid for all rational agents as such.

The latter proposition certainly seems to rest on direct insight into the *concept* of rational activity as such, and if this is enough to constitute an analytic proposition, then an analytic proposition it will have to be. If, however, it is claimed that the subject-concept present in every analytic proposition must be purely arbitrary, then we must insist with Kant that our proposition is not analytic, but synthetic, and also that, since it states a necessity, it must be *a priori*: it rests, not on the analysis of an arbitrary concept, but ultimately on direct insight into the necessary activity of a rational being such as we ourselves are.

The whole question raises problems of logic which cannot here be discussed. We can only say that if this is an analytic proposition, it is an analytic proposition about reality.[1]

The really essential point which should not be obscured is that in the last resort Kant claims a special and direct insight into the necessary activity of a rational being as such, no matter what be the logical character of the propositions in which this insight is expressed. In this respect, as he himself recognises elsewhere, our insight into the principles of practical reason is on the same footing as our insight into the principles of theoretical reason. Indeed our consciousness of pure practical reason and of pure theoretical reason alike springs from our consciousness of the necessary and unconditioned principles which a rational being as such must follow in action and in thought.[2]

---

[1] See Chapter XII §2. [2] *K.p.V.*, 30 = 140 (= 53).

I need hardly add that direct insight into the principles on which a rational being as such must act could not be attained without personal experience—if we may call it so—of ordinary moral actions and of ordinary moral judgements. We have gradually to separate these principles from their empirical concomitants; but when we have successfully disentangled them, we may find in them a necessity and intelligibility such as could not characterise any mere empirical generalisation. In this respect also the parallel with theoretical reason is complete.

§7. *The imperative of autonomy.*

So far we have considered the principle of autonomy only as a principle on which a rational agent would necessarily act, if reason had full control over his passions. It may be suggested that we have still to explain how this principle can be an imperative, a principle on which a rational agent *ought* to act if he is irrational enough to be tempted to do otherwise. Is it perhaps in its special character as a categorical imperative that Kant describes this principle as a synthetic *a priori* proposition?

The answer to this question is in the negative. Once we have accepted the principle of autonomy as one on which a rational agent as such would necessarily act, we require no further synthetic *a priori* proposition in order to assert that it is also a categorical imperative for imperfect rational agents.

Kant's whole procedure bears out this view, which is also confirmed by his treatment of hypothetical imperatives. Once he has established the principle that a rational agent as such, if he wills the end, must necessarily will the means, Kant finds no difficulty—perhaps he should have found more—in turning it into a hypothetical imperative: he takes it for granted that if anything is what a rational agent as such would necessarily do, it is also what a rational agent ought to do, should he be tempted to do otherwise. Exactly the same assumption is made in the case of the categorical imperative, and the passage from a moral principle to a categorical imperative is in no need of further justification, although it may be defended by the contention that the intelligible world is the ground of the sensible world.

If a hypothetical imperative is an analytic proposition, this is because it is founded on a principle which is analytic; and if a categorical imperative is a synthetic *a priori* proposition, this is because it is founded on a principle which is itself a synthetic *a priori* proposition.

§8. *The objective principles of reason.*

Kant's justification of the categorical imperative is reduced in the end to this—that a rational agent as such has direct insight into the principle of autonomy as a principle on which a rational agent, with full control over his passions, would necessarily act. That is the fundamental contention from which the categorical imperative follows. This contention is supported by a similar insight of theoretical reason into its own necessary principles, and the whole doctrine is claimed to be the only one which can render ordinary moral judgements intelligible. The latter claim would receive strong confirmation if the doctrine were worked out into a complete system, though this confirmation by itself would be by no means a certain proof.[1]

We need not be surprised at this ultimate claim to direct insight: it accords both with Kant's general view that reason must be transparent to itself, and also with his moral view that the common reason of the plain man is an adequate guide to conduct.

In the case of practical reason the principles into whose necessity we have direct insight are the principles which are at the base of our five formulations of the categorical imperative, and in particular the principle of autonomy. In the case of theoretical reason it is not so easy to specify the principles. I believe them to cover the necessary and universal forms of thought, which Kant identified partly with the table of judgements and of syllogisms as given in traditional logic (somewhat modified by himself). They cover also the principles of the understanding (though these are complicated by reference to time and space) and presumably the supreme principle of the necessary synthetic unity of apperception. Finally, though this need not exhaust the list, they cover the Ideas of reason, the principles of reason in Kant's own technical sense.[2]

Such an appeal for corroboration to the complicated doctrines of the *Critique of Pure Reason* can carry no weight with those who have not read that work and may only encourage in their scepticism those who have; nor is it any part of my contention that Kant's pioneer labour in this difficult field is not in need of the most drastic revision. But we may, I hope, see at least the plausibility of his general doctrine if we consider one Idea of reason—the Idea of a system.

As a *thinker* every rational being as such must necessarily aim—and knows that he must necessarily aim—at a complete system:[3] he cannot rest in contradictions and inconsistencies nor can he let himself be satisfied with loose ends, though he may have practical grounds for doing both. Such a system of thought must be based on sense, but it is not given to sense. Can this necessary ideal of a rational thinker as such rest on anything other than the insight of theoretical reason into its own necessary activity?

As an *agent* every rational being as such must necessarily aim—and knows that he must necessarily aim—at a complete system: he cannot be satisfied with limited ends or with antagonism and conflict between desire and desire, between man and man, between State and State. Such a system must be a system of actions whose ends are based on the desires of men, but it is the aim of a rational will, not the object of any desire or aggregate of desires. Can the necessary ideal of a rational agent as such rest on anything other than the insight of practical reason into its own necessary activity? The five formulae of Kant are nothing but a philosophical

[1] *Gr.*, 392 = 9.   [2] *Gr.*, 452 = 85–6.
[3] See Chapter IX, Appendix §6.

analysis of such a necessary—that is, objectively necessary—system of action, beginning with the universal law which is its form and ending with the complete ideal of a kingdom of ends to be realised in time.

This parallel between theoretical and practical reason might be elaborated indefinitely, and the differences might be as illuminating as the resemblances. All I suggest is that this is a line of thought not to be rejected lightly without due consideration. Unless we accept the ideal, in practice if not in theory, of an objective principle of reason, the result in the long run is lunacy. Unless we accept the ideal of objective principles of practical reason, the result in the long run is criminal lunacy; and recent events suggest that the run need not be very long.

§9. *Reason and the unconditioned.*

There is one further point, which is brought in at the very end of the *Groundwork*. On Kant's view practical reason must conceive and seek to realise an unconditioned moral law, which for human beings must be an unconditioned or categorical imperative.[1] Apart from this there can be for us no unconditioned or absolute good.

As rational agents we can all understand that if we will the end Z, we ought to will the means Y. This gives us a conditioned obligation and a conditioned good, a good as means. But as rational agents we cannot be content to pursue only goods which are good as means: practical reason cannot be satisfied unless we can pursue a good which is unconditioned and good in itself, and without this all our pursuit of means is sheer futility.

In this again Kant sees a close parallel with theoretical reason. The function of theoretical reason, when it finds itself confronted—as it does in experience—with the conditioned, is to conceive and to seek the unconditioned.

For example, we suppose that every event is necessary and that we understand its necessity by discovering its cause. In this way we explain a conditioned necessity by discovering its condition. But to understand the necessity of the cause, we must discover the cause of the cause, and so *ad infinitum*. However far back we go, we never come to anything other than a conditioned necessity, and this is no more satisfying to human reason than the conditioned necessity with which we started. Theoretical reason must conceive the totality of causes, which, because it is a totality of causes, cannot itself be caused. It is this Idea, as we have seen,[2] which gives us the conception, however empty, of an uncaused cause or a free cause. In the same way theoretical reason must conceive the totality of conditions for every conditioned necessity, a totality which must itself be an unconditioned necessity, if there is to be any necessity at all. The conception of the moral law as unconditionally necessary is only a further example of the activity of reason (here of practical reason) in conceiving —and seeking to realise—an unconditioned necessity.

[1] *Gr.*, 463 = 99–100.   [2] Chapter IX, Appendix §4.

If we suppose that we can understand a necessity only by stating its condition, then manifestly we cannot understand an unconditioned necessity: to explain it by stating its condition involves us in direct contradiction. Hence Kant declares, with a rather unnecessary appearance of paradox, that the unconditioned necessity of moral law is incomprehensible, but we can comprehend its incomprehensibility. It would be truer to say that we understand it well enough as a necessary ideal of reason, though we cannot without self-contradiction profess to understand it by discovering its condition.

Those who ask why we should do our duty are falling into this contradiction. They are assuming that we should do our duty only if we want something else, such as happiness in this world or the next. They are in short asking what is the condition under which we should obey an unconditioned imperative. This is merely to deny that there can be an unconditioned imperative or to show that they do not understand what a categorical imperative is.

The theoretical Idea of a totality of conditions or an unconditioned necessity cannot give us knowledge; for no object of this kind can be given to us in experience. We can, however, act in accordance with our Idea of an unconditioned moral law, and thereby we can realise in time an unconditioned and absolute good.

APPENDIX

KANT'S ADDITIONAL ARGUMENT

WHAT I have called Kant's additional argument consists of three propositions,[1] of which the second is supposed to follow from the first, and the third is supposed to follow from the second.

Proposition A: *The intelligible world contains the ground of the sensible world.* Presumably Kant has in mind here the doctrine that the thing-in-itself is the ground of the sensible world so far as it is the ground of the *matter* (sensa) of the sensible world. This was brought out in the argument from the passivity of sense.[2] But he may also have in mind the doctrine of the *Critique of Pure Reason*, namely, that the I-in-itself is the ground of the *form* of the sensible world: sensibility is the ground of the forms of space and time, while understanding is the ground of the categories. We must not forget that in experience the mind must contribute something to the world as known by it.[3]

Proposition B: *Therefore the intelligible world contains also the ground of the laws of the sensible world.*

This new assertion is misleading unless we take into account *both*

[1] *Gr.*, 453 = 87–8. See also Chapter XXIV above, §2.
[2] Chapter XXII §6.   [3] Chapter XXII §7.

the doctrines mentioned above. According to Kant it is the I-in-itself—or the understanding and sensibility of the knower—which is the ground of the ultimate and necessary and universal and formal laws of the sensible world, and in particular of the ultimate law that every event must have a cause. So far as the laws of the sensible world are empirical, they may be said to have their ground in the thing-in-itself; for the thing-in-itself is the ground of the sensa on the basis of which these empirical laws are formulated by science. Yet empirical laws, though they neither are nor can be deduced from the ultimate *a priori* laws, are nevertheless specifications of them: we could not, for example, discover that an absence of Vitamin C leads to scurvy except on the presupposition that every event must have a cause.[1]

Proposition C: *Hence the intelligible world is, and must be thought to be,*[2] *the source of laws immediately*[3] *governing my will (which belongs wholly to the intelligible world).*

This statement so palpably fails to follow from the previous ones that it is hard to see what kind of telescoped argument Kant has in his mind. Granted that the intelligible world is the ground of the laws of the sensible world, we cannot infer that it is the source of the laws immediately governing my will; for my will, as he expressly says, belongs, not to the sensible world, but to the intelligible world.

We may try to reconstruct his argument in the light of the passage immediately preceding these three propositions. He has just recapitulated his preparatory exposition and affirmed that so far as we consider ourselves to belong to the intelligible world, we must conceive all our actions to accord completely with the principle of autonomy; and that so far as we consider ourselves to belong to the sensible world, we must conceive our actions to be wholly under the heteronomy of nature.[4] Hence he has already taken it as established that my will—from one point of view—must be conceived as governed by the laws of the intelligible world, and he has no need whatever to re-establish it by a new inference. What he has to do is to meet the objection that it is impossible both to conceive my will as belonging to the intelligible world and as governed by its laws, and also to conceive my actions as governed by the quite different laws of the sensible world—the laws, namely, of cause and effect. His answer is that there is nothing unique or miraculous about such a double conception, since—quite apart from the case of my will—the intelligible world must always be conceived as the ground of the sensible world and

---

[1] The nature of particular empirical laws as a system is worked out fully in the *Critique of Judgement*. See especially *Erste Einleitung* III, 15 ff.

[2] Strictly speaking, all this should surely be a question *only* of what must be thought to be: we are here concerned only with Ideas, not with knowledge of fact.

[3] This means that these laws do not govern my will through the medium of an end already desired, as do hypothetical imperatives.

[4] This is identified with the law of nature governing desires and inclinations—that is, with a law of psychological, not physical, causation. This is in turn identified with the principle of happiness. The difficulty of this is that the principle of happiness cannot be a complete account of the psychological laws of human nature; for men in fact often act in ways which conflict with the attainment of happiness.

of the laws—particularly the causal laws—by which it is governed. In spite of the difficulty of recognising two kinds of law the relation between my will and my actions is only a special case of the generic relation which must be conceived to hold between the intelligible and the sensible world.

If this reconstruction is regarded as too hazardous, it may be noted that the first two propositions, which assert that the intelligible world is the ground of the sensible world and of its laws, are emphasised by special type, which is not used for the third and most difficult proposition. The argument would seem to run smoothly enough if the third proposition were simply omitted; but it seems to me that the general sense of my interpretation is assumed in what follows.

CHAPTER XXV

SOME FURTHER QUESTIONS

§1. *Further questions to be considered.*

So far we have considered only what may be called the logical character of Kant's attempt to justify the categorical imperative. It may perhaps seem disappointing if his deduction is reduced to a claim to have direct insight into the principle of autonomy as one which is valid for all rational agents as such and is the ground of moral goodness as well as the basis of the categorical imperative. Even so, Kant is in no worse a position than those philosophers who claim to know by direct insight that pleasure is the only good or again that certain kinds of thing are good or that certain kinds of act are right. Indeed he is in a better position; for the hedonistic claim—to speak dogmatically—is both paradoxical and false; while the claim to have a series of independent and unrelated intuitions into the goodness of certain kinds of thing or the rightness of certain kinds of act is unsatisfactory unless we can grasp some single intelligible principle in the light of which these intuitions can be brought into relation with one another and applied to particular situations where different goods or different obligations may appear to be in conflict with one another.

There are, however, other difficulties in Kant's ethical doctrine, particularly its connexion with his metaphysics, its relation to feeling, and above all its insistence on a difference between theoretical and practical insight. Without some reference to these topics our discussion cannot be complete.

§2. *The real self.*

Kant may be thought to justify the categorical imperative by saying that it accords with the will of my real self as a member of the intelligible world, and this is why I ought to obey it.[1] If there is anything of this in the present argument, it is certainly not emphasised: Kant's emphasis is on the rationality of the moral will, and not on its supposed metaphysical reality. It is true that in his appeal to ordinary moral judgement[2] he claims that even a bad man wishes to be a better one, that in so doing he transfers himself to another order of things than the sensible, and that in thus transplanting himself into the intelligible world he is conscious of a good will in himself which constitutes the law for his bad will; but even here there seems no suggestion that he should obey his rational will

---

[1] See also Chapter XXII §2.   [2] *Gr.*, 454–5 = 88–9

because it is his real will rather than because it is his good or rational will. In his more philosophical account[1] Kant is far from laying any weight on the reality of the pure rational will. On the contrary, he says that in addition to my sensuously affected will there comes the *Idea* of the same will as a pure will belonging to the intelligible world.[2]

In other passages Kant identifies a man's intelligence and his rational will with his 'proper' self.[3] This must be so, since it is the possession of intelligence which distinguishes man from other animals and makes him a self. Only as a rational agent can man be subject to the categorical imperative (or indeed to any other), and it is not clear whether Kant is saying more than this when he declares that man is bound by the categorical imperative because he is a member of the intelligible world.

One of the passages, however, does suggest that Kant is at least reinforcing the appeal to the rationality of the self by ascribing to the rational self a special metaphysical status.[4] He has insisted that the moral law is valid for us as men because it springs from our will as intelligence, that is, from our proper self; and he goes on to say—with all the emphasis of special type—*that what belongs to mere appearance is necessarily subordinated by reason to the character of the thing as it is in itself.*

The implications of this are somewhat obscure, but it looks like saying that intelligence is real, desires are mere appearance, and therefore a rational agent will subordinate his desires to his intelligence.

This kind of metaphysical argument for morality makes little appeal to the modern man, and the reason why desires ought to be controlled is surely because they may lead to irrational action, and not because they are themselves unreal.

We may properly hold—as Kant does[5]—that because man is a rational being, he will always be dissatisfied and in conflict with himself so long as he devotes his reason merely to the pursuit of pleasure and even of happiness. Since his reason has another and more essential function, his proper self cannot be realised in a life of self-seeking, and such a life must inevitably produce a feeling of frustration. This contention, if true, as I believe it is, seems to be in no need of metaphysical support, though it may be in need of metaphysical defence.

§3. *The conflict of reason and desire.*

The moral law must appear to us as an imperative because we are rational agents with a rational will which may come into conflict with desire. In some ways such a conflict may be hard to understand: in other ways we understand it only too well. Kant seeks to make it more intelligible by distinguishing the self considered as a member of the intelligible world from the self considered as a member of the sensible world.

[1] *Gr.*, 453 = 88.
[2] The relation between the Idea and my sensuously affected will is compared with the relation of the categories to sensuous intuition.
[3] *Gr.*, 457 = 92–3; 458 = 93; 461 = 96–7: '*Das eigentliche Selbst*'.
[4] *Gr.*, 460–1 = 96–7.　　　　　　　　　　　　　[5] *Gr.*, 394–6 = 13–15.

If we take this as a metaphysical theory (not merely as a practical Idea on which we are entitled to act), it does not seem to make the conflict of reason and desire more intelligible. It is hard to see how there could be a conflict between the self as it is and the self as it appears. It is hard to see how the self as it is could be in any way affected by the self as it appears. It is in short hard to see how desires could be either a help or a hindrance to a rational will, if such a will belongs to an intelligible and non-sensible world.

If this is so, the distinction between the intelligible and sensible worlds does not help us to understand how the principles of autonomy must appear to us as a categorical imperative: indeed it makes difficult what is otherwise comparatively easy.

The objection may be due to the crudity of our interpretation in taking a practical Idea as a speculative theory, but it was already raised in Kant's time, and it is perhaps worth while merely to note his answer.[1] Nature, he says, does not help or hinder freedom; but nature as an appearance helps or hinders the *effects* of freedom as appearances in the sensible world.[2]

§4. *Ethics and metaphysics.*

Kant's ethics—in spite perhaps of occasional lapses—is not based on his metaphysics: it would be truer to say that his metaphysics, so far as we take this to be concerned with a supersensible reality, is based primarily on his ethics. Whatever confusion or error there may be on this topic in the *Groundwork* is to a great extent cleared away by the *Critique of Practical Reason.*

Even in the *Groundwork* the somewhat hesitating attempt to justify the principle of autonomy by the necessity of presupposing freedom in all rational activity is not wholly an appeal to non-moral considerations. For Kant freedom is essentially a moral ideal. What arouses his awe and admiration is the spectacle of a minute rational creature, thinking freely and acting freely, in accordance with his own principles, in an endless physical universe governed throughout by iron law. This spectacle is only the concrete embodiment of the Idea of law for its own sake; but perhaps Kant's emotional attitude towards it may be put down, at least partly, to his personal passion for freedom, a passion which is also shown in his political and religious thinking. In any case it is clear, and it becomes

---

[1] *K.U., Einl.* IX, 195–6 n. (= LV n.).

[2] For the sake of completeness we must add the rest of his answer, which perhaps raises more problems than it solves. Even the causality of freedom (that is, of pure and practical reason) is, he says, itself the causality of a natural cause subordinated to freedom (that is, of the subject as a human being and consequently considered as an appearance.) The intelligible which is conceived under the Idea of freedom contains the ground of the *determination* of this latter causality in a way which is admittedly inexplicable. In a somewhat telescoped parenthesis he indicates further—and we may compare §2 above—that a similar relation holds between the intelligible, conceived as the supersensible substratum of nature, and the series of causal events which constitute nature as an appearance.

clear to Kant himself later, that the necessity of presupposing freedom of the will rests on direct insight into the objective principles of morality. Once that is seen, his ethics becomes manifestly independent of his metaphysics and must be judged on its own merits.

The metaphysical beliefs about God and immortality which Kant justifies on the basis of his ethics lie beyond the scope of the present work. They do not alter the content of his ethics, nor can they add either to the supreme value of the moral will or to the binding nature of the categorical imperative. Nevertheless, as Kant recognises,[1] it is a great stimulus to moral effort and a strong support to the human spirit, if man can believe that the moral life is something more than a mortal enterprise in which he can join with his fellow men against the background of a blind and indifferent universe until he and the human race are blotted out for ever. Man cannot be indifferent to the possibility that his puny efforts towards moral perfection may, in spite of appearances, be in accord with the purpose of the universe, and that he may be taking part in an eternal enterprise under a divine leader. There may still be some today, and they are fortunate, who can honestly claim to know by pure theoretical reason that this is not a mere possibility but a reality. Most men who are at all touched by the modern spirit would be well content if with Kant they could hold this as a reasonable faith based on their moral convictions; but the discussion of this topic belongs to Kant's philosophy of religion, not to his ethics.

There are some who hold that Kant's belief in a timeless and intelligible world undermines morality, since it makes the moral struggle unreal. This may be so, if we take him to be propounding a scientific theory about two wholly different worlds. It is not so, if we regard him as teaching that our task as men is to manifest in time eternal principles of reason on which we may rationally believe that this mysterious universe is governed. And indeed his view is not so different from that of some of the theologically minded who gibe at it, inasmuch as they too regard the activity of God as timeless and the temporal universe as the manifestation of a timeless will.

§5. *Moral interest.*

No human being—it is obvious enough—will be convinced of moral obligation by the purely intellectual recognition that a fully rational agent would necessarily act in accordance with a universal law unconditionally valid for all rational agents as such. This should not surprise us, nor should it be used as a ground for rejecting Kant's philosophy. Even the purely intellectual ideal of system would mean nothing whatever to a man who had not thought, and very little to a man who had not thought a great deal; but it is no less a necessary ideal of thought because of that. If Kant's analysis of the moral ideal is to mean anything to us, we

[1] *Gr.*, 462–3 = 99.

must not only have a capacity for highly abstract thinking: we must also have a certain experience of moral action.

Perhaps it is the apparent thinness of the moral ideal as analysed by philosophy which makes Kant so insistent on the question 'How can I take an interest in morality?'[1] He returns to this question at the very end of his book,[2] and declares that we can no more explain this than we can explain how freedom is possible or how reason can be practical.[3]

An 'interest' on Kant's view always belongs to beings who are partly rational and partly sensuous. Moral interest, so-called, is identified by him with the feeling of reverence,[4] and it is natural enough that he should turn to consider the feeling element in morality after he has established the categorical imperative. It may seem strange, it must seem strange, that so strong a feeling should be aroused by a morality which has been so abstractly analysed. How is it that man believes himself to *feel* his personal worth in obedience to the categorical imperative and to estimate the worth of mere pleasure as nothing in comparison with this?[5] Kant may even be returning to the second form of his main question about the possibility of a categorical imperative—the form which is concerned with an absolutely good will rather than with a rational agent.[6] Or at least he may be asking how we can explain the feelings which accompany the judgement that in obedience to the categorical imperative there is manifested an absolutely good will.

The feeling concerned he regards in this passage as one of pleasure or satisfaction at the fulfilment of duty, though that is clearly an inadequate account of reverence. He adds little to what he has said already[7] beyond perhaps making it clear that we have to consider a relation between a mere Idea and an emotion, not a relation between two events, which alone can be 'explained', if the explanation of anything is a statement of its cause. He denies that it is possible to understand *a priori* how a mere thought can produce a feeling of pleasure or pain—a view which is considerably modified in the *Critique of Practical Reason*.[8]

It would be impossible from a philosophical account even of such a thing as skill to understand the feelings aroused by an outstanding exhibition of skill. The same is even more true as regards a philosophical account of art. Kant is perfectly right in insisting that if we are to feel the supreme value of moral goodness we must separate it in thought from all regard to a man's own advantage in this world and the next;[9] but it must be added that for partly sensuous and partly rational beings like men this feeling will be aroused in its full intensity only if they see or imagine goodness manifested in individual men and so brought nearer to intuition.[10]

---

[1] *Gr.*, 449–50 = 82–83.
[2] *Gr.*, 459–60 = 95–6.
[3] See Chapter XXV §7.
[4] *Gr.*, 401 n. = 22 n.
[5] *Gr.*, 449–50 = 82.
[6] Chapter XIX §2.
[7] See Chapter V, especially the Appendix.
[8] *K.p.V.*, 73 = 198 (= 130).
[9] *Gr.*, 411 n. = 34 n.
[10] *Gr.*, 436 = 66 and 437 = 67.

§6. *Interest and obligation.*

Kant once more warns us, as so often, against supposing the moral law to be binding upon us because it arouses our interest or affects our emotions. On the contrary, it arouses our interest and affects our emotions because it is binding and is recognised as binding.

This is a truth which is overlooked by those who today bid us to be moral because of the higher satisfaction which it will bring. Once we have ceased to believe that the moral law is binding and that there is supreme goodness in the life of obedience to the moral law, these alleged higher satisfactions will melt into thin air. Apart from this it is always a denial of morality to bid men pursue it for what they will get out of it—whether this takes the old form of promising that God will reward them or the new form of promising that they will find a higher happiness in their present life. The older form is the more plausible of the two inasmuch as by postponing our reward to a future life it is less likely to be contradicted by obvious facts. It is also less removed from a moral standpoint, and makes a stronger appeal to the human heart, inasmuch as it bids us face, at least for a season, the effort and the trials without which no great thing can be done. Nevertheless to cajole or threaten men into being good is always to assert implicitly that goodness is of less value than feelings of pleasure or satisfaction and that the moral law has in itself no binding force. There is no morality—other than the not too estimable quality of prudence—unless there is, independently of our emotions, an unconditioned goodness and an unconditioned obligation.

§7. *Practical insight.*

The most difficult, and yet the most valuable, element in Kant's doctrine still remains to be considered, hard as it is to express this clearly and unambiguously. There is a difference between theoretical and practical insight, and it is the special characteristics of practical insight with which we are now concerned.

Hitherto I have dealt with the resemblance rather than with the difference between these two kinds of insight. In both of them we have gradually to separate out from their empirical concomitants the principles at work in ordinary judgements, and to grasp the necessity of these principles alike in themselves and as conditions of the judgements in which they are embodied. In both of them the apprehension of principle is ascribed by Kant to the self-consciousness of reason.[1] But in moral insight the self-consciousness in question is a self-consciousness of practical reason; it is not merely self-conscious thinking but is at the same time a self-conscious attitude of the rational will

This attitude of the will must be present in ordinary moral judgements

[1] See Chapter XXI §5.

as well as in philosophical ones. Thus even a bad man is said to be conscious of a good will in himself which constitutes the law for his bad will. The very principle of autonomy itself brings out this kind of self-consciousness: a rational agent knows that, considered as a rational agent, he would necessarily act always as a law-making member of a kingdom of ends. The moral 'I ought' is always a necessary 'I will' of a person who is conscious of himself as a rational agent. Kant says even of the bad man that 'he believes himself to be this better person'—at least when he adopts the point of view from which he regards himself as free and as a member of the intelligible world.[1]

Our thought of the good will present in us is, it is true, spoken of as an Idea.[2] An Idea is not the concept of any actual object in space and time; and Kant, as we have seen, is the last man to claim possession of a good or holy will either for himself or for others.[3] Nevertheless this does not mean that we have here merely a theoretical conception divorced from all actual volition. Every Idea, though it is not constitutive of actual objects, is regulative: that is, it is a principle actually employed, however feebly, in the thinking of the rational being who conceives it. And the Idea of a good will is a practical Idea, one which is regulative for our actual will and employed, however feebly, in the volition of the rational agent who conceives it. If we were not conscious of, as it were, the stirrings of a good will in ourselves, if the Idea were wholly without influence at least on our wishes, morality would mean nothing at all to us. We should be brutes and not men, and to speak of duty in such a context would be absurd.

This view is fundamental to Kant's conception of morality. The bad man recognises the authority of the law even in transgressing it.[4] We all recognise the validity of the categorical imperative even when we sophistically reduce its universality to mere generality, and pretend we are only making an inconsiderable exception to it under the pressure of circumstances.[5] Our feeling of reverence for the moral law, a feeling which we cannot eradicate without ceasing to be men, arises from consciousness that our will is subordinated to the law.[6] All these statements must be taken to imply that a good will is in some degree present in us.

§8. *Modern intellectualism.*

This doctrine of Kant is unfortunately seldom taken seriously today. This general neglect seems to me largely due to the modern tendency to split things up instead of trying to see them as a whole. Analysis is more popular than synthesis.

Thus even the modern defenders of reason in morals seem to regard reason as a purely intellectual faculty whose function, so far as it is not concerned solely with inference, is to apprehend immediately a number of

[1] *Gr.*, 454–5 = 89.　　　　　　　　　[2] *Gr.*, 454 = 88.
[3] Chapter III §5.　　　　　　　　　　[4] *Gr.*, 455 = 89.
[5] *Gr.*, 424 = 51.　　　　[6] *Gr.*, 401 n. = 21 n. See also Chapter V §§2–3.

separate and isolated truths—truths, for example, about the kinds of thing that are good or the kinds of act that are right. When reason is thus divorced from volition, it is hard to believe it capable of apprehending truths of this kind, which seem to be bound up with emotional and volitional attitudes in a way strangely different from the truths of mathematics or of logic. The fact that such apprehensions are claimed as knowledge, and therefore as infallible, does not make them easier to stomach by an age which is only too conscious of the relative element in moral judgement; and there is a widespread and not unplausible tendency to maintain that purely intellectual apprehensions can have no influence over the passions.

The further development of this tendency is a general revolt against reason. This is marked even in theoretical matters, as is indeed inevitable once the synthetic activity of theoretical reason is ignored or denied. It is still more marked in morals, where undiluted relativism has passed from the scholar's study to the chit-chat of general conversation. Moral judgements tend to be regarded as mere expressions of personal emotion or of likes and dislikes, and moral action so-called is viewed as mere convention or habit, or as based at most on intelligent self-interest.

Thus the two views which Kant described as dogmatism and scepticism are as prevalent today as ever, scepticism, however, being well in the lead. They must arise if we split the whole personality of man into separate and unrelated faculties, theoretical reason on the one hand and a mysterious entity called the will, which operates blindly after thinking has taken place and produces actions which may be objects of subsequent thinking. It is easy to see that such an entity could not be a will at all, and certainly not a free or rational will: so far as it operated, its operations would be the result of some preceding intellectual activity or apprehension. It is almost inevitable that the very existence of such an entity should be denied, and that the so-called will should be reduced to a mere complex of impulses, having, perhaps, their origin in the unconscious. This last theory is still intellectualistic: it is formed from the point of view, not of an agent, but of a spectator—which is what most philosophers, and perhaps even most psychologists, tend to be from the very nature of their profession.

In contrasting these views I am putting my own interpretation on modern movements, and a summary interpretation at that. I am not asserting that the doctrine of separate and unrelated faculties is explicitly taught: my complaint is rather that it appears to be taken for granted,[1] and that the rationality of will receives no adequate discussion. Expressly though Kant repudiates any attempt to construct a philosophy of action, his account of practical reason on its different levels is at least an effort to consider the way in which human volitions are themselves rational. Until philosophers recognise with him that willing may be as rational as thinking, it is hard to see how we can have any satisfactory moral philosophy.

[1] This is as true of modern psychoanalysis as it is of other doctrines.

§9. *Kant's teleology.*

Kant's treatment of the problem may be sketchy and his solutions inadequate, but if we accept his view of willing as itself a rational activity, we begin to see the relations between skilful and prudential and moral action; we begin to understand the emotional factors which undoubtedly accompany moral judgement; above all we begin to realise that duty is neither a mystery nor an illusion, but an intelligible conception and a necessary ideal in the whole context of our practical experience.

The adoption of Kant's view of willing need not commit us to claims of a special metaphysical status for the real and rational self,[1] though it raises metaphysical questions about the possibility of freedom. On the other hand, if we regard rationality as the distinguishing character of man and of his will, it does commit us to the doctrine that the end of man is to realise rationality in thought and action, not indeed as an isolated individual, but as a member of a community of rational beings. A failure to seek the realisation of this end must inevitably result in a feeling of frustration.

It may be objected that the suppression of natural desires will equally lead to feelings of frustration, and that these must have their place in life as well as practical reason. This is true, but it is irrelevant as a criticism of Kant. He always rejects a 'monastic' asceticism which goes to work with 'self-torture and crucifixion of the flesh' and can in the end produce only a secret hate against the commands of virtue. What he calls 'ethical gymnastic' consists only in resistance to natural desires to the extent necessary to become their master in cases where they may threaten danger to morality; and this makes a man hardy and also cheerful in the consciousness of his recovered freedom.[2] The Idea of my pure moral will stands to my will as affected by sensuous desires in somewhat the same relation as the categories stand to my intuitions[3]—that is, as a principle of organisation, not as a principle of suppression. Furthermore, we must remember Kant's teleological principles in applying the moral law:[4] everything in human nature has its proper function and purpose, and, on Kant's view as on Plato's, it will perform its proper function only under the governance of a rational will. Nor must we forget that a rational will must concern itself, not only with my desires, but also with the desires of others, and that a harmony of human purposes is possible only on the condition that all men seek to obey the same moral law.[5] Kant always holds both that man has a right, and even an indirect duty, to seek happiness so far as his doing so does not transgress the moral law, and that only so far as all men subordinate their search for happiness to the fulfilment of their duty can happiness be widely attained—though even then happiness would to some extent depend on other considerations which are not under human control. For him the realisation of a rational

---

[1] See §2 above.
[3] *Gr.*, 454 = 88.
[5] *K.p.V.*, 28 = 137–8 (= 50–1).
[2] *M.d.S.*, *Tugendlehre*, §53, 485.
[4] Chapter XV §6.

will is not opposed to, but is rather the condition of, the fullest possible realisation of human powers and human desires.

§10. *The self-consciousness of practical reason.*

When we have cleared away misunderstanding, Kant's justification of the categorical imperative is seen to rest, not on purely theoretical argument or insight, and not on some emotional experience, still less a mystical one, but on what may be called the necessary self-consciousness of practical reason. Does this contention really amount to anything, or are we merely using fine phrases as a sort of cloak under whose disguise amiable aspirations may be able to pass muster as serious philosophical theories?[1]

If we are to do justice to Kant's view, we must see it in the context of a whole philosophy in which the self-consciousness of reason holds the central place. According to him, to entertain any concept, or at least any complex concept, is to be conscious of the plan or pattern of one's own mental activity (including the activity of imagination). Thus to entertain an empirical concept is to be conscious of the plan or pattern followed in combining sense-data into a physical object. To entertain a geometrical concept is to be conscious of the plan or pattern followed in constructing a geometrical figure. To entertain a logical concept like that of ground and consequent is to be conscious of the pattern of the necessary activity of reason as such. To entertain a category like that of cause and effect is to be conscious of the pattern of a necessary activity of the imagination in combining objects in one time and space and of its correspondence with the concept of ground and consequent. To entertain an Idea of reason is to be conscious of the pattern of the necessary activity of reason in passing beyond the conditioned to the totality of conditions and so to the unconditioned.[2]

We have a similar consciousness or self-consciousness of the pattern of the activity of practical reason. In our maxims we are conscious of willing our actions as having a certain character or as conforming to a pattern or a rule; and this consciousness is a self-consciousness of practical reason, not merely a theoretical consciousness super-added to a blind and unconscious volition. In our objective principles of skill and prudence we have a similar self-consciousness of the pattern or rule of a necessary activity of practical reason, of the pattern or rule which a rational agent would necessarily follow if he had full control over passion, and ought to follow if he is irrational enough to be tempted to do otherwise. But in all this the pattern or rule is subject to a condition, the condition that a particular end is sought. In moral principle we have a similar self-consciousness of the pattern or rule of the necessary activity of practical reason, but in this case the principle is no longer subject to the condition that we happen to be seeking a particular end.

All this is far too summary to be precise, and it omits many necessary qualifications, but it may be sufficient to indicate the general lines of

---

[1] Compare *Gr.*, 453 = 87.   [2] See Chapters IX, Appendix, and XXIII §5.

Kant's thinking to a reader of good will, if he is more anxious to understand than to refute.

The central point, and the central difficulty, is that as regards the objective principles of practical reason we are still supposed to have a self-consciousness of the necessary activity of practical reason, not merely a theoretical consciousness super-added to a blind or unconscious will. Yet we cannot suppose, as we do *ex hypothesi* in the case of a maxim, that the objective principles are in fact being followed. Hence the necessary self-consciousness of practical reason appears to be a misnomer. How can we say that a good will must be present in men as rational agents, when it so very manifestly is nothing of the kind?

§11. *Thought and action.*

It is extraordinarily difficult to think out clearly the relation between moral judgement, especially philosophical moral judgement, and moral action, if we are dissatisfied with the view that moral judgement is a purely theoretical activity not fundamentally different from logical or mathematical judgements. I have suggested that our philosophical grasp of moral principles is in some ways analogous to our philosophical grasp of logical principles. The latter must be present in our thinking and yet, especially before we have formulated them, they may be almost as obscurely and imperfectly present in our thinking as moral principles are in our acting. This is particularly true of what Kant calls Ideas of reason, which set before us the ideal of seeking for the condition of every condition until we have completed the totality of conditions, which itself must be unconditioned. This theoretical ideal is no more capable of complete attainment than is the moral ideal, which is also an Idea of reason, although of practical reason. Yet in both cases the ideal, when abstractly formulated, is seen to be a necessary ideal of reason, and not merely a principle actually at work, even if imperfectly, in rational thinking or rational action.

The difference is, however, that in conceiving our Idea of theoretical reason we are ourselves thinking; the thinking thought about does not differ in kind from the thinking which thinks about it; and consequently there seems to be less difficulty in claiming direct insight into the necessity of this Idea. If, however, in conceiving an Idea of practical reason we are merely thinking, then what we are thinking about seems to be something different in kind from the thinking which thinks about it; and consequently there seems to be more difficulty in claiming direct insight into the necessity of the practical Idea. Is this greater difficulty due to our incorrigible habit of thinking about action as if it were something essentially unintelligent, a mere object thought about and not an activity of practical reason? Ought we not to deny the divorce between thinking and acting and to say that the apprehension of the necessity of the moral ideal is something more than mere theory and somehow contains in itself an activity of will? Is this apprehension in short properly described as self-consciousness of the necessary activity of practical reason, a self-consciousness which is volitional as well as theoretical, as indeed it must be even in our moral actions?

Such a view is certainly difficult and hard to make precise in words, yet our experience of moral judgement seems to suggest that there is expressed in it something more than theory, some attitude of the will. This aspect of moral judgement—or of what is sometimes thought to be moral judgement—is brought out by some positivists,[1] although they do not go on to ask whether this attitude of the will may be rational or irrational: they seem to assume that whatever is not purely theoretical must necessarily be irrational, an assumption which seems to me in need of some justification.

Perhaps I am making too many difficulties, and it may be sufficient to say here that we cannot expect to grasp the necessity of moral principles, or even to make moral judgements, unless we are conscious of some sort of moral volition in ourselves. One thing at least is certain. A moral philosopher cannot argue men into being good. All he can do is to separate out the principles by which good men think and act, principles which are not nearly so obscure as some modern intellectuals pretend; and he can claim—as nearly all moral philosophers do—that he has a direct insight into the necessity of these principles. Kant goes further and claims that such insight is an insight on the part of reason into its own necessary practical activity, and that it is intelligible when we consider the nature of reason as a self-conscious activity, not only in thinking but also in acting.

If this is the proper view, all we can say to a man who asks us why he should be moral is something like this: 'We can set before you in a more or less clear and systematic form certain principles by which good men have judged and to some extent acted down the ages; but if you want to be convinced that it is your duty to act on these principles and that such action is a pre-eminent good and the one source of human dignity, then you must act on them yourself. You cannot attain moral insight without acting morally any more than you can attain logical insight without thinking correctly. Indeed in either case you must take a decision and make a venture of faith. You must give yourself up to the activity which you wish to understand, and this is as true about morality as it is about logic, or indeed about science or about art. Do not make the absurd mistake of supposing that you can understand and judge the moral life without any personal experience, a mistake which you would never dream of making in regard to any other kind of human activity.' Whatever be the theory of the matter, this is the practical answer, and it appears to be in accordance with Kant's doctrine.

To many such a view may appear nonsensical and absurd, the product of a moralistic prejudice; but they ought at least to ask whether their condemnation may not spring from an intellectualistic prejudice, which may be just as misleading as a moralistic one.

[1] See *The Philosophy of G. E. Moore*, pp. 71 ff., for an interesting article by C. L. Stevenson.

§12. *Some practical objections.*

No adequate discussion of the theoretical difficulties in this view can be attempted here, but it may be well to note some objections on the level of practice.

It may be thought that almost any kind of life will be judged good if it is freely chosen and persistently followed, so that this method of seeking moral insight will result in purely arbitrary judgements. This, however, is true only within limits and mainly as regards what is good for the individual: the moral life I claim to be good in itself and not merely good for me—to be good in itself even when, in a narrow sense, it is *not* good for me.

It may also be thought that a great deal of spurious morality has been advocated, and may be advocated, along precisely these lines. In this there is nothing surprising, for men grasp moral principles slowly and clutter them up with nonsense; yet the strength of their advocacy may rest on the genuine moral principles mixed up with the nonsense, and the nonsense may be cured by further living and by further thought. The fundamental principle of Kant's moral philosophy is not that we should live blindly, but that we should live intelligently.

Finally it may be thought by some that the doctrine is insufficient: the moral decision must be supplemented by the grace of God. If this is true, it belongs to the philosophy of religion and not of morals; and in any case the moral decision is essential, and by itself it will carry us a long way.

CHAPTER XXVI

THE DEFENCE OF FREEDOM

§1. *The antinomy of freedom and necessity.*

WHETHER we regard the principle of autonomy as following from the presupposition of freedom or consider the presupposition of freedom to follow from our recognition of a categorical imperative, it is necessary to defend freedom against the charge that it is incompatible with the causal necessity which we know to prevail in nature. This fundamental problem has hitherto been kept in the background; and only after Kant has explained how a categorical imperative is possible does he turn explicitly to the task of reconciling spiritual freedom with the causal necessity which governs the phenomenal world.[1]

The new argument is comparatively easy in the light of the preceding discussion. Freedom and necessity seem to be equally necessary, the first for action, the second for science; and yet they seem to be contradictory. Since we cannot afford to give up either, we must suppose that there is no real contradiction between them, and we must try to see whether the seeming contradiction can be removed; otherwise of the two it is freedom which we should have to give up.

The contradiction will be removed only if we are able to show that freedom and necessity can, and indeed must, be conceived as combined in man. It is manifestly impossible to hold that man can be both free and causally determined, if we conceive man in the same sense, or in the same relation, in both cases. Freedom and necessity can be reconciled only if man can be conceived in two senses or in two relations (that is, as thing-in-himself and as phenomenon). It is the task of speculative reason to resolve the antinomy by establishing this double standpoint (or double point of view) and so to *defend* practical reason and moral beliefs against all possible attack. Practical reason legitimately requires this service from theoretical reason, and in so doing it is not going beyond its proper limits.

§2. *The solution of the antinomy.*

The solution which Kant offers for the antinomy[2] is the one we have already found in our attempts to escape from the alleged vicious circle of the argument.[3]

There is no contradiction in supposing *a thing as it is in itself* to be

[1] *Gr.*, 455 ff. = 89 ff.   [2] *Gr.*, 457–8 = 92–3.
[3] Chapter XXII §§3 and 4

independent of the laws to which the same thing is subject *as an appearance* or as belonging to the sensible world. Man must look upon himself from both these points of view. He must regard himself, *qua* intelligence, as independent of the causal laws which govern his sense-impressions: his reasoning must be determined by grounds of quite another kind. Similarly —though here again it is not clear whether Kant regards this as an inference or as due to independent insight—he must conceive himself as an intelligence possessed of a will and so as exercising causality in the phenomenal world; and here too he must regard his rational willing as determined by quite other grounds than the causal laws which must govern him considered as a temporal series of impressions, feelings, desires, and actions. Hence he must regard himself from two different points of view: he must consider himself, as a rational being and a rational agent, to be a thing-in-itself and a member of the intelligible world under the laws of freedom; and he must also consider himself, as a sensuously affected being and an object of inner sense, to be an appearance in the sensible world completely governed by the laws of cause and effect. Once we understand that man must regard himself from these two points of view the supposed contradiction disappears.

§3. *The two standpoints.*

Kant seems to be right in saying that there are two standpoints from which we must regard ourselves. The two standpoints I have described on a humble level as the standpoint of the agent himself and the standpoint of the observer. In the light shed by Kant's account of theoretical and practical reason this description is seen to be too simple. The two standpoints are rather the standpoint of the self as consciously thinking and acting, and the standpoint from which the self is considered as something thought about and acted upon. Both these standpoints seem to be necessarily present in anything we can call self-knowledge.

The standpoint of the self as thinking and acting does seem to be one which in a curious way is outside appearances and even outside time.[1] Yet by itself such a view is quite unsatisfactory. Not only can we know our thinking and acting as events in time, but our thinking and acting, besides always taking place *at* a time, also take place *through* a time, as Kant himself admits.[2]

Even if in our thinking we seem to survey all time in the light of timeless principles, we do so from a particular point in time, and one which is continually changing. Our view of the future is not the same as our view of the past.

Our acting is based on such a view and such a survey, but it seems even more closely bound up with time; for however timeless be its principles, its very essence is, as it were, to thrust out of eternity into time

[1] Compare Chapter XXIII §§3-4. See also *Gr.*, 458 = 93 for a standpoint 'outside appearances'.
[2] *K.r.V.*, A210 = B255.

and to affect the course of changing events as these pass before us at a particular moment.

It is hard to describe the double standpoint from which we seem necessarily to regard ourselves, but it would surely be unwise to suggest that there is no double standpoint at all, and that Kant's problem is artificial. The main troubles arise when we begin to consider his attempt to justify this double standpoint and to treat it as falling under a more general principle.

What Kant maintains is that this special double standpoint is only a particular case of a more general standpoint from which we must necessarily regard every object of knowledge. Everything must be conceived as a thing-in-itself and as an appearance to us. All things as appearances must be governed by the causal laws of the sensible world, but the very same things as they are in themselves may be exempt from these laws.

§4. *How is freedom possible?*

It is not unnatural to suppose that Kant, in propounding this doctrine, is offering us a theory about the intelligible world which will explain how freedom is possible. There are two main and obvious objections to such a theory. The first is that he seems to claim knowledge of the intelligible world to which he is not entitled; and the second is that even if this knowledge were admitted, his theory would offer a very poor explanation of freedom indeed.

As to knowledge of the intelligible world, considered as the totality of things-in-themselves, we may perhaps grant him, on his premises, that the intelligible world cannot be conceived as temporal or as subject to causal law, which is essentially temporal. But he seems to go very much further than this. Even to call the world as it is in itself an 'intelligible' world is unnecessarily ambiguous, if by 'intelligible' he means only that although it must be conceived, it is inaccessible to our senses. He has, however, already described it as an 'intellectual' world,[1] and so presumably as one which is actively intelligent. There seems to be little doubt that he conceives the intelligible world as 'the whole of rational beings as things-in-themselves'.[2] Man, as he tells us in the present passage,[3] knows nothing more of the intelligible world than this—that in it reason alone, and indeed pure reason independent of sensibility, is the source of law; and it is added that the laws of the intelligible world apply to man categorically because only in that world is he his proper self.[4]

All this suggests that Kant claims a surprising amount of knowledge about the intelligible world and is prepared to base his present defence of freedom, and even his justification of the categorical imperative, on such knowledge. It is hard to see why he permits himself to use language which he knows to be misleading.

Let us suppose, however, for the sake of argument, that we know

---
[1] *Gr.*, 451 = 85.   [2] *Gr.*, 458 = 94.   [3] *Gr.*, 457 = 93.
[4] For objections to this doctrine see Chapter XXIV §9.

ultimate reality to be a society of rational beings engaged in timeless activity. In what way are we in a better position to deal with the problem of freedom? It is admittedly impossible to understand how such a society of timeless beings could be the ground of a changing world in space and time governed by causal law. What is more, since timeless activity is inconceivable to us, a free timeless activity is equally inconceivable, and could not possibly explain our freedom to act here and now in accordance with the moral law. Yet it is precisely this freedom which we are attempting to defend.

It is unnecessary to elaborate further criticisms of such a theory: they can be found in almost any book on Kant. The only defence of Kant, if there is one, is that in spite of his admittedly misleading language he is not offering such a theoretical explanation at all. It is at least worthy of remark that he himself explicitly denies the possibility of explaining how freedom is possible.[1]

§5. *Phenomena and noumena.*

In trying to interpret Kant we must take seriously his insistence that the distinction between phenomena and noumena, or between the sensible and intelligible worlds, is to be understood in a negative sense.[2] He holds that the thing-in-itself which we are bound to conceive as the reality which is the ground of appearance is *not* an object of our senses and consequently cannot be known by us. If we suppose that it can be known by means of our conceptions, this on Kant's view is to suppose that we know it by some kind of intuition which is not, like ours, sensuous and passive, but intellectual and active. We then take 'noumenon' in a positive sense as an object known by means of a non-sensuous intuition; and to do this is always illegitimate.

On the basis of this distinction some commentators tend to regard the thing-in-itself as unnecessary to Kant's system; what we cannot know we cannot consider to be in any sense real. Kant is far too much of a realist to accept this. For him appearances are always appearances of a reality; and I see no reason to doubt that he always regarded the thing-in-itself as real in itself but unknown by us.[3]

With the difficulties of this view—such as the meaning of the 'real' in this connexion—we are not here concerned. What should be noted is that the concept of a noumenon is attained by making complete abstraction from our sensuous intuitions under the forms of time and space.[4] This method of abstraction, when applied to objects of experience in general, leaves us with the pure concept of an object in general or of a thing in general. When applied, as Kant applies it, to particular classes of objects, it leaves us with different concepts of noumena, and these at first sight seem to have little to do with things-in-themselves.

---

[1] *Gr.*, 458–9=94.   [2] *K.r.V.*, B311; B306–7.
[3] *K.r.V.*, B xx . See also *K.M.E.*, Chapter LVI §3.
[4] Compare *Gr.*, 462 = 98 for the Idea of an intelligible world.

There are many examples in Kant of such a procedure. Thus when we abstract from the temporal reference in the category of cause, we are left with the concept of *causa noumenon* (cause as a noumenon), that is, of a ground. When we abstract from the sensible characteristics of man, we are left with the concept of *homo noumenon*, which is—at least often—identified with humanity or personality. This tendency becomes more marked in Kant's later works. For example, legal possession is described as *possessio noumenon* inasmuch as the concept abstracts from the empirical conditions which belong to the physical occupation or use of some object in time and space.[1]

If we abstract from all the sensible and temporal characteristics of moral action, what are we left with? All we are left with is the concept of a timeless universal moral law considered as the ground (not the cause) of the action. When we conceive a moral action in this way we are considering action to be free in so far as it can have its ground in such a timeless law. The action is considered, not in relation to temporal antecedents, but in relation to its rational ground.

This seems a much more satisfactory way of conceiving free moral action: it does not involve any unintelligible theory that a moral action is in reality the timeless activity of an unknown I-in-itself. Here we have one point of view from which actions must be regarded—and the same of course applies to thoughts. Has this point of view anything to do with the point of view whereby objects are conceived as grounded in unknown things-in-themselves?

It is easy enough to see how commentators may hold that the thing-in-itself is superfluous and that Kant requires no more than the concept of action as grounded in a universal moral law. But it is also easy to see why Kant—if I may be dogmatic—rejects such a contention. For him, if the sensible world were the sole reality, we should not be entitled to conceive actions in this way; the laws of cause and effect as necessarily applied to our observed actions would exclude such a possibility. If, however, all sensible objects must be conceived as grounded in an unknown reality not governed by cause and effect, then, and then only, are we entitled to the presupposition on which as rational agents we must act, the presupposition that our actions can be willed in accordance with a universal and timeless moral law. And it is only on the same hypothesis that we are entitled to think—as we do—on the presupposition that our judgements and inferences can be made in accordance with the timeless principles of theoretical reason.

Hence if Kant is to think of a man as acting freely in accordance with timeless moral laws, and in that sense as a member of the intelligible world, he has at the same time to think of that world as the world of things as they are in themselves and not as they appear to our senses. But this involves no claim to know the world as it is in itself. Still less does it involve a claim to understand how an intelligible or intellectual world, considered as a thing-in-itself, can through its timeless activity be manifested in temporal actions.

[1] *M.d.S.*, *Rechtslehre*, §§6 and 10, 251 and 259.

We must also remember that for Kant freedom is a *practical* Idea, and that this is something very different from a speculative theory of reality. All he has to show is that there is no theoretical reason why we should not be entitled to act—as the categorical imperative enjoins—in accordance with a universal moral law. This he does by arguing that we could exclude the possibility of such action only if the sensible world, with its causal laws, were the sole reality. If he can justify the view that it is not to be conceived as the sole reality, there is no need for him to go farther.

§6. *The thought of the intelligible world.*

It may be objected that all this is special pleading and that it is illegitimate thus to water down Kant's crude statements by making an appeal to a vague general conspectus of his doctrine.

To this the answer is that Kant himself immediately proceeds to water down, or rather to make more precise, his doctrine, and that he does so along the lines suggested. This is his first approach to the question of the *limits* of practical reason with which the whole of the final section of the *Groundwork* is supposed to concern itself. As his exposition is difficult and the subject controversial, the passage requires careful study.[1]

Practical reason, he maintains, does not go beyond its limits when it conceives the intelligible world and *thinks* itself into the intelligible world. It does go beyond its limits when it wants to *intuit* or *sense* itself into the intelligible world. In other words it must not claim to *know* the intelligible world or to *know* itself as belonging to the intelligible world.

To conceive or think oneself into the intelligible world is only a *negative* thought—the thought that the sensible world does *not* give laws to a rational will.[2] The thought of self as belonging to the intelligible world becomes *positive* only in one point: we conceive ourselves, not only negatively as exempt from the laws of the sensible world, but also as possessing a positive faculty or power, the power which we call a will, the power of reason to cause events in the sensible world. How does Kant regard this positive power? He is very careful to insist that it is only a power to act in accordance with a universal moral principle. If we go further and try to hale some motive, some object of the will, out of the intelligible world, practical reason is going beyond its limits and is claiming acquaintance with something of which it knows nothing. This should exclude the possibility that we can know our real self to be some sort of timeless intellectual activity in the intelligible world and can for this reason regard ourselves as bound by the categorical imperative.

[1] *Gr.*, 458 = 93–4. Compare also *Gr.*, 462 = 98.
[2] Here the intelligible world is conceived as a noumenon in the negative sense—that is, as *not* known to our sensuous intuition. and consequently as not under the causal laws of the sensible world.

If I am not to abandon consciousness of myself as intelligence—that is, as thinking and acting in accordance with rational principles—I must so far conceive thoughts and actions as not determined by sense in accordance with merely causal laws. In order to do this I must conceive myself as a member of a non-sensible world. My concept of a non-sensible—or as Kant calls it intelligible—world is thus said to be only *a standpoint* which reason sees itself compelled to adopt outside appearances *in order to conceive itself as practical*.

To say this is not to say that the intelligible world is unreal. The concept of the sensible world is as much a standpoint as the concept of the intelligible world.[1] Incidentally to say that the *concept* of the intelligible world is only a standpoint is not to say that the intelligible world itself is only a standpoint. On the contrary, unless the intelligible world were real, although unknown by us, we should not be justified in claiming to act, and to judge our actions, from this standpoint, as I have already tried to explain.[2]

The thought of myself as a rational agent acting in accordance with a universal moral law does, Kant admits, carry with it the *Idea* of another order and another kind of law than that which governs the sensible world: it makes it necessary for us to conceive the intelligible world, and to conceive it as the totality of rational beings considered as things-in-themselves.

It is very clear from this that Kant is far from abandoning the thing-in-itself. It is equally clear that his concept of a totality of rational beings considered as things-in-themselves is, like his belief in God and immortality, based on his ethics:[3] it is not an independent and metaphysical conception—and still less is it metaphysical knowledge—from which his ethics can be deduced.

There follows a difficult passage[4] in which Kant disclaims all knowledge of the intelligible world. There is not the slightest pretension to do more than think in accordance with the purely *formal* condition of such a world. But what is this formal condition? The formal condition is nothing other than the principle of morality itself, the principle of acting only on maxims which are valid as universal laws, or in other words the principle of autonomy which alone is compatible with freedom.

What we *know* is only the ultimate universal law on which a rational agent as such would necessarily act. We cannot conceive a rational agent as so acting unless we distinguish the intelligible from the sensible world and suppose him to be—from one point of view—a member of the intelligible world. But this formal principle gives us no knowledge of any *object*, least of all of an intelligible world. On the contrary, all laws which give us knowledge of a determinate object are the causal laws of nature; and these govern only the sensible world and constitute what Kant calls 'heteronomy'.

[1] *Gr.*, 452 = 86.   [2] See §3 above.
[3] This concept, however, receives support from considerations urged in the *Critique of Judgement*.
[4] *Gr.*, 458 = 94.

§7. *There is no explanation of freedom.*

Any attempt to explain how freedom is possible is definitely excluded by Kant.[1] To explain anything is to bring it under the laws of nature, especially the causal laws. More simply, to explain anything is to state its cause. Obviously we cannot explain free action by showing that it is caused by something other than itself; and indeed the *Idea* of freedom is *ex hypothesi* not the concept of an object of possible experience, and so not the concept of any object in nature falling under causal law.

To explain how freedom is possible would be the same thing as to explain how pure reason can be practical—that is, how pure reason can have effects in the phenomenal world. In order to do this we should have to intuit pure reason as well as to conceive its formal law. This assumes that we can know the intelligible world by intuition as we know the phenomenal world; and indeed it treats the intelligible world as if it were the phenomenal world, and as if it were under the laws of the phenomenal world. To attempt a task of this kind would be indeed to go beyond the limits of practical philosophy.

All we can do is to *defend* freedom against attack by showing that it must be conceived to belong to man as rational and so as a member of the intelligible world and not as a member of the sensible world. Once we have understood that two standpoints are necessary and that from one of them we must conceive things-in-themselves to be the hidden ground of phenomena, there is no contradiction in supposing man to be both free and determined, free as a member of the intelligible world and determined as a member of the sensible world.

It should be observed also that this passage comes very much nearer to the doctrine of the *Critique of Practical Reason*. Apart from its insistence on the *defence* of freedom, the Idea of freedom is based on consciousness of the moral law. The Idea of freedom is said to be valid only as a necessary presupposition of reason in a being conscious of a rational will as a power of determining himself to act in accordance with laws of reason.

§8. *Timeless action.*

I have done my best to show the reasonableness of Kant's doctrine by keeping strictly within the limits he has set himself. A rational agent as such would necessarily act in accordance with principles unconditionally valid for all rational agents and would regard such principles as imperatives if, because of non-rational elements within him, he were tempted to act otherwise. He would also necessarily presuppose himself to be free to act in accordance with such principles. All this is borne out by our moral consciousness, and it is true of our thinking as well as of

---

[1] *Gr.*, 458–9 = 94–5.

our acting. It makes a claim that there is more in the world than energy or motion governed by physical laws and that a rational agent is something more than such energy or motion, and even something more than a series of mental events succeeding one another in accordance with the causal laws of psychology. Kant's metaphysical doctrine of the thing-in-itself cannot be adequately expounded, and still less defended, here; but at least it is a reasoned attempt to justify the view that there is such a something more.[1] It gives us an answer to those dogmatists who, on the ground of their special insight into the nature of reality, are boldly prepared to deny the possibility of freedom.[2] We can always say to such a man with justice 'There are more things in heaven and earth, Horatio, than are dreamt of in your philosophy.'

Furthermore, the relation between the principles of reason and our changing thoughts and actions is not one of temporal succession or of cause and effect. No doubt we must think the premises before we think the conclusion, but the validity of the argument is independent of this temporal succession: an argument is sound because it accords with timeless principles. Similarly we must conceive both the actual situation and also the maxim of a proposed action, as well as the moral law, before we act morally,[3] but an action is not moral because it follows, or is caused by, a previous act of thinking; it is moral because it is willed in accordance with timeless principles.

Unfortunately, because of this timeless element in temporal action Kant—and this is specially marked in the *Critique of Pure Reason*[4]—speaks as if our actions in the intelligible world were timeless. In so doing he gives a handle to his critics of which they take full advantage. Such a view, we must remember, was propounded during a period in which thinkers were more ready than they are now to explain events as due to the timeless activity of God. Nevertheless a doctrine of this kind is surely contrary to Kant's own principles: it is an example of that 'swarming about' or 'fluttering about' in the intelligible world which he consistently repudiates.[5] The objection to it is not merely that it cannot explain our temporal actions: this Kant would certainly admit. The objection is rather that timeless activity is itself inconceivable, at least by us: and on Kant's own principles we could defend it, if at all, only as a piece of mythology. What we can conceive is only the timeless principles in accordance with which as rational beings we think and act; and indeed no one insists on this more than Kant himself.

On the other hand it is only fair to Kant to remember that he repudiates a doctrine of two selves such as we are apt to attribute to him, not

---

[1] *Gr.*, 462 = 98.   [2] *Gr.*, 459 = 95.
[3] We must also conceive the moral law in acting upon it, but equally in inferring we must grasp the principles in accordance with which we draw the conclusion. Both thinking and acting, successive though they are, yet rise in a curious way above succession; and in both an obscure grasp of principles may be present in the activity itself before these have become clear to conscious reflection.
[4] *K.r.V.*, A539 ff. = B567 ff.
[5] *Gr.*, 462 = 98. The German word is '*herumschwärmen*'.

unnaturally, because of the language which he employs. If we are to extract any satisfactory doctrine from him, we must insist that there are not two selves, but one self considered from two points of view. Similarly there are not two actions, one temporal and the other timeless; there is only one action which has both temporal and timeless aspects. The truth which he is setting out is that an action may be a temporal event and may yet be grounded on a timeless principle.[1]

§9. *Freedom to act badly.*

So far freedom is freedom to act in accordance with the principles of autonomy. But, as we have seen,[2] Kant supposes man to be free when he acts badly. If this were not so, man would not be responsible for his bad actions; nor could he regard the moral law as an imperative if it were not possible for him to obey the moral law. Man, as Kant says, is not responsible for his desires; but he is responsible for the indulgence with which he allows his desires to influence his maxims to the detriment of the moral law.[3]

This view is fully in accord with common sense. The difficulty of it for Kant's philosophy is that the ground of immoral action must somehow lie in rational agents as members of the intelligible world. There must be an I-in-itself for each separate rational agent as known to experience, and each I-in-itself must somehow contain in itself, not only a pure rational will, but also some kind of irrationality which is manifested in its actions. In this way irrationality is introduced into the intelligible world.

This difficulty, however, concerns the origin of evil, and perhaps Kant may be allowed to plead that this can have no intelligible ground.[4] All that any one can say of evil is that it must spring from irrationality in a rational will; but Kant's theory seems to make this contention more difficult rather than more easy.

If we are free in acting badly, then we must be free, not only in so far as we act according to objective principles of reason, but also in so far as we act on subjective principles, or maxims, even when they are opposed to the moral law. This is Kant's explicit view, especially in his later works.[5] He holds that no desire or interest can influence our actions unless it is taken up into our maxim by an act of free choice.[6]

Such a view seems to bring us back very near to the liberty of indifference, with all its difficulties, in spite of Kant's denial that freedom can

---

[1] *K.p.V.*, 99 = 230 (= 177). 'When the law of our intelligible existence (the moral law) is in question, reason recognises no differences of time.'
[2] Chapter XX §7. Compare also *K.p.V.*, 99–100 = 231 (= 178–9).
[3] *Gr.*, 458 = 93.
[4] *Religion*, 43 = 49 (= 46–7); 21 = 21–2 (= 7–8).
[5] *Religion*, 21 n. = 22 n. (= 7 n.).   [6] *Religion*, 24 = 25 (= 12).

be defined in this way.[1] Nevertheless his recognition of two senses of freedom, even if it is not altogether clear, seems necessary at least as a first approach to the problem. On the one hand, freedom seems merely a power to act rationally with a full knowledge of the circumstances in which we act. On the other hand, if this were all, the extent to which we were able to act rationally might be wholly determined by something other than ourselves; and this seems to be a denial of freedom. It looks as if we must be free to act both rationally and irrationally, or at least to act both more rationally and less rationally: without this there could be no responsibility for our actions and apparently no meaning in the statement that we ought to pursue a particular course of action. If so, to adopt any maxim or principle of action is to act freely, and behind this we cannot go. It still remains true that only rational actions—actions in accordance with maxims—can be free; and we must not forget that every maxim has some rationality, even if this rationality be displayed only in relation to a set of circumstances which seems to be arbitrarily limited.[2] It is hard to understand why we should regard ourselves as free even in limiting the scope of our own rationality, but the fact remains that we do. Indeed unless we do, responsibility and obligation alike seem to disappear.

Although Kant recognises freedom even in acting badly, he does not cease to regard a free will as a power to produce effects without being determined to do so by anything other than itself; and although our will is often said to be influenced, not determined, by desires, this influence is apparently possible only through our free choice.

This view seems to deny that there are degrees of freedom, but other passages suggest the contrary.[3] Clearly this is a topic which requires more discussion than Kant has given it.

§10. *Freedom and necessity.*

Although from one point of view all actions are free, we must not forget that from another point of view all actions—moral and immoral alike—are determined.

I believe Kant to be completely sound in saying that we can and do, and even must, take these two points of view. I even think he must be right in maintaining that the first point of view must in some way have a deeper insight into reality than the second: it is at least looking for something without which there could be neither action nor thought, not even the thought of determinism. Such a belief, however, cannot be upheld except by an elaborate metaphysic. The Critical Philosophy is a remarkable effort to supply such a metaphysic, although the attempt to put

---

[1] *M.d.S., Rechtslehre, Einl.* IV, 226 = 28.
[2] See Chapter IX §1.
[3] See Chapter XX §9.

freedom into the intelligible world and necessity into a phenomenal one breaks down if we take the doctrine to mean that there are two different kinds of action in two different kinds of world.

It is also a question whether it is possible to take these two points of view without allowing either to influence the other.

The possibility of degrees of freedom must suggest that there are also degrees of determinism, or at least that a rational will may be influenced to a greater or lesser extent by nature in a way not wholly dependent on a free choice. Kant indeed maintains that what he calls our empirical character as an appearance is grounded in our intelligible character as a thing-in-itself; but he also says of our empirical character that no man can fathom how much should be ascribed to mere nature.[1]

On the other hand it is also hard to believe that a free will can in no way influence or deflect the course of events. According to Kant, if we had enough knowledge of a man's nature and environment we could calculate his future behaviour with as much certainty as an eclipse of the sun or moon.[2] In these calculations we must admittedly take into account the man's 'empirical' character; and so far as this is grounded on his intelligible character, he may still be said to influence events, if only in a way that could be foretold with sufficient knowledge. But even his empirical character must itself be regarded as the effect of events happening before he is born; and if this is so, it is hard to see how any remnant of freedom can be saved. Kant never properly faces this difficulty. It would surely be fantastic to suggest that the intelligible character of each individual prepared the way for his empirical character by being the ground of events happening before he was born.

§11. *The defence of freedom.*

It is impossible within the limits of the present book to discuss adequately Kant's defence of freedom. This is only a part of the vast metaphysical structure for which he clears the ground in his discussion of theoretical reason, but which is itself based primarily upon his ethics and is for him a matter of faith and not of knowledge. I have sought only to indicate the method of approach to the problem, to clear away some misconceptions, to suggest certain difficulties, and above all to show that Kant's ethics, so far from being deduced from the Idea of freedom, is itself the ground on which the Idea of freedom is based. Hence Kant's ethics is independent of his metaphysics and has a claim to our acceptance, or at least to our consideration, no matter what be our attitude towards his metaphysics. But he is surely right in maintaining that there can be no morality, as it is understood, however obscurely, by ordinary

[1] $K.r.V.$, A539 = B567 and A551 n. = B579 n.
[2] $K.p.V.$, 99 = 230 (= 177); $K.r.V.$, A549–50 = B577–8.

men, without the presupposition of freedom. The defence of freedom is necessary for the defence of morality, and if Kant's defence is not to be regarded as successful, at least he has shown us the character of the problem and perhaps even suggested some of the lines on which it may be solved.

INDEX OF PROPER NAMES

ABBOTT, 113n., 134n., 143n.
Addison, 162
Alexander, S., 236
Aristotle, 29n., 108, 160n.
Ayer, A. J., 35n., 122n.

BARFORD, C. B. H., 17
Beck, L. J., 17
Borowski, 150n.
Bullock, A. B., 48n.

CAIRD, Edward, 63n., 237n.
Cassirer, Ernst, 140n.
Churchill, Winston, 92
Cicero, 38n.
Collingwood, R. G., 195
Cook Wilson, 74
Croce, 50

DARWIN, 109

FALK, W. D., 187n.
Francis I, 140
Francis, St., 26

GANDHI, Mahatma, 92
Gentile, G., 236

HARDIE, W. F. R., 17
Hegel, 30
Hitler, 138
Hoernlé, 205n.
Hoffmann, Alfons, 150n.
Horatio, 274
Hume, David, 30, 210, 227
Huxley, T. H., 161

JACHMANN, 150n.
Jones, Bobby, 91
Joseph, H. W. B., 121n.

KANT, I., 197
Kydd, Mrs. R. M., 210n.

LEIBNIZ, 121, 209, 227, 230

MELLIN, 147n.
Mill, John Stuart, 176
Moore, G. E., 110, 123n.

NERO, 36, 39
Newton, 131, 161, 162, 191, 227, 230

PLATO, 29n., 160n., 261n.
Price, H. H., 88n., 227n.

RASHDALL, Canon, 48n.
Reich, Klaus, 33n., 38n., 238n.
Ross, Sir David, 36, 117n.
Rousseau, J. J., 42, 162
Russell, Bertrand, 74

SCHILLER, 48, 50
Schilpp, P. A., 16, 30, 42n., 53n., 57n.
Schopenhauer, 70
Schroeder, Professor, 48n.
Seneca, 189n.
Smith, Adam, 190
Stevenson, C. L., 264n.

TAYLOR, A. E., 218n.

VARDON, Harry, 91
Victoria, Queen, 62

WASIANSKI, 150, 198
Webb, C. C. J., 60n.
Wells, H. G., 114n.
Wilder, Thornton, 40n.
Wolff, Christian, 33

GENERAL INDEX

ABGELEITET, 134
Ableiten, 80
Absolute, 34
Action, philosophy of, 32-3
——, impulsive, 82
——, moral, matter of, 73, 75, 185-6
——, timeless, 273
Activity, mental, knowledge of, 236
——, pure, 237
——, timeless, 237-8, 269, 273
Agent, rational, 128, 200-1, 246
Agents, rational, 70, 89-90, 176
Analogy, 158, 159, 160, 190-1
Analysis, method of, 25-6
Antagonism, 124, 139
Anthropology, practical, 32
Antinomies, 231
Antinomy, of freedom and necessity, 266 ff.
Apperception, pure, 237
Arbitrium, and will, 213
—— *brutum*, 210, 215
—— *liberum*, 210, 215
Argument, analytic or regressive, 130
Arguments, analytic and synthetic, 26-7, 29
——, progressive and regressive, 27, 29
Attention, 235
Autonomy, imperative of, 247
——, principle of, 180, 199, 243, 246

BEAUTY, 144, 184
Behaviour, animal, 219
Bonum consummatum, 43, 192

CATEGORIES, 143, 231, 238-9
—— of the understanding, 97, 100
Category, pure, 97
——, schematised, 99
Causality and law, 211
——, two senses of, 209
Cause and effect, 97
Christianity, 196-7
Circle, vicious, 28, 224 ff.
Coherence of wills, 139, 151, 194
Concept, different kinds of, 100
Condition, limiting, 141-2, 178
Conditions, human, 46
Conflict of reason and desire, 254
Consequences, 153
——, ignoring of, 76
Contentment, 50, 57

Contradiction in wills, 124, 139
Culture, 155, 173, 195

DARWINISM, 150, 161
Deduction, 28, 203
——, failure of, 244
——, transcendental, 200, 202, 242 ff.
Definitions, 27
Dignity and price, 188
Due, 117
Duties, perfect and imperfect, 147, 150, 171-2
—— to self and others, 148, 172
Dutiful, 117
Duty and a good will, 46
—— and necessity, 22
——, motive of, 50 ff., 118
——, sense of, 118

EMOTIONS, generous, motive of, 53 ff.
Empiricism, 30
Ends, 166 ff.
—— and grounds, 167, 169
—— in themselves, 167 ff.
——, kingdom of, 185 ff.
——, —— ——, realisation of, 191
——, private, 187
Enlightenment, 196
Enthusiasts, moral, 40, 51
Epicurean, 57
Ethics and metaphysics, 255
——, applied, 23, 32
——, Aristotelian, 155
——, pure, 23 ff.
Examples, use of, 24-5
Exhibition, 158
——, practical, 162
——, symbolic, 159, 184
Experience, 22

FALLACY, naturalistic, 110
Feeling, moral, 57, 118
Formalism, 74, 186
Freedom, 214
—— and autonomy, 212
—— and ends, 175, 181
—— and maxims, 214
—— and necessity, 209, 276
——, defence of, 266 ff., 277
——, degrees of, 215, 276, 277

280

INDEX

Freedom, Idea of, 99, 211, 271
——, law of, 69, 211, 212
——, no explanation of, 273
——, positive concept of, 211
——, possibility of, 268
——, presupposition of, 217
—— to act badly, 275

GOD, 256
——, conception of, 159
——, existence of, 188
——, Kingdom of, 188, 196
Good, absolute, 34
—— at, 104
——, conditioned, 39
—— for, 104
——, highest, 41
—— in general, 103
——, moral, 107
——, my, 105 ff.
——, perfect, 43, 192
——, realistic view of, 110 ff.
——, teleological view of, 108 ff.
——, unconditioned, 34
—— without limitation, 34
Good-heartedness, 54
Goodness and obligation, 116
——, contributory, 36-7
—— is fundamental, 45
——, motive of, 52
Goods, *prima facie*, 36, 38-9
Gymnastic, ethical, 261

HAPPINESS and duty, 49, 55 ff.
——, pursuit of, 85
——, two views of, 85, 92, 106, 126
Hegelians, 84
Heteronomy, 212
——, two kinds of, 214
History, philosophy of, 195
Holiness, 52
Honour, 53
Humanity, 165, 198

IDEA, 93n.
—— of reason, 93, 97, 99 ff., 143, 263
—— of system, 248
——, practical, 190, 263, 271
——, practical and theoretical, 191, 263
——, use of, regulative and constitutive, 100
Ideal of imagination, 127
—— of reason, 187

Imagination, 143, 144, 229n.
Immortality, 256
Imperative, categorical, 115, 127
——, ——, application of, 131, 184-5, 192 ff.
——, ——, possibility of, 127, 199, 204
——, definition of, 114
——, hypothetical, 115
——, kinds of, 114
Imperatives, categorical, 127
——, ——, ground of, 168, 170, 176, 181
——, hypothetical, ground of, 168, 169
—— in general, 113
——, possibility of, 120 ff.
Inclinations, 49-50, 55 ff.
Indifference, liberty of, 214, 275-6
Insight, direct, 245 ff.
——, practical, 258 ff.
Intellectualism, modern, 259
Interest and obligation, 258
——, mediate and immediate, 75
——, moral, 223, 256
——, pathological, 75, 83, 182
"I ought' and 'I will', 114, 223, 259
Isolation, method of, 47 ff.

JUDGEMENT, moral, canon of, 137
Judgements, *a priori*, 20 ff.
——, moral, 20

KINDNESS, 152, 173
Knowledge, composite, 22

LATITUDE, 91, 92, 137, 148, 194
Law-abidingness, 71
Law and universality, 69
—— as command, 70
—— as such, 69
——, form of, 157
——, moral, and moral imperative, 70
—— of freedom, 69, 211, 212
—— of nature, 69, 146 ff.
——, teleological, 149 ff.
——, universal, 133 ff.
Laws, moral, 23, 70
Legalism, 75
Legislation, universal, 180
Liberty of indifference, 214, 275-6
Life, 234n.
——, organic, 191
Loans, promises to repay, 152, 172
Love, 65, 196
——, motive of, 54, 57n.

MATTER of moral action, 73, 75, 185-6
Maxim, 59 ff., 60n.
——, formal, 72, 77
—— of duty, 61-2
Maxims, 135
——, formal and material, 61
——, legislating through, 182
——, material, 137
Means and end, 83
——, constituent, 105
Method, the Critical, 19 ff., 27 ff.
Mind affects itself, 235 ff.
Morality, commands of, 116
——, laws of, 116
——, paradox of, 192
——, principle of, 93
Morals, metaphysic of, 31
Motive of reverence, 66 ff.
——, two senses of, 67
Motives, 117-18

NATURE, kingdom of, 185, 190
——, law of, 69, 146 ff.
——, perfection of, 150
——, purposes of, 154
Necessitation, 113
Necessity and duty, 22
——, natural, 209 ff.
Noumenon, different senses of, 269

OBJECTS of a good will, 43
Obligation and goodness, 116
Obstacles, 46

PERMISSIBLE and obligatory, 141
Pflichtmässig and *pflichtvoll*, 117
Phenomena and noumena, 269
Philosophy, the task of, 23
Pleasure, 106-7
Politics, philosophy of, 194
Practical reason, 80, 81
—— —— and its presupposition, 218
—— —— and purpose, 155-6
—— ——, critique of, 31
—— ——, denial of, 87
—— ——, function of, 78
—— ——, limits of, 271
—— ——, principles of, 59 ff., 89, 113, 220, 240, 248
—— ——, pure, 94
—— ——, self-consciousness of, 262 ff.
Prerogative, 189
Price, 189
Principle, 59

Principles, application of, 17, 131, 174, 183
——, *a priori*, 28
——, conditioned and unconditioned, 95
——, objective, of reason, 247 ff.
——, practical, subjective and objective, 59 ff., 89, 113
Progress, moral, 194
Propositions, analytic, 120 ff., 246
——, self-evident, 28
——, synthetic, 122
——, synthetic *a priori*, 122, 127
Prudence, 51
——, counsels of, 115
——, imperatives of, 126
Psychology, general, 32
——, practical, 32
Purposiveness, logical, in nature, 191
—— without a purpose, 149n.

RATIONALISM, 30
Realm or kingdom, 187
Reason, activity of, 238
—— and the unconditioned, 249
—— as a power of Ideas, 239
—— as such, 219, 221
——, different senses of, 79, 96
——, fact of, 221
——, function of, 44-5, 78
——, logical and real use of, 97
——, practical—*see* practical reason
——, principles of, 240, 247 ff.
——, pure, fact of, 203
——, self-consciousness of, 220, 258 ff., 262 ff.
——, theoretical, and action, 81
——, ——, and its presupposition, 218
——, ——, principles of, 200, 238, 248
Religion, 188, 196
Respect, 64, 65n.
Results of action, and moral value, 58
Reverence, 42, 63 ff., 224
Revolution, Copernican, 227
Rules, moral, 23

SACRIFICE, 166
Schema of regular succession, 98
Schemata, 144, 158
——, transcendental, 143, 144, 159
Schwärmerei, 52
Self, phenomenal and noumenal, 234
——, ——, and substance, 234n.
——, real, 253
Self-evidence, 237
Self-love, principle of, 91
Sense, inner, 233
——, moral, 65

INDEX

Sense, passivity of, 228 ff.
Skill, imperatives of, 123 ff.
———, principle of, 90
———, rules of, 115
Soul, 234n.
Space, 230
Spontaneity, aesthetic, 144
———, intellectual, 142
Standpoint, 272
Standpoints, two, 225 ff., 240, 267
Stoic, 57
Stoics, 189, 216
Succession, objective and subjective, 98
Suicide, 154, 172
Symbols, 159
Synthesis, method of, 29
System, Idea of, 248

TELEOLOGY, 44, 109, 191, 261
Term, third, 128, 213, 244–5
Theories, empirical and mystical, 163
———, positivistic, 20
Thought and action, 263
Thing-in-itself, 269 ff.
Things-in-themselves, 227 ff.
Time, 230
Type, 160

UNDERSTANDING, 239
———, intuitive, 100 ff.
Universal, concrete, 101
Utilitarianism, 58

VALUE, aesthetic, economic, and moral, 189
Virtuous, fantastically, 40, 51

WILL, 82, 103, 166, 208, 211, 212, 219, 260
——— and *arbitrium*, 213
———, good, 34 ff., 177, 201
———, holy, 46, 52
———, individual, unity of, 193
———, supreme, 193
——— under moral laws, 213
World, intellectual, 238
———, intelligible, 190, 223 ff.
———, ———, and sensible, 227 ff., 243
———, ———, ground of sensible world, 250 ff.
———, ———, knowledge of, 243, 268, 272
———, ———, membership of, 233 ff.
———, ———, thought of, 271
———, noumenal and phenomenal, 227 ff.
Worth, moral, 47 ff.

CPSIA information can be obtained
at www.ICGtesting.com
Printed in the USA
BVHW03s1016280518
517490BV00019B/492/P

9 780282 382346